International Human Resource Management

This essential book provides a thorough foundation for anyone studying or working in International Human Resource Management (IHRM). Featuring data and examples from international business, consulting practice, academic research, and interviews with IHRM managers in multinational and global organizations, it covers almost everything that is currently known in the field. The approach offers both a theoretical and practical treatment of this important and evolving area, relying heavily on the authors' varied and international backgrounds.

Thoroughly updated and revised, this third edition includes learning objectives, key terms, discussion questions, and end-of-chapter vignettes for application of the ideas in the text. It is designed to lead readers through all of the key topics in a highly engaging and approachable way. The language is very 'reader friendly' and thoroughly global in scope and examples. The book focuses on IHRM within multinational enterprises throughout the world, featuring topics including:

- Globalization of business and HRM
- Global strategy and structure
- Global HR planning and forecasting
- Global talent management
- Global training and management development
- Global compensation and benefits
- Global employee performance management
- New trends in International HRM

Uncovering precisely why IHRM is important for success, this outstanding textbook provides an essential foundation for an understanding of the theory and practice of IHRM. It is essential reading for all students, lecturers and IHRM professionals.

Dennis R. Briscoe is Professor (emeritus) of International Human Resource Management at the University of San Diego, California, where he taught for 30 years.

Randall S. Schuler is Professor of Strategic International Human Resource at the School of Management and Labor Relations at Rutgers University, New Brunswick, NJ, and Research Professor at GSBA Zurich, Switzerland.

Lisbeth Claus is a Professor of Global HR at the Atkinson Graduate School of Management of Willamette University, Salem, Oregon.

Routledge Global Human Resource Management Series

Edited by Randall S. Schuler, Susan E. Jackson, Paul Sparrow, and Michael Poole

Routledge Global Human Resource Management is an important new series that examines human resources in its global context. The series is organized into three strands: content and issues in global human resource management (HRM); specific HR functions in a global context; and comparative HRM. Authored by some of the world's leading authorities on HRM, each book in the series aims to give readers comprehensive, in-depth, and accessible texts that combine essential theory and best practice. Topics covered include cross-border alliances, global leadership, global legal systems, HRM in Asia, Africa and the Americas, industrial relations, and global staffing.

Managing Human Resources in Cross Border Alliances
Randall S. Schuler, Susan E. Jackson, and Yadong Luo

Managing Human Resources in Africa
Edited by Ken N. Kamoche, Yaw A. Debrah, Frank M. Horwitz, and Gerry Nkombo Muuka

Globalizing Human Resource Management
Paul Sparrow, Chris Brewster, and Hilary Harris

Managing Human Resources in Asia-Pacific
Edited by Pawan S. Budhwar

Managing Human Resources in Latin America
An agenda for international leaders
Edited by Marta M. Elvira and Anabella Davila

Global Staffing
Edited by Hugh Scullion and David G. Collings

Managing Human Resources in Europe
A thematic approach
Edited by Henrik Holt Larsen and Wolfgang Mayrhofer

Managing Human Resources in the Middle East
Edited by Pawan S. Budhwar and Kamel Mellahi

Managing Global Legal Systems
International employment regulation and competitive advantage
Gary W. Florkowski

Global Industrial Relations
Edited by Michael J. Morley, Patrick Gunnigle, and David G. Collings

Managing Human Resources in North America
Current issues and perspectives
Edited by Steve Werner

Global Leadership: Research, Practice and Development
Mark E. Mendenhall, Joyce S. Osland, Allan Bird, Gary R. Oddou, and Martha L. Maznevski

Performance Management Systems
A global perspective
Edited by Arup Varma, Pawan S. Budhwar and Angelo DeNisi

International Human Resource Management
Policy and practice for multinational enterprises (Third edition)
Dennis R. Briscoe, Randall S. Schuler, and Lisbeth Claus

International Human Resource Management

Third Edition

Policies and practices for
multinational enterprises

Dennis R. Briscoe
Randall S. Schuler
Lisbeth Claus

Routledge
Taylor & Francis Group

LONDON AND NEW YORK

First published 1995
by Prentice Hall

Second edition 2004
by Routledge

Third edition 2009
by Routledge
2 Park Square, Milton Park, Abingdon, Oxon OX14 4RN

Simultaneously published in the USA and Canada
by Routledge
270 Madison Avenue, New York, NY 10016

Routledge is an imprint of the Taylor & Francis Group, an informa business

© 2009 Dennis R. Briscoe, Randall S. Schuler and Lisbeth Claus

Typeset in Times New Roman by
Florence Production Ltd, Stoodleigh, Devon
Printed and bound in India by
Replika Press Pvt, Ltd

British Library Cataloguing in Publication Data
A catalogue record for this book is available from the British Library

Library of Congress Cataloging in Publication Data
Briscoe, Dennis R., 1945–
    International human resource management: policy and practice
    for multinational enterprises/Dennis R. Briscoe, Randall S. Schuler, Lisbeth Claus. – 3rd ed.
        p. cm. – (Routledge global human resource management series)
    1. International business enterprises – Personnel management.
    I. Schuler, Randall S.   II. Claus, Lisbeth M.   III. Title.
    HF5549.5.E45B74 2007
    658.3 – dc22   2007051264

ISBN10: 0–415–77350–4 (hbk)
ISBN10: 0–415–77351–2 (pbk)
ISBN13: 978–0–415–77350–8 (hbk)
ISBN13: 978–0–415–77351–5 (pbk)

Contents

List of illustrations

List of tables

List of boxes

IHRM in Action

List of vignettes

Foreword

Global Human Resource Management is a series of books edited and authored by some of the best and most well known researchers in the field of human resource management. The series is aimed at offering students and practitioners accessible, coordinated and comprehensive books in global human resource management. To be used individually or together, these books cover the main bases of comparative and international human resource management. Taking an expert look at an increasingly important and complex area of global business, this is a groundbreaking new series that answers a real need for serious textbooks on global HRM.

Several books in this series are devoted to human resource management policies and practices in multinational enterprises. Some books focus on specific areas of global HRM policies and practices, such as global leadership, global compensation, global staffing and global labour relations. Other books address special topics that arise in multinational enterprises, such as managing HR in cross-border alliances, developing strategies and structures, and managing legal systems for multinational enterprises. This third edition serves as the foundation text for all the other books that focus on specific areas of global HRM policies and practices, and for the books that address special topics such as alliances, strategies and structures, and legal systems. As such its nine chapters provide the broadest possible base for an overview of all the major areas in the field of international human resource management. As with all the books in the series, the chapters are based upon the most recent and classic research, as well as numerous examples of what multinational enterprises are doing today.

In addition to books on various HRM topics in multinational enterprises, several other books in the series adopt a comparative approach to understanding human resource management. These books on comparative human resource management describe the HRM policies and practices found at the local level in selected countries in several regions of the world. The comparative books utilize a common framework that makes it easier for the reader to systematically understand the rationale for the existence of various HRM activities in different countries and easier to compare these activities across countries.

This series is intended to serve the growing market of global scholars and professionals who are seeking a deeper and broader understanding of the role and importance of human resource management in companies as they operate throughout the world. With this in mind, all books in the series provide a thorough review of existing research and numerous examples of companies around the world. Mini-company stories and examples are found throughout the chapters. In addition, many of the books in the series include at least one detailed case description that serves as convenient practical illustrations of topics discussed in the book. The internet site for this volume contains additional cases and resources for students and faculty to use for greater discussion of the topics in all the chapters.

Because a significant number of scholars and professionals throughout the world are involved in researching and practicing the topics examined in this series of books, the authorship of the books and the experience of companies cited in the books reflect a vast global representation. The authors in the series bring with them exceptional knowledge of the HRM topics they address, and in many cases the authors have been the pioneers of their topics. So we feel fortunate to have the involvement of such a distinguished group of academics in the series.

The publisher and editor also have played a major role in making this series possible. Routledge has provided its global production, marketing and reputation to make the series feasible and affordable to academics and practitioners throughout the world. In addition, Routledge has provided its own highly qualified professionals to make the series a reality. In particular we want to indicate our deep appreciation of the work of our series editor, Francesca Heslop. She has been very supportive from the very beginning and has been invaluable in providing support and encouragement to us and to the many authors in the series. Francesca, along with other Routledge staff, including Simon Whitmore, Russell George, Victoria Lincoln, Jacqueline Curthoys, Lindsie Court, Simon Alexander, Gemma Anderson, Dan Wadsworth and Asha Pearse, have helped make the process of completing the series an enjoyable one. For everything they have done, we thank them all.

Randall S. Schuler, Rutgers University and GBSA Zurich
Paul Sparrow, Lancaster University
Susan E. Jackson, Rutgers University and GSBA Zurich
Michael Poole, Cardiff University

Acknowledgments

There are many individuals who have provided valuable information, insights, and assistance in completing this book. They include: Susan Jackson, Rutgers University; Paul Sparrow, Lancaster Business School; Michael Poole, Cardiff University; Chris Brewster, Reading University; Paul Evans, INSEAD; Vlado Pucik, IMD; Yadong Luo, University of Miami; Ingmar Björkman, the Swedish School of Economics; Wes Harry, Lancashire University, Shaun Tyson and Michael Dickmann, Cranfield School of Management; Gary Florkowski, University of Pittsburgh; Cal Reynolds, Calvin Reynolds and Associates; Hugh Scullion, National University of Ireland; Stu Youngblood, Texas Christian University; Bruno Staffelbach, University of Zurich; Martin Hilb, University of St. Gallen; Christian Scholz, University of Saarlandes; Gerold Frick, Fachhochschule, Aachen; Michael Morley, University of Limerick; Charles Galunic and Isable Assureira, INSEAD; Ibraiz Tarique, Pace University; Shimon Dolon, ESADE; Georges Bachtold, Blumer Machines Company; Darryl Weiss, Lockheed Martin Orincon, San Diego; Jerry Edge, RMC Consultants; Joann Stang, Solar Turbines (retired); Bernie Kulchin, Cubic Corporation; Ben Shaw, Bond University; Ed Watson, KPMG; Gardiner Hempel, Deloitte and Touche; Wayne Cascio and Manuel Serapio, University of Colorado–Denver; and Bob Grove, San Diego Employers' Association (retired). Dr. Schuler thanks many students at Rutgers University in the Department of Human Resource Management for their teaching and writing suggestions, and the department's webmaster, Joanne Mangels for her work on the construction of his global web site. Dr. Briscoe thanks his graduate students at the University of San Diego, particularly his most recent assistant, Chanyu Miao, for their help in research into IHRM and country HR practices and in development of Dr. Briscoe's web site (http://www.internationalhrm.com), particularly Mario D'Angelo, who is now web designer for Globe[3]. Dr. Claus would like to thank the past board members of the SHRM Global Forum and members of the current SHRM Global Expert Panel. Special thanks to Carolyn Gould, PricewaterhouseCoopers LLP; Brian Glade and Howard Wallack, SHRM; Thomas Becker, OBI; Gerlinde Herrmann, The Herrmann Group Limited; Ian Benson, Simona Bucur, Brian Coon, Leah Daniels, Alin Hutanu, Erin Landers, and Margaret Stearns, her research associates at Willamette University; Mary Stout, faculty administrative assistant at Willamette University; her global HR students in the early career MBA at Willamette University; and the many "now GPHR-certified" global HR practitioners that she taught in the SHRM/GPHER certification preperation courses in the US, Europe, and China.

Finally the authors thank the many great people at Routledge for their wonderful assistance and support throughout this project. Dr. Briscoe also acknowledges the support from his wife, Georgia, who provided the inspiration and example for "going for the summit" in completing this third edition (she's a serious mountain climber), without whom the climb would have been much harder, and the inspiration provided by our son, Forrest, who is now making his own climb. He also acknowledges how great it was to work with his co-authors, Lisbeth Claus and Randall Schuler. They provided the support necessary to complete the project within tough deadlines, and whose contributions improved the final product beyond measure.

List of acronyms

ADA	Americans with Disabilities Act
ADEA	Age Discrimination in Employment Act
Aka	also known as
APEC	Asia–Pacific Economic Cooperation
ASEAN	Association of South East Asian Nations
BOK	body of knowledge
BRIC	Brazil, Russia, India, China
BT	business traveler
C&B	compensation and benefits
CBT	computer-based training
CEE	Central and Eastern Europe
CEO	chief executive officer
CFO	chief financial officer
CIPD	Chartered Institute of Personnel and Development
COLA	cost of living allowance
CSR	corporate social responsibility
EEA	European Economic Area
EFTA	European Free Trade Agreement
EPI	efficient purchaser index
ESOP	employee stock ownership plan
ESPP	employee stock purchase plan
ETUC	European Trade Union Confederation
EU	European Union
FCN treaty	Friendship, Commerce, and Navigation Treaty
FCPA	Foreign Corrupt Practices Act
FDI	foreign direct investment
FTAA	Free Trade Area of the Americas
Fx	exchange rate
GATT	General Agreement on Tariffs and Trade
GEC	global employment company
GI	global integration
GLOBE	global leadership and organizational behavior effectiveness
GPHR	global professional in human resources

GHRIS	global human resource information system
GUFs	global union federations
HCN	host country national
HQ	headquarters
HR	human resources
HRCI	Human Resource Certification Institute
HRIS	human resource information system
HRM	human resource management
IA	international assignee
IB	international business
ICC	International Chamber of Commerce
ICFTU	International Confederation of Free Trade Unions
IE	international employee
IHR	international human resources
IHRM	international human resource management
IJV	international joint venture
ILO	International Labour Organization
IPM	international performance management
IMF	International Monetary Fund
INS	Immigration and Naturalization Service
IPM	international performance management
IPO	Intellectual Property Office
IT	information technology
ITUC	International Trade Union Confederation
JV	joint venture
LR	local responsiveness
M&A	mergers and acquisitions
MNE	multinational enterprise
NAALC	North American Agreement on Labor Cooperation
NAFTA	North American Free Trade Agreement
NGO	non-governmental organization
OECD	Organization for Economic Cooperation and Development
OEEC	Organization for European Economic Co-operation
PA	performance appraisal
PCN	parent country national
PCT	Patent Cooperation Treaty
PM	performance management
PRC	People's Republic of China
R&D	research and development
SAR	stock appreciation rights
SEC	Securities and Exchange Commission
SHRM	Society for Human Resource Management
SIHRM	strategic international human resource management
SME	small and medium-sized enterprises
SOX	Sarbanes–Oxley

TCN	third country national
T&D	training and development
TI	Transparency International
TNC	transnational corporation
TUAC	Trade Union Advisory Committee
UN	United Nations
UNCTAD	United Nations Conference on Trade and Development
UK	United Kingdom
US	United States
WCL	World Confederation of Labour
WFTU	World Federation of Trade Unions
WLB	Work–life balance
WIPO	World Industrial Property Organization
WTO	World Trade Organization

Introduction

This book is about International Human Resource Management (IHRM). That is, it is about human resource management in a global context. The conduct of business is increasingly global in scope and managing human resources has become critical to the successful conduct of global business. This third edition has been written to update this most important but fast changing discipline. The majority of the book discusses the IHRM issues faced by multinational enterprises (MNEs), primarily from the perspective of the parent company or headquarters. However, MNEs increasingly manage their work forces on a global basis, so this edition not only examines management of parent companies' work forces, but provides increased focus on management of work forces in subsidiaries, international joint ventures, and global partnerships, as well as issues related to human resource management of global work forces, with globalized policies, shared services, and global centers of HR excellence.

New effort was made to globalize the information, to present it from the perspectives of as many different MNEs, from as many different countries, as possible. So the examples in the chapters as well as the end-of-chapter vignettes draw from many small and medium-sized companies (many of which will be new to the reader), as well as the traditional and well known large firms, which come from both large and small countries.

PARTS AND CHAPTERS

This book is divided into two parts (see the chapter map, Figure 1, to understand how the topics relate to each other). Part I describes the key components of the context within which IHRM operates. Each of these components contributes a critical part of the environment which determines the nature of IHRM. Part II describes the policies and practices that result from that context. The first part of the book sets the scene and explains why IHRM is so important to the success of international business, describing the nature of global commerce as it relates to IHRM. These chapters include (1) the globalization of HRM; (2) creating the international organization; (3) HRM and culture; and (4) global employment law, industrial relations, and international ethics.

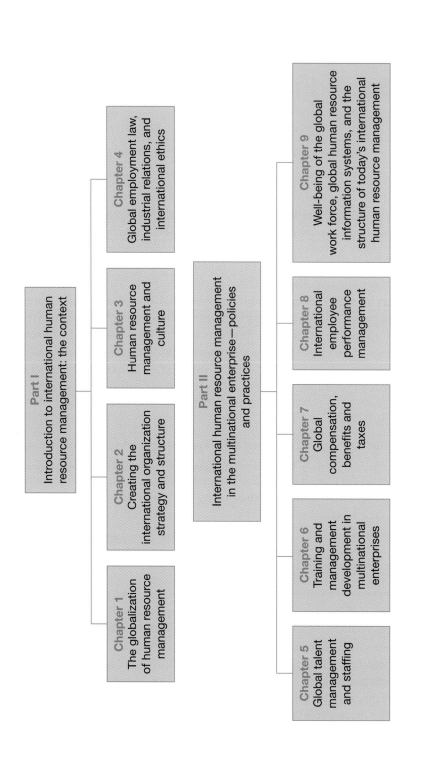

Figure 1 Chapter map

Chapter 1 introduces the globalization of business and describes how that has changed the nature of HRM. It describes the evolving nature of HRM as it meets the needs of changing MNEs and explains how this has led to the development of strategic IHRM in helping MNEs attain sustainable competitive advantage in the global marketplace. Chapter 1 describes the basic nature and development of IHRM, differentiates IHRM from domestic HRM, and discusses some of the difficulties experienced in that development.

Chapter 2 examines international business (IB) strategy, focusing on how varying approaches to international business affect the nature and design of multinational firms and the important role that IHRM plays in those design decisions. The conduct of international business is increasingly complex, involving the need to—at the same time—focus on centralized control and influence and local adaptation to customers and culture. This chapter describes the many different approaches to international business and explains how IHRM changes and contributes to the design and management of those various options.

Chapter 3 discusses national and organizational culture and the critical role it plays in determining IHR policies and practices. National cultural differences sometimes need to be accommodated and sometimes they are influenced by corporate culture. This chapter describes the nature of culture and how it influences in particular IHRM policies and practices, as described throughout Part II.

Chapter 4, the last chapter in Part I, describes international aspects of the legal, regulatory, labor relations, and ethical environments, all key components of the external context of IHRM. As is true for HRM in a domestic context, there are many aspects of the external (to the firm) environment that have a major impact on the importance and practice of HRM when operating in the global arena. This chapter discusses a number of these issues: (1) international employment law and the institutions that develop and apply it; (2) the extraterritorial application of country laws outside the countries of origin, particularly the application of US laws outside the US; (3) immigration law, in particular the role IHR plays in obtaining visas for increasingly mobile employees of the MNEs; (4) elements of international labor relations that are especially important to MNEs, and (5) ethical standards, behavior, and decision making in the international arena, particularly as they impact IHRM. All of these areas are increasingly important to MNEs and to IHRM and all have growing impacts on the successful contribution of IHR managers and the growing impact on IHR and enterprises operating in the global marketplace.

All of these components of the environment constitute the context within which IHRM creates and performs its policies and practices and, therefore, also sets the stage for the rest of the text, which provides a comprehensive overview of the policies and practices of IHRM. These policies and practices are described both from a centralized, headquarters-focused perspective as well as from the local perspective of subsidiaries, joint ventures, partnerships, and contractors. Part II is concerned with the global HR management of all employees of MNEs. Thus the chapters in this section include: (5) global talent management and staffing; (6) training and management development in MNEs; (7) global compensation, benefits, and taxes; (8) international employee performance management; and (9) the well-being of the global work force, global HRIS, and the structure of today's IHRM.

The first chapter in Part II, Chapter 5, focuses on the importance of talent management for the MNE and provides an overview of global staffing, including an explanation of global employment forecasting and planning and description of the many different types of international employees used by MNEs today. The central focus of this chapter is on description and analysis of international assignees (IAs), including their selection and preparation for foreign assignments as well as difficulties with and best practices in their management while on assignment.

Chapter 6 describes the function of training for a global work force as well as methods of management and leadership development in MNEs. In this chapter, attention is also paid to global (virtual) teamwork and the development of a global mind-set among employees of the MNEs. Chapter 7 describes the complex area of compensation, benefits, and taxes for both international assignees as well as for local work forces. Chapter 8 describes the topic of performance management with respect to a global work force. Chapter 9, the last chapter, looks at a number of issues of importance to today's MNEs, from maintaining and protecting employees' health, safety, and well-being, to the provision of a number of important services, such as a global human resource information system, relocation services, and IHR research, and lastly, the professionalization of IHR managers and design of HR departments and the services they provide.

CHAPTER AND BOOK FEATURES

This edition has been shortened, combining chapters in order to make the presentation more concise, and the language has been simplified in order to make the text more reader-friendly, particularly for those who are not native speakers of English. Each chapter begins with "learning objectives" and a list of "key terms" introduced in that chapter. The learning objectives provide a focus for readers as they consider the material in each chapter. Similarly, the key terms allow the reader to focus on IHR-specific terminology as the global HR body of knowledge is becoming more codified.

All chapters also contain one or more "IHRM in Action" illustrations of current experiences of multinational enterprises, both large and small, and well known and some probably not known at all, and from major countries and lesser-known countries. All of the examples have been chosen to point out to the reader how firms from around the world have implemented the policies and practices described in the text. At the end of each chapter there is a set of questions to guide class discussion of the themes and topics in the chapter as well as one or more "vignettes" written specifically for this text and for illustration and discussion of the central concepts in each chapter.

The end-of-book materials include the notes that document the text in each chapter, including relevant classic resources and up-to-date worldwide research, and the experiences and stories of multinational enterprises. To add even more relevant information as it unfolds, the reader is encouraged to visit numerous websites that are available, many of which are referenced in the notes and throughout the text. Additional websites and other materials are found on the website for this text, which is maintained by the publisher at www.routlege.com/textbooks/9780415773515.

Finally, there are thorough subject and author indexes. These provide the reader with further information about the various topics covered in the book as well as the many authors whose work has been used to compile this book and facilitates locating topics and authors throughout the text.

TERMINOLOGY

In this book, a number of terms are used to refer to organizations that conduct international business. In general, the term MNE (multinational enterprise) is used to refer to all organizations that conduct business outside their countries of origin. The term MNE is used rather than MNC (multinational corporation—which is often a more commonly used term) because in many countries there is no form of legal ownership equivalent to the American corporation, from whence derives the term MNC. So we chose a term that can be used with wider application without being tied technically to the legal structure of one particular country. Thus, in this text the generic term "enterprise" is used to refer to any type of organization involved with international business. For small and medium-sized MNEs, the term SME is sometimes used. Generally, the term MNE is used throughout the book. When appropriate, SME will be used to highlight special characteristics of small and medium-sized MNEs.

MNEs can be described as operating multinationally, internationally, globally, or transnationally. While these terms often seem to be used interchangeably, some distinctions can be made. For example the term "global" refers to enterprises that operate all over the world and have consistent policies and practices throughout their operations. Such MNEs have a high percentage of international turnover or sales (over 50 percent) outside their home countries, and a high percentage of employees outside their home countries, as well, with operations in a large number of countries, and a global perspective and attitude reflected in their business strategies and in their mission statements. These firms tend to have highly centralized (or, at least, regionalized) policy, at least as it applies to financial issues and sharing of resources and innovations, and world-class standards for their global products and services. In contrast, transnational firms are global in scope but decentralized and localized in products, marketing strategies, and operations. That is, they take advantage of their global presence to gain access to resources (ideas, technology, capital, people, products, and services) and develop economies of scale, while at the same time maintaining a local presence that is seen as comparable to that of domestic competitors. The other terms, such as "multinational" or "international," generally refer to MNEs that have not yet developed their levels of international operations to this extent. Because more and more enterprises are moving in the direction of being more global, in thought at least, if not in action, the word "global" is used in both the subtitle of this book as well as in the title of the entire series. Thus most of the topics, policies, and practices discussed throughout this book are currently applicable to most enterprises, and are likely to soon apply to most others. In this book, if the terms global, multinational, or international enterprise make a difference to the particular topic, policy, or practice being discussed, then an attempt is made to make it clear through explanation or the use of the terminology as to which type of enterprise is being described.

Introduction to international human resource management: the context

1 The globalization of human resource management

This book is about Human Resource Management (HRM) in organizations that operate in the global economy. That is, it is about the globalization of HRM (referred to in this text as International HRM or IHRM). Over the last fifty to 100 years, the economies of the world have become increasingly integrated.[1] This has been driven by many forces and led by what is now referred to as the multinational enterprise (MNE). As enterprises have increased their global activity, all of their business functions have required adaptation, including human resource management. This book is about the nature of HRM in the multinational enterprise.

This first chapter provides an introduction to and overview of the evolution of the globalization of commerce and its impact on human resource management. HRM has become one of the most important business functions, today, particularly in terms of a global enterprise's ability to build sustainable competitive advantage in the global economy.

The pace of globalization is continuing to increase. Markets for most goods and services are global, investment across borders continues to increase, the number and value of cross-border mergers and acquisitions, international joint ventures, and alliances continues to increase, and the amount of money and number of people (legal and illegal) that cross borders are on the rise. Thousands of firms and millions of people work outside their countries of origin and millions of people work at home for foreign-owned companies. Competition almost everywhere is global in scope, meaning almost all enterprises face real or potential competition from foreign products or services or from foreign-owned subsidiaries and domestic firms that are now foreign-owned. In addition, inputs to business activity (including financial capital, materiel, ideas, technology, parts, insurance, legal services, office equipment and, of course, employees) are available everywhere at world-class quality, price, and speed, creating global standards and competition in virtually every industry and sector.

What this means is that there is no way for anyone or any business to escape from constant global pressure. It affects everyone and all aspects of every organization. The conduct of business has become a truly global activity. And so has HRM. This is the purpose of this introductory chapter: to provide understanding of how this pervasive globalization is affecting HRM—and to show how today's HRM is carrying out its new obligations and how it is changing to meet the demands of this newly interconnected world.

THE INTERNATIONALIZATION OF BUSINESS

Enterprises, large and small, from all countries (developed and developing) are already or are in the process of going global. The names of the largest businesses from the wealthiest countries are well known. However, large firms from developing countries and small to medium-sized enterprises (SMEs) from both developed and developing countries may not be as well known, but their presence is also being felt ever more strongly throughout the world. Because of this, a strong effort has been made throughout this book to provide examples from not only the large, well known, companies, but also from lesser-known firms. For example, IHRM in Action 1.1 tells the story of one such firm, Harry Ramsden's Fish and Chips, from the UK, as it decided to "go international." Harry Ramsden's provides a classic example of what has happened—and is continuing to happen—to small and medium-sized firms everywhere.

What is driving this interest in and need to globalize? There are many pressures, including the following:

- *Increased travel.* International travel has become much easier, quicker, and cheaper. Hundreds of millions of people travel across national borders every year, for business and pleasure. They see how people in other countries live and they experience goods and services that are available in other countries. They then take back home either some of those products or, at least, new expectations for what is possible. Many either decide to trade in these products or recognize new opportunities to sell their own products or services in the countries they visited.

- *Rapid and extensive global communication.* Global communication has also become much easier, quicker, more varied, and cheaper. Global television, music, movies, telecommunication, the internet, the worldwide web, and print media all spread information about how people around the world live and their standards of living, about what they think and want, which also helps to create expectations for an ever-increasing quality of life.

- *Rapid development and transfer of new technology.* New technologies are developed around the world and because of modern transportation, education, and communication, are made available everywhere. In addition, new technologies make it possible to manufacture products and deliver services with world-class quality and prices everywhere in the world. And modern education and information technology make it possible for just about every country to play a part in the global economy.

- *Free trade.* Trade between countries and within regions of the world is constantly increasing, as trade agreements (on a global basis, through the World Trade Organization, and regionally, through trade treaties, such as the EU, the North American Free Trade Agreement, and the Association of South East Asian Nations) decrease trade barriers and open markets. Often, local and national governments go even further, supporting and encouraging growing trade and foreign investment with tax incentives and free trade zones.

- *Education.* Improving education around the world is enabling firms everywhere to produce world-class products and services and raises expectations for those products and services. This also makes it possible for firms to produce and offer their products and services everywhere, using local talent.[2] Global communications and travel also facilitate the sharing of knowledge and information, so that no country or set of countries any longer has advantages based on better educational systems.

- *Migration of large numbers of people.* Not only do millions of people move to other countries to work (either because their employers ask them to relocate,

HARRY RAMSDEN'S GOES INTERNATIONAL

Deep-fried fish and chips have long been a popular snack in England. One of England's premium fish-and-chip shops, Harry Ramsden's, which was founded in Guiseley, Yorkshire, in 1928, is one of the few that have opened shops at multiple locations. By 1994 the company had eight branches in Britain, with more scheduled for opening, and one in Dublin, Ireland, and one recently opened in Hong Kong. Its busiest UK location was in the resort town of Blackpool, generating annual sales of over £1.5 million (US$2.3 million). Harry Ramsden's managers, however, dissatisfied with this success, wanted to turn Harry Ramsden's into a global enterprise.

To this end, the company set up its first international operation in Hong Kong. According to finance director Richard Taylor: "We marketed the product as Britain's fast food, and it proved extremely successful." Within two years the Hong Kong venture was generating annual sales equivalent to its Blackpool operations. Half of the initial clientele in Hong Kong were British expatriates, but within a couple of years, more than 80 percent of customers were ethnic Chinese, illustrating the relative ease with which at least some products and services, such as a country's favorite food, can transfer to another country and culture.

Emboldened by this success, Harry Ramsden's began to open additional overseas branches, in such logical places as Dublin, Ireland, and Melbourne, Australia, as well as in other more exotic locales, such as Singapore, Dubai in the United Arab Emirates, Saudi Arabia, Walt Disney World in the US, and Japan. In the first experimental shop in Tokyo, the Japanese took to this product, despite their traditional aversion to greasy food. This experience led to Harry Ramsden's looking for a Japanese partner to establish a joint venture in Japan and, thus, to facilitate the opening of more shops in Japan.

Richard Taylor stated its international strategy: "We want Harry Ramsden's to become a global brand. In the short term the greatest returns will be in the UK. But it would be a mistake to saturate the UK and then turn to the rest of the world. We'd probably come a cropper when we internationalized. We need experience now." As of 2006, Harry Ramsden's had 170 owned and franchised outlets in the UK and internationally.

Source Abrahams, P. (1994), Getting hooked on fish and chips in Japan, *Financial Times*, May 17, updated in 2006 from web sites www.harryramsdens.co.uk, http://en.wikipedia.org/wiki/Harry_Ramsden's, and www.market-reports.co.uk.

usually for a limited time, or they are recruited to fill jobs for which there are not enough local workers), but many millions more emigrate, legally and illegally, to other countries seeking work or are relocated because of natural disasters or political conflicts.

● *Knowledge sharing.* The impact of global enterprises, as they "export" their management philosophies and techniques, as well as their technologies, products, and services, around the world.[3]

● *Pressure on costs.* Because of local and global competition, firms are always seeking lower costs, in order to compete with local and global firms that have access to lower-cost materials and lower-cost inputs such as land, utilities, and labor. In addition to other reactions, this has led to outsourcing and offshoring of business activities and processes.

● *Search for new markets.* The mature markets and limited opportunities for growth in developed countries push many firms to seek markets in other countries in order to grow revenue and market share.

● *Homogenization of cultures.* The integration of cultures and values through the impact of global communication and the internet and the spread of products and services such as music, food, television, movies, and clothing, have led to common consumer demands around the world.

● *E-commerce.* The worldwide web, credit cards, and global transportation and logistics services, have made it possible for large and small firms to conduct business over the internet. If a business has a web site, its business is global, such that anyone—from anywhere in the world—who has access to the web can access that web site.

Together these pressures have created a new set of global realities for large and small enterprises—publicly traded, privately held, family-owned, and government-owned. These new global realities impact every aspect of enterprises, including—if not especially—their HRM functions. When businesses internationalize, HRM responsibilities, such as talent management, executive and leadership development, performance management (PM), compensation, and labor relations, take on global characteristics, requiring globally savvy HRM professionals to facilitate international business (IB) success. This chapter introduces and explores the connection between international business and IHRM and the rest of the book describes in detail the nature of IHRM and its connection to international business success.

The increasing importance of international business

Thomas Friedman, the *New York Times*'s senior foreign news correspondent, defines globalization as:

> . . . the inexorable integration of markets, nation-states, and technologies to a degree never witnessed before—in a way that is enabling individuals, corporations, and nation-states to reach around the world farther, faster, deeper,

and cheaper than ever before and in a way that is enabling the world to reach into individuals, corporations, and nation-states farther, faster, deeper, and cheaper than ever before.[4]

In other words, globalization is the ever-increasing interaction, interconnectedness, and integration of people, companies, and countries. Globalization is creating the political, economic, and social structure of the new world. There are some people who don't like the consequences of globalization; but the reality is that the expanding connections between people, companies, countries, and cultures are real, powerful, and increasing in importance. International business continues to grow in terms of enterprises conducting business across borders, foreign direct investment (FDI), and the value of trade between countries.

The United Nations estimates that there are approximately 70,000 transnational enterprises (those with assets and investments in other countries) with more than 690,000 affiliates that report total annual sales amounting to almost US$19 trillion as of 2005 and that employ more than 75 million people worldwide.[5] These numbers have more than doubled since 1990. The overall level of FDI has expanded rapidly to where it is now estimated to total at least US$9 trillion, with approximately 65 percent coming from and going to developed countries, which represents a large increase in FDI into (and from, if the large emerging markets are considered) the developing countries. (As will be illustrated later, this number is likely to be a low estimate, and certainly does not reflect the size of foreign trade or the volume of cross-border currency flows, as a function of stock market investments, currency exchanges, government interactions, etc., or other forms of international trade, such as exports and imports, outsourcing, offshoring, licensing, franchising, and subcontracting.) Indeed, the amount of FDI and trade coming from and going to developing countries, particularly the large emerging markets, including India, China, Russia, Brazil, Indonesia, Mexico, South Africa, and the countries of Central and Eastern Europe, is also increasing quite rapidly[6] and will likely surpass the gross domestic products of today's wealthiest countries by the mid-point of this century. And even though the total value of trade from large countries like the US, UK, Japan, France, and Germany continues to increase, there are many smaller countries, such as Belgium, the Netherlands, Austria, Switzerland, Denmark, Sweden, Canada, and Singapore, where exports already represent more than 30 percent of their GDP. In addition, of course, the emerging economies like Brazil, India, China, and Russia (referred to as the BRIC countries) are increasing their international trade (both exports and imports) at a rapid pace. Even the value of international acquisitions continues to grow at a rapid pace, reaching over US$3 trillion in 2006![7]

The following paragraphs provide a few examples to further illustrate the expansion of global commerce. Fifty years ago the US economy accounted for 53 percent of global GDP; but today it accounts for less than 28 percent of global GDP (or less than 20 percent in terms of global purchasing power parity), albeit both of a much larger US GDP and of a very much larger global economy.[8] Not only is the world economy much larger in absolute terms, but an ever-increasing number of countries are developing a significant presence in that economy. It is no longer just a few large countries, such as Great Britain, Germany, France, Japan, and the US, that play important roles in the global economy. There is an ever-growing number of countries whose enterprises are represented among the world's largest MNEs and there are many thousands more SMEs which don't show up in the surveys or rankings but which also play a significant role in the conduct of international commerce.

The *Fortune* Global 500 (which is a ranking of the largest publicly traded firms in the world, based on their amount of revenues) includes firms from an ever-increasing number of countries.[9] The 2006 list (for the year 2005) included firms from 229 cities in thirty-two countries. (Just three years earlier, there were only twenty-five countries represented.) *Business Week*'s Global 1000 (a ranking of the largest publicly traded firms based on their market capitalization), which for the first time included the top publicly traded businesses from emerging markets, included firms from thirty-eight countries in its 2006 list.[10] *Forbes'* Global 2000 (a ranking of the largest public companies based on a composite of sales, profits, assets, and market value) included firms from fifty-four countries in its 2006 list.[11] The London *Financial Times'* Global 500 (based on market capitalization in all the major stock markets from around the world) included firms from thirty-three countries in their 2006 list.[12] *Fortune* magazine has even developed a list of the fifty most powerful women in the global economy, which in late 2006 profiled women from twenty different countries.[13]

The point is that international business is no longer only the domain of large firms from the large and/or developed countries. These surveys show that now enterprises from such small, developing, and/or emerging markets (in alphabetical order) as Argentina, Bermuda, Brazil, Chile, China, Colombia, the Czech Republic, Egypt, Greece, Iceland, India, Indonesia, Israel, Jordan, Liberia, Luxembourg, Malaysia, Mexico, Morocco, Pakistan, Panama, the Philippines, Poland, Portugal, Russia, Saudi Arabia, Singapore, South Africa, South Korea, Thailand, Taiwan, Turkey, the United Arab Emirates, and Venezuela are contributing in a big way to global trade.

All of these surveys focus on large, publicly traded firms. The key reason, of course, is that data about these firms are readily available from their stock market filings. They do not, however, include the thousands of SMEs nor private and family-held businesses or government-owned enterprises, which most of the time do not publish their financial results. Some privately owned firms (such as Superbrands in the UK and the Hangzhou Wahaha group in China), family-owned firms (such as Ikea in Sweden and Gianni Versace in Italy), as well as government-owned enterprises (such as Japan Post and China National Pharmaceutical Group) are among the world's largest and/or most global firms. Of course, there are also millions of small to medium-sized firms that sell and purchase in the global marketplace. Since there is no way to track their size or numbers, there is no way to be sure of their importance to global trade. But certainly it is very large. And the HR issues in their global operations are just as important to them as they are to their larger competitors.

Hermann Simon's book *Hidden Champions: Lessons from 500 of the World's Best Unknown Companies*, focused on relatively little known SMEs with worldwide market shares of 50 percent to 90 percent.[14] These SMEs do not always follow the management and organizational practices—including HR practices—of their better-known, larger, MNE counterparts, yet they often also dominate their market niches. Indeed, in many countries, many of the firms that conduct international business are quite small. It is estimated, for example, that there are in Germany about 350 small to medium-sized firms (SMEs with fewer than 300 or so employees) that dominate their global niche markets.

Adding to the complexity is the growing number of firms that derive over half their revenues outside their home countries and the increasing number of firms whose ownership is held by firms from another country. Some of the larger (and more familiar) firms with greater than 50 percent of their revenues from outside their home countries (in alphabetical order) include ABB Asea Brown Boveri, BP Amoco, Coca-cola, Dow Chemical, Exxon, Fuji Film, Hewlett-Packard, Honda Motors, IBM, Ikea, Intel, Manpower, McDonald's, Nestlé, Nokia, Royal Dutch Shell, Siemens, Unilever, Volkswagen, and Xerox. In addition, many well known firms are now owned by firms from another country, including Firestone Tire (owned by Bridgestone, Japan), Guinness (owned by Diageo, UK), Holiday Inn (purchased by Bass, UK, but now a part of Intercontinental Hotels, UK), RCA (owned by Thomson, France), Braun (purchased by Gillette, which has now been purchased by Procter & Gamble), Godiva Chocolate (purchased by Campbell Soup, US), Nissan (majority ownership by Renault, France), etc. Sometimes, it is the case that the foreign owner is a large firm that has purchased a smaller firm in another country, e.g., Ford Motor Company's ownership of Volvo or Unilever's ownership of Best Foods (US) and Ben & Jerry's Ice Cream (US). And sometimes, it is a fairly large family-owned business from a small country that purchases a business in a larger country, such as Badger Manufacturing, from El Salvador, a family-owned manufacturer of plastic-wrap for grocery stores throughout Latin America, that purchased the major producer of such plastic wrap in the US.

And, beyond this, firms of all types and sizes, in addition to acquiring and establishing foreign subsidiaries, are increasingly licensing, subcontracting, outsourcing, offshoring, and forming alliances with foreign partners.

As a result of these international acquisitions and partnerships, the nationality of firms, products, and services is becoming ever more difficult to identify and, for practical purposes, even irrelevant. This is also true for the nationality and location of a firm's human resources. The management of these "borderless" human resources is a complex and difficult task (largely because it is usually still anchored in the national identities that govern their legal, institutional, and cultural characters)—but nevertheless a task that can be successfully and satisfyingly accomplished. The core challenge of IHRM is to operate in these seemingly borderless firms yet within the constraints of multiple national laws and cultures.

In summary, the point being made here is that the globalization of business is proceeding at an unexpected and unprecedented rate.[15] The opening of markets and the appearance of competitive foreign firms places pressure on virtually every major industry in virtually every country. These developments impact human resource management on a number of fronts. The increased intensity of competition places great pressure on firms to develop the capacity to operate at lower costs and with greater speed, quality, customer service, and innovation, both at home and abroad. HR is called upon to recruit, select, develop, and retain the work force talent that can achieve this global competitiveness, often in dozens of countries.

The strategic decision to "go international"

MNEs, in order to be successful in the global marketplace, must develop business strategies that take advantage of global resources and markets, including their human resource functions. In order for IHR managers to make an effective contribution to that success, they have had to learn how to contribute to the global strategic management of the enterprise. Since firms differ in their levels of international development and in the scope of their international operations, IHR managers must be able to assist in the development of those global operations, no matter their scope. Variances in the strategic international development of firms influences IHRM and how strategic IHRM has developed to support those varying global strategies and activities.

In an *ideal* world, firms will regularly analyze their external environments and their internal capabilities and resources in order to develop strategies for competitive advantage and continuing success. Strategy management is an ongoing process to develop internal consistency within the firm (alignment of every function with the firm strategy) and adjustment to the external environment (fit of firm capabilities and resources with opportunities).

> Among all the things managers do, nothing affects a company's ultimate success or failure more fundamentally than how well its management team charts the company's long-term direction, develops competitively effective strategic moves and business approaches, and implements what needs to be done internally to produce good day-in/day-out strategy execution. Indeed, *good strategy and good strategy execution are the most trustworthy signs of good management.*[16]

In that same *ideal* world, all business functions of the firm will be closely integrated into the planning and will be involved with parallel strategic planning within their own areas of responsibility (see Pucik and Evans, *People Strategies for MNEs*, in this series, for more detailed discussion of how this looks for HRM). In terms of HR, many of the same issues arise—albeit in a much more complex way—when a firm's strategic planning "goes international" as when its strategic planning is concerned only with domestic issues. When management begin to develop and implement global strategic plans, they also begin to concern themselves with global HR issues.[17] Indeed, the HR issues are among the most critical issues for successfully competing in the global marketplace. Because of that, HR—in this *ideal* world—will be involved in the international strategic decision making at every step.

The new, global, complex, and often chaotic world of the MNE requires a new strategic focus and new capabilities from HR just as it does from other management functions. Only limited studies have been made of the extent to which multinational firms actually involve their HRM functions in their global strategic planning. These studies suggest that HR does not tend to be as involved as would be hoped. Often the HR department is one of the last areas of management to be impacted by internationalization and HR managers are among the last to personally internationalize. However, experience and observation suggest that this situation is rapidly improving.

How do the various HR practitioners play this strategic role in the MNE? First, we assume (in an ideal world) that the senior HR executive of an MNE has a seat at the table among other senior executives of the C-suite. In that role, the senior HR executive is an active participant in the development of the global strategy and guides the firm in terms of global talent management issues. Second, the senior HR executive develops the HR strategy with the global HR team (usually made up of the country HR directors and the senior HR experts in the functional areas of HR talent management). The global HR strategic plan supports the corporate strategic objectives. Then, each business unit, regional, and country HR unit develops an HR work plan to achieve the HR strategic objectives and develops metrics to evaluate timely results.

International orientation

One aspect of international strategy that has been relatively well studied involves the international orientation of senior executives, usually referred to in terms proposed by Perlmutter, such as ethnocentric, regiocentric, polycentric, and geocentric.[18] The central strategic issue in a firm's orientation is the degree of domination of the MNE headquarters over subsidiary management and HR practices. Thus this headquarters orientation goes a long way toward determining the level of autonomy that subsidiaries enjoy in their management and HR practices.

Ethnocentrism

The initial orientation of most managers in MNE headquarters, especially those from a relatively homogeneous national population and culture (or from a country with a strong nationalist or patriotic culture), is one of *ethnocentrism*. In this orientation, managers are most likely to use a home country standard as a reference in managing international activities. The outlook is one of centralized decision making and high control over international operations that are centered in the headquarters. Managers with such a mind-set are likely to follow an international strategy of replicating home country systems, procedures, and structure abroad.[19] This mind-set is likely to make extensive use of expatriates from headquarters to establish and manage the subsidiary operations.

Polycentrism or regiocentrism

Over time and as a result of increased experience, managerial orientation tends to evolve or develop into *polycentrism* or *regiocentrism*. Here, as international investment and involvement increase, the host country culture and traditions assume increased salience. This may be extended to include a number of similar countries in a region, with host country standards and practices increasingly used as a reference point for managing company operations. The strategies typically followed are likely to be multinational (or multidomestic) strategies that emphasize decentralized and autonomous operations within wholly owned subsidiaries. Under this mind-set, HR managers in the foreign subsidiaries tend to be local and relatively autonomous from headquarters influence and oversight.

Geocentrism

When a firm reaches the level of a global orientation, a *geocentric* mind-set will develop and be adopted. Here the managerial outlook is one of creating a global network and a preference for following a transnational strategy that is integrative and interdependent among various elements of the global organization. Under the geocentric mind-set HR practices will include extensive use of expatriates and inpatriates (these and related terms will be fully defined and explored in Chapter 6 on staffing) with a broad global sharing of HR practices and adoption of the best practices, no matter their origins.

It would be expected that HR policies and practices would be as centralized or decentralized as the overall strategic mind-set of the enterprise. Indeed, in one study relating these concepts to IHR practices, it was found that IHR practices do indeed correlate with these mind-sets.[20] That is, in firms with an ethnocentric orientation, HR practices for international operations tend to copy parent company practices and are very centralized. In firms with a polycentric mind-set, HR practices tend to be decentralized and local subsidiaries tend to be much more likely to be left alone, managed by a local HR manager who will follow local HR practices. And in firms with a geocentric orientation, HR practices tend to be more eclectic, borrowing best practices from around the world, rather than giving preference necessarily to either headquarters or local practices. However, more recent developments into HR shared service centers, where transactional HR activities are shared by various users in the organization and user-level agreements and charge-back systems are developed, are proving that centralized services can be developed to service localized internal HR customers.

THE INTERNATIONALIZATION OF HUMAN RESOURCE MANAGEMENT

Broadly defined, the field of IHRM is the *study and application of all human resource management activities as they impact the process of managing human resources in enterprises in the global environment.* HRM in the MNE is playing an increasingly significant role in providing solutions to business problems at the global level. Consequently there is a need to re-examine how HR policies can best support the rapid advance of globalization.[21] The challenges facing HRM in the MNE, as the function strives to become the crusader of globalization, include the following:

1. *Developing* a global mind-set inside the HR function, particularly awareness and understanding of the new global competitive environment and the impact it has on the management of people worldwide. The global HR challenge consists of how to effectively attract, engage, and retain the thousands of MNE employees in many different countries to achieve strategic objectives. This not only includes engaging employees in different countries of the MNE but also the role and importance of globally mobile employees such as expatriates, inpatriates, and short-term international assignees.
2. *Aligning* core HR processes and activities with the new requirements of competing globally, while simultaneously responding to local issues and requirements.
3. *Enhancing* global competencies and capabilities within the HR function.[22]

Forms of international human resource management

Internationalization of HRM can take many forms. For practical purposes, HR managers in most types of firms will confront at least some aspects of internationalization. That is to say, the globalization and technology factors that have led to there being "no place to hide" for business, in general, have also led to there being no place to hide for the HR professional. HR practitioners can find themselves involved in—and therefore must understand and become skilled at dealing with—IHRM issues in almost every job situation. The following provides a short summary of the most significant of these situations.

Headquarters of multinationals

This situation involves working as an HR professional in the central or regional headquarters of the traditional MNE, such as depicted by firm X in country A in Figure 1.1. This is the situation that receives almost all of the attention in literature about the internationalization of business and is, by far, the best-known for HR managers. The focus is from the center out to the subsidiaries and alliances, dictating and overseeing HR practice in all foreign operations and administering the movement of employees between locations. In the past, this primarily involved the relocation of expatriates from headquarters to foreign subsidiaries and back. But now it also

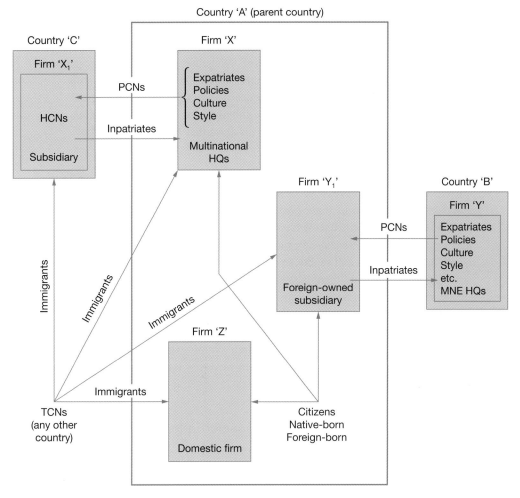

Figure 1.1 International human resource management.
Source Briscoe, D. R., for this book

involves the movement of international assignees across all borders and the development of HR policy and practices throughout the firm's global operations. Increasingly, this can also mean for HR professionals, themselves, working as expatriate HR managers in foreign subsidiaries or alliances.

This situation involves, for example, an HR manager working in her or his home country in the MNE headquarters for a firm like Nokia (Finland), Nestlé (Switzerland), Samsung (South Korea), or Citibank (US), all firms that have extensive foreign business operations. Typical headquarters IHRM responsibilities might include helping to select and prepare employees for international assignments, determining and administering compensation packages for these international assignees, developing safety programs for business travelers and international assignees, and establishing HRM policies and practices for the firm's foreign subsidiaries. Increasingly, however, the case in at least some MNEs, involves IHR becoming a major strategic partner in the firm's global planning and in talent management of the global work force, relegating many of the international assignee responsibilities to centralized shared service centers, or outsourcing them to specialized service providers. Typically, the headquarters either applies its parent country HRM practices directly to its foreign subsidiaries, or it tries to merge its personnel practices with those that are common in the host countries.

In terms of HR management in the foreign subsidiaries of MNEs, as a matter of practice and probably necessity, local HR managers are almost always host country nationals (HCNs). That is, these positions do not tend to be filled with HR managers from the parent firm. The use of local HR managers as part of the subsidiary management team makes sense because the host country work force is normally hired locally and work rules and practices must fit local laws and customs. Host country nationals are more likely than expatriate HR managers to be effective in the subsidiary HR position, even though HR policy is often "dictated" from the parent company headquarters. This centralization of HR policy can create problems with interface for host country (subsidiary) managers—including local HR managers—who will differ in their orientations from the parent country (headquarters) HR managers. As a matter of management development, however, in large firms, even HR managers may be rotated through foreign assignments.

Home country subsidiaries of foreign-owned enterprises

The second possibility for IHR involves the HR manager who works in his or her home country but works in a subsidiary of a foreign MNE, such as firm Y in country A in Figure 1.1. This often involves working for a home country firm that has been acquired by a foreign firm, although it may also involve working in a subsidiary established by a foreign firm. Now the HR manager may be on the receiving end of policy and practice as sent out from the (now) foreign headquarters (particularly when the foreign firm practices a centralized approach to its HR and management practices, applying its parent country policies and practices). This will involve working with the foreign headquarters (and, often, expatriate managers sent from the foreign enterprise) and typically will involve having to integrate a foreign philosophy and organizational culture into the local operations. This particular perspective has received little research attention, but is by no means uncommon. This situation would involve, for example, host country HR managers working in the local subsidiaries of MNEs that have set up operations in places like Central Europe (pharmaceutical companies, tobacco companies, telecommunications firms), India (software developers, call centers), China (manufacturing facilities, services), Africa (energy companies), and Latin America (commodity and natural resource firms), or even, maybe especially, HR managers working in the local subsidiaries of the large multinationals in Asia, the US, and Europe, such as Siemens, Toyota, and IBM.

The different communication styles, worker motivation philosophies, and organizational structures and frequent lack of understanding of the host country cultures, markets, employment laws and practices, even language itself, by the parent company can cause major problems for the local HR manager, and thus force that host country HR manager to confront aspects of internationalization that are just as difficult as those confronted by the home country HR manager working at headquarters and dealing with the "export" of policy and practice.

Domestic firms

The situation of firm Z in Figure 1.1 depicts what is "on the surface" a purely domestic firm, such as a hospital, farm, dry cleaner, ski resort, road or building construction contractor, or restaurant (or the purely domestic operations of an MNE, such as a local fast food franchise or a local petrol station). In many countries (particularly true in many locales in the US and Europe), these types of firms also confront many of the complexities of international business, particularly as they relate to IHRM. These complexities include: (1) the hiring of employees who come from another country, culture, and language (recent immigrants) or their families (who may have been born in the new country, and may be, therefore, now citizens, but who may still be more familiar with the language and culture with which they grow up at home than with that of their new country); as well as (2) having to deal with competition from foreign firms for customers and suppliers, or for capital which may well come from foreign-owned firms, or competition from these firms for resources, including employees. While outside of the West, these domestic firms tend to be relatively small, we now also see the phenomenon of what has been called "domestic multinationals." These are successful domestic companies in emerging markets that are going abroad and becoming MNEs themselves. Examples of such firms include Pliva (generic pharmaceuticals, Croatia), Mittal (steel, India), Tata Consulting Services, Infosys, and Wipro (IT services, India), Lukoil (oil company, Russia), Gazprom (oil and gas, Russia), Haier (home appliances, China), Mahindra & Mahindra (tractors and cars, India), Sadia (food and beverages, Brazil), Embraer (aereospace, Brazil), Koc (diversified industries, Turkey) and Cemex (building materials, Mexico), to name just a few. These emerging market companies are global players in their respective industries and have the potential of reaching the top rank of global corporations.[23]

The hiring—or recruiting—of immigrants (or, even, the first generation since immigration) in local, domestic firms can lead to many of the same internationalization concerns as those faced by MNEs, such as how to merge the cultures, languages, and general work expectations of employees from different countries, and how to respond to employees who bring to their new work situations sometimes very different languages and very different attitudes toward supervision and have very different expectations related to the practice of management. Even in the domestic firm, HR managers must develop all the knowledge and experience necessary to succeed in an internationalized environment.

IHRM in Action 1.2 illustrates how Aldrich Kilbride & Tatone, a Salem, Oregon-based accounting firm, dealt with the challenge of adding offices in Hillsboro (Oregon), San Diego (California), and two local offices in India. Rather than following the traditional outsourcing trends in accounting, the firm decided to establish Indian offices and hire full-time year-round staffs. Their experiences illustrates that in some (maybe many) communities, even in quite small firms, employers (and their HR managers) must rely on global expansion and staffing to serve their business needs and, thus, have to cope with many of the same international and global HR issues as do larger global firms.

In many countries, particularly in the European Union (EU) and in the US, shortages of certain types of employees, both highly educated and skilled as well as unskilled, have made it necessary to recruit such employees from other countries. This is even one more aspect of the global complexities that HR managers in all types of firms must confront and learn to deal with.

IHRM in Action 1.2

INTERNATIONAL EXPANSION FOR A LOCAL US ACCOUNTING FIRM

A 200-employee accounting firm may not top your list of global businesses with IHRM issues, but it should. Aldrich Kilbride & Tatone (AKT), an Oregon accounting firm, has operated since 1973 in the small town of Salem. Poised to grow the business, it made a number of strategic decisions to add services and locations. It opened two offices in Mumbai and Coimbatore (India) and merged with Grice Lund & Tarkington, a San Diego, California-based accounting firm. Rather than outsourcing, a route commonly used by accounting firms, AKT decided to establish its Indian offices through direct investment and hire its own year-round staff. Yet, because of the cyclical nature of their tax business, it had to overcome major hurdles to increase efficiency and create sustainable careers for its employees regardless of location. The biggest hurdles, initially, included computer security, file sharing, and time zones. But, it soon realized that cultural differences and maintaining a similar organizational culture in each of its locations was an additional challenge. While each office allows it to form teams of experts who can focus on specific customer needs, it also faced the challenge of deploying its Indian tax professionals when the frantic US tax season was done. AKT decided to partner with one of England's top firms. Now, from May through December, AKT's India staff work to prepare the tax returns of their partner's clients. The global expansion of this small US accounting firm proved to be successful for employees and customers alike because of the attention paid to people issues.

Source Kerr, J. (2007), Balancing AKT, *B2B Willamette Valley Magazine*, March 2007.

Government agencies and non-governmental organizations

Even though this text primarily discusses IHRM in a business context, many other types of organizations are also global in scope and are concerned about many of the same international issues. For example, government agencies such as the Foreign Ministries of countries and their embassies and the hundreds of non-governmental organizations (NGOs) that send representatives to other countries such as many organized religions (Catholic Church, LDS Church, Moon Church, Life Church, etc.), humanitarian organizations (international relief agencies, World Vision, Care, Mercy Corp, Red Cross, Habitat for Humanity, or Doctors Without Borders) all send hundreds of people from their parent headquarters to their overseas operations and often also employ many local and third country people to staff their activities around the globe.

In addition, there are an increasing number of agencies that are global by purpose and function, such as the United Nations and all of its agencies,[24] the World Bank, the World Trade Organization (WTO), the Organization for Economic Cooperation and Development (OECD), the Association of South East Asian Nations (ASEAN), and the EU with its large concentration of employees in Brussels, Strasbourg, and Luxembourg). Many IHR activities for these organizations are similar to those faced by their commercial counterparts. Indeed, many of them have experience with international operations over a longer period of time than is true for most firms and have accumulated much significant expertise on how to best handle global HR problems. Problems associated with recruiting, compensating, and managing employees in multiple countries are not much different for the International Red Cross or the World Health Organization than they are for IBM. HR managers in these types of organizations must also be globally savvy in order to effectively carry out their responsibilities and they often have much that they can teach their private sector counterparts.

The development of international human resource management

HR managers, no matter the type of organization for which they work, can and do confront aspects of IHR. The extent of this involvement will vary according to a number of factors, such as the degree of development of the global strategy of the enterprise, and will invariably increase with time. But as the general internationalization of business increases in extent and intensity, HR managers are being called upon to contribute increasing expertise to that internationalization.

Some of the HR-related questions that need to be answered within the MNE as it establishes its international strategy include:

- *Country selection.* Which countries make the most sense for locating international operations, and where will the firm be most likely able to recruit and hire the kinds of employees it will need at a competitive wage?

- *Gobal staffing.* How many employees will need to be relocated to foreign locations to start up the new operations and how many will be needed to run them (and does the firm have those people or know how to find or train them—or will the necessary people be found locally in the host countries)?
- *Recruitment and selection.* What will be required to find and recruit the necessary talent to make the new international operations successful?
- *Compensation.* How will the firm compensate its new global work force, both the international assignees from the home office as well as the new local employees?
- *Standardization or adaptation.* Will the firm want its HRM policies to be uniform across all of its locations (standardization or global integration) or will they be tailored to each location (adaptation or localization)?

Whether the local HR manager is from headquarters, from the host country, or from a third country, he or she will be sandwiched between his or her own culture and legal traditions and those of the firm, whether headquarters or local affiliate. HR managers at the local, regional, and headquarters levels must integrate and coordinate activities taking place in diverse environments with people of diverse backgrounds as well as with their own diverse backgrounds. Plus they are frequently also looked to for expertise in helping other managers be successful in their international endeavors, as well.

Since most organizations, today, experience one or more aspects of international HR, the success or failure of those enterprises is often a function of how they handle their IHR concerns. As a consequence, a new set of responsibilities has developed within the HR function.

Differences between international and domestic human resource management

It should be clear to the reader by now that international HRM differs from purely domestic HRM in a number of ways.[25] Some of these differences include IHR being responsible for:

- *More HR functions and activities*, for example, the management of international assignees which includes such things as foreign taxes, work visas, and assistance with international relocations.
- *A broader expertise and perspective*, including knowledge about foreign countries, their employment laws and practices, and cultural differences.
- *More involvement in people's lives*, as the firm relocates employees and their families from country to country.
- Dealing with and *managing a much wider mix of employees*, adding considerable complexity to the IHR management task—with each of the various types of global employees requiring different staffing, compensation, and benefits programs.
- *More external factors and influences*, such as dealing with issues stemming from multiple governments, cultures, currencies and languages.

● As a result, a greater level of risk, with greater exposure to problems and difficulties and, thus, exposure to much greater potential liabilities for making mistakes in HR decisions (for example, political risk and uncertainties, early repatriation of employees on foreign assignments, etc.).

In addition to these factors, the geographic dispersion, multiculturalism, different legal and social system(s), and the cross-border movement of capital, goods, services and people that the international firm faces adds a need for competency and sensitivity that is not found in the domestic firm.[26] The personal and professional attitudes and perspectives of the IHR manager must be greatly expanded to handle the multiple countries and cultures confronted in the international arena—both to manage their IHR responsibilities and to contribute to successful international business strategies by their firms—beyond those which the domestic HR manager must develop. The typical domestic HR manager does not have the contacts or networks that become necessary to learn about and to handle the new global responsibilities. He or she doesn't typically have any experience with the business and social protocols needed to interact successfully with foreign colleagues or with the forms of organizational structure used to pursue international strategies (such as joint ventures or cross-border acquisitions). And the still relatively limited body of literature and publicly available seminars and training programs make it much more difficult to develop the competencies needed to manage successfully the IHRM function.

Development of the international human resource management function

Some large MNEs, such as Nestlé, Unilever, Royal Dutch Shell, Colgate, and Ford Motor Company, have quite long histories of international activity, going back 100 years or more. By necessity of having to manage operations in many countries, these firms have developed—at least at their headquarters level—considerable international HR expertise. Even so, the specific business function called "international human resource management" is relatively new as a professional and academic activity.

The only professional society (what is now referred to as the "Global Forum" and used to be called the "Institute for International HR") was organized by the HR professional society in the US (the Society for Human Resource Management, SHRM) about thirty years ago. However, it has only been during the last twenty years or so that the annual meeting of the Global Forum has involved much more than a fairly small group of senior IHR managers from the large US MNEs (plus a few HR executives from MNEs from other countries). These meetings were largely an opportunity for these senior HR executives to share experiences and learn from each other about the issues they faced with the management of expatriates and the HR issues confronted in the establishment of local subsidiaries in foreign countries.

It has only been in the last ten to fifteen years that IHR service providers (such as cross-cultural training firms, international relocation firms, and global HR consultant firms) have focused on the globalization of HRM. SHRM, and a few universities, have begun to provide training seminars and courses in topics related to IHRM. Gradually, large professional societies similar to SHRM in other countries (such as the Chartered Institute of Personnel and Development, CIPD, in the UK), as well as the World Federation of Personnel Management (with over sixty national HR professional societies as members) are beginning to offer conferences and seminars focused on IHRM, as well. For details about CIPD, for example, see Sparrow *et al.*, *Globalizing Human Resource Management*, in this series.

A turning point in the professionalization of IHRM occurred with the establishment of the GPHR (Global Professional in Human Resources) certification by the Human Resource Certification Institute (HRCI) of the US in 2003. (For more information about the professionalization of IHRM, see pp. 333–334). The body of knowledge for this exam was codified into six domains (most of which are covered in this book and the additional books in the series). The domains include: (1) global strategic HR; (2) global organizational effectiveness and employee development; (3) global staffing; (4) global compensation and benefits; (5) international assignment management; and (6) international employee relations and regulations. Not only is GPHR the fastest-growing HR professional certification program, it attracts HR practitioners from around the world (see www.hrci.org).

As a business discipline and an academic field of study, IHRM may well still be in its infancy; yet it is very real and firmly established. There are many reasons for its youth, some of which have to do with the generally limited role of HRM within many firms, including some of the large MNEs, and some of which have to do with HR managers themselves. Suddenly, in the last twenty years or so, as business in general around the world has rapidly internationalized, HR professionals have been called upon to manage a number of new activities for which they have no preparation, to work alongside HR professionals from other countries with whom they have no prior experience, and to adapt their HR practices to multicultural and cross-cultural environments, with which they have little experience. Until quite recently, HR managers have not needed to embrace globalization as a part of their development. And business schools and professional societies have also been slow to add courses in international HR to their curricula.

Since HR, by its nature, focuses primarily on local staffing and employment issues, its practitioners are often the last ones in their firms to focus on the impact of increasing globalization, the last ones to take on international assignments, and thus often the last ones on the management team to contribute as fully fledged strategic partners in the internationalization of their firms.

A number of reasons have been put forth to explain this late awakening by HR to the importance of international business in firms and its impact on HR.[27] They include the lack of professionalization of HR (and IHR); the deep fragmentation into functional areas within HR practice, so that what limited international responsibilities there might be were not "seen" or evaluated as important by other HR practitioners; the lack of awareness and understanding among domestic HR practitioners of cross-cultural and IHR issues; the preoccupation with domestic legal and other practice issues; and the tremendous gap between the academic IHR body of knowledge and the international practitioner's expertise and concerns.

Clearly there is an identifiable body of knowledge and practice (such as that developed for SHRM's GPHR certification) that provides an important starting point for studying IHRM. A few journals focus specifically on this subject, such as the *International Journal of Human Resource Management.* And there are others that are more generically devoted to HR that have added frequent articles and special editions devoted to IHR. (See the web site for this book for a list of such journals, and for a complete listing of all of the books—about twenty, now—in this series on various aspects of IHRM, as well as professional associations.) And, gradually, the number of texts and readings books has increased while the number of courses and seminars at universities and provided by firms and professional societies has also gradually increased.

STRATEGIC INTERNATIONAL HUMAN RESOURCE MANAGEMENT

As HRM has become more involved with helping organizations be successful in their international endeavors, it has had to also develop a strategic global focus for itself. It has had to develop strategies to hire, manage, and retain the best employees throughout the enterprise's international activities, as well as attracting and retaining HR managers with global HR expertise so that HR can contribute effectively to the firm's overall global strategic planning.

The level of impact of an MNE's international activity on HR (and vice versa) varies according to a number of considerations, including the stage of internationalization, the global nature of the particular industry, and the particular choices the firm makes to structure its international operations. International HR activities are very different based on the stage of internationalization of the firm (i.e., in the transition from being a domestic to becoming a transnational organization).[28] When a firm is basically domestic or only exports its products/services and all employees are in the headquarters country, there may be little apparent need for IHRM. However, the HR experience of many of these largely domestic firms is that they "suddenly become global"[29] and that HR practitioners, with little or no international experience, are almost overnight dealing with setting up offices and staffing in countries outside of the home country. At other times, there may be considerable demand for global services from the HR function (for example, when the need for increased numbers of expatriates arises to staff foreign operations). These HR activities may not be housed within the essential core of the HR function—partially because many of these services can be provided by consultants or through other forms of temporary assistance, and partially because HR doesn't, at least initially, have the expertise and it must seek help outside the firm. The main role of IHRM at the typical already established MNE is to support the global activities of the firm (and the local HR functions) in the firm's foreign subsidiaries and other local operations, such acquisitions, joint ventures, partnerships, and alliances. HR activities may also vary by the type of industry. When the firm's industry is a global industry, such as oil, automobiles, airlines, or consumer personal care products, and it is pursuing a global business strategy, the need for coordination and centralization for worldwide consistency of HR policy and practice becomes more important. Some other industries, such as the insurance industry, are rather latecomers to globalization. Finally, the factor that will affect HR practices the most is the firm's international strategy (global integration versus local responsiveness) and accompanying decision-making structure (centralized versus decentralized decision making). This tension between standardization (global integration) and adaptation (local responsiveness) often becomes the major conflict within the MNE's strategic management planning and, specifically, within IHRM's support of those plans.[30]

> In order to build, maintain, and develop their corporate identity, multinational organizations need to strive for consistency in their ways of managing people on a worldwide basis. Yet, in order to be effective locally, they also need to adapt those ways to the specific cultural requirements of different societies. While the global nature of the business may call for increased consistency, the variety of cultural environments may be calling for differentiation.[31]

Often, MNEs begin their international "experiments" with reliance on expatriates to found and manage their foreign operations (with the usual exception of HR, normally provided by local expertise). Then, as they gain international experience and grow more comfortable with their foreign hosts, they typically evolve toward increasing reliance on local control and management. Today, however, many MNEs develop toward a common set of values and organizational culture, trying to ensure a centralized, common corporate vision and objectives throughout their global operations. In this stage, cross-national management training, cross-national assignments for management development and promotions, and cross-national project teams are relied on to embed this global vision in the global enterprise. In deed, as will be described throughout this book, many firms are now seeking ways to develop globally consistent HR practices throughout all of their operations as a way to reinforce a common corporate culture.

As Percy Barnevik, former CEO of the merged Swedish–Swiss firm ABB Asea Brown Boveri, put this issue:

> You want to be able to optimize a business globally—to specialize in the production of components, to drive economies of scale as far as you can, to rotate managers and technologists around the world to share expertise and solve problems. But you also want to have deep local roots everywhere you operate— building products in the countries where you sell them, recruiting the best local talent from the universities, working with the local government to increase exports. If you build such an organization, you create a business advantage that's damn difficult to copy.[32]

This tension between global centralization and integration (standardization) and local responsiveness (adaptation) is often a major dilemma for global firms and their IHR managers. There is no simple solution to this conflict, as is pointed out throughout this book. The extent to which HR is integrated with a firm's international strategic planning usually takes place only in the context of discussions concerning a very limited set of global issues, such as acquisitions or divestitures of overseas facilities and operations, entering or withdrawing from foreign markets, proposed corporate structures and management systems to accommodate different nations and cultures, the means for controlling relationships between overseas subsidiaries and headquarters, and procedures for effectively managing the fundamental elements of the HRM system (e.g., staffing policies and practices in multiple countries, compensation and benefit systems, labor relations, etc.).[33] Even these discussions are likely to take place at a strategic level only when there is a close personal relationship between senior HR executives and the firm's CEO and its other senior executives. It is still not as common as might be expected for firms to engage their HR executives in their overall globalization discussions.[34]

Research on strategic international human resource management

It has been only recently that researchers have focused on strategic IHRM (SIHRM).[35] This research has extended our understanding of SIHRM, yet there is still much that is not known about the factors that influence it. The existing research on SIHRM has found, as would be expected, that local culture and national managerial orientation influences the nature of HR practice, that the degree of global mind-set influences the nature of an MNE's global strategy, and that influences the degree of global focus in the HR strategy.[36] In addition, it has been found that following appropriate global HR practices—rather than using only the parent firm's HR practices—was associated with the later stages of an organization's life cycle (as the MNE matures) and with better organizational performance.[37] And large global Japanese and European MNEs were found to be more likely to pursue global HR practices than was the case for similar American firms. Or, stated the other way around, American firms are more likely to pursue localization of IHR than are their Japanese or European counterparts.[38]

In general, this research has dealt with some form of linkage between headquarters' (corporate) international focus (for example, their degree of ethnocentrism or geocentrism) and HR policy and practice in foreign subsidiaries. If HR strategy must implement corporate strategy, then the extent to which HR practice in foreign subsidiaries reflects corporate international business strategy is an important consideration.[39] But, as is typically observed by researchers, the examination of IHR strategy is in its infancy. Even though a number of models have been put forward to speculate on the possible linkages (with limited supporting data), there is still much more to examine to understand the complexities of SIHRM. Both the responses and the choices are more numerous and complex in practice than these models have yet demonstrated.

THE EVOLVING INTERNATIONAL HUMAN RESOURCE FUNCTION

The last chapter of this book describes in some detail the ways in which HR is increasingly structured in today's multinational enterprises. This last section of the introductory chapter provides just an introduction to and overview of the typical IHRM responsibilities.

Support of the strategic objectives of the multinational enterprise

It is commonly said that strategy is only as good as its implementation. IHR plays a major role in developing tactical plans to support the organizational objectives. Achieving desirable results from ever more complex global business activities requires MNEs to pay increasing attention to the human aspects of cross-border business, to the merger of global work forces and cultures in the establishment of foreign subsidiaries and in cross-border acquisitions, joint ventures, and alliances, and to the development of individual employees who represent multiple corporate and national cultures, speak multiple languages, and have widely varying perspectives on customer, product, and business issues. It is usually expected that IHR will provide these capabilities and advise the rest of the enterprise on how to ensure performance in this cross-border complexity.

Transactional services at global and local levels

IHR is expected to solve the problems associated with global HR issues, such as global staffing, global compensation, pension, and health care systems, management development throughout the global enterprise, global employee and management recruitment and selection, global labor relations, global training programs, etc. Many of these HR services will have to be provided at all levels: local, cross-border, and global. In the end, the global and cultural aspects of international business boil down to finding ways for individuals with varying backgrounds and perspectives to work together; that is, finding ways to develop a corporate "glue" that will hold the organization effectively together across multiple international boundaries.[40]

This type of organizational glue—effective cross-border assignments, global social and professional networks, and effective cross-national task forces and work teams— will need to be increasingly used to pull together employees from disparate country and corporate cultures and far-flung business units. And it is IHR that is expected to provide the global enterprise with the expertise to help design and administer such strategies.

International human resource services to support the multinational enterprise

Given the many HR problems that MNEs encounter in conducting business on a global scale, IHR is expected to carry out the following agenda:[41]

- Ensure IHR contribution as an integral partner in formulating the global strategy for the firm.
- Develop the necessary competency among senior IHR staff so that they can contribute as partners in the strategic management of the global firm.
- Take the lead in developing processes and concepts with top management as they develop the global strategy: these contributions might include developing capacities for environmental scanning about HR issues throughout the world (particularly for the countries of existing or contemplated operations), for decision making (particularly related to global HR concerns), and for the learning processes that the firm needs to adapt to new global requirements.
- Develop a framework to help top management fully understand the increasingly complex organizational structure and people implications of globalization: that is, help management, individually and as a team, develop the necessary global mind-set to conduct successful global business.
- Facilitate the implementation of the global strategy by identifying key skills that will be required, assessing current global competencies and creating strategies for developing the skills needed internally or locating them on the outside.
- Distribute and share the responsibilities for IHR: increasingly, IHR will become a shared responsibility, with line management, IHR managers, and work teams all sharing in the objective of ensuring the effective hiring, development, and deployment of the global firm's human resources, both at home and abroad.[42]

This may lead to the decentralization of IHR decision making, possibly even outsourcing the administration of the basic functions, only leaving the strategic role for senior IHR executives. There may be less use of a separate headquarters IHR department, with IHR responsibilities delegated out to the global business units or, at least shared and developed with them. Many of the basic administrative activities (particularly for international assignee program administration, including relocation, cultural and language training, health and safety orientation and management, and compensation and benefits administration) will be outsourced to vendors with special expertise in these particular areas of IHRM. At any rate, the senior IHR executive and team will be responsible for ensuring that all of these traditional administrative IHR functions are managed effectively. Thus, the resulting IHRM responsibilities are both strategic and tactical and require that the new IHR professional be competent to play such a global role.

CONCLUSION

This chapter has introduced international human resource management and the context of international business. It described the pervasive nature of globalization and its impact on the development and practice of HRM in the MNE. The chapter showed how economic activity around the world had become increasingly integrated and, thus, increasingly global in nature. One of the most difficult challenges to international operations is the management of human resources. An effective and informed HR function is vital to the success of all firms with international operations. As a result, as firms have internationalized, so has HRM.

Because of rapidly developing global competition, firms are increasingly pressured to develop global strategies, which leads to the internationalization of HR at all levels: headquarters, subsidiary, and domestic, for profit and not for profit, private and public, commercial and government. The result is that almost all HR has become IHR. This chapter explained why all HR professionals must master at least some aspects of internationalization in their jobs and described how international HRM differs from purely "domestic" HRM. The chapter makes the point that IHRM encompasses and reflects many international business and management characteristics such as the determination of strategy and structure, which impacts the day-to-day operations of the core IHR policies and practices related to global staffing, training and development, compensation, employee relations, and health and safety.

This chapter concluded with an introduction to the evolving nature of IHR and outlined the newly expected contribution of senior IHR executives in the global development of the enterprise.

GUIDED DISCUSSION QUESTIONS

1 What forces have been driving the increased internationalization of business?

2 Explain the different orientations to international business that can be found among executives.

3 What are the various situations in which an HR manager might be involved with various aspects of internationalization?

4 What are the major differences between domestic and international HR?

5 How is HR changing in order to support an MNE's strategic decision to "go international"?

VIGNETTE 1.1 GLOBAL INTEGRATION IN ACTION

Career development at IBM

IBM states that there are three laws of global integration: the law of economics, the law of expertise, and the law of openness. These same three laws apply to a global work force. The law of economics is one of work force supply and demand. The law of expertise assures that the right people with the right skills are at the right place at the right time and at the right cost. The law of openness relates to transparency when identifying and finding people with the requisite knowledge, skills and expertise, while living the company's values.

IBM's CEO, Sam Palmisano, speaking on October 6, 2006, asserted that: "Work flows to the places where it will be done best—that is, most efficiently and with the highest quality." If one accepts this principle, then the most pressing questions for companies, nations, and individuals become: "What will cause work to flow to me? And on what basis will I differentiate and compete?" IBM has decided to compete on expertise and openness. To do so, it needed to transform career development to meet its strategic goals. IBM's commitment to change, reinvent itself, and innovate applies to both the company at large and its employees alike.

In 2003, IBM conducted a ValuesJam, an in-depth exploration of its values and beliefs by employees. Over 22,000 employees participated in the seventy-two-hour event and defined the company's new core values. From ValuesJam came the realization that in order for IBM to be innovative with its clients, it had to be innovative from the inside out. This meant that IBM needed to apply its three laws of global integration to the careers of its employees. Seen in this light, the law of economics focuses on the marketplace for jobs within IBM, the law of expertise deals with skills and experience needed now and in the future, and the law of openness is about access to learning, knowledge, people, opportunities, and living the values.

The IBM career development solution models the three laws of global integration and focuses on six integrated components:

- *Personalized learning* focuses on formal and informal development.
- *Pervasive mentoring* is about connecting IBMers to amplify the power of learning by working together.
- *Expertise management* enables targeted career development as well as broader work force management.
- *Career tracks* helps employees navigate development for future opportunities.
- *My development* is about personalized guidance enabled via an interactive web interface.
- *Blue pages* is the employees' online space to share their expertise and "brand."

According to Brussels-based Mia Van Straelen, director of learning, IBM EMEA region: "Career development at IBM will be supported by a clearly aligned business model." To this end, career development is included in IBM's core management systems. Both BUs and Geos determine time allocation targets for career development, while managers are held responsible for career development through specific measurements already in place. Additionally, management reviews follow a cadence throughout all levels of IBM. All this is rolled up in annual reviews with the SVPs and CEO.

Career development is vital from both business and employee perspectives. From a business perspective, it allows IBM an opportunity to innovate, grow and lead the IT industry. It also enables them to attract, motivate, and retain top talent. Just as important, career development has a positive impact on employee satisfaction and retention. From an employee perspective, it provides an environment where each employee can realize his/her potential and an opportunity to work in a stimulating environment. Finally, it also provides opportunities to advance and grow while making a difference to IBM clients and the world.

Questions

1 How do the three laws of global integration apply to career development?

2 How attractive is the new career development model for the new millennium generation of knowledge workers?

Source Claus, L. (2007), Global HR in Action Vignettes, Willamette University, www.willamette.edu/agsm/global_hr.

VIGNETTE 1.2   FROM STARUSA TO STARGLOBAL (1)

Bob Lewis, president and CEO of StarUSA, was heading back home to the Midwest from his quarterly visit to StarEuro in Brussels, Belgium. Settling down on the plane for a long flight, he reflected on last night's dinner conversation with Herman Wouters, general manager of the European Star subsidiary. Wouters, now in his early fifties, informed him of his desire to retire next year and pursue a more leisurely life. Financially, Wouters had done very well with his relationship with StarUSA. First, for more than ten years he was their leading independent distributor of Star products in the Benelux and then, for fourteen years, general manager of StarEURO. As Herman confided, business was not standing still and he was ready to enjoy life. He reassured Bob that he intended to stay on until a new general manager was in place and the transition was complete. Totally shocked by Wouter's resignation and this turn of events, Bob had time to think during the eight-hour flight and sort out what all of this would mean to the company.

StarUSA, a $3.5 billion company headquartered in a Midwestern metropolitan area, was established in 1949 by an engineer/entrepreneur. The company is known as a business-to-business provider of world-class customized engineering solutions. Another trademark of the company is the attention it pays to providing superior customer service. Originally named after its founder, it became a public company in 1956. The founder ran the company until the early 1980s, a period which saw the firm grow to 550 employees and attain the $1 billion sales mark (in 1981). At that time, StarUSA's customer base was mainly in the US, with 5 percent overseas sales, originating mostly from Canada and Europe. International sales were handled by local independent distributors and coordinated by international sales reps through the company's international export division.

In the 1980s, a number of internal and external changes affected the company dramatically. In 1984, the founder of the company retired and Bob Lewis, a non-family member, was appointed president and CEO. He had experienced a meteoric rise in his career since he joined the company just a few years earlier as national sales manager. At the same time, many of StarUSA's existing business clients started moving production outside of the US to their overseas subsidiaries. To respond to demand from their multinational company customers, StarUSA established StarEuro, a wholly owned subsidiary outside of Brussels, Belgium, to support growing European sales. Herman Wouters, a Belgian who at that time was the largest European distributor, was asked to join the company and head the European operations as general manager. He reported directly to the president of the company. Except for product and service specifications, quality assurance and financial controls, the wholly owned subsidiary was run like a local operation with limited managerial or operational controls from US headquarters. There was little interference from corporate. As Lewis said in his speech at the opening ceremony of the new European headquarters building in Belgium: "We don't want to meddle in the daily running of the company in Europe." Today, the European subsidiary has 348 employees, most of them at its headquarters and manufacturing facility outside of Brussels and less than two dozen employees at sales offices in eight different European national markets.

In the early 1990s, an Asia-Pacific hub was set up in Singapore. Today, StarAsia is staffed with twenty-six local employees (mainly sales and customer service people) scattered in key Asian markets. StarCanada is supported by sixteen Canadian employees and there are plans to open two new sales offices, one in Mexico and the other in Brazil. International sales for the company in 2001 were 14 percent of total sales and growing faster than overall revenues. Most of the international sales growth has been coming from the southern hemisphere as StarEuro sales have been slightly under plan. As many as 20 percent of the company's 2,056 employees now work outside of the US with a physical presence in nineteen countries. This rapid worldwide growth of the company's sales and operations put greater demands on corporate headquarters to plan and coordinate activities at a global level.

Cindy Fratelli joined StarUSA in 1988 as director of human resources. During her tenure at the company, she has gained the confidence and respect of the close-knit corporate management team. Prior to joining StarUSA, she was a compensation manager for a large insurance company. She grew up near the company's headquarters and attended college in the southern part of the US. Since she joined the company, her major accomplishments include the introduction of a performance management system, a performance-based compensation plan (with an aggressive sales and service incentive plan for sales people), an MBO (management by objectives) bonus plan for management, and a profit-sharing plan for staff employees. She also introduced extensive HR training and development initiatives. She worked closely with the IT team to select an HR information system that integrates with the company's existing manufacturing control system. Bob credits her for maintaining the family-oriented corporate culture that was established by the founder despite the rapid growth of the company. In 1998, she was promoted to vice-president and became the first woman on an all-male executive team. Her attention to detail and metrics is matched by a bubbly people-oriented personality. Her HR responsibilities have been limited to the domestic market where most of the company's employees reside. In Europe, the general manager assumes the HR task-related activities with the help of an administrative assistant. In other markets, the recruitment function is outsourced.

As Bob's plane was pulling into the arrival gate, he had outlined a plan to "globalize" the company to coincide with the search for a new general manager for StarEuro.

Questions

1 Why did Herman Wouters resign?

2 What is the international strategy of StarUSA?

3 How has StarUSA's development affected its HR function?

FROM STARUSA TO STARGLOBAL (2)

Cindy Fratelli, SPHR, vice-president of human resources, had just left the meeting that Bob Lewis, president and CEO of StarUSA, called upon his return from Brussels, Belgium. For over an hour, Bob laid out his plan to search for a new general manager for StarEuro after Herman Wouters had turned in his resignation. Bob also wanted to realign his organization to take advantage of the growing internationalization of the business and its customers. The entire executive team was present at the meeting: Mike Vincent, chief finance officer and vice-president of finance; Andrew Kling, vice-president of sales and marketing, Rich Gomez, vice-president of operations, Cindy Fratelli, vice-president of human resources, and Josh Lansberger, director of IT.

Bob elaborated that he wanted to use his headquarters management time to lead the effort of integrating the different functions globally while at the same time continue to be responsive to local conditions. Bob emphasized that HR would play a major role in the internationalization process as knowledge sharing of best practices and global teamwork were needed to give the company a competitive advantage. There would be more teamwork within business functions between people at headquarters and the various subsidiaries around the world.

Cindy was excited at the challenge while at the same time apprehensive. Although a certified professional in her field, she had no international experience, knowledge or training whatsoever. International issues were rarely covered at the professional conferences she attended or in the professional journals she read to keep up with new developments in her field. She had vaguely heard about a new certification program called the GPHR. She was not even aware of outside management consultants that could lead her in the right direction. As she pondered what role she was to play in this change process, she went on the web site of her professional HR organization (www.shrm.org) and searched for "international" with the hope of getting some direction as to how to respond to the challenge. She had one week to present Bob with a detailed implementation plan on how to support this new strategic objective of StarGlobal.

Questions

1 Why is Cindy Fratelli unprepared to play an IHR role?

2 How can she prepare herself?

3 What areas of IHR will Cindy need to learn?

Source Claus, L. (2007), Global HR in Action Vignettes, Willamette University, www.willamette.edu/agsm/global_hr.

2 Creating the international organization: strategy and structure

LEARNING OBJECTIVES

This chapter will enable the reader to:

- Describe the evolution of the MNE and explain the global organizational structures used by MNEs
- Describe the choices for entry into IB
- Explain the IHR implications of cross-border acquisitions, IJVs, and alliances
- Describe the record of success and failure of cross-border acquisitions and joint ventures
- Design a proper due diligence program in cross-border acquisitions and partnerships and explain its importance
- Describe the HR issues in managing cross-border acquisitions and partnerships

KEY TERMS

- Export
- International division or global product division
- Multi-country and multi-domestic organizations
- Regionalization
- The global firm
- The transnational firm
- The born-global firm
- The globally integrated enterprise
- Licensing and subcontracting
- Outsourcing

- Offshoring
- Wholly owned subsidiary
- Global mergers and acquisitions
- International joint ventures
- International alliances, partnerships, and consortia
- *Maquiladoras*
- Cross-border/dispersed/virtual teams
- Informal global networks
- Global learning organization
- Global integration
- Local responsiveness
- Due diligence

One of the challenges for IHR is to become organizational architects of the global firm. Global organizations need appropriate structure in order to effectively conduct business in the chaotic and complex global economy. Not only does the MNE need to be organized to achieve the strategic objectives of the firm, but IHR also needs an appropriate organizational structure to effectively become a business partner, itself. The first chapter looked at the foundations of strategic IHRM and its relation to strategic international business. This chapter examines the reasons for internationalization and the ways in which organizations "go international," particularly the use of cross-border acquisitions, international joint ventures, and alliances or partnerships, and the central role that IHRM plays in the implementation of these choices. And, then, the chapter examines how these choices influence the design of the organizations that global firms use to carry out their international activities. The notion that "structure" always follows "strategy" implies that once an internationalization strategy has been developed by the firm, effective organizational structures need to be identified to support the attainment of that globalization objective. It is the role of this chapter, then, to describe the organizational designs and business structures that MNEs (and their IHR managers) evaluate in carrying out their internationalization mandates and provide a summary of the kinds of concerns that IHRM must consider in order to ensure effectiveness in the carrying out of these decisions.

The developing complexity of international business is forcing firms to create new forms of organization and new applications of old forms which are creating new challenges for MNEs and thus for IHRM. Firms now have to cope with a greater number of countries (and their politics, governments, and cultures), protect a greater level of foreign investment, deal with greater overall political uncertainties and operating risks, develop new mental mind-sets throughout their leadership and down through their work forces, and manage an increasing number of sites and partnerships.[1]

For virtually all enterprises in this global economy, market opportunities, critical resources, cutting-edge ideas, potential partners, and new competitors can be found not only just around the corner in the home market but increasingly also in distant and often little understood regions of the world as well.[2] How successful an enterprise is at exploiting these emerging opportunities and at tackling the accompanying challenges and new global competitive pressures depends essentially on how intelligent it is at observing and interpreting the dynamic world in which it operates and at figuring out how to deal with it, capitalizing on all the available global resources. Choosing or designing the most appropriate and most effective organizational forms and learning how to manage these new organizations are key to dealing with these challenges and pressures and thus to competing effectively in this new environment.

Firms that have operated in a domestic environment for a long time may suddenly find themselves operating in a more global environment and domestic HR managers become, almost overnight, confronted with the "suddenly global"[3] nature of their enterprises. As an example, IHRM in Action 2.1 highlights what has happened to Comex, a Mexican paint manufacturer that has begun to internationalize. Comex is a family-owned and run firm, but it has found that it needs to examine carefully the structure and management it requires to operate in its new international environment. As will be illustrated throughout this chapter, IHRM is often the department expected to provide key strategic advice and/or support in these organizational efforts, since many of the issues in internationalization are often related to HR issues. It is the goal of this chapter to provide the basic understanding that IHR requires to effectively manage these new responsibilities.

GLOBAL ORGANIZATIONAL STRUCTURE

Once a firm has built, acquired, or negotiated a global presence in multiple countries it must convert that presence into global competitive advantage. To accomplish this, firms must take advantage of five opportunities:[4]

- Adapting to local market differences.
- Exploiting global economies of scale.
- Exploiting economies of global scope.
- Tapping into the best locations for activities and resources.
- Maximizing knowledge and experience transfer between locations.

That is, the major challenge is both to effectively take advantage of local differences and to facilitate integration across the firm's many locations and operations of what is learned from those differences. Most of this chapter provides a discussion of the choices and decisions that global firms make related to these two dimensions: local adaptation and centralized integration. All of the sources of global competitive advantage are—at their core—HR issues. They require integrated and skilled work forces in order to achieve—the primary responsibility of HR. In order to fully

A MEXICAN FIRM GOES INTERNATIONAL

Comex

There are many reasons for "going international"—and many paths for getting there. The reasons may be proactive or reactive. Proactive reasons for internationalization include a seach for new markets and resources (materials and labor), increased cost pressures, and incentives provided by governments and trade agreements. Reactive reasons include following existing customers into foreign markets and being closer to suppliers and customers. Comex, a Mexican paint manufacturer, provides an example of one firm's reaction to the global economy in an industry and from a country which have not, historically, operated across borders. Comex was started fifty-four years ago in an old mill in Mexico City by Jose Achar, descendant of Syrian immigrants to Mexico, producing water-based and oil paints. When the company moved to new facilities in 1958, it began to manufacture vinyl paint, which turned out to be so successful that competitors banded together and convinced hardware retailers to stop selling Comex paint. That emergency forced the Achar brothers to establish their own paint stores, selling their own paint exclusively. This approach—franchising—was a first in Mexico. Within a year, Comex had established 100 stores.

Because the Achars decided to manage their stores as concessions, turning store managers into business owners, they created a new career path for Mexicans who otherwise had limited opportunities to advance economically. Under this scheme, Comex was able to grow quickly while circumventing the need for enormous amounts of fresh capital to finance a chain of retail stores. Despite the strains associated with such growth, the firm is still family-owned. "There are many family members at the company, but we have three main principles which have made family ownership successful at Comex. We maintain openness to our brothers, respect for our elders, and right-of-way to the most capable," says Marcos Achar, nephew of the founder, who began his career at the firm in 1988 and became CEO in 2004.

Though Comex started as a small family hardware business in Mexico City, it now has more than 3,000 retail stores and captures an estimated 54 per cent of domestic paint sales. However, to maintain its growth rate, the company has realized, it must expand internationally. And it has recognized that the most effective way for it to gain access to new markets is through acquisition. Acquisitions, including those in the US, will drive sales to US$1.4 billion, making Comex the fifth-largest paint manufacturer in North America. A surprise move was the acquisition of Professional Paints, based in Lone Tree, Colorado, in 2004, which was one of the first cross-border acquisitions involving a Mexican company acquiring a US company. The marriage is expected to substantially enhance each firm's product line, enabling each to expand its special products and approaches into the other's markets, and illustrating some of the benefits of going international through acquisition—and some of the challenges of merging firms from two very different countries and cultures.

Source Makeover artists: How key principles helped a tiny family-owned hardware store grow to an international behemoth, *Business Week*, Special Advertising Feature, December 4 2006.

understand how these challenges link to IHRM, a short synthesis of the development of the MNE is provided with a description of how the stages in this evolution have led to the globalization of HR.

Evolution of the multinational enterprise

One of the most common approaches taken to understanding the evolution of the global enterprise focuses primarily on the geographic scope of their operations (or the process by which domestic firms increase their international involvement).[5] Firms generally do not (or should not) enter international markets haphazardly but use deliberate strategies for market selection and entry. The notion of gradual international involvement was first introduced by Bartlett and Ghoshal[6] who identified distinct stages of internationalization of a company (domestic, international, multinational, global and transnational), each stage reflecting specific conditions for the firm and a corresponding organizational mentality. Extending on this typology, eight forms of internationalization are described here with their corresponding HR implications and focus.

Internationalization through export

In the early stages of a firm's decision to "go international," international activity is often limited to efforts at export and import. At this stage, there is relatively little impact on the organization and IHRM, other than possible training opportunities to ensure that employees have the knowledge necessary to carry on cross-border commerce (or staffing to recruit the few employees whose responsibilities under this scenario are international). The export and/or international purchasing desks are usually side activities of marketing or purchasing. There is little impact on the form of the organization.

International division or global product division

When international sales and/or purchases reach a significant level (usually above 10–20 percent of revenues or purchases), a new international division is often established, with full responsibility for all international operations.[7] Although the firm's focus is still on domestic operations, the growth opportunities for international sales are becoming noticed. Many service-oriented businesses begin at this stage, often with the hiring of host country nationals as sales people, the acquisition of foreign counterparts, or numerous small startups in major foreign locales. Under this strategy, MNEs begin to consider local (foreign) assembly, and eventually, complete manufacturing of their products and/or services, either for sale and delivery in the foreign country or for export back to the home market or to other foreign markets. This division may initially be located within the marketing function, but as sales and investment increase, it may become an independent division, equivalent to domestic product or regional divisions and with little integration with domestic operations.

At this level of development, the international responsibilities of the HR department can expand dramatically and become much more complex. Not only will the number of parent company employees on international assignment increase significantly (creating the demand for new skills in the HR department) but there will be a need to hire host country nationals. As a result, the HR department will now need to become involved with development of HRM policies and practices (especially for international assignees), and staffing decisions for the foreign operations. In addition to staffing and compensation issues, one of the other major impacts on HR at this stage involves new areas for training. Many parts of the firm will need to gain new multicultural skills and understanding, including HR.

It is possible the firm will recruit a manager with international experience, with the direction for this—and probably also the actual selection—most likely to come from marketing or operations, not from HR. HR may have only the implementation responsibilities at this level, meaning administering pay and benefits. If sales offices are established abroad, it is likely, at least in the beginning, that local nationals will be hired to staff these offices. Or, if someone from the home office is relocated to the new foreign sales office, they will be selected by the marketing and/or operations managers and, again, HR may have little involvement. But if those making these decisions—in these early stages—lack experience and understanding of international business (which is often the case), HR may be expected (or, at least, may have the opportunity) to provide the training or staffing necessary to ensure good international decision making. HR may finally have a major role to play here, but may not be very involved if they do not yet have the IHR competencies and global mind-set to be able to make a significant contribution. At this point in time, HR will also begin to be exposed to new IHR concerns, such as pay, benefits, and taxes in foreign locales, work visas in other countries, and international relocation issues, as well as the training programs for themselves as well as for everyone else. Indeed, some anecdotal evidence suggests that firms are increasingly wanting their HR managers involved at earlier stages in their internationalization planning.[8]

Multi-country/multi-domestic strategy

In many industries, the next step in the evolution of international business is for firms to establish copies of their home offices and operations in relatively self-standing foreign subsidiaries. Initially, international assignees from the home office will be relocated internationally to transfer the firm's technology, set up the new operations, and to manage the subsidiary's early activities.

Up to the late 1980s or so, firms that pursued this "multicountry or multidomestic" internationalization strategy were likely to locate primarily in the large developed countries and countries with geographic or cultural contiguity (e.g., American firms setting up in Canada or the UK; or French firms setting up in other French-speaking countries). Thus they were managing a dozen or so country operations. Only a limited number of industries had firms with operations in a larger number of countries (twenty to thirty countries) and/or in other resource markets (e.g., mining, oil, automobile manufacturing, consumer products, and transportation—such as shipping and airlines). But in the last decade, these industries have expanded into many more countries and on to most, if not all, continents around the globe (with the possible exception of Antarctica), and so have most other industries. Today, it is common for firms to operate in dozens of countries, with many MNEs operating in 100 to 200 countries, with all of the attendant complexities and problems.

As independent as subsidiaries often become, in this strategy the organization's operations in a number of countries may reach such size and importance that there is increased need for integration with corporate headquarters. The firm may develop global product divisions that provide global coordination of finance, HRM, marketing, and research and development (R&D). Or the MNE may organize its country subsidiaries into regional operations with a regional headquarters to coordinate operations on a regional basis. Nevertheless, at this level of international strategy, the MNE will have significant operations (assembly, manufacturing, sales and marketing, service centers, R&D, branch offices) in many countries and may well reach the condition where half or more of its sales and employment are in countries outside of headquarters.

Key personnel in the subsidiaries and regional offices are usually from the company's home office with many decisions made at corporate headquarters. Thus, although the subsidiaries are largely staffed by people from the countries in which they are located, managers from the home office may retain authority in key areas (such as profitability and compensation bonuses). The MNE at this level of development generally views each national market as a specialized market for its particular subsidiaries' products. Each subsidiary concentrates its efforts on the nation in which it is located.

The HR department's role at this stage becomes more complex and difficult. Now HRM must not only provide services—such as relocation, compensation, and benefits for often hundreds of employees (international assignees) working in foreign (to them) locations—but it must also coordinate HRM activities and practices of the many subsidiaries, seeking both consistency with the culture and policies of the parent company and accommodation of local values and practices. In addition, the need for training for international assignees (from the parent company or from foreign locales), local nationals, third country nationals, and parent company employees to handle foreign assignments and interaction with foreign counterparts will increase dramatically. At this stage, coping with cultural differences (addressed in the next chapter) becomes an overriding concern.

Regionalization

In an alternative to the multidomestic strategy, a firm may decide initially (or, possibly after first pursuing the multidomestic strategy) to conduct its international business on a regional basis. This evolution is described in IHRM in Action 2.2. Ford's experience was pretty typical of the early multinational corporations. This approach initially involves first organizing to conduct business in only one or two

FORD MOTOR COMPANY GOES INTERNATIONAL

Ford Motor Company has been in business for over 100 years and when it comes to a global mind-set, Ford is ahead of most of its competitors.

For a number of historical reasons, over the years Ford evolved into a collection of country and regional fiefdoms. Early in its history, Ford was like many large firms, which often sent people off to other major countries to run a company just like the one back home. The first Henry Ford, the founder of the Ford Motor Company, was in many ways an internationalist, because within a very few years of establishing the company in the US he was opening assembly and manufacturing plants all over the world—the first of which was a Model T assembly plant in Trafford Park, England, in 1911—that were essentially smaller versions of the original company in Detroit.

But by the mid-1920s a sense of local pride had developed in countries around the world. Countries began to develop their own automotive companies. Suddenly, there were automotive companies in the UK, in France, Germany, Australia, and they were all making their own vehicles. Nations wanted to assert their independence and saw the automotive industry as a means of investing in their own economies. The Europeans exported, the Americans exported, and that's how the competitive game was being played. (This was the beginnings of the "multidomestic" structure for large multinational corporations, as explained in this chapter.)

In the 1960s, though, regionalism began to develop, with the emergence of the European Common Market, NAFTA, ASEAN, and other regional trading groups. Countries kept their own political systems and social values but formed economic trading blocs. So . . . big companies established regional headquarters within the various major trading blocs. Ford Europe was established in this period. This was when most of the regional and functional fiefdoms (with each region becoming very independent) became firmly entrenched at Ford. (This is what is referred to in the text as the "regional" corporate structure, an extension of the "multidomestic" structure.) The fiefdoms were excellent at what they did: they squeezed every last ounce of efficiency out of the regional model. For example, back in the period of nationalism, Ford had multiple accounting activities around the world—there were fifteen in Europe alone. The regional model got it down to four: one in Europe, one in the US, one in Asia-Pacific, and one in South America. But even with that efficiency, Ford felt that the model didn't work any more.

Today Ford is moving to a fourth stage of economic evolution with the globalization of all aspects of its international operations: capital, communications, economic policy, trade policy, human resources, marketing, advertising, brands, etc. The auto industry around the world has become globalized. Germany and Japan produce cars in the US, Korea produces cars in Eastern Europe, and Malaysia, China, and Mexico export cars and parts throughout the world. Ford now manufactures and distributes automobiles in 200 markets on six continents, with 330,000 employees in more than 100 plants worldwide. In addition, the automotive industry has become an electronics-driven industry. It is increasingly a business that requires huge investments in technology and intellectual capital, not only for constant innovations in development and manufacturing, but in automobiles, themselves.

So the leadership of Ford feels there is no longer a choice about globalization. For a company of Ford's background and size, remaining a national or regional company is no longer a viable alternative. Auto companies around the world have global ambitions, and many of them are world-class players, such as Toyota, Honda, Volkswagen, Daimler-Chrysler, Renault and, quite soon, Geely Motors and others from China and Tata Motors from India. In this environment, Ford sees an incredible challenge: more markets open for business, more competitors fighting for dominance, more need for very smart people and fresh ideas.

Ford feels that it can't build such a company if it holds on to a mind-set that doesn't respond swiftly to (the global) consumers' needs or pay attention to the (global) capital markets. So, under the leadership originally of Jacques Nasser, then of William Ford III, and now of Alan Mulally, Ford has begun to reinvent itself as a truly global organization with a single strategic focus on consumers and shareholder value. Ford realizes that, in this process, it must not try to eliminate the role of national cultures or eliminate the idea that it makes sense to have people with expertise in one function or another, but it wants to develop a Ford-wide corporate DNA that drives how it does things everywhere. That DNA has a couple of key components, including a global mind-set, an intuitive knowledge of Ford's customers around the world, and a relentless focus on growth, where every employee contributes to the company and to business results. Many large, experienced, multinational firms are now trying to develop a global structure and frame of mind similar to what Ford is doing, as they all see it as necessary for successful operation in today's globalized economy. And it is HR which must take the responsibility to develop this corporate DNA.

Sources Lapid, K. (2006), Outsourcing and offshoring under the General Agreement on Trade in Services, *Journal of World Trade*, 40 (2): 341–364; Neff, J. (2006), Ford announces corporate realignment, *Autoblog*, December 14; Wetlaufer, S. (1999), Driving change: An interview with Ford Motor Company's Jacques Nasser, *Harvard Business Review*, March–April: 77–80; and Whitney, K. (2006), Ford: Driving learning and developing the "Way Forward," *Chief Learning Officer*, 5 (5): 44–47.

regions, such as Europe or Latin America (typical for an American or Asian firm) or maybe North America (for a European or Asian firm) or Asia (for an American or European firm). The HRM impacts here are similar to those in the previous strategy, although they will be managed from a regional headquarters.

An assumption often made here, is that countries within a region share some common characteristics, such as similarities in national culture, geographical proximity, or stage of economic development. Sometimes, however, the reality is that there is as much diversity between countries in a region as there is between regions. And, thus, the complexities and difficulties are just as challenging under a regionalization strategy as is the case with the multi-domestic strategy.

The global firm

In recent years, many MNEs have reached the state of internationalization where their operations are becoming blind to national borders. Even though most businesses still organize on a regional basis (the number of countries being managed is often just too many to be adequately managed from a single headquarters) and adaptation to local customer preferences may still be necessary, products and services are increasingly designed for and marketed to customers all over the world. This is particularly true for industrial products (i.e., for products sold from business to business, such as computer chips or office supplies) and for many services (i.e., banking, retail, insurance, package delivery, and many consumer products). The best technology and innovative ideas are sought everywhere and applied to markets throughout the world. Products and services are created where costs are the lowest, quality is the highest, and time to delivery is the shortest, and delivered wherever the demand is sufficient. And resources (money, material and parts, insurance, even people) are sought from wherever the best quality for cost can be found.

Firms that operate this way are increasingly referred to as "global."[9] Reaching this stage of development is not merely a matter of company size or experience in internationalization. Sometimes it is a reflection of the nature of the pressures of the particular industry. And, often, it reflects a purposeful, strategic decision to "go global."

The experiences of global MNEs suggest that running a global company is an order of magnitude more complicated than managing a multinational or international firm.[10] The global corporation looks at the whole world as *one market*. It manufactures, conducts research, raises capital, and buys supplies wherever it can do the job best. It keeps in touch with technology and market trends all around the world. National boundaries and regulations tend to be irrelevant, or a mere hindrance. Corporate headquarters might be anywhere. In general, such companies have extremely strong corporate cultures that become the glue that bonds their diverse operations.

At this level of development, the role of the HR department must again shift. Employees are hired everywhere in the world, wherever the necessary skills, training, and experience can be found. Yet, these globally sourced employees must also be socialized into the corporate culture. IHR efforts in this regard include global onboarding programs (such as orientation and on-the-job training) and continuous development into the standardized practices of the MNE. Worldwide policies are developed and implemented for many aspects of HR responsibility, possibly based on practices followed in numerous different places around the world. Management promotions require international experience and managers and executives are developed who come from all major countries and regions of operation. At the same time, increased sophistication in locating certain HRM practices becomes even more important, as the firm tries to be a global enterprise.

This usually means developing global brands and creating global company name recognition, with fewer expatriates in local subsidiaries, and increased use of third country nationals, more transfers of employees between subsidiaries, common training for managers and executives from throughout the global operations, and broader-based multinational composition of corporate boards and top management and technical teams. And in most firms this means trying to develop or maintain an international corporate culture that transcends national boundaries and national cultures. Although the official corporate language is usually (business) English, key employees need to be multilingual, experienced in a number of countries, and culturally sensitive, with their countries of origin making little difference. In addition, executive development becomes a major role of HR in conjunction with top management, with close tracking of top talent and high potential managers from around the world.

The transnational firm

Bartlett and Ghoshal suggested that many firms are evolving into a new form of international business that they termed "transnational."[11] In the sense that the transnational firm (TNC) has a global focus, it is similar to the global firm, described in the previous section. But it differs from the global firm in that, rather than developing global products, services, brands, and standardized processes and policies and procedures, the transnational organization works hard to localize, to be seen, not only as a global firm, but as a local firm as well, albeit one that draws upon global expertise, technology, and resources.[12] In a transnational firm, the focus is simultaneously on global integration, local responsiveness, and knowledge sharing among the different parts of the organization.

The transnational firm[13] is often put forth as the direction in which all international firms are headed. The salient management and HR question may be how to manage the complex, national (cultural) diversity that this level of global business activity experiences. When integration is needed (as in joint ventures and in the development of global work forces), cultural diversity needs to be valued and utilized while minimizing its negative impacts; but when cultural diversity is needed to differentiate products and services to meet the needs of local markets, new corporate practices and organizational designs are required. IHRM in Action 2.3 describes a major transnational firm—CAP Gemini–Sogeti—and the IHR implications of "going transnational."

A TRANSNATIONAL ORGANIZATION

IHRM in Action 2.3

Cap Gemini–Sogeti

Cap Gemini–Sogeti (CGS) is Europe's largest computer software and services group. CGS has taken all available means (organic growth, acquisitions, and alliances) to become Europe's No. 1 in computer services and consulting and, as of 2006, among the top five of the world's outsourcing services providers. The original merger of Cap, a computer services group, and Sogeti, a business management and information processing company, brought together operations in the UK, the Netherlands, Switzerland, and Germany, with a head office in France. Further acquisitions brought in a large number of small groups throughout Europe and the US. This expanded its coverage to IT consulting, customized software, outsourcing services, and education and training. CGS was already highly decentralized, but when any of its branches reaches 150 personnel, it is split in two. This gives the firm greater flexibility in responding to variations in local demand. Decision making and direct customer service are facilitated with smaller teams.

CGS has developed information pooling systems to ensure that innovative solutions developed in one country or business will be rapidly disseminated to other countries and businesses. These include electronic bulletin boards and extensive electronic and voicemail facilities, plus the organizational culture of informal networks of professionals who work frequently together in project teams.

The challenges for this fast-growing transnational have major HR components, e.g., integrating its wide variety of organizations into a group with a common culture capable of working within a complex web of ownership relationships, while benefiting from the strengths of the relationships that exist among its "family" of committed, semi-autonomous professionals. Internally, CGS and its IHR team work to clarify and coordinate roles, objectives, systems, and resources, particularly its skilled professional staff, across countries and markets. Its Genesis project took two years to achieve this integration, but now CGS sees itself as coming much closer to achieving its aim to be a modern transnational enterprise.

Source Cap Gemini web site (2007), www.capgemeni.com/about/; Segal-Horn, S. and Faulkner, D. (1999), *The Dynamics of International Strategy*, London: International Thomson.

The born-global firm

Although many existing firms internationalize through stages, some new enterprises, especially in the IT industry, are "born global" and almost immediately operate across the globe. The reasons they operate in key global markets from their inceptions essentially stem from the nature of their products (internet products, IT applications, and other highly specialized products with global niches) and their marketing through the worldwide web. In addition, the lowering of market entry barriers as a result of the democratization of the sources of competitive advantage (venture capital, IT resources, intellectual capital, etc.) in a "flat" world also provide global access. The HR activities of these firms are focused primarily on frequent international business travel of key individuals and legal protection of intellectual property rights (patents and trademarks) in the various countries in which they operate, the hiring of key local staff, and the management of international project teams for local client service. As mentioned in the first chapter, any firm creates a web site (announcing either a product or service)—it is global. Anyone, anywhere, can (and will) access that site and some will want to buy the site's products or services. In addition, many "born global" enterprises are created by people from multiple countries who have met each other online or at global professional or trade conferences who decide to work together in a new enterprise to use their joint skills and ideas.

The globally integrated enterprise

The emerging model of the twenty-first century is not the multinational company described above, but a globally integrated enterprise that is very different in structure and operations.[14] Samuel Palmisano, chairman and CEO of IBM, describes the difference between a twentieth century multinational and a twenty-first century globally integrated enterprise as follows. In a multinational model, companies build local production capacity within key markets, while performing other tasks on a global basis. In contrast, in the globally integrated enterprise, strategy, management, and operations—which take place in many different locations—are integrated into production of goods and services to deliver value to clients worldwide. This integrated model is made possible because of shared technologies, global IT systems, and global communications infrastructure. In a globally integrated structure, different operations, expertise, and capabilities (especially as is the case for service organizations, as IBM now describes itself)—again, located around the world—allow the enterprise to connect with its customers, using all the resources of the firm, and engage in collaborative innovation to solve the customers' problems and challenges. HR activities in the globally integrated firm internally reflect the same laws of global integration as those provided to the external clients. Talent and expertise within the MNE flow to where it creates most value. (For an example of internal talent management and development in a globally integrated enterprise see Vignette 2.1.)

However, the differences between multinational/multidomestic and global/transnational and born-global and globally integrated firms is significant. In the traditional multinational enterprise, free-standing subsidiaries or stand-alone foreign operations may be so loosely affiliated that valuable opportunities for economies of scale, joint marketing efforts, or shared technology and innovations may be lost. As illustrated in the Ford Motor Company description (see IHRM in Action 2.2), country or regional operations and functional experts can develop attitudes of strong independence that can result in the loss of benefits that arise from sharing product ideas and technologies across national boundaries. The transnational firm creates a structure and management system that take advantage of global capabilities while allowing local subsidiaries to operate as independent businesses. The born-global firm and the globally integrated enterprise tend to be more network-based. Whichever the structure developed, the global HR roles and activities must shift to meet the needs of the organizations.

The MNE philosophy of primarily staffing with locals (which is one of the consequences of pursuit of a multidomestic or regional structure) sounds reasonable. But if only Frenchmen work in France, only Japanese in Japan, and only Americans in the US, a firm may well lose the input of talented individuals and teams with different backgrounds and perspectives on products, services, organizational and management practices, markets, and international needs and limit the firm's ability to learn, innovate, and adapt skills which are absolutely critical to success in global competition. This may limit the firm's awareness of new technologies and product ideas enough so as to create a definite competitive disadvantage relative to more global competitors. Such diverse perspectives are also important to IHRM, bringing multiple viewpoints and experiences to bear on HR problems in the parent company as well as in the foreign subsidiaries and partnerships.

Most of the discussion in this book focuses on IHRM policies and practices as they apply to multinational/multidomestic (traditional) MNEs, global, transnational MNEs and the (newly emerging) born-global and globally integrated enterprises. The rest of this chapter discusses these organizational and managerial implications. And the next chapter provides extensive discussion of the cultural implications which override—or, at least, influence—everything that happens in international business.

CHOICE OF METHOD FOR ENTRY INTO INTERNATIONAL BUSINESS

As the previous section describes, the global scope of business activity has expanded dramatically since the 1970s. But not only has the scope increased, so also has the number of ways in which firms carry out their international operations. The ways that global organizations evolve were described. Now, this section examines the many forms that enterprises use to build their global businesses. These processes are critically important because IHR is expected to play a major role in advising on these strategies and in the implementation of these approaches. Often, when HR concerns are not adequately addressed—as will be discussed in the section after this—the approaches taken to conduct international business fail.

As a firm internationalizes, it must make a choice of methods for market entry. These market entry choices will partially be dictated by its own internationalization strategy, the options it has in particular countries (due to legal requirements and opportunities), the timing of its entry into the market (early versus late entrant) and the risks it wants to bear. Common international market entry choices are licensing and subcontracting, outsourcing, offshoring, wholly owned subsidiary, merger or acquisition, international joint venture, and strategic alliance/partnership. The definitions and uses of these terms often overlap, but enough description is provided here to illustrate how important HR issues are to the success of each of them. The rest of this section provides a summary of the market entry choices that firms make when they decide to go international, with a special emphasis on the choices that have a direct impact on HR management. All of these forms of international involvement create major coordination and integration challenges, and thus are aspects of international business that IHR professionals must thoroughly understand in order to provide senior managers with the advice they need for designing effective global businesses. So following this section is a description of the IHRM ramifications of these various structural choices. The objective, here, is to provide enough background so that IHR managers can participate effectively in decisions that implement their firms' international business choices.

Licensing and subcontracting

One of the earliest approaches to international business was subcontracting, i.e., contracting or licensing (generally by a manufacturer) with a firm in another country to assemble or manufacture its products, usually for export back to the home country. The primary reason for "going international" in this way was to take advantage of lower costs in the foreign locale. In manufacturing, this form of market entry is often referred to as contract manufacturing. A special form of licensing (especially for service models) is franchising where franchisees buy into the brand and business model of the franchisor in return for operational and marketing expertise. IHR activities in this area are usually focused on two types of activities. In licensing and contract manufacturing, the MNE wants to make sure that the human rights of the production workers are guaranteed and that the manufacturing and production activities are done in a responsible manner. In franchising, the main IHR focus is on management development and training so that the franchisee adheres to the operational and customer service standards established by the franchisor.

Outsourcing[15]

This is a form of subcontracting. Beginning in the 1990s, firms began to subcontract with foreign firms to do more than produce their products. With the development of computers and the internet, firms began to contract out other business processes, such as information technology and business processes such as call centers, accounting, claims processing, customer service, and data analysis, to other firms in their home country and in other countries. The primary reason for outsourcing to a third party (whether a single function or an entire business process) was to reduce costs, but improving quality (because the service provider specializes in the outsourced function) and freeing company resources for greater focus on core competencies are also among the reasons given for outsourcing. The term "outsourcing" was developed to describe this process of contracting with an external firm to provide products or services that would otherwise be completed internally. Because these "outsourced" functions are important to the operation of the business (they are usually not core competencies), they are more directly linked into the management of the business (than was often the case with earlier forms of licensing and manufacture subcontracting), and thus there is more likely to be closer managerial and technical involvement by the parent firm with the service provider. At a minimum there is usually technology transfer and training in the parent firm's processes. International outsourcing (to a firm located outside of the home country) leads to the posting of international assignees, ongoing business travel, and continual training, to negotiate and oversee the relationships with the vendors that have the outsourced contract. All of these activities involve HR in planning, managing, and execution. Frequently, the people performing the work internally for the client firm are transferred and become employees of the service provider.

In all cases, outsourcing success depends on three factors:[16] executive-level support in the client organization for the outsourcing mission; ample communication to affected employees; and the client's ability to manage its service providers, ensuring delivery of quality service and support to the client and to customers. The outsourcing professionals in charge of the work on both the client and provider sides (including HRM) need a combination of skills in such areas as negotiation, communication, project management, human resource management (employee assignment and management, compensation and benefits, training, employee relations, performance management, outplacement, etc.), and the ability to develop and understand the terms and conditions of the contracts and agreements.

Offshoring[17]

Often the terms offshoring and outsourcing are used interchangeably. However, as originally developed, the concepts have different meanings. As used here, offshoring differs from outsourcing in that offshoring involves the relocation of one or more aspects of a firm's business processes to a location in another country for the purpose, at least initially, of lowering costs. That is, the function is now performed by an entity of the firm but in an offshore location. This can include any business process, such as operations, manufacturing, or services. So, the unit performing the process in a foreign country is still a part of the parent firm and the employees are still employees of the parent. Thus the HR responsibilities of staffing, training, compensating, employee relations, and performance management are the same, albeit in another country, legal system, and culture, as they are with the function being performed "at home." Though offshoring (and offshore outsourcing) saves businesses labor costs as well as other expenses associated with personnel, it also contributes to an atmosphere of anxiety among workers who feel their jobs are being threatened.[18]

> With job security as one of the most critical factors in determining how satisfied employees are with their jobs, the threat of off-shoring could cause significant damage to employee morale. Dealing with the functional, structural and strategic aspects of the off-shoring process will put HR at the center of the off-shoring debate. But dealing with the repercussions of off-shoring on employee satisfaction, recruitment and retention may prove to be its greater challenge.[19]

The primary issues that companies should think about when they think about relocating services offshore are their expertise in managing remote locations, the caliber and skill sets of the foreign labor force, the cost of labor, language skills on both sides, telecom bandwidth (to handle the necessary flow of data and information), cost, and reliability at the foreign location, infrastructure, political stability, enforceability of intellectual property rights and business contracts, and the general maturity of the business environment.[20] Obviously, many of these issues are of primary focus for IHR and thus must be understood by IHR and the IHR department must develop the expertise to deal effectively with them.

Wholly owned subsidiary

Until quite recently, the most common way to enter international business (beyond subcontracting and exporting) was to conduct business through wholly owned foreign subsidiaries. Still, this is a popular form of entry into another country's economy. Subsidiaries can be developed in a number of ways, including through greenfield or brownfield projects or through acquisition of existing foreign-owned businesses. The development of a subsidiary through a greenfield project involves acquiring an open (green) "field" in order to build the subsidiary facilities from scratch. A brownfield project involves the purchase of existing facilities (buildings) and developing the subsidiary inside those facilities (sometimes referred to as a turnkey operation). The third alternative is often seen as providing the easiest access to new (foreign) markets and involves the acquisition of an existing enterprise that is already established in the target country.

From an HR standpoint, a startup project (greenfield or brownfield) requires staffing and creating all HR policies and practices for a totally new work force. (There is a choice of transferring all policies and practices from the parent's headquarters or basically adopting the policies and practices that are common in the new country —or, possibly, a combination of these two options.) An acquisition, however, poses different challenges—either accepting the HR practices of the acquired firm or partially or totally changing them to those of the new parent firm. In both choices, however, the major challenge for the firm and for HR is to integrate the acquired firm's practices (and its work force) with those of the parent. In all cases, the knowledge base and competencies required of the parent firm's HR department are clearly more complex and complicated than is the case prior to investment in any foreign subsidiaries. The effectiveness with which HR and the firm manages these issues goes a long way toward determining the success or failure of the venture.

Mergers and acquisitions (M&As)

Although this form was discussed briefly above as a wholly owned subsidiary market entry method, it deserves special attention because of the large volume of global M&A activity (now reaching more than US$3 trillion per year)[21] and the special ramifications for IHR's role. For many MNEs and industries, M&A is the preferred market entry method in both developed and emerging markets in order to consolidate the scope of activities and the parent firms' positions in the global market place. Foreign acquisitions often face national economic protectionism sentiments and antitrust laws. IHR activities in international M&As are especially important in the pre-merger due diligence phase (for example, the liabilities involved in acquiring the compensation and benefit components of the acquired work force) and in post-merger integration (which usually involves downsizing, integration of international HR systems, and developing a new people management culture). It is also important to note that some M&A partners may have acquired rights that must be continued (more about that in Chapter 4 on legal regulations). For more extensive coverage of the IHR issues involved with global mergers and acquisitions, the reader should refer to *Managing Human Resources in Cross Border Alliances* by Schuler, Jackson and Luo in this Global HRM series.[22]

International joint ventures (IJVs)

In recent years, the international structure of choice for many businesses is the IJV, in which two or more firms (at least one from each of at least two countries) create a new business entity with shared ownership and managerial responsibilities in the country of one of the partners. This new entity is often created with limited objectives and a limited life, with a specific date set for the dissolution of the IJV. Employees will normally be assigned to the new entity from each of the partners, possibly with the hiring of some new employees, with specific managerial and employee responsibilities (hopefully) negotiated prior to the establishment of the joint venture. Many new problems arise for HR, from the adoption or development of HR practices for a multinational work force to issues concerning the merger and interaction of two or more national and corporate cultures (or, as sometimes happens, the design of a new culture).

When a firm acquires an existing firm in another country, the central problem is to integrate an existing (acquired) firm and its culture and practices into the (acquiring) parent firm. However, in the situation of an IJV, a new entity is created. Although there are a number of definitions of an IJV, a typical definition is: "a separate legal organizational entity representing the partial holdings of two or more parent firms, in which the headquarters of at least one is located outside the country of operation of the joint venture. This entity is subject to the joint control of its parent firms, each of which is economically and legally independent of the other."[23]

Thus the central HR (and managerial) challenge in an IJV is always to create this new entity, with all its dimensions, work force, culture, and practices. This new firm can emulate one or more of the partners; that is, it can be some form of integrated entity, drawing on the culture and practices of the partners. Or it can be designed to be an entirely new organization, separate from the cultures or practices of the partners.[24] One of the keys to success of an IJV is for the partners to agree on and to be clear about which one of these choices is being pursued. Lack of clarity on this issue can lead to conflicting expectations for the performance of the resulting organization and will typically lead to unmet expectations and conflict between the partners—and eventual early dissolution of the venture.

The reasons for entering into IJV agreements are not so different from those for cross-border acquisitions, except for the reduced risk, since the risk is shared in the IJV in a new, separate, legal entity. These include:

- To gain knowledge about local markets, culture, and local ways of doing business in order to transfer that knowledge back to the parent firm(s), i.e., to learn from the joint venture partner(s).
- To gain access to the partner's product technology, product knowledge, or methods of manufacturing.
- To satisfy host government requirements and insistence.
- To gain increased economies of scale.
- To gain local market image and channel access.
- To obtain vital raw materials or technology.
- To spread the risks (with the IJV partners).
- To improve competitive advantage in the face of increasing global competition.
- To become more cost-effective and efficient in the face of increased globalization of markets.

The overriding motive in most joint ventures seems to be the desire by one or all parties to gain knowledge and learn from their partner(s). Obviously, for a firm to learn from a partner, the partner must have some level of willingness to share what it knows. If all partners wish to learn from the others, then, to be successful, all the partners must be willing to share. This is often a source of conflict, in itself, particularly where there is not a sufficient level of trust among the partners. In this case, sharing will tend to be minimized and the original objective may be stymied. Often, the central strategy for learning from the IJV has to do with the choices for staffing—and thus is an IHR concern. "Transfer of staff between the JV and the parent firms can provide a mechanism for sharing information, for learning from each other's abilities and expertise, and for the creation of synergies related to product development."[25] But if the wrong people are chosen to staff the IJV, that is, people with poor interpersonal or cross-cultural skills or limited technical ability, this objective of the partners may be difficult to achieve.

Strategic alliances, partnerships (e.g., research), and consortia

Firms using this structure do not necessarily replace their traditional multidomestic or global/transnational structures. But increasingly, MNEs are developing and using alliances, partnerships, joint ventures (described in the previous paragraphs), and other forms of linkages to operate internationally. Sometimes these structures are used to gain access to technology, research, and laboratories that the firm might not otherwise have access to, or as a strategy that can provide additional flexibility in a fast-moving global economy. Since, typically, no new legal entity is created, the firms involved can relatively quickly and easily dissolve the relationship as the situation warrants. Dissolving legal entities such as subsidiaries and joint ventures is usually not easy—and, sometimes, not possible.

MCI Corporation (acquired by WorldCom and then by Verizon, in 2006), provides a classic example of this sort of international partnership at work. MCI was one of the most important early providers of global telecommunications services (and now, as a part of Verizon, operates in sixty-five countries). From early in its telecom history, MCI was one of the leaders in internet and wireless technologies.[26] MCI got its technology from more than fifty major research partners located all over the world, including from its major competitors, such as AT&T. Even though MCI owns a large R&D complex, it doesn't develop its new technologies there. Instead, this is where MCI takes leading-edge technologies developed by its independent research partners and tests, perfects, and integrates them into the MCI (and, now, Verizon) telecommunications networks. In an industry where new products (e.g., cellphones) routinely become obsolete in less than thirteen months, MCI finds it to be more efficient (and practical) to spend time looking for innovative people and labs around the world than to develop its own technology. MCI's executive vice-president of a few years ago explained: "I have access to the intellectual assets of [other firms'] 9,000 engineers. If I did my own development, what would I have? Five hundred engineers?"[27]

Because of this sort of logic, cross-border partnerships of various types are increasingly becoming the organizational choice for many MNEs, large and small. In these international alliances, the HR activities associated with coordinating work forces and managements of firms from different countries and cultures remain the primary stumbling blocks to gaining the desired business benefits. IHRM in Action 2.4 showcases how a relatively small Indian (Mumbai) architectural firm has partnered with a similar firm in New York to combine their skills on projects in both countries. The cultural differences have become strengths, rather than barriers to their success.

A GLOBAL PARTNERSHIP

Links between Mumbai and Manhattan firms open doors for two architects

A mutual friend introduced Manhattan architect William Leeds to Indian architect Bobby Mukherji. Mukherji, founder of what was at the time a five-person firm in Mumbai (but is now much larger), was interested in entering the US market. Leeds was also eager to tap into India's thriving economy. Since then, the two architects have designed a variety of projects, including a fabric showroom, a trendy Chicago restaurant, a major Indian government office opening in New York, and a major multinational hotel in India. They enjoy sharing their talents and views. And their collaboration has led to significant recognition for both firms. Indeed, Mukherji has become one of the award-winning and renowned architects in India, winning major projects in India and the US.

"To be working with somebody from a place as far away as India gives us a new perspective on architecture and a new approach to planning," said Leeds, who has about half a dozen employees. "Bobby brings in new ideas that we wouldn't necessarily have at our fingertips." Besides new ideas, Mukherji provides Leeds and his US clients with access to unique Indian building materials and a team of twenty-five Indian craftsmen and artisans on his payroll in Mumbai. Many Mukherji projects, especially at his nightclubs, feature original artwork and hand-carved details.

Although they live thousands of miles apart, Leeds and Mukherji communicate frequently by phone, fax, and the internet. They have added the ability to communicate via teleconferencing. And, now, with Skype and other similar technologies, they can communicate easily "face-to-face" to problem-solve and share ideas for meeting client needs.

The firms work together project by project, based on a handshake, not a written agreement. They split the expenses and profits, depending on who does what. Projects with Mukherjinow make up about 10–15 percent of Leeds's total billings. Leeds says that eventually he hopes 25 percent of his total projects will be with Mukherji's firm. Both say one of the greatest benefits of the relationship is acting as each other's marketing representative. "We look out for his interests and for him to grow," Leeds said. "In India, Bobby helps us because he can determine who is real and who is not. Between the two of us, we can accurately target the right clients."

"India is extremely friendly," Mukherji said. "Personal relationships are very important. There is a lot of weight given to word-of-mouth agreements, and people respect that." Obviously, this is one partnership that was built on relationships and has helped both parties achieve business objectives in each other's countries. The development of these kinds of cross-border and cross-cultural communications and merged working relationships is a HR concern. Obviously, an effective IHR function can facilitate this kind of experience.

Sources "Architecture academy celebrates jubilee," *India Times*, Real Estate Section, retrieved from http://www.realestate.indiatimes.com/articleshow;1344726.cms, July 25 2007; Applegate, J. (1996), Alliances quick way to grow: Links to Bombay firm open doors for architect, *Denver Business Journal*, October 4–10: 3B.

Maquiladora (a special form of subsidiary)

Since the 1960s, a unique form of international partnership has developed between the US and Mexico. In 1965, Mexico agreed to the creation of what are referred to as *maquiladoras*, which are a special form of foreign subsidiary with special characteristics favorable to the foreign parents.[28] These "twin plants" (one in the US and one in Mexico) were established to attract investment and create jobs in Mexico along the US–Mexican border, with the intention to reduce the numbers of Mexicans entering the US illegally in search of jobs. The parent firms (originally from the US, but eventually from Europe and Asia, as well) receive special customs treatment, allowing the foreign firms to import, duty-free, the equipment, parts, and materials needed for assembly or manufacturing in Mexico, with cheap Mexican labor, of products which are then to be exported to the US or other countries, with only the labor value added subject to import and export tax.

The idea has been so successful that there are now about 3,000 of these operations, employing about 1 million Mexican workers. Some of these operations are wholly owned subsidiaries. And some are subcontracted to firms that handle everything from setting up the operations to employing and managing the work forces. From an IHR perspective, every HR issue becomes important, from the hiring of the work force in Mexico to determining which labor laws apply to that work force, to pay and benefits, to training, to skill development, to selecting and managing home country transferees to work in the *maquiladora*, to learning how to operate in two very different cultures and legal systems, and to management of the labor force from the perspective of two cultures.

The situation between the US and Mexico may be unique (for example, the only situation where a developed economy shares a long common border with an emerging economy), nevertheless, other countries are taking a close look at the *maquiladora* example as a possible solution to their needs to limit immigration/emigration, create jobs, and attract investment. Even this particular US–Mexico opportunity (*maquiladoras*) can offer an additional option for many firms—from any country —who want to internationalize and who want to take advantage of low-cost Mexican labor.

Managing the cross-border acquisition and joint venture/partnership

Even though these options have become the dominant choices for entry into business in many countries, firms' experiences are not always positive. Critical to the success of all of these options are the compatibility of the parties' cultures (both corporate and country), styles of management and decision making, and HR practices. Indeed, the HR practices are so important that the next section focuses on specifically the IHR implications.

Record of success and failure

With these many choices come many challenges and complexities. With these challenges and complexities come risks and dangers. And with these risks and dangers come possibilities of failure. Indeed, success is not as likely as might be assumed. Some surveys suggest that 40 percent or more of international combinations fall short of their objectives and one-third are dissolved within a few months or years.[29] Interviews with top financial services executives found that 90 percent of alliance negotiations fail to reach agreement and that only 2 percent create deals that last more than four years.[30] At least half of all cross-border combinations (acquisitions, joint ventures, and partnerships) fall well short of expectations.

Typically, the reasons for pursuing cross-border acquisitions or alliances are financial or strategic (due to perceived synergy from combining operations, products, services, markets, or technology) with the goal of achieving increased profits, market value, and improved market position. Yet these objectives are less commonly achieved than would be expected.

Human resource implications of cross-border acquisitions, international joint ventures, and alliances

When acquisition, joint venture, or partnership is the choice for entry into a new market, it is often seen as a quicker and more effective way to develop a presence in a local market than to build such capability from scratch. IHRM in Action 2.5 illustrates what one large MNE, General Electric Corporation, has learned about how to ensure the success of these cross-border acquisitions. As is discussed in the rest of this section, there can be a multitude of problems encountered when acquiring or merging with firms in other countries. The Schuler, Jackson, and Luo book in this series provides additional detail about the IHR implications of cross-border acquisitions, joint ventures, and partnerships and alliances.[31]

The high failure rate and managerial complexity of cross-border mergers and acquisitions, joint ventures, and partnerships are often blamed on inadequate examination of human resource issues. One reason for this is that the planning for these actions all too often minimizes or ignores the HR management implications. The following section gives a short summary of the HR issues that impact the success or failure of these internationalization choices. Even though there are differences between the three major forms of global structure discussed above (acquisition, joint venture, and partnership), the following discussion focuses on the many similar HR considerations of importance to all three.

Due diligence

One of the keys for firms to achieve their financial and strategic objectives through these cross-border combinations requires them to conduct a very thorough "due diligence" of the potential partner(s) in order to assess carefully the "real" values to be gained. However, all too often:

ACQUISITION INTEGRATION

GE Capital lessons learned

Over the years, and as the result of experience with many, many acquisitions, GE Capital Services' acquisition integration process has been discussed, debated, tested, changed, and refined. It is now well established and codified. The following are some of the lessons they have learned about how to ensure the success of any acquisitions.

- Acquisition integration is not a discrete phase of a deal and does not begin when the documents are signed. Rather it is a process that begins with due diligence and runs through the ongoing management of the new enterprise.
- Integration management is a full-time job and needs to be recognized as a distinct business function, just like operations, marketing, or finance.
- Decisions about management structure, key roles, reporting relationships, layoffs, restructuring, and other career-affecting aspects of the integration should be made, announced, and implemented as soon as possible after the deal is signed—within days, if possible. Creeping changes, uncertainty, and anxiety that last for months are debilitating and immediately start to drain value from an acquisition.
- A successful integration melds not only various technical aspects of the business but also the different cultures. The best way to do so is to get people working together quickly to solve business problems and accomplish results that could not have been achieved before.

Even with the ten and more years spent on refining the acquisition integration process and making "best practices" available via the intranet, including things like communication plans, 100-day plans, functional integration checklists, workshop agendas, consulting resources, and HR department support, the process remains an ongoing challenge. Every acquisition is unique, with its own business strategy, personality, and culture. Thus, GE Capital continues to strive to make every new acquisition integration better than the last. Maybe the most important lessons that GE Capital has learned is that the competence to make the integration process work must always be worked on—it is never fully attained.

Sources Ashkenas, R. N., DeMonaco, L. J., and Francis, S. C. (1998), Making the deal real: How GE Capital integrates acquisitions, *Harvard Business Review*, January–February: 165–178; and DiGeorgio, R. M., Making mergers and acquisitions work: What we know and don't know, Part I (2002, vol. 3, no. 2: 134–148) and Part II (2003, vol 3, no. 3: 259–274), *Journal of Change Management*.

> People . . . just jump into the deal and then comes the realization that you have to work at it . . . There are no easy mergers or acquisitions [or joint ventures or alliances]. Mergers need to be more thoughtful, more precise with regard to their objectives, more deliberate with regard to their people and processes and yet be done in a rapid time.[32]

As a result, the typical due diligence review of target firms during the pre-combination phase rarely considers the critical people, organizational, and HR issues that often provide the reasons for the success or failure of the combination.[33]

The reasons for failure usually have more to do with the incompatibility of people, cultures, and/or HR systems (such as compensation, pension plans, and union contracts) than with problems with the originally perceived financial or strategic benefits. These HR complications often include issues such as overestimation of the abilities of the target firm, an exaggerated assumption of the synergies available from the combination, inadequate attention to the incompatibilities of the firms' programs, ways of conducting business, and cultures, and unwillingness to prepare for the frequently experienced loss of productivity and staff after the merger is completed. Add to these problems the typical differences experienced between legal and cultural systems in different countries, and it becomes easier to understand the necessity of HR due diligence prior to any international acquisition or alliance and of paying close attention to the necessary post-merger people integration issues.

And yet "globalization mandates alliances [and cross-border acquisitions], makes them absolutely essential to strategy . . . Like it or not, the simultaneous developments that go under the name of globalization makes alliances—*entente* —necessary."[34]

Process of integration

Once the due diligence is completed, and the formal process of combination is complete, the firm(s) must implement the integration of the firms. Yet, organizational integration in the aftermath of acquisitions and alliances is often reported as being problematic. First, the firms involved need to determine the desirable end result. There are at least three options: one dominant firm, a shared model, with the firms drawing on culture and practices from all parties involved, or a model in which a new organizational culture and management style are purposely developed.

All three of these choices require a process of acculturation, i.e., the process of individual employees and the organization itself adapting and reacting to each others' cultures and practices, which can take place in a number of different ways, not all of them healthy for the new organization. As much as both parties typically state the new combination involves the linking of equals, in practice one group always dominates in the acculturation process. Thus the process of acculturation can result in any of the following:[35]

● *Assimilation.* The non-dominant group relinquishes its identity.
● *Integration.* The non-dominant group maintains its cultural integrity but becomes at the same time an integral part of the dominant culture.
● *Rejection.* The non-dominant group withdraws from the dominant culture.
● *Deculturation.* The non-dominant group loses cultural and psychological contact with both its own original culture and the dominant culture.

The point is that assimilation is not always the end result of the acquisition or partnership. When there is lack of agreement on the preferred adaptation process by the parties involved, problems will occur and integration may not happen at all.

ORGANIZATIONAL STRUCTURE AND DESIGN

As the preceding paragraphs illustrate, cross-border mergers, acquisitions, and alliances of various types are increasingly used by firms to gain access to new global markets and global resources, even though they are often unsuccessful in their attempts. In some countries, joint ventures or partnerships are, if not the only way to enter the marketplace, at least the "smartest" way, either because foreign firms and individuals can, for practical purposes, do business in the country only through such local partnerships (either because the local culture places primary importance on relationships in order to do business there or the government requires such local partnering). And yet, adequate due diligence and planning for and implementation of the integration of the firms often need more attention than they get, particularly as it relates to issues of concern to IHR.

The last issue we deal with in this chapter involves the organizational structure necessary to conduct this international business. Like everything else that has gone before in this chapter, this too is increasingly complex. The more assets and employees a firm has in its foreign subsidiaries and partnerships, the more products and services the firm markets around the world, the more aspects of its business it locates abroad (such as advertising, research and development, service centers, as well as manufacturing and sales offices), the more forms of foreign activity the firm uses (such as outsourcing, offshoring, wholly-owned subsidiaries, M&As, joint ventures, and alliances), and the more languages, cultures, and time zones it has to cope with, the more complex the structure will need to be. This applies both to the overall design of the organization as well as the structure of the HR department itself.

The basic organizational challenge to MNEs has always been twofold: first, the integration of activities that take place in multiple countries and, second, the coordination of policies and practices in multiple foreign subsidiaries with those developed in and pursued by headquarters. This balancing act between global integration and local autonomy has been the primary task of managers with global responsibility for both the production and delivery of products as well as for functions like HR, finance, and research and development. The basic organizational structure of global firms, then, has been a blend of multiple organizational components: (1) global product lines; (2) regional and country headquarters; (3) country subsidiaries and international alliances; and (4) global business functions. Varying global strategies and international problems have led to various combinations and foci across these four dimensions. And, now, increased foreign direct investment—with more cross-border M&As, joint ventures, and strategic alliances than ever before and with constantly evolving product innovations and new technologies—is causing the convergence and realignment of whole industries in such a way as to blur the traditional boundaries between these four dimensions and making the design and management of MNEs even more complex than before.

In addition to the common organizational design influencers (such as strategies, goals, environment, technology, people, and size), four additional factors determine how MNEs organize for global business:[36]

- The firm's forms and stages of international development.
- The amount of cross-border coordination required by the firm's strategy (that is, the degree of desired standardization and centralization versus the degree of acceptable and/or necessary localization and decentralization).
- The nature of the host governments' involvement in the economic process.
- The diversity and complexity of the MNE's business operations.

To a large degree, these factors concern the level of development and required interconnectedness of the MNE's various subsidiaries and alliances. Such subsidiaries and alliances can range in form from simple sales offices to offshored business functions to complete, stand-alone operations (wholly or partially owned), formal joint ventures, and less formal partnerships of various kinds.

In the past, MNEs have dealt with the complexity of international business by trying to simplify (read: standardize) their operations and organizations. This typically led to development of common policies and practices throughout a firm's global operations and to simpler forms of organization (usually copying their domestic organizational structures in the subsidiaries) and the use of global product divisions or independent country subsidiaries, reporting through the traditional marketing or manufacturing chains of command. This minimized the problem of command and control in the global context, since the assumption was that if managers could handle domestic operations, then they could also effectively manage the structures and systems that were duplicated internationally, to handle the firm's global commerce, transferring parent company products, technology, and management style to their foreign operations. Often, international business was viewed as a relatively unimportant side-light of the overall enterprise activities, and thus limited attention was paid to its management and structure.

However, MNEs (especially the ones with longer-term experience and with greater foreign investment and number of foreign employees) have discovered that this strategy does not work very well. Doing business internationally is too complex and unpredictable. Other countries and cultures don't always accommodate the MNE's products, styles, and culture. The result is that MNEs have needed to develop more sophisticated organizational structures in order to deal effectively with this complexity and to develop new managerial skills to deal with multiple cultures, languages, and ways of conducting business internationally.

This has created many new challenges to develop the necessary organization and management coordination mechanisms and to train and develop global managers that can manage these more complex forms of structure and systems.[37] The systems need to be able to cope with the challenges global firms confront and their managers need to have the mind-set and ability to manage those new systems.

The basic problem that underlies the ability of firms to organize in such a way in their international operations as to be able to exploit global opportunities is the challenge of figuring out how to coordinate and balance the opposing forces of integrating their foreign operations with each other and with the parent firm while at the same time allowing the necessary autonomy and local control needed to meet unique national and cultural interests.[38] MNEs need integration and sharing of learning and experience, so they typically seek common policies in a number of areas related to overall performance, such as financial objectives, yet they also need to allow localized adaptation to cultural differences, particularly in product characteristics and in management. The emphasis on increased layers of organization and size of formal structure and more sophisticated systems has in fact slowed down communication, learning, and decision making, and limited international firms' abilities to adapt effectively to local differences. Thus MNEs are increasingly turning to reduced size of business units (as illustrated by Cap Gemini, in IHRM in Action 2.3), increased numbers of smaller business centers, and informal networks linking these business centers and managers and employees around the world for improved communication, control, and coordination. As Jay Galbraith, one of the foremost researchers on issues related to the design of the global corporation, says: "Organizing a company to do business on a global scale remains one of the most complex organizational responsibilities."[39] And coping with the challenge of combining centralized control and integration with localized products and managerial adaptation creates one of the most significant of these complexities.

It should be obvious that no one type of international organization structure embodies the right system for all firms. Rather, the MNE needs to be a multidimensional network of businesses (product lines and services), countries, and functions. Global customers are demanding single points of business contact and global strategies seek simplified reporting structures. In response, firms are being forced into four and five (or more) dimensional networks, linking traditional functional areas (e.g., R&D, finance, and marketing—which will be located where the talents and costs will be best), product lines and business groupings of products, country headquarters, subsidiaries, joint ventures, design and development centers, partnerships and alliances, regional headquarters, shared service centers in areas like HR and customer service, and combinations of all of these. Global firms (and individuals) which can develop and build global networks, including global electronic networks, will be best positioned to meet these challenges. The virtual teams that will be formed from these networks (and developed to do the planning, customer service, and research and development work of the global firm) will allow companies to continue to organize and reorganize along whatever new dimensions may yet be needed. And managers will need to be developed who will be able to operate effectively in these global firms with both multidimensional structures as well as multiple types of structures. As concerns for cost control compete with concerns for integration and cross-fertilization across national borders, firms tend to look for ways to coordinate all the many critical components of the firm. Managers often have to report to multiple offices, such as local national bosses plus their product group and regional or headquarters functional offices, as well. And often the critical interactions include a number of other centers, such as design or R&D centers, financial centers, planning centers, and/or service centers.

INTERNATIONAL HUMAN RESOURCE MANAGEMENT AND GLOBAL ORGANIZATIONAL DESIGN

Designing the MNE is increasingly complex and to a large degree presents mostly new and complex people and organizational issues, such as cross-border negotiations, cultural sensitivities, coordination and control across national boundaries and time zones, cross-border and cross-cultural teamwork, and global learning and integration. As the number of countries and cultures and variety of international business activities, as well as the use of cross-border teams and task forces, continue to increase, the more important IHR has become in helping firms make sure that their globalization works.

International human resource management and the management of global organization structure

IHRM should not only be able to support the organizational structure of the MNE and deliver the "glue" technology that these different groupings need to integrate, but it must also organize itself to deliver HR transactional services for all locations of the MNE. The traditional IHRM view of how to best organize itself, in the early stages of internationalization, was focused on either servicing the subsidiary's HR needs (with outsourced help) at arm's length from the headquarters, or hire local HR country managers to deliver these services on location. However, both options had major drawbacks. Headquarters HR managers are simply incapable (and dangerously unknowledgeable) in managing HR practices outside of their own countries (due to both their lack of international exposure and to the legal and cultural complexity of host countries) and locals, although knowledgeable to deliver transactional HR services in their local countries, may not be cost-effective and often lack the strategic HR component in their jobs and are used by headquarters to implement corporate programs in the local environment.

To remedy some of these shortcomings, and as a result of the capabilities provided through modern IT and communication technologies, a new organizational form has been emerging to deliver HR transactional services in the MNE. This new structure for the delivery of HR services throughout an MNE's global operations is referred to as "shared services." In a shared service model, individual country operations can specialize in varying aspects of international HR services and then, given the power of intranets, countries can access these expertises without having to develop them all themselves. In this way, all of an MNE's foreign operations can have available world-class IHR capabilities.

It's more than formal structure

The challenge for the management of MNEs and their IHR departments is to learn how to manage all of these networks and linkages. This is one of the most important objectives of leadership development in the MNE and is discussed in a later chapter. Here is a short introduction to networks, one of the most important forms of linkage. HR issues with global and/or virtual teams are discussed throughout the text, for example in Chapter 6 on training and development and in the last chapter.

Networks

One of the most important competencies that holds together these complex global businesses are the informal networks that individual managers develop throughout the many centers of the firm. These networks work only if the managers who interact with each other to get their planning and implementation done know and trust each other well enough to work out their different purposes. It requires constant attention to the skills of integration and to management development programs that have as one of their major foci the building of such networks and the competencies of integration.

RESEARCH ON THE STRUCTURE AND PERFORMANCE OF THE MULTINATIONAL ENTERPRISE[40]

Even though international corporations have been around for a long time, "surprisingly little academic research has focused on this complex and fast-changing field until recently."[41] There is a particular shortage of empirical studies, partly because of the late interest shown in the operations of these corporations and partly because their sheer complexity and geographical dispersion make access difficult. Most available studies suffer one or more of three shortcomings. First, the overwhelming majority are of manufacturing enterprises.[42] And, although the differences between goods production and service provision are widely described,[43] little attention has been paid to whether the management and organization of global firms varies by type of industry, e.g., the differences between industries such as extraction (oil and mining), consumer products, banking, and transportation (e.g., automobiles and airlines), all of which are very global industries. Particularly ignored are organizations that deliver professional business services, for example accounting, law, architecture, engineering, and consulting services.[44]

A second shortcoming is that more attention has been given to understanding issues of strategy[45] than to issues of management and organization.[46] And yet, as Ghoshal and Westney note, "it is easier to develop appropriate international business strategies than it is to build organizational systems to carry them out."[47] Hout, Porter, and Rudden similarly declare that organization, not strategy, is the "Achilles heel" of global firms.[48] Studies that do focus on management and organization frequently equate organization with structure and ignore or downplay decision processes and HR practices that activate and give purpose to structural architecture.[49] Studies using broader definitions mostly pre-date current debates on global strategy.[50] Of the small number of studies that examine organizational arrangements in the wider sense, the focus is almost entirely on manufacturing industries, and thus little attention has been paid to the many other industries which have become global.[51]

The third shortcoming is that most studies of international management fail to capture the temporal context of organizations, with a few exceptions.[52] Insufficient attention is given to the circumstances within which an organization is operating and to how those circumstances may be changing and impelling organizational adjustment. Instead, snapshots of organizational mechanisms are provided without full analysis of the circumstances that influence their adoption and evolution. These usually ignored circumstances include not only the "administrative heritage" of the organization but also the history of the industry. And now IHRM has the challenge to understand all of these circumstances in order to help their organizations cope with them.

THE GLOBAL LEARNING ORGANIZATION: THE TIE THAT BINDS

Ultimately, the "tie" that binds the global firm together is the intellectual and social capital it has in the experience, knowledge, and skills held by its employees around the world and its abilities to share, and use, that knowledge on a global basis. In today's world, where the only sustainable competitive advantage any firm has is its ability to learn faster than its competitors, creating a culture of learning and nurturing and facilitating that learning across borders may be the only avenue to success.[53] In today's global economy, "change is complex and messy, [so] many stick with the known for fear of the unknown . . . It is much more reassuring to stay as you are . . . than to try to make a fundamental change when you cannot be certain that the effort will succeed."[54] Yet a firm has to do it, in order to survive and thrive in today's environment. It has to take the risk to find ways to facilitate learning so that change is possible. As John Browne, CEO of BP Amoco, put it: "learning is at the heart of a company's ability to adapt to a rapidly changing environment."[55] From a global perspective, this means a firm must facilitate learning on a global basis—across borders, across parts of the organization in different country locales, in global and virtual teams, with people on foreign assignments and after they return from those assignments, and in international joint ventures and cross-border partnerships and alliances.

As Peter Senge says, "perhaps for the first time in history, humankind has the capacity to create far more information than anyone can absorb, to foster far greater interdependency than anyone can manage, and to accelerate change far faster than anyone's ability to keep pace."[56] Thus the challenge to firms is that learning on a global basis must become a central managerial focus. Technology alone (such as creating IT databases and repositories of knowledge and experience) will not solve the challenge. Nor will merely stating principles and values of collaboration. People must want to use such knowledge sources and must be willing to contribute their own "learnings" to them. In the end, people must be committed to: (1) the importance of learning; and (2) the need to share and use information. In turn, the MNE (and IHR) needs to create the organizational culture and structure and the HR policies and practices that encourage and facilitate such attitudes and behaviors. This is the essence of learning in organizations and knowledge management.[57]

The global firm must use its people who have international experience and knowledge and who have been posted to international assignments, spreading them throughout the organization. It must ensure that individuals coming back from overseas assignments are provided new jobs that use the knowledge and skills learned overseas and are given opportunities to share that learning. In order for a firm to reap the benefits of global learning, it is imperative that its valuable expatriate employees remain with the organization long enough to share their experience. Since learning is so important, and learning across borders (taking advantage of the global experiences and multinational learning of a global firm's global work force) is so necessary, carefully managing employees on foreign assignments to ensure successful expatriation and repatriation would seem essential. (These issues are discussed in detail in Chapter 5 on staffing.)

Special efforts also need to be made to expose employees and managers "at home" to the products and processes of foreign subsidiaries and foreign acquisitions and partners, and vice versa, including visits to each other's operations to observe and learn through direct interaction. The firm must spread employees and managers from the countries of its operations throughout its organization, including at the very highest levels of the executive team and the board of directors itself. Only in these ways can the global firm make effective use of any technology that has been adopted to facilitate learning on a global scale, such as talent directories, intranets for sharing information, etc.

CONCLUSION

This chapter has focused on the difficult task of designing organizational structure for the complexities of the modern global enterprise. First, it described the evolution of firms in the expansion of their global reach. Then it discussed the choices that firms consider in their decisions about how to "go international." The evolution of the global firm from a simple headquarters–subsidiary model to the very complex matrix structures that link hundreds of business centers located in dozens of countries was discussed, with the goal of providing guidance on options for designing effective organizational structures that enable MNEs to integrate and control their far-flung, and often locally centered, operations.

Next, the chapter described the international mergers and acquisitions and alliances of various types that have become so popular in recent years. Because issues of culture and HR are at the core of the success or failure of these approaches to international business, the processes of pre-combination due diligence and post-combination integration are discussed in the particular context of identifying and working with critical people (HR) concerns. And lastly, the chapter described the current state of research into global organizational design and the power of global organizational learning as the "glue" that has the power to hold together these global operations.

GUIDED DISCUSSION QUESTIONS

1 How has the MNE evolved? How have the changes in MNEs affected HR?

2 What are the various choices that MNEs have for entry into IB? How do the functions of HR vary with these various choices?

3 How can IHR help to ensure the success of cross-border acquisitions and joint ventures?

4 How do networks and learning organizations help to ensure an MNEs competitive advantage?

VIGNETTE 2.1 INTEGRATED RECRUITMENT STRATEGY IN ACTION

Internationalization of human resources at OBI

Renowned for its orange big box stores, OBI is one of the leading DIY/home improvement retail brands in Europe. Founded in Germany in 1970, the company currently operates about 500 stores in ten European countries and boasts 40,000 employees. OBI's expansion strategy is geared towards market leadership in Central and Eastern Europe. Its share of international sales is expected to grow from one-third to one-half of the organization's total revenue within four years.

While most of the stores are owned and operated by OBI, some operate under franchise agreements. In some countries, such as Russia and Ukraine, OBI entered into joint ventures with local partners to expand its business while maintaining full operational control. Until 2006, OBI's subsidiaries operated, for the most part, independently in each country—a textbook multidomestic situation. Any coordination with the parent company headquarters depended more on an individual manager's ability and willingness to network within the informal structure than on any formal corporate policies.

As OBI expanded in the international market, its HR department realized that in order to realize economies of scale and draw upon global expertise and resources while still localizing the business in its different national markets, the company would have to change its multidomestic approach. OBI needed to create a more centralized mode of operations and become a transnational company.

Thomas Belker, managing director of HR, remembers:

> When I started my job in 2006, many line managers came and asked for support. The international business was growing so fast that we were in dire need of expatriates to build up new country headquarters and to support the development of new stores. As a result, one of our most daring endeavours, the expansion in Russia, was at risk. The recruiting activities for the 2,000 employees OBI needed to hire that year came almost to a standstill because we couldn't find a sufficient number of expats for the management team.

No standardized HR management practices existed, and in those countries where practices had been developed, they were rarely followed. As a result, some line managers typically requested individualized guidance from headquarters as needed, and would then tailor the suggested solutions to their specific situation. In other cases, managers were accustomed to formulating their own solutions, as headquarters did not always provide the necessary support. Once faced with a potentially huge shortage of qualified employees to support its international expansion, however, OBI realized that it needed standardized recruitment procedures. "I knew that my first meeting with all the country managers would be crucial if I wanted to convince everyone to understand multi-domestic as a deadlock," Recalls Thomas Belker. "But how could I take away the fear of the dreaded centralization of processes that would cut off individual solutions by the country managers?"

Local managers were concerned that a standardized competency model would give them less control over their hiring decisions. OBI had previously developed several competency models, although none of them had been uniformly applied. While creating a standardized model would undoubtedly have the advantage of providing clear guidance, OBI was concerned that managers might not comply if the model could not address local concerns.

First and foremost, OBI realized that standardizing all of its HR practices would not necessarily lead to a well integrated organization, and that there was considerable resistance in some countries to adopting centralized HR management. Therefore, it forbade the use of the term "centralization" and instead encouraged each country's managers to help develop the core processes. While the standards would eventually become company-wide, they could be formulated at any level of the organization. Second, recognizing that each domestic operation could develop its own unique solutions to problems facing its country's operations, OBI sought to determine which country addressed which problem the most efficiently. OBI named certain countries "centers of competency" for specific core processes. Thus, the guidelines for recruiting, training, performance management, etc., were established independently in one country and then later applied to other countries' operations. This had the added benefit of increasing interaction among HR managers and developing an international mind-set throughout the corporation. By assigning each country's operations a key function in developing HR policies, OBI was able to transform itself from a multidomestic operation to a transnational organization.

Questions

1 How did OBI capitalize on the strengths of its multi-domestic strategy when shifting the structure to a transnational organization?

2 Why did OBI create "Centers of Competency"?

3 How does shifting from a multi-domestic to a transnational model affect the organization's culture?

4 How did it affect HR?

Source Claus, L. (2007), Global HR in Action Vignettes, Willamette University, www.willamette.edu/agsm/global_hr.

International human resource management and culture

3

LEARNING OBJECTIVES

This chapter will enable the reader to:

- Define culture
- Explain the importance of culture in international business
- Explain the concept of culture as three layers of meaning
- Describe the basic research findings of G. Hofstede and F. Trompenaars
- Describe the differences between convergence, divergence, and cross-vergence
- Explain the importance of culture to IHRM
- Describe the importance of culture to the conduct of research in IHRM
- Explain the difficulties encountered when performing cross-cultural research
- Define the universal, situational, and convergence assumptions underlying cross-cultural research

KEY TERMS

- National culture
- Organizational (MNE) culture
- Surface, hidden, and invisible culture
- Convergence, divergence, and cross-vergence
- Universalism and particularism
- Low context and high context

Many of the most important and difficult challenges to the conduct of international human resource management stem from the differences encountered in various countries' and MNEs' cultures. National and organizational cultures vary significantly from one country and firm to another. Often these differences clash when firms conduct business in multiple countries and with enterprises located in various countries. This can become a particularly salient challenge when business people lack knowledge of or sensitivity to these differences, resulting in their making mistakes in both their business and their personal interactions. Even when they know the differences, they can mistakenly assume that their own country or company way of doing things provides the best way to conduct business. Thus they can make decisions and behave in ways that alienate their foreign counterparts, the people with whom they interact from other countries or companies, such as foreign customers, suppliers, and employees, or they make mistakes that lead to business and/or personal problems. Of course, a second—and maybe just as important—consequence in today's global economy is the likelihood that this attitude of giving preference to one's own country and company culture will result in the overlooking or dismissing of better ways of doing things that can be found in other countries and their enterprises.

As two long-time participants in the international business environment put it:

> More than any other aspect of the business experience, our knowledge and understanding of culture affects the outcome of business ventures. Without insight into the ways of others, we can't expect to develop credibility, nurture goodwill, inspire a work force, or develop marketable products. And that directly translates to bottom-line results. Culture affects the way we develop and maintain relationships. It plays a significant role in determining success with colleagues and partners, and helps us grasp how to evolve into respected leaders around the world. Understanding culture fundamentally affects how we run our business, what characteristics to look for in selecting people, how to develop global talent, how to conduct meetings, and how to manage employees and work with teams.[1]

Knowledge about and competency in working with varying country and organizational cultures is one of the most important issues impacting the success of international business activity, in general, and of IHRM, in particular. The impact of differences in national and organizational cultures lies at the center of every aspect of international business and IHRM. Therefore, this chapter provides both an overview of the nature of national and organization (and corporate) culture and their impact on IHRM as well as provides guidance as to how IHRM can perform the role within MNEs as the advisor and trainer on how to learn from cultural differences and to use those differences in ways to help build global competitive advantage. This chapter also examines research in IHRM (since it is so closely impacted by culture) and its role in understanding the impact of culture on the global organization and on IHRM, itself. Of course, the concept of culture and its influence on IHRM is discussed in every chapter in this book, as its impact on the particular topic of each chapter is described.

THE NATURE AND IMPORTANCE OF CULTURE

Every country has at least some variances from all others, e.g., its history, government, and laws. The more countries with which an MNE interacts (sells, sources, hires or transfers employees, develops joint ventures and partnerships, etc.), the more complex and difficult conducting business becomes. And, today, it is common for MNEs to interact with dozens of other countries. So, one of the central causes of this complexity and high level of difficulty has to do with the importance and critical nature of the differences between the national cultures of all these various countries.

Variances in people's values, beliefs, and behavior patterns (for example, what they consider to be right and wrong, normal and not-normal) are critically important to such international business activities as cross-national negotiations, sales interactions between people from different countries, management of the performance of employees from different countries, the understanding and treatment of contracts between firms from different countries, and all HR responsibilities, such as recruiting and hiring, compensation, training, labor relations, and performance management.

Often, people—particularly those with limited international experience—operate with the expectation that the business methods and models to which they are accustomed will work just as well in other countries as they do at home. Yet, people and companies with long experience in the global arena suggest that such positive overlap is rarely the case. A few years ago, the World Economic Forum asked over 3,000 executives from around the globe to rate countries on how well developed "intercultural understanding" was in those countries' business communities.[2] As would be expected, some countries were perceived to have more highly developed "cross-cultural competencies" than other countries. At the top of the list were countries such as Switzerland, Singapore, the Netherlands, Hong Kong, and Malaysia, countries which have built their economies on international trade. While at the bottom of the list were countries such as Poland, the Czech Republic, South Africa, China, and Russia, countries which, until quite recently, have had economies basically closed to international trade. What this survey illustrates is that, at least in these executives' perceptions, people from some countries—such as Switzerland and Singapore— exhibit a much greater degree of intercultural understanding than do people from other countries—such as China and Russia. Presumably, therefore, people from the countries with the highest degrees of intercultural understanding have an advantage in their conduct of international business, while those with lower scores on their intercultural understanding have much ground to make up to gain these advantages for themselves.

People working for organizations that operate in the international arena (whether in business, government, or the non-profit sector), including HR practitioners, need a context into which they can place the culture(s) they know and the new ones they encounter, so they can modify their own and their firms' behaviors in order to be more effective in both business and social situations. They need a way to cope with the significant constraints imposed by cultural differences between countries. Indeed, dealing with these cultural differences may provide the most important factor in determining whether or not their international ventures succeed or fail.

The next few pages present a model for developing this awareness and understanding so as to enable IHR managers to more effectively cope with their international responsibilities, to interact more effectively with their international colleagues, and to enhance their learning from their exposure to and experience with HR practices in other countries.

A definition and description of culture

There have been many definitions of "culture" offered over the years. For the purposes of this text the following definition is used: *Culture is the characteristic way of behaving and believing that a group of people have developed over time and share.* In the context of this book, the "groups" whose cultures will be discussed are the people from a particular country or region and the members of a particular company. Of course, the concept is also used to describe the values and behaviors of other groups, such as members of particular professions, certain industries, age groups, and racial groups. With this definition, then, a group's culture:

- Gives them a sense of who they are, of belonging, of how they should behave.
- Provides them the capacity to adapt to circumstances (because the culture defines what is the appropriate behavior in that circumstance) and to transmit this knowledge to succeeding generations (in the case of countries) or to new employees (in the case of organizations).
- Affects every aspect of the management process—how people think, solve problems, and make decisions (for a country or firm).

As Schell and Solomon phrase it:

Learned and absorbed during the earliest stages of childhood, reinforced by literature, history, and religion, embodied by . . . heroes, and expressed in . . . instinctive values and views, culture is a powerful force that shapes our thoughts and perceptions. It affects the way we perceive and judge events [and other people], how we respond to and interpret them, and how we communicate to one another in both spoken and unspoken language. Culture, with all of its implications [and forms], differs in every society. These differences might be profound or subtle; they might be obvious or invisible. Ever present yet constantly changing, culture permeates the world we know and molds the way we construct or define reality.[3]

When a firm enters a new country and performs activities such as hiring, using only its home country practices, it can cause significant alienation and lack of trust, which can have further ramifications, for example, in making it difficult to attain a quality work force.

Understanding culture as layers of meaning

One of the complexities that makes "culture" so difficult to deal with is its multiple layers of meaning. There are many readily observable things about the culture of a country, a region, or a firm that differ quite obviously from those of other countries, regions, and firms. These characteristics, including such things as food, art, clothing, greetings, and historical landmarks, are clearly visible. Sometimes these are referred to as artifacts, or manifestations, of underlying values and assumptions.[4] The underlying values and assumptions are much less obvious.

One way to understand this concept is illustrated in Figure 3.1, which represents culture as a series of concentric circles, or multiple layers.[5] The layers of culture, or "onion", model provides a way to understand culture as a series of layers, with each

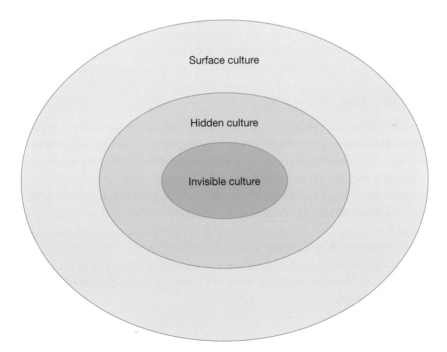

Figure 3.1 The three layers of culture. Outer layer, or *surface* culture: dress, food, architecture, customs; middle layer, or *hidden* culture: values, religions, and philosophies about child rearing, views of right and wrong; core, or *invisible* culture: the culture's universal truths.

Sources Briscoe, D. R. Based on Hofstede, G. (1991), *Cultures and Organizations*, Maidenhead: McGraw-Hill; Trompenaars, F. (1992/1993), *Riding the Waves of Culture*, Burr Ridge, IL: Irwin; and Schell, M. S. and Solomon, C. M. (1997), *Capitalizing on the Global Workforce*, Chicago: Irwin.

layer, moving from the outside to the inside, representing less and less visible, or less explicit, values and assumptions, but correspondingly more and more important values and beliefs for determining attitudes and behaviors. These layers include:

- *Surface or explicit culture* (the outside layer): things that are readily observable, such as dress, food, architecture, customs, body language, gestures, etiquette, greetings, gift giving.
- *Hidden culture* (the middle layer): values, religions, and philosophies about things like child rearing, views of what is right and wrong.
- *Invisible or implicit culture* (the core): the culture's universal truths.

This approach to an understanding of culture is used throughout this book as various business and IHR practices, such as preparing employees for international assignments or developing compensation and motivation practices for application in foreign operations, are described and evaluated.

As people develop an ability to work successfully with differing cultures, they typically go through a process such as that illustrated in Figure 3.2, "Development of cross-cultural competence." This approach to building knowledge about another person or group's behavior and values and eventually adapting to or being able to integrate with that other person's or group's behaviors and attitudes assumes that a person must first understand her or his own cultural values and beliefs before she or he can develop an appreciation and respect for cultural differences, which precedes the eventual movement toward reconciliation and integration with differing national and organizational cultures.

All three stages are challenging. All three stages require progressing from basic education and training about one's own and others' cultures through gaining experience with other cultures to reflecting on and then developing an openness about and finally a willingness to seek feedback about one's own values and behaviors in relation to the foreign culture(s). Ultimately, as was found in an extensive study of the development of global executives, people learn best to deal with the complexities of culture by living in a different culture.[6] But the other steps illustrated in Figure 3.2 are also important in developing what is referred to here as "cultural competency." For more information about preparation and training for learning to accept and adapt to one or more "foreign" cultures, refer to Chapter 6, on global training and management development.

National and regional cultures

An increasing number of researchers are assessing whether or not the wide variety of cultures around the world can be reduced to a more limited set of cultures with similar characteristics. If so, it would greatly reduce the number of problems associated with determining management and HR practices in various countries.

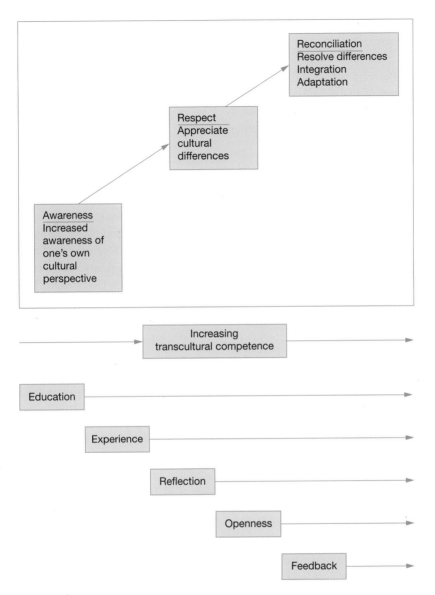

Figure 3.2 Development of cross-cultural competence.

Source Briscoe, D. R., developed for this book

The research of Geert Hofstede

The best known of the studies of national culture (and the first major study of cultural values in a large sample of countries) was performed by Dr. Geert Hofstede in the subsidiaries (initially in fifty-three countries) of one of the major multinational corporations, now known to have been IBM.[7] In particular, this study focused on identifying country differences and regional similarities on the basis of a series of work-related factors. The following provides a short summary of the factors identified in this research:

- Degree of acceptance of *power distance* between bosses and subordinates.
- Degree of *individualism* or collectivism.
- Degree of *masculinity* or femininity in social values.
- Degree of *uncertainty avoidance* or tolerance for ambiguity.

Hofstede found not only that certain countries consistently show similarities based on the presence of these characteristics but also that there are clearly differences between the various groupings of countries on these value dimensions. The significant conclusion for MNEs was that the idea was wrong that managerial and organizational systems as developed and practiced in the parent country and parent company of an MNE should be—or could be—imposed upon the MNE's foreign subsidiaries.[8] As is discussed in more detail toward the end of this chapter, such large-scale research is difficult and expensive. And, not surprisingly, such research has been very difficult to replicate, although ongoing research in the original firm of Hofstede's research (IBM) is confirming both the cultural characteristics and the country profiles.[9]

The research of Fons Trompenaars

Dr. Fons Trompenaars published results of a similar large-scale study (over 15,000 employees from over fifty countries, again from one firm with long-term global experience, Royal Dutch Shell).[10] Even though Trompenaars focused on different aspects of culture—such as how different cultures accord status to members of their cultures, the varying attitudes toward time and nature, and differing attitudes toward individuals and groups and resulting relationships between members of society—his overall conclusions are quite similar to those of Hofstede. Trompenaars identified five distinct cultural factors into which the countries in his study could be categorized. These included the following:

- Universalism versus particularism (emphasis on rule versus relationships).
- Collectivism versus individualism.
- Range of emotions expressed (neutral versus emotional).
- Range of involvement with other people (diffuse versus specific).
- Basis for according status to other people (achievement versus ascription).

In the words of Trompenaars:

> These five value orientations greatly influence our ways of doing business and managing, as well as our responses in the face of moral dilemmas. Our relative position along these dimensions guides our beliefs and actions through life. For example, we all confront situations in which the established rules do not quite fit a particular circumstance. Do we do what is deemed right, or do we adapt to the circumstances of the situation?

If we are in a difficult meeting, do we show how strongly we feel and risk the consequences, or do we show admirable restraint? When we encounter a difficult problem, do we break it apart into pieces to understand it, or do we see everything as related to everything else? On what grounds do we show respect for someone's status or power, because they have achieved it or because other circumstances (like age, education, or family lineage) define it?[11]

Since the reporting of these studies by Hofstede and Trompenaars, other researchers and consultants have reported similar findings or developed alternative ways to categorize cultural values. For example, the Global Leadership and Organizational Behavior Effectiveness (GLOBE) research project (one of the most comprehensive studies yet, performed by a large multinational team of professors) categorized countries on nine cultural dimensions including assertiveness, future orientation, gender differentiation, uncertainty avoidance, power distance, institutional collectivism, in-group collectivism, performance orientation, and humane orientation,[12] which exhibits much overlap, even synthesizing of, the factors reported by Hofstede and Trompenaars.

National cultural clusters

Because the number of different national and ethnic cultures is so great, the efforts by Hofstede, Trompenaars, and others, to cluster countries with similar cultural profiles and to identify a limited set of variables with which one can understand cultural differences have of course been welcomed by firms working in the international arena. The hope and expectation for these efforts is that they can simplify the problems encountered in adjusting to varying national cultures by limiting the number of significantly different countries or regions for the purpose of facilitating international management. The results of several studies suggest cultural groupings of the following countries:[13]

- *Anglo.* Australia, Canada, Ireland, New Zealand, South Africa, United Kingdom, United States.
- *Arab.* Abu-Dhabi, Bahrain, Kuwait, Oman, Saudi Arabia, United Arab Emirates.
- *Far Eastern.* Hong Kong, China, Indonesia, Malaysia, Philippines, Singapore, Vietnam, Taiwan, Thailand.
- *Germanic.* Austria, Germany, Switzerland.
- *Latin American.* Argentina, Chile, Colombia, Mexico, Peru, Venezuela.
- *Latin European.* Belgium, France, Italy, Portugal, Spain.
- *Near Eastern.* Greece, Iran, Turkey.
- *Nordic.* Denmark, Finland, Norway, Sweden.
- *Independent.* Brazil, India, Israel, Japan, South Korea.

People with extensive international experience will probably suggest that some of these groupings hide significant within-group (between countries that are in the same group) differences (such as would be experienced among the different countries in the

Far Eastern cluster).[14] Nevertheless, the various research efforts to identify countries with similar cultural characteristics do suggest that the countries in each group do indeed exhibit significant similarities in their cultural profiles.

These kinds of studies—even if they only confirm managers' assumptions about certain country characteristics—can provide some guidance to general managers and HR managers as they structure policies and practices in foreign operations and activities. At a minimum, these studies provide support for decentralizing many aspects of organizational structure and management and offer a suggestion for creating regional divisions for managing at least some aspects of the highly complex global firm.

The observations of an experienced practitioner

One interesting and practical approach to understanding cultural differences has been developed on the observations and experiences of Richard Gesteland over a thirty-year career as expatriate manager and international negotiator in many countries.[15] Gesteland has observed that variances in four general patterns of cross-cultural business behavior provide critical help in understanding international marketing, negotiating, and managing. These four patterns include:

- *Deal focus versus relationship focus.* Gesteland states that this focus on "making or doing the deal" rather than "building relationships" provides the "Great Divide" between business cultures, with differences in this focus often proving to be exceedingly difficult to bridge.
- *Informal versus formal cultures.* Problems occur here when informal business travelers from relatively egalitarian cultures cross paths with more formal counterparts from hierarchical societies.
- *Rigid-time (monochromic) versus fluid-time (polychromic) cultures.* One group of the world's cultures worships the clock while another group is more relaxed about time and scheduling, focusing instead on the people around them.
- *Expressive versus reserved cultures.* Expressive people communicate—verbally, non-verbally, and in writing—in radically different ways from their more reserved counterparts, which often causes great confusion that can spoil the best efforts to market, sell, source, negotiate, or manage people across cultures.

These four patterns, as offered by Gesteland, suggest some similarities to and additional verification of those published by researchers, such as Hofstede and Trompenaars. And they suggest some slight differences, with an emphasis on what has been crucial to the practice of international management and negotiation.

The dangers of oversimplification

The attempts to isolate country variances and then to group countries and regions with similar profiles and to minimize the variables with which we try to understand cultural differences can simplify the management (and IHR management) task of figuring out how to interact effectively in various countries. But this may oversimplify the understanding of cultural differences.[16] For example, Brannen expresses the concern that the focus on country differences falls short on two levels: (1) that it provides little explanation of within-group differences, that is, it treats countries or cultures as homogeneous wholes, with everyone within the country or culture being alike; and (2) it provides little understanding of how cultures change, that is, it tends to treat cultures as a given—impermeable and static.[17] Brannen suggests that experience shows that cultures are not nearly as homogeneous or as static as these studies suggest. There are considerable differences within cultures and cultures do, in fact, change over time.

COUNTRY CULTURE VERSUS COMPANY CULTURE

Just as countries develop unique patterns of values, norms, beliefs, and acceptable behavior, so also do companies. Most MNEs take great pride in their "organizational cultures," which reflect, at least initially, the values of their founders and evolve to create corporate personalities that give employees a template for how to behave, including in areas like the making of decisions, the acceptance of continual improvement, and the treatment of fellow employees and customers.

For many firms, these organizational values take precedence over country cultures, particularly when there is a conflict between the two. For example, many large MNEs that originate in the US or UK may feel very strongly about the assignment of women to senior management positions and will do this even in cultures where it is rare (and not supported by cultural norms) for women to have these types of appointments. Or MNEs from Western countries may feel strongly in favor of egalitarian and participative management styles and compensation practices and may decide that these values are so important that they will pursue strategies to implement these practices in their foreign operations, even though local culture supports a very different set of values (and often even in the face of resistance from the local culture—even legal—norms). Asian MNEs might emphasize strong group loyalty and discussion, with deference to senior employees, in the ways they operate, even in their foreign subsidiaries, and even when this is not an accepted or understood way to operate by local employees and managers.

The conflict between centralization/standardization and localization/customization has been discussed a number of times already in this book. This dilemma may never be fully resolved, and it will come up again, as it affects various aspects of IHRM policy and practice. This is one of the consequences of the major cultural differences as described in this chapter. IHRM in Action 3.1 helps to illustrate how this issue plays out in one well known global company, McDonald's. McDonald's continuing insistence on aspects of standardization while adopting numerous local ideas and adaptations is an approach being adopted by many MNEs.

McDONALD'S IN GLOBAL ACTION

An example of how even mass-market suppliers are heeding cultural diversity is provided by McDonald's. The Big Mac hamburger is so quintessentially American that "McWorld" has become an epithet for the homogenization of world tastes by the US. But the global popularity of McDonald's products has been increasingly supplanted by local exceptions.

The international division sustained McDonald's throughout much of the 1990s and continues today to create new products that are adopted back in the US and in other countries. When domestic US sales are in trouble, as they were during the 1990s, it has often been the company's local adaptations, introduced by franchisees and national coordinators, which have shown the greatest sales successes, enabling the firm to register over fifteen years of sustained growth. More important, the autonomy first ceded to foreign operators now has become the policy of the whole corporation.

When the Indonesian currency collapsed in 1998, potato imports became too expensive. Rice was substituted and later maintained. In Korea, roast pork was substituted for beef, while soy sauce and garlic were added to the bun in much of Southeast Asia. Austria introduced "McCafes", a variety of local coffee blends (and now McDonald's coffee in the US is voted in polls as the best). And there are many other adaptations, as well, such as beer in Germany and soy and lamb-based burgers in India.

Yet in key values of issues like quality, cleanliness, speed, and branding, McDonald's remains uniform. "Decentralization does not mean anarchy," says the CEO. "Those things are not negotiable."

Sources Adapted from Trompenaars, F. and Hampden-Turner, C. (2001), Cultural answers to global dilemmas, *Financial Times*, January 15: 14; Watson, J. L. (ed.) (1997), *Golden Arches East: McDonald's in East Asia*, Stanford, CA: Stanford University Press; and www.mcdonalds.com.

CULTURAL CONVERGENCE AND/OR DIVERGENCE

One of the continuing controversies that surrounds any discussion of the role of culture in international business is whether or not, due to increasing globalization, there is a growing convergence of national cultural values and characteristics.[18] There is some evidence to support both the point of view that modern technology and the modernizing of industries around the world are influencing firms to adopt similar "best practices" (convergence)[19] as well as support for the view that countries' cultural values and practices continue to exert quite strong influences on their business and HR practices (divergence).[20] It is likely that reality is somewhere in between:

Convergence and divergence perspectives may represent polar extremes. As most firms struggle to find the optimal trade-off between globalization and localization, that is, "glocalization," perhaps the reality is closer to a more balanced or middle-ground view called "cross-vergence," or the intermixing of cultural systems between different countries.[21]

This issue of convergence versus divergence in cultural variance around the world is discussed throughout this book as it applies to various HR practices, such as in Chapter 8 in the discussion of global performance management. But, as the global economy continues to grow, it is likely that cultural differences will influence international business practices in multiple and complex ways. Management and HR practices are likely to be both influenced by the practices of large MNEs from the developed economies as well as by the values and practices from the largest emerging economies, referred to as the BRIC (Brazil, Russia, India, China) economies, and from smaller, yet successful economies, such as Korea and Hong Kong, creating potentially many different, yet successful, hybrid management systems.

RESEARCH IN INTERNATIONAL HUMAN RESOURCE MANAGEMENT

One of the reasons for the apparent slow pace of development of IHRM stems from the problems inherent in researching international organizational issues. This is largely due to the significant and complex impact of culture on such research.

International business research began to develop in the 1970s (along with the expansion of international business).[22]

Cross-cultural management research, however, remained largely limited throughout the 1970s and 1980s and, even now, represents only a small percentage of published research on management and organizational topics.[23] Much of the published research has been from an American perspective, performed by American (or American-trained) researchers,[24] and mostly done in the top industrialized or developed countries.[25] Research published by non-Western scholars (or published in non-English language sources) has gone largely unnoticed in the US, in particular, and in Western Europe and Japan to a lesser extent.[26] And among the business disciplines, management, organization, and HRM have been among those topics receiving the least attention.[27] All of this has contributed to the lack of research related to IHRM.

The limited research published on international and comparative management and organization in general, and IHRM in particular, has been criticized as lacking in analytical rigor, relying too heavily on description of organizational practices (as opposed to critically evaluating such practices), being expedient in research design and planning, and lacking the sustained effort needed to develop case material and other types of longitudinal studies.[28]

There are numerous reasons for this. Multinational—or cross-border or cross-cultural—research is expensive, takes more time and typically involves more travel than domestic research, and often requires skills in multiple languages, sensitivity to multiple cultures, and cooperation among numerous individuals from different countries, companies and, often, governments. All of this combines (and conspires) to make such research quite difficult, if not impossible. Throw in problems with cultural differences among researchers and at research sites, translation problems (see the next few paragraphs), interpretation variances among multinational research teams, and difficulties with research designs such as the use of control groups and the creation of equivalent groups for comparison purposes, and one can see some of the reasons for the lack of rigorous research in IHRM in particular, and to a lesser extent, international management in general.[29]

Even though the amount of research into topics of relevance to IHRM continues to be quite limited,[30] the quantity and quality are growing.[31] As described above, and as with all research into topics related to international business (if not all areas of international research), there are a number of issues that make such research difficult to perform, difficult to describe, and difficult to get published.[32] The following is a short introduction to issues related to the conduct of research into IHRM which should help those interested in both the conduct and the reporting of such research as well as help readers to evaluate the research that is reported, both of an empirical and of a more general, anecdotal, nature.

General frustrations

International management researchers have reported frustration with four particular problems:

- Inconsistent and vague definitions of terms like *culture*.
- Inaccurate translation of key terminology (see the next few paragraphs).
- Difficulty in obtaining representative or equivalent samples of research subjects. It is very hard to isolate the variables of interest in different cultures.
- Difficulty in isolating cultural differences—versus identifying cultural characteristics which might be common across varying cultures—amid varying national economic and political realities (such as stages of development of the countries or cultures being studied and the nature of their political systems).

Forms of research in international human resource management

IHRM research has basically taken one of three forms. These are:

- Cross-cultural, i.e., the study of issues or practices, comparing one country to another.

- Multicultural, i.e., the study of a practice or issue in a number of countries.
- HR practices in other countries, i.e., describing HR practices in one or more countries that are "foreign" to the researcher.

However, the majority of the published research has been of the first variety, primarily due to the many problems with conducting cross-border studies, as described earlier.

The specific case of employee surveys[33]

Although most IHRM research is conducted by academic researchers (with some done by consultants and practitioners), some is conducted by in-house scientists. One of the functions of IHRM research is to help firms evaluate their IHRM practices. One of the common methods used for such in-house research is employee surveys. Even though surveys may be relatively simple in terms of research design, they are still impacted by all of the issues described in this section. Every issue, from translation and item equivalence to union or works council reviews to length of time to administer to varying privacy guidelines or attitudes to methods for administration, to difficulties in working with multinational teams, can cause problems.

Basic assumptions

The basic models and/or assumptions that underlie cross-cultural research have been described as falling into the following three "camps." The perspective of a particular researcher will obviously influence the approach taken, the types of questions examined, the type of data or information sought, and the interpretations of the results.[34]

- *Universal.* A researcher with a universalist assumption has the attitude that there exist some universal cultural characteristics; his or her research task is to identify them and thus demonstrate that certain management and HR practices will work anywhere.
- *Situational.* A researcher with this perspective maintains that there are different managerial practices for different situations; thus his or her task is to identify the cultural situations in which HR or management practices differ or which practices differ based on which cultural variables.
- *Convergent.* A researcher with this perspective begins with a view (and tries to verify) that countries with similar industrial and cultural backgrounds will converge to a common set of management practices as they approach similar levels of economic maturity.

Specific difficulties

Some of the specific reasons for the difficulties in doing international/comparative management and IHR research and getting it published include the following.

The particular focus of the researcher(s)

There are often the following two foci described:

- *Emic.* Trying to identify culture-specific aspects of concepts/behavior, i.e., differences across cultures.
- *Etic.* Trying to identify culture-common aspects, i.e., the same across all cultures.

These terms have been borrowed from linguistics: a phon*emic* system documents meaningful sounds specific to a given language, and a phon*etic* system organizes all sounds that have meaning in any language. Both approaches provide legitimate research orientations, but if a researcher uses an *etic* approach (i.e., assumes universality across cultures) when there is little or no support for doing so, or vice versa, it makes the results difficult to interpret—or leads to errors in interpretation—and will cause problems with review and publishing.

These approaches obviously interact with the universalist versus situational perspectives. A universalist approach will look for evidence to suggest that there is really only "one best way" and that countries that have practices that diverge will eventually converge to the best way. Thus a longitudinal perspective becomes quite important. Most cultural research is pretty static—that is, it doesn't take into account a long enough perspective to show that pressures even within a culture (or, broader, within the global environment) can lead to significant changes and adaptation. So, if the distinction between *emic* and *etic* approaches is ignored in research design, or if unwarranted universality assumptions are made, major methodological difficulties can arise.

Language problems

Language problems are at the root of many of the problems encountered in conducting cross-national research. (This is discussed in more detail later.)

Measurement and/or methodological problems

Measurement and methodological problems can occur when conducting research in multiple cultures and/or languages (for example, attempting to get equivalence in the meaning of terms in various languages, particularly in questionnaire and interview research).[35] "Measurement error occurs when the measure or scale employed fails to reflect the correct extent to which the subject possesses the attribute being measured."[36] These errors can arise because of flaws in scale design or mathematical properties, problems with instrument validity, or because of incorrect application of the scale. These are general methodological problems and can occur in any type of research. However, the complexities of cross-national research add additional problems involving issues such as the reliability of the measures in terms of equivalence of language in different versions of the instrument and equivalence in various versions of the instruments, themselves.[37] In addition, the cross-cultural researcher needs to be aware of the need for equivalence of administration of research and of response to the research in different national or cultural locales.

Equivalence problems in cross-cultural research

The three critical equivalence issues that arise in conducting cross-cultural and cross-national research include:[38]

- *Metric* (stimulus) equivalence. This deals with trying to ensure that the psychometric properties of various forms of the research instruments, such as questionnaire surveys or interviews, which have to be translated into languages different from the original form, are the same; this is usually accomplished through back translation, i.e., having translators convert the translated forms back into the original language, to see if the back-translated questionnaire is the same as the original. Most cross-cultural research focuses here, and this step is pretty much required of all such research, in order to get published. But, as is demonstrated in the next few paragraphs, more is needed.
- *Conceptual* equivalence. The concern here is to ensure that not only do the words translate the same, but that they have the same meaning in different cultures and produce the same level of consistency in results, i.e., the measurement results are similar. For example, in a cross-cultural survey administered in China, South Korea, Japan, and the US, researchers found significant effects attributable not only to country differences but also to the type of scale used, e.g., Likert or semantic differentials.[39] The authors' conclusion was that reactions to various attitude scales are culturally bound and, thus, the scales need to be matched to country situations.
- *Functional* equivalence. This form of equivalence is concerned with ensuring that the terms used and the translations developed are viewed in each culture in similar ways, which requires having "insider" knowledge about the culture, adequate to determine what various cultures value and what the concepts really mean in each culture so as to produce "functional" similarity. In addition, functional equivalence is concerned with ensuring that the concepts work the same way and are implemented the same way in each culture.

The point here is that the results achieved through cross-cultural research may be due to the nature of the research itself (the scales, the language, the wording, the translations, administration, etc.) rather than with any "real" differences in the variables being studied. In addition, there are two more issues that need to be considered:

- *Subjectivity of the topics themselves.* There can be differences between cultures in how they approach the very concept of doing research. The emphasis in Western research is on objectivity and specificity (at least, as viewed within Western cultural norms). But there are potentially a number of points at which people from non-Western (and, even, some from within Western) cultures would view research differently. For example, the choice of topics to research, that is, the topics that are seen as most important to research, are likely to vary from country to country. And topics, themselves, are likely to be viewed very differently and approached very differently in different cultures. For example, US business (males) have traditionally shown a bias for action but French business (males) prefer thought before action. Whether action or thought comes first could well be researched using objective measurement; but which is the "correct" managerial bias is subjective. And, indeed, women in either culture may view this issue differently yet.
- *Factors other than culture.* Lastly, there may also be factors other than culture that make interpreting the results of cross-cultural and cross-national research very problematic. For example, a review of research published in Arabic showed conflicting results over preferences for various leadership or management styles in Arab countries.[40] The author concluded that management styles used in these countries varied with situational factors other than culture.

Research content in international human resource management

Traditionally, the majority of published IHRM research and writing has been related to the selection and preparation of expatriates (now more commonly referred to as international assignees). Gradually more research interest has been focused on local foreign work forces and on other HRM practices in MNEs and in foreign operations. Clearly there are many practices of importance in IHRM that are gaining increased attention from researchers and writers. This is reflected in the chapters throughout the rest of this book.

IMPACT OF CULTURE ON INTERNATIONAL HUMAN RESOURCE MANAGEMENT

The discussion in this chapter has illustrated just how important culture is in the conduct of international business and international HRM. Indeed, every aspect of international business and IHRM is impacted by national and organizational culture. Every topic throughout the rest of this book is influenced by the realities of varying country and company cultures. This is true for the HR management of international assignees as well as for the HR management of local work forces in subsidiaries and joint ventures.

CONCLUSION

This chapter has described the concepts of national and MNE cultures and discussed their importance to the successful conduct of international business and international human resource management. Cultural differences impact international business and IHRM in ways that make both much more challenging and complex. MNEs and their managers need understanding and appreciation for these differences as well as cultural competencies in working within these varying cultural contexts.

This chapter has provided only an introduction and a frame of reference. The concepts and ideas are utilized throughout the rest of the book to help describe the complexities and challenges of IHR. The chapter has provided a framework within which the rest of IHRM and this book can be understood.

GUIDED DISCUSSION QUESTIONS

1 How would you define or describe the concept of culture?

2 How is the research of Trompenaars similar to or different from that of Hofstede?

3 What do you consider to be the most important factors of culture in terms of their impact on business?

4 Are national cultures converging or diverging?

5 What are the most important difficulties in conducting research on IHRM that stem from differences in national cultures and languages?

VIGNETTE 3.1 "GLUE TECHNOLOGY" IN ACTION

Post-merger integration at Teva Pharmaceuticals

Teva, Israel's largest, and one of its oldest, companies, operated as a domestic Israeli company for almost a century. In the 1990s, Teva undertook an internationalization strategy through acquisitions. As a result, Teva grew from fewer than 3,000 employees (1992), primarily located in Israel, to more than 13,000 employees (2005) on three continents.

At Teva, post-merger implementation focuses mainly on cultural integration, with specific attention to talent management, retention, and adaptation to local cultures. Once the acquisition of a company has been approved, cultural and economic issues are key to integration. Cultural integration focuses on socialization into the Teva vision. Because HR people (even in different firms) tend to speak the same professional language, HR people at Teva are the first to make contact with the acquired organizations. HR economic issues revolve around developing a working plan budget (focusing on planning, controlling, and compensation), alignment of HR worldwide working plans (with an emphasis on cost differentials), and monthly tracking of labor costs and number of employees. Teva has a track record of a variance between HR plan and actual of less than 1 percent. This successful record has positioned HR as a strategic business partner with Teva's senior management in terms of supporting the acquisition strategy.

While there is a focus on HR metrics at the global level, Teva's corporate culture is strongly decentralized, focused on lateral services rather than functional silos and hierarchies, devoid of written policies, and embedded in a dynamic Israeli management style. Teva has "policy guidelines," not policies. Management in Teva's headquarters in Israel, Petach-Tikva, does not tell division management how to run its business. For example, HR has performance appraisal process guidelines, but there is no formal process, standard appraisal form, or performance review timetable for all units. Teva's informality is a core cultural aspect of the company and reflects the strategic orientation of the company, which emphasizes decentralization. Teva is a company that is built on relationships among people, not among roles.

In such a structure, Teva attributes an enormous importance to people. The focus is on constantly enriching the experience of people through brainstorming and participation. Everyone can say anything and is encouraged to contribute. There are no functional silos; people work laterally. In functional organizations, the culture is such that questions are directed to the person responsible for the function. At Teva, Israeli management asks the same question from everyone. Unlike in France or the US, where managers respect the domain of responsibility, Teva management crosses information from different sources in order to enrich the response. At first, working this way resulted in a lack of trust and miscommunication among the managers of the acquired companies. Now they attribute much of Teva's business success to the flexibility of the organizational structure.

Another example of lateral services is the establishment of Shared Service Centers (SSC) as part of HR's organizational structure. According to Avi Robinson, Vice-President HR International: "The Shared Service Centers give lateral services to all sites in a particular geographic location. The two major parameters of success are service and efficiency." These SSCs are focused on HR measurement in order to show results. In addition to SSC responsibilities, country HR managers play an active business partner role for all local Teva activities.

In addition to the formal post-integration mechanisms described above (such as lateral services and HR shared services), a number of initiatives are aimed at forging global work force integration, both of general employees and of HR professionals. HR development projects such as the Teva Way, "Shaar" (or "Gateway"), and Global Leadership operate at a global employee level. They are intended to integrate training and development activities, push strategy-derived issues, and provide some of the "glue technology." At the HR professional level, the global HR team (made up of country HR managers) meets face-to-face on a regular basis and works virtually on lateral projects.

The Teva Way is very aspirational and informs every employee what kind of a company Teva wants to be. The Teva Way is about shared values and the alignment of local activities to global initiatives so that every Teva employee, regardless of location around the world, can share the trademark Teva culture. The focus is on accepting local cultural differences while still making a commitment and contribution to Teva and its success. It is not just a slogan, but a concerted effort to identify and disseminate Teva's core values.

Another development project is "Shaar" (called "Gateway" in other countries). Designed to aid in the development of younger managers, Shaar has been running for nine years in Israel and has now expanded globally. Middle managers with various functional areas of expertise are selected early on in their careers and socialized into business development and leadership. This is an accelerated program where trainees are exposed to Teva's senior management and asked to work on lateral team projects, often in areas outside of their comfort zone. The objectives of Gateway are both lateral integration and employee development.

Finally, Global Leadership Development is one of the mechanisms for the development of senior managers. This program provides cross-border and lateral project opportunities and greater exposure to the senior management team.

Remaining an Israeli company in spite of its rapid growth is very important to Teva. There may be a sense of loss in Israel as the company grows from a domestic company to a major global company. As Teva grows through acquisition outside of its domestic market, the majority of its employees will reside outside of corporate headquarters country. What it means to be a global Israeli company is much clearer in Teva Israel than in the company's operations around the world. From an Israeli perspective, Teva is the crown jewel of corporate success in a competitive global business environment. With regard to HR, they are the most advanced and a best practice to be emulated by other Israeli companies. Being a global Israel company is also part of the company's strategic vision with important HR implications.

Questions

1 What is HR's role in developing glue technology?

2 What does it mean for Teva to be an Israeli global company?

Source Claus, L. (2007), Global HR in Action Vignettes, Willamette University, www.willamette.edu/agsm/global_hr.

Global employment law, industrial relations, and international ethics

4

LEARNING OBJECTIVES

This chapter will enable the reader to:

- List and describe the activities of international organizations that affect labor standards
- List and describe the goals of the various international trade agreements
- Describe how EU directives impact IHRM
- Identify sources of international laws that affect an organization's international operations and IHRM
- Compare employment laws and regulations in various countries and analyze their effects on IHRM
- Identify the major issues impacting HR with regard to immigration/visas, data protection, anti-discrimination and harassment, termination and reduction in force, and intellectual property
- Integrate existing labor and employment laws and regulations, ethical standards, and other rules into IHRM policies and practices
- Describe the nature of employee and labor relations in different national contexts
- Describe the role of ethics, CSR and corporate governance in IHRM

KEY TERMS

- Andean community
- Asia–Pacific Economic Cooperation (APEC)
- Association of South East Asian Nations (ASEAN)
- Chapeau agreement
- Conventions

- Corporate social responsibility
- Corporate governance
- Cultural relativism
- European Union (EU)
- Extraterritoriality
- Friendship, Commerce and Navigation (FCN) treaty
- Free Trade Area of the Americas (FTAA)
- Foreign compulsion defense
- General Agreement on Tariffs and Trade (GATT)
- Global Compact
- Governance
- International Labor Organization (ILO)
- Individual relativism
- Mercosur/Mercosul
- NAALC
- North American Free Trade Agreement (NAFTA)
- Organization for Economic Cooperation and Development (OECD)
- Presumption of non-extraterritoriality
- Rule of law
- Safe harbor
- Transparency
- Transposition
- United Nations (UN)
- United Nations Conference on Trade, Aid and Defense (UNCTAD)
- Universalism
- Visa
- World Bank
- World Trade Organization (WTO)

This chapter is about labor relations, employment law, and ethics in the global economy. Each of these topics deserves a chapter for itself. However, each is covered in other books in this series. Accordingly, what is provided here is an introduction to these topics, so as to illustrate their contribution to the context that defines the role of the IHR manager in the multinational enterprise.

MNEs do not operate in a vacuum. There is a broad institutional, legal, and regulatory environment, which they must take into account as they conduct their global commerce. International organizations, national trade agreements, and commercial diplomacy efforts with governments all impact how MNEs must operate. National, supranational and extraterritorial laws have varying legal and regulatory impacts on nation states and their actors (firms, labor organizations, regulatory bodies, and individuals). In addition to legal compliance, a number of other regulatory issues also have impact on the activities of the MNE (such as, immigration controls, data privacy/protection, discrimination controls, termination and reduction in force regulations, and intellectual property protection). MNEs must maintain successful industrial relations with employees and their representatives in the many countries in which they do business. And, finally, moving beyond a pure concern with compliance with the law, MNEs must also promote ethical conduct in their activities with all of their stakeholders, be responsible corporate citizens, and establish transparent corporate governance mechanisms.

This social, political, and legal framework—as it applies to the employment context in which MNEs operate—is the subject of this chapter. The chapter describes the institutions, standards, laws, regulations, and relations that affect the employment activities of organizations that operate internationally. Compliance with these employment regulations, and the extent to which they are voluntary or binding, is very complex and, as a consequence, IHR departments often end up having to consult with specialized international service firms (law firms, labor relations consultants, etc.) to guide them through these regulatory and labor issues. Because of this complexity, therefore, this chapter provides only a general overview of the broad structural context in which MNEs operate and its impact on IHR activities.

THE INSTITUTIONAL CONTEXT OF INTERNATIONAL BUSINESS

A number of international institutions are involved with establishing labor standards that apply to most (or many) countries and to their enterprises that conduct business across borders.[1] Gradually these institutions are developing a certain level of consensus on basic employment rights. Box 4.1 provides a list of these general standards.[2] These rights are now becoming accepted not only by the various international groups, but also by regional political affiliations and by national legislatures, which are beginning to incorporate them into local law and jurisprudence.

International organizations

A number of international organizations such as the United Nations (UN), the International Labour Organisation (ILO), the Organization for Economic Cooperation and Development (OECD), the World Bank, and the International Monetary Fund (IMF) have all promoted labor standards that impact employees and labor relations within MNEs. Some of these standards are voluntary while others are technically binding for member states of the international body. The following provides a short description of these bodies and the standards they have promulgated.

BOX 4.1 **EQUIVALENT EMPLOYMENT STANDARDS AS STATED BY VARIOUS INTERNATIONAL ORGANIZATIONS**

- Freedom of association (i.e., the right to organize and to bargain collectively)
- Equal employment opportunity and non-discrimination
- Prohibitions against child labor and forced (prison or slave) labor
- Basic principles concerning occupational safety and health
- Consultation with workers' groups prior to carrying out substantial changes such as work force reductions and plant closures
- Grievance or dispute resolution procedures
- Use of monitors (internal or external) to audit employment practices

Sources ILO Core Labour Standards, 2006, http://www.adb.org/Documents/Handbooks/ Core-Labor-Standards/default.asp; OECD, Guidelines for Multinational Enterprises, www.oecd.org/daf/investment/guidelines.

United Nations

The UN plays a relatively insignificant role in establishing employment laws or standards. Until quite recently, the UN operated in this domain only through related agencies, such as the International Labour Organisation (see below). The UN has mostly focused on the social dimensions of international trade through its Conference on Trade and Development (UNCTAD), its focus on the transnational corporation, within the work of UNCTAD,[3] and through regional economic commissions (such as the Economic and Social Commission for Asia and the Pacific), and this was primarily through the convening of conferences and commissioning studies to focus on the social impacts of liberalized trade and the increased importance of transnational corporations.

However, the UN is beginning to take on a more active role, within the context of developing and giving visibility to its Statement of Universal Human Rights. In July 2000, the United Nations General Assembly adopted the Global Compact that calls on businesses around the world to embrace nine universal principles in the areas of human rights, labor standards, and the environment.[4] The Global Compact is a voluntary initiative that purports to provide a global framework to promote sustainable growth and good citizenship through committed and creative corporate leadership.

International Labour Organisation (ILO)

Established in 1919, the ILO has as its primary goal the improvement of working conditions, living standards, and the fair and equitable treatment of workers in all countries. It is composed of member states with representatives from governments, employers, and workers. This tripartite structure has remained as the mechanism through which the ILO carries on its work. The ILO currently has 177 member countries and is the only really global organization that deals with labor issues, such as stating generally accepted employment standards that apply to all members.

The ILO sets two types of labor standards in twelve industrial categories. These standards are issued as either *conventions* or *recommendations*. Conventions are international treaties which are legally binding for the member states once they are ratified by them. Recommendations are non-binding guidelines that usually assist countries in the implementation of conventions. Ratification of an ILO convention consists of a two-step process: (1) once a convention has been adopted by the ILO labor conference, a member state may choose whether to ratify it or not; (2) once ratified by a member state, it is binding for the country without reservation (i.e., the national legislation must be in compliance with it).

Organization of Economic Cooperation and Development (OECD)

Established in 1960, the OECD evolved from the Organization for European Economic Cooperation (OEEC) that was formed by a number of European nations to administer the US Marshall plan to rebuild the war-ravaged economies of Europe at the end of World War II. Its focus is broader than that of the ILO as it coordinates economic policy among the industrialized countries and addresses globalization issues through the promotion of economic, environmental and social policy among its members. OECD membership has gradually expanded to its current thirty members —all industrialized countries that have developed to an agreed-upon threshold of *per capita* GDP and a demonstrated willingness to adhere to OECD standards and agreements plus seventy non-member states that act as observers.

Since the OECD is a voluntary organization, it cannot set binding labor standards but only sets forth voluntary guidelines. These guidelines are issued under the umbrella of a "chapeau" agreement (i.e., a guiding framework for local laws and regulations) and provide recommendations on responsible business conduct for MNEs operating in or from adhering countries. The guidelines address numerous areas of business, including employment and industrial relations, and are supported by a dispute resolution mechanism.

World Bank and International Monetary Fund (IMF)

Both financial institutions have undertaken extensive research on the relation between trade policy reform and labor markets (wages, unemployment, etc.). Their primary interest has been in protecting "social safety nets" in the phasing and sequencing of their programs. For example, where structural reforms that they have introduced (such as privatization of government-owned sectors of the economy or reductions in protective tariffs) have led to significant retrenchment of jobs (such as in the public sector), they have introduced programs including severance payments and worker retraining schemes. These institutions also provide grants and loans for the development of infrastructure in emerging markets.

International trade organizations and agreements

There are a number of international trade organizations and regional trade treaties that are pursuing, to a greater or lesser extent, common labor standards throughout their areas of treaty. The best known (and most fully developed) of these is the European Union (EU), but they also include the North American Free Trade Agreement (NAFTA), Mercosor/Mercosul, and ASEAN, among other less developed regional agreements. The following provides a short overview of their key efforts in the arena of labor and employment standards.

World Trade Organization (WTO)

The WTO is the international body in which multilateral tariff reductions are negotiated, non-tariff trade barriers are reduced, and international trade disputes are reviewed and adjudicated.[5] It replaced the earlier General Agreement on Tariffs and Trade (GATT). To this point in time, the WTO has not taken any direct action to define labor standards. But it is under constant pressure, primarily from the developed countries, and among them, primarily the US and the EU, to examine ways to link labor codes and human rights issues with tariff reductions.

Some industrial nations and labor advocates think the WTO should use trade sanctions as a means of pressuring countries that, in their opinion, are violating "core labor rights," a term that covers such matters as the use of child labor and forced labor and denial of the right to organize free trade unions. Advocates of such WTO sanctions argue that a country with lower standards for labor rights has an unfair advantage for its exports. Thus, they argue, it is an appropriate topic for consideration by the WTO. There has been considerable discussion within the WTO about ways to be involved with labor issues, such as linking with the ILO. But thus far, there is no consensus to do so. Indeed, the general consensus appears, for now at least, to be for the WTO to defer to the ILO in the pursuit of global labor standards.

North American Free Trade Agreement (NAFTA)

This treaty, between Canada, the United States, and Mexico, signed in 1992, aims at promoting greater trade and closer economic ties between the three member countries, provoked considerable protests from groups, such as labor unions, concerned about possible negative consequences that such freer trade might have on employment, wages, and working conditions. As a response, the three member countries negotiated a supplemental (side) agreement on labor issues. This agreement (North American Agreement on Labor Cooperation, NAALC) was concluded in 1993. Under this agreement, all countries are committed to respect and enforce their own labor laws but, in addition, the NAALC provides mechanisms for problem-solving consultations and evaluations of patterns of practice by independent committees of experts.

Since 2000, the US has negotiated three additional bilateral trade agreements which, for the first time, have incorporated within the body of the trade treaties (not as a side agreement, as with NAALC) a linkage between labor standards and the liberalization of trade. These treaties provide that the parties to the agreements will "strive to ensure" that internationally recognized standards on specific labor matters (those stated by the ILO) are "recognized and protected by domestic law." These bilateral agreements have been signed with Jordan, Chile, and Singapore.

Since the 1990s, pretty much out of the scrutiny of the public or the media, all countries in the western hemisphere (with the exception of Cuba) have been meeting to negotiate a free trade agreement for the hemisphere (referred to as FTAA, or the Free Trade Area of the Americas).[6] One of the objectives of the FTAA is to include labor standards that will be even more inclusive than those enumerated in the Social Charter of the EU or any other existing trade agreement. Originally, the plan was for the negotiations to be completed by 2005 and for the member countries to implement the agreement by 2006. But various countries expressed difficulties with parts of the agreement during the late negotiations in 2005 and now the final signing of this agreement has been postponed until the problems can be resolved. Some critics have suggested that it may be impossible (maybe even a good thing) to resolve these difficulties.[7]

Mercosur/Mercosul

Mercosur is a "common market" agreement signed in 1991 for the free circulation of goods and services and the adoption of common trade and tariff policies between four Latin America countries (Argentina, Brazil, Paraguay, and Uruguay). Shortly after conclusion of the treaty, the Ministers of Labor of the four countries issued a declaration noting the need to take into account labor issues to ensure that the process of integration of the members' economies would be accompanied by real improvement and relative equality in the conditions of work in the four member countries. In 1994, the Presidents of the states issued a joint statement stressing the relevance, for the establishment of a common market, of issues related to employment, migration, workers' protection and the harmonization of the labor legislation of the four countries. A tripartite (labor, management, and government) working subgroup was set up to deal with labor relations, employment, and social security issues. In the final structure, established in 1994, an Economic and Social Consultative Forum was established to make recommendations to the central commission about labor and social issues. Thus, labor and social issues form a part of the institutional structure of Mercosur, but it remains an advisory role.

Andean Community

Originally established as the Andean Pact in 1969, it has been known since 1997 as the Andean Community. Member countries include Bolivia, Colombia, Ecuador, Peru, and Venezuela. The goal of the Andean Community is to achieve a balanced and harmonious development of the member countries under equitable conditions through integration and economic and social cooperation.

Association of South East Asian Nations (ASEAN)

ASEAN was founded in 1992 with the goal to accelerate economic growth, social progress, and cultural development in the region and promote peace and stability in South East Asia. The original ASEAN member states included Brunei, Indonesia, Malaysia, Philippines, Singapore, and Thailand, with these countries joining since then (and their years of membership): Brunei Darussalam (1984), Vietnam (1995), Laos and Myanmar (1997), and Cambodia (1999). ASEAN has undertaken a number of studies concerning the social dimensions and impacts of the liberalization of trade within the member states. So far, however, the members have not developed standards for member states, although it is to be expected that this will happen in the near future.

Asia-Pacific Economic Cooperation (APEC)

APEC's purpose is to facilitate economic growth, trade, investment and cooperation among twenty-one member economies in the Asia-Pacific region. It operates in a cooperative and open dialog manner based on non-binding commitments. It has not yet focused specifically on labor issues.

European Union (EU)

What began as the Treaty of Rome in 1957 as an economic union (a "common market") of six Western European countries (France, Germany, Italy and the Benelux countries), the European Economic Community has now (2007) grown to an enlarged EU of twenty-seven member states and has become a social and political union (in addition to a pure economic free trade zone) as well. As the number of countries increases, so also does the size of the population covered, with a population approaching 500 million people. Thus, the EU is the largest single integrated market in the world. The structure of the EU consists of five distinct institutions (the European Parliament, the Council of the EU, the European Commission, the Court of Justice, and the Court of Auditors), each with specific responsibilities.

A particular issue of interest for IHR is what is referred to within the EU as the social dimension.[8] The Social Charter of the EU, first adopted in 1989 and implemented in 1992, sets out twelve principles of the fundamental rights of workers. Since the original adoption of these principles, the EU has been translating them into practice through directives, with the intent of defining a minimum set of basic rules to be observed in every member country. The intent is to raise the standards in the poorer countries, while encouraging countries that want to do so to move to even higher levels of worker protections or to, at least, maintain their already higher standards.

Of course, these principles and standards apply to all firms, locally owned or foreign owned, that operate within the EU.

Under the Maastricht Treaty of 1991, the following protocols for EU-wide adoption with regard to the various areas of social policy were agreed to:

- Require unanimous agreement by all member states: social security, social protections, individual terminations, representation/collective defense including co-determination, third country national employment conditions, and financial aid for employment promotion.
- Require a qualified majority vote: issues related to the environment, safety and health, working conditions, information and consultation, equal opportunity— labor market opportunities/treatment at work, and integration of persons excluded from the labor market.
- Exempt (i.e., left to the discretion of individual states): levels of pay, right of association, and right to strike or lockout.

Under the Treaty of Amsterdam in 1998, the EU included an Employment "chapter" in the basic treaty, with the purpose of promoting throughout all member states a high level of employment and social protection. Employment policy remains the responsibility of individual member states, but the new chapter on employment policy has the intention of providing a common and central focus on employment policy, including improving the employability of the labor force (particularly young workers and the long-term unemployed), encouraging and facilitating entrepreneurship, encouraging greater adaptability of businesses and their employees (by modernizing work arrangements, such as flexible work arrangements and tax incentives for in-house training), and strengthening the policies for equal opportunity (tackling gender gaps in some economic sectors, reconciling conflicts between work and family life, facilitating reintegration into the labor market, and promoting the integration of people with disabilities).

The EU has passed many directives (discussed later) that address specific areas of concern with the overall objectives of the Social Charter. It is necessary for IHR managers in any enterprise doing business within the EU to understand these regulations and to ensure that their firm's policies and practices abide by them. It is no longer possible to locate an MNE's operations in any specific country within the EU with the strategy of hoping to find "softer" employment standards and regulations. Now they apply to all member states and as the number of member countries has increased to twenty-seven, the task of ensuring compliance within the EU has become even more extensive and complicated.

The Social Charter also established the European Social Fund, whose purpose is to promote the geographical and occupational mobility of workers by focusing development funds on training and retraining schemes, particularly for younger workers and women, migrants, workers threatened with unemployment in restructuring industries, workers with disabilities, and workers in small and medium-sized enterprises.

Commercial diplomacy

MNEs expand across the globe to engage in international commerce. As a result, they must manage their relationships with the various governments and the complex set of regulatory issues that affect their activities and business sectors. Commercial diplomacy is an emerging interdisciplinary field that aims at influencing foreign government policy and regulatory decisions that affect global trade. It is not just restricted to commercial attachés and trade officials who negotiate tariff and quotas on imports, but it also involves many other areas of international business that affect the MNE, such as:

- Trade negotiations (tariff and non-tariff trade barriers; political interests, trade agreements, etc.).
- Impact of policy decision making (business interests, macro-economic impact, public opinion).
- Government regulations (affecting banking, accounting, telecommunications, etc.).
- Legislation (anti-trust/competition law, EU directives, Sarbanes–Oxley, etc.).
- Standards (health, safety, environment, data privacy, product safety, labeling, etc.).
- Industrial subsidies (agricultural, R&D, etc.).
- Corporate conduct (human rights, corruption and bribery, corporate governance, CSR).

While commercial diplomacy efforts are usually conducted by trade officials, they also include bureaucrats in various governments and ministries, industry and professional associations, unions, non-government organizations (NGOs) and the international departments of MNEs. Because of IHR's concern with international organizational behavior issues, they will often need to add value (provide information, analyze, consult, negotiate, etc.) to these commercial diplomacy activities.

THE GLOBAL LEGAL AND REGULATORY CONTEXT OF THE MULTINATIONAL ENTERPRISE

One of the most important areas of global context for IHR is the area of employment law. Even though there is only limited employment regulation developed by international organizations (i.e., employment law developed by bodies with global reach and/or jurisdiction, and what international development there has been involves quite limited ability of enforcement), every firm that operates in the global economy must contend with the varying employment laws in every country in which it operates, as well as abiding by whatever international standards also exist.[9] Typically, these foreign laws and practices differ drastically from what MNEs are familiar with in the headquarters (home) country. Thus, there can be considerable risk of making mistakes, pursuing risky strategies, and putting the enterprise at considerable potential liability for not understanding adequately what these laws, standards, and codes require of the MNE.

Whether an MNE establishes new foreign offices, expands across borders through acquisition, or develops cross-border joint ventures or partnerships, and whether it operates through wholly owned subsidiaries, partial equity arrangements, joint ventures, partnerships, or subcontractors, licensees, or franchisees, it must acquaint itself and comply with all local employment laws and any regional or international employment standards that apply to its international operations. Failure to do so can carry liabilities at many levels, including, of course, legal and financial liabilities, but also including the potential consequences of negative public opinion, consumer dissatisfaction, and hostile local governments.

MNEs typically approach these issues in one or more of the following ways:

- *Understanding international labor standards and regulations* that apply to the labor and employee relations of enterprises that operate in more than one country, such as those developed by the EU, the ILO, and the OECD.
- *Conducting an analysis of the labor and employment laws and practices in each of the countries* within which the MNE operates, such as rules related to discrimination and worker terminations.
- *Determining the extent to which extraterritorial laws apply* especially for countries (such as the US) that have enacted such laws.
- *Analyzing labor and employment issues that are common to all MNEs,* such as problems with adaptation to labor relations and local cultural practice.

Obviously these approaches overlap. The strategic IHR manager will try to understand international employee relations from all these perspectives. For many IHR managers, their responsibilities usually allow them relative autonomy to develop IHR policy and make decisions that can be applied in all countries. There is a "patchwork" of different legislative powers (national, international, extraterritorial). IHR must:

- Comply with the laws of the countries in which it operates. This requires knowledge of local laws and regulations.
- Comply with international standards and supranational regulations. This requires knowledge of international labor standards and supranational binding regulations.
- Comply with the extraterritorial laws of its own country. This requires knowledge of extraterritorial laws.

Complying with these laws and regulations adds an extra layer of concern that requires considerable local input and involvement.

National laws and regulations

Every country's employment laws vary significantly from every other country's employment laws, making this area of the IHRM environment very complex.

In addition, as more and more firms operate in countries outside their original "home" borders, judicial systems within many countries are beginning to take into consideration laws from the parent countries of the MNEs that now operate within their jurisdictions, in addition to their own laws, making it increasingly difficult for MNEs to ignore either their own home country laws in their foreign operations or the laws in their host countries.

When an employee is in Japan one day and Mexico the next, subject to different cultural and social norms as well as contrasting laws and regulations, or an employee in the US meets with a colleague from Sweden to finalize a project in Spain, today's MNE must make sure that any number of standards that apply in the different jurisdictions are not violated. And compounding the complexity is the fact that the legal statutes and regulations not only vary from country to country, but they are also continually being revised and updated.

One of the greatest mistakes IHR can make is to think that corporate HR at headquarters can navigate alone the myriad of local laws and regulations. Most MNEs, employ domestic HR practitioners (local HR generalist, HR country and regional managers) in the local countries in which they operate. In addition, they use international employment lawyers to advise them with compliance. Even understanding the local laws is not sufficient, as the basis of the legal system can be radically different in different countries.

Supranational laws

International organizations, like the ILO and the OECD, and treaties like the EU and NAFTA have developed binding agreements and legal instruments for the affected member states. Note that the notion of "binding" in many of these supranational organizations implies that it is either "directly" or "indirectly" binding. Directly binding, at the member state level, requires "transposition" of the "law" or "treaty" into the national legislation of the countries. Therefore, based on the overall agreement, the member states must guarantee implementation via their national laws usually within a specific time frame. Indirectly binding, at the individual level of companies and individuals, means that employees enjoy certain rights and obligations under these agreements.

The EU has been the most prolific in passing laws that apply to its member states. The EU employs a variety of legal instruments, such as regulations, directives, decisions, opinions, and recommendations, with the first three being binding for member states. Several EU regulations (automatically binding when member states join the EU) and directives (provisions which are binding for member states within eighteen months of their establishment) affect HR and labor relations. Of the different EU legal instruments, the directives have the greatest impact on the practice of IHR as there are several EU directives that deal with employment issues. Selected EU directives affecting labor and social policy are summarized in Box 4.2.

BOX 4.2 **THE SCOPE OF SELECTED EU DIRECTIVES AFFECTING THE LABOR AND SOCIAL POLICY OF BUSINESSES OPERATING IN MEMBER STATES**

Acquired Rights (77/187/EC)

Protects and preserves the rights of workers when the undertaking, business, or part of a business in which they are engaged is transferred between employers as a result of a legal transfer or merger.

Transfer of Undertakings (TUPE) Regulations (2001/23/EC)

Governs the transfer of undertakings and protects the rights of employees in a transfer situation. Employees enjoy the same terms and conditions, with continuity of employment, as they did with the previous employer (transposition of the acquired rights directive into the laws of the member states). Includes business transfers of a stable economic entity retaining its identity and service provision changes (outsourcing, insourcing and subcontracting) for labor-intensive activities. TUPE regulates whether dismissals, as part of the transfer of operations, will be fair or unfair and affects information and consultation requirements and pension liabilities.

European Work Council (94/45/EC, 97/74/EC)

Regulates transnational information and consultation (I&C) on matters as soon as there are two member states involved. It establishes the rights and procedure to information and consultation by requiring the establishment of European works councils (EWC) in undertakings of 1,000 employees in member states combined, or at least 150 in each of at least two member states. If there is a pre-existing agreement on transnational I&C that covers the EU work force, the directive does not apply but the agreement can be renewed when it expires; if not it falls under the directive. If there is no pre-existing agreement, the directive applies and central management is responsible for setting up EWC and I&C procedures.

Redundancies (consolidated Directive: 98/59/EC)

Provides procedures (I&C phase) for making a defined number of employees redundant within a defined period of time.

Fixed Term Work (99/70/EC)

Deals with the use of contract workers and protects fixed term contract employees from comparable less favorable employment practices and benefits. Stipulates that a continuous fixed term contract for four or more years is considered employment as a permanent employee.

Information and Consultation (2002/14/EC)

Establishes a general framework and obligation of employers for I&C with employees. Applies to "undertakings" with at least 100 employees/establishments of at least fifty employees (until March 2008). The directive sets only a general framework for I&C and leaves the practical arrangements (such as works councils, trade unions, etc.) to be worked out by the member states.

Working Time (2003/88/EC)

Provides a definition of working time and determines minimum rest periods, the maximum working week (forty-eight hour average over sixteen weeks), minimum annual leave, paid holidays, night and shift work.

Protection of Individuals with regard to the Processing of Personal Data and the Free Movement of such Data (95/46/EC)

Protects the right to privacy via strict limitations on the processing and transmission of personal data, wholly or partly, by automatic means. Affects HRIS, payroll systems, but also transmission of personal information via corporate internet, email, fax, and voicemail to countries outside the EU that do not provide adequate data protection. The US is considered by the EU as a country that does not provide "adequate data protection" and has negotiated a special agreement with the EU (Safe Harbor).

Pregnancy and Maternity Leave (92/85/EEC); Parental Leave (96/34/EC; extended to UK through 97/75/EC)

Establishes measures to protect the health and safety of pregnant women, new mothers, female workers who are breastfeeding, including minimum leave time for pregnancy and childbirth and later to working parents.

Social Security (1408/71)

Avoids the loss of social security benefits when employees move within the EU for employment. Applies to employed and self-employed workers who reside in a member state and to whom legislation of a member state applies. The general principle is that the employee is subject to the social security legislation of the work state. Exceptions (subject to social security legislation of home country) include secondment and simultaneous employment in two or more member states.

Terms of Employment (91/533)

Regulates the terms of the employment contract and requires a written statement of the main terms of employment. If no written contract has been drafted, one is implied.

EU Pension Funds (under consideration)

Aims to harmonize pension legislation across EU member states, protect pension funds and their beneficiaries, and reduce the cost of operating multiple pension funds. Pension Funds Directive of 13 May 2003 allows the establishment of pan-European pension funds subject to detailed rules.

Service (under consideration)

Proposed directive on services in the internal market to increase freedom to provide cross-border services by removing legal and administrative barriers.

Source Keller, W. L. & Darby, T. J. (Editors in Chief) (2003), *International Labor and Employment Laws*, Vol. 1, 2nd edn, Washington, DC: Bureau of National Affairs. For individual directives see http://ec.europa.eu/atoz_en.htm.

The intention of EU directives is to harmonize legislation between the various member states by setting a common framework. Although member states must ensure transposition into their national legislation that conforms to the general principles of a directive, the actual transposition details may vary substantially in the different member states. Overall, EU directives have been very effective (i.e., all member states have transposed the desired protective measures into their legislation). But, in spite of the EU's attempts to harmonize employment legislation, there is still an enormous degree of legal diversity in the member states and the differences in employment laws between the three major European countries (UK, France, and Germany), the Old Europe, and the New Europe (enlargement countries) remain considerable. With the failure in 2005 at developing an EU constitution and the fact that all EU "social matters" must be decided with unanimity of the member states, it is today's legal expert opinion that not much new EU legislation affecting HR is to be expected in the near future (although there are still several directives impacting the workplace in the pipeline). As a result, a lot more is expected from EU case law in the future (as existing directives and legislation are interpreted through the judicial systems of the EU) in terms of its impact on employment matters. IHR practitioners must remain cognizant of these developments.

Extraterritorial laws

In general, laws have the presumption of non-extraterritoriality, meaning that they only apply to the sovereign territory of the nation that enacted them. Unless a law explicitly states that it applies to a territory outside of that country, it is presumed to apply only within the country of jurisdiction. Some laws, however, have been designed with extraterritorial intent written into them. As a result, every MNE must consider the application of its parent country laws to its overseas operations (referred to as the extraterritorial application of national law). In general, international jurisprudence holds that MNEs are accountable to the laws of the countries where they operate. However, there are some exceptions to this general rule.

More than any other nation, the US has enacted a number of extraterritorial laws. US laws with extraterritorial intent include most of its anti-discrimination legislation (such as the Civil Rights Act, the Age Discrimination in Employment Act, and the Americans with Disabilities Act), the Foreign Corrupt Practices Act (FCPA), and Sarbanes–Oxley (SOX). In particular, US multinationals must comply with the extraterritorial application of three particular US anti-discrimination statutes, meaning these laws provide protection for US citizens working for US companies in their overseas operations. In 1991, the US Congress amended the Americans with Disabilities Act (ADA) and Title VII of the Civil Rights Act of 1964 to give extraterritorial effect to those laws. Earlier, in 1984, the Age Discrimination in Employment Act of 1967 (ADEA) was also given extraterritorial effect. Title VII prohibits discrimination and harassment on the basis of sex, race, national origin, color and religion. The ADA prohibits discrimination against disabled individuals, and requires employers to make reasonable accommodation for those disabilities. And the ADEA prohibits discrimination on the basis of age against individuals age forty and older and sets standards for retirement age. The effect of these amendments was to grant American citizens working anywhere in the world, for a US-owned or controlled company, the right to sue in US court for alleged violations of these acts, wherever they occur. Hence, an employee of an American firm (who is a US citizen) and who believes she has been subjected to sexual harassment in Japan or who believes he has been terminated because of his age in Germany, may bring a lawsuit in the US to pursue these claims. Under any circumstance, the law of the foreign country in which a firm operates takes precedence, although, in US courts, the viability of the defense of an otherwise in the US illegal action on the basis of the foreign law restriction is still unsettled. There is no doubt that US extraterritorial laws apply to US citizens when working for US companies worldwide. An interesting legal question is whether the US extraterritorial laws also apply to non-US citizens working in the foreign subsidiary of a US company.

How does an MNE determine which nation's laws will govern a company's labor practices? Is it the extraterritorial law of the headquarters/home country of the MNE or the local host country law? The fact that a law is an extraterritorial law (in this case usually from the US) does not necessarily mean that it applies universally (e.g., to all its employees everywhere). Which law applies (home or host) depends on the dynamics of control, location, and citizenship of the MNE. The standard that is used to resolve this question is what is referred to as the "integrated enterprise test"; the more integrated the global operations of the MNE, the more likely the extraterritorial law will apply in the host country and extend to non-US citizens. Four factors determine the extent to which two operations are determined to be integrated:

- The interrelation of their operations.
- Common management.
- Centralized control of labor relations.
- Common ownership or financial control.

There are also some exceptions in the applicability of extraterritorial law due to conflicting laws in other territories. An extraterritorial law of one country may be unenforceable if complying with the extraterritorial law would cause the firm to violate host country law. This is referred to as the foreign compulsion defense (i.e., because it would be illegal in the other country, the MNE would not be able to comply with the extraterritorial law). For example, in some countries it may be illegal to hire women for certain jobs, therefore a US company operating in that country and following that law may use as a defense that it was compelled to follow the local law. Note that this defense usually does not apply to a local cultural practice that is not written in a local law.

Application of national law to local foreign-owned enterprises

Every firm must abide by the laws of the countries in which it does business. Thus the issue of whose laws apply can also be viewed from the perspective of any country in terms of how it applies its laws to foreign owned and operated firms within its national borders. Or it can be viewed from the perspective of the firm, as it tries to understand how it must operate its foreign subsidiaries and joint ventures. At a minimum, the MNE must understand that the local laws apply, not its home laws, although, as described above, MNEs from some countries, such as the US, may also find themselves subject to their home laws, at least in terms of treatment of their home citizen employees in their foreign operations. And this may well apply to the firm's parent country international assignees in the foreign locales as well as to how they manage their local employees. So, for example, giving preference in job assignments or promotions to a firm's expatriates over qualified local employees may run afoul of local laws.

Treaty rights can also impact the operations of foreign companies within national jurisdictions. For example, since the end of World War II, the US has negotiated treaties with some twenty countries that are referred to as Friendship, Commerce, and Navigation (FCN) treaties. Among other things, these treaties provide that companies from each country can make employment decisions within the territories of the other party that give preference to key personnel from their home countries.[10] Specifically, an FCN treaty gives foreign companies who establish themselves in the US the right to engage managerial, professional and other specialized personnel "of their choice" in the US, even if giving such preferences might violate US anti-discrimination laws. For example, a Japanese company in the US can reserve its most senior executive positions for Japanese only. A number of foreign companies that have been sued in US courts for national origin discrimination (i.e., giving preference in employment decisions in their local subsidiaries to their parent country nationals) have used a defense that their FCN treaties give them the right to do that. US courts and legal experts have not developed a consensus as to whether or not such treaties provide that type of protection.

Additionally, the US Sovereign Immunity Act states that US operations that are owned, or are controlled by, a non-US government entity may be safeguarded from certain civil claims. In other words, they may not need to comply with US anti-discrimination laws in their employment practices. However, the key word here is government entity, since this exemption does not apply to a commercial activity of a foreign government (such as for example a tourist office from a foreign country established in New York) but only for a government's "diplomatic" functions.

There are other complexities in US law that often require that each specific situation—particularly those involving treatment of US employees and parent country nationals in foreign owned subsidiaries in the US—to be interpreted separately. The bottom line is that IHR managers in MNEs that operate in foreign countries need to make sure they understand the local legal landscape before establishing employment policy and practice in those foreign operations.

Comparative law

There is not enough space in this treatment of international employment laws and regulations to provide very much detail about the employment laws in separate countries. Other books in this series provide regional information about employment laws and *Managing Global Legal Systems*, by Gary Florkowski, provides additional information about the global employment-related legal system. Rather, the intention here is to provide a short overview of particular important areas of concern to the MNE IHR director, including immigration, data privacy, anti-discrimination laws, termination laws, and intellectual property protection. Many of these areas overlap, making it important for IHR managers (and their firms' legal advisors) to know these connections and to consider them as firms make decisions that affect their work forces in the countries in which they operate.

Immigration/visas

Every country exercises control over its definition of citizenship and the immigration that it allows into its territory. Some countries, such as Japan, allow very limited immigration. Others like the US, Canada, and Israel, even though they may exercise control over who is granted immigration rights, admit large numbers of immigrants every year. Indeed, in many years, the US admits more immigrants (legal and illegal) than the rest of the countries of the world combined. Most other countries fall somewhere in between these two extremes. A country's attitudes about immigration vary according to its particular employment needs at any point in time (as well as according to other political and humanitarian concerns). And these change over time, as attitudes and needs change.

Virtually every country requires a work permit or visa whenever a "foreign" person is transferred to or takes on a job in their country for a period of six months or more. Of course, there are typically many other situations that can also trigger the requirement for a visa, even if the work will only last a couple of days. The activities that will trigger the need for such special visas and the amount of time required to process such a visa vary from country to country and from situation to situation. Because of this, IHR managers must be sure, when decisions are being made about sending employees on foreign assignments that can involve everything from short-term business trips to longer-term relocations for a number of months or years, that the necessary visas are applied for and that an adequate amount of time is allowed to be able to gain the necessary approvals for such travel and transfers. Immigration law firms that specialize in helping firms acquire the necessary visas and work permits often provide the information needed to make such judgments.

The destruction of the World Trade Towers in New York City on 11 September 2001 by individuals who had been living in the US, legally and illegally, on student and tourist visas, led to a major tightening of immigration rules and procedures and increased scrutiny of visa applicants of all types in the US. For example, the Immigration and Naturalization Service (INS) that has held the responsibility for customs, border control, and immigration and citizenship issues, has been closed and its responsibilities have been taken over by the new Department of Homeland Security, with the mandate to tighten scrutiny of visa applications and immigration. Gradually, most of the forms and procedures of the INS are being revamped. The events of 9–11 also led to increased scrutiny of legal immigration issues in other areas of the world, as well, partially due to pressure from the US. This is especially true for certain countries and areas of the world that are perceived to be involved with international terrorism, as the US has pressured them to tighten their own procedures and to aid the US in its tightened procedures.

Many countries follow procedures which are similar to each others' and require visas prior to arrival for people to enter and/or work in the country. These visas are usually divided into temporary (non-immigrant) and permanent (immigrant) types of visas. And in most countries and most situations, family and significant others who accompany foreign workers do not qualify for a worker visa in the host location.

Gaining approval of these various visas can be complicated and very time-consuming, expensive, and difficult, as countries tighten their procedures for even business-related and tourist visas. Firms that hire immigrants, move people around the globe, and seek talent all over the world must manage this complexity in order to effectively staff their global operations.

IHR has both a strategic role and tactical role to play with regard to immigration and visa issues. Strategically, IHR must know the company's risks, liabilities, and burden of employing foreign nationals and understand the legal repercussions for non-compliance. In addition, global staffing (and international recruitment) approaches require a comprehensive compensation and immigration strategy and advance planning to avoid delays in terms of obtaining the required visas for employees. HR's tactical role consists of anticipating roadblocks in the visa application process, being aware of application procedures to follow in different countries (or using the services of a specialized firm), and complying with the necessary record keeping and tracking of visas.

The EU is a special case in terms of visas because of the free movement of labor within its member countries which also includes European Economic Area (EEA) nationals and European Free Trade Association (EFTA) nationals. For transfers within the European region, there is no need to obtain a visa. Having a valid identity card or passport is sufficient, as EU nationals have the right of residence in any EU host country and the host country will issue a residence permit for any national of a member state. There are still some exceptions for some of the enlargement countries (new EU member states) where transition measures for free movement of labor for citizens are in place. A number of other countries have facilitated the visa application process to multiple countries within a region as a result of agreements (e.g., APEC Business Travel Card, European Economic Area, NAFTA, and the Schengen

Agreement). For example, the Schengen Agreement among some European countries eliminates systematic border controls

Data privacy/protection

With the advent of the internet and the ease of global communication, allowing information to be shared and distributed quite readily, concern over the protection of information about individuals (for example, employees and customers) has become of increasing concern in many countries.[11] Often, that concern is based in those countries' constitutional guarantees of protection of individual privacy.

In Europe, these protections are particularly strong.[12] Because of this, in 1998 the EU issued a directive on the protection of employee privacy. Of particular interest to MNEs operating in Europe, under the terms of the directive, personal data on European employees, including international assignees working in Europe, cannot be transferred out of the EU unless the country in which the data recipient resides has acceptable privacy protection standards in place. In any case, any firm transferring employee data from Europe to the US (or anywhere else outside Europe) must pay close attention to how such information is managed and shared with third parties. This has been of particular concern to American MNEs in Europe, since there has not been consensus in the US on how to provide adequate privacy protections, as of now wanting to rely more on self-regulation and laws applying to only particular sectors, such as health care and financial institutions. In late 2000, the EU agreed to a "safe harbor" principle from the US in which American firms which agree to abide by the basic European privacy standards will certify to the US Department of Commerce that they are in compliance, which will be reviewed by the EU. Such certified firms will be able to transfer data on European and international assignees from Europe to the US. The potential liability for American firms that do not certify compliance with basic European privacy laws through this "safe harbor" procedure is to lose their right to do business anywhere in the EU.

Several challenges face American firms in implementing the principles of the EU directive. These include logistical difficulties in getting consent (starting from the beginning) in companies with large numbers of employees; limited power to persuade employees to consent to data releases, since employers cannot use consent in hiring decisions and thus will have to find different ways, such as the use of pseudonyms, for transferring data without compromising the privacy of the employee; and a risk of public exposure from a number of privacy rights groups that have threatened to draw public attention to firms that they consider to employ substandard privacy practices. Box 4.3 summarizes the data privacy principles as protected under the EU's Data Protection Directive. A reading of these principles (which are well established, accepted, and protected in European firms but may not so well established or accepted in other parts of the world) helps to understand both why Europeans are so concerned about their enforcement and why American firms (and presumably firms from other countries, such as Japan and South Korea, that also have extensive operations in Europe and also may not have such extensive privacy protections in place) are concerned about their implications and implementation.

BOX 4.3 EUROPEAN UNION DATA PROTECTION PRINCIPLES

Legitimacy
The necessity of the data to execute a contract or comply with a legal obligation; employee consent

Proportionality
Relevant and not excessive

Finality
Cannot be used for other purposes than its stated use

Notice
Collection and use must be disclosed to employees

Accuracy and retention
Data must be up to date and maintained only as long as its stated use

Security
Safeguards to prevent unauthorized access

Access
Employees have right to access and are allowed to correct personal data

Source Keller, W. L. & Darby, T. J. (editors-in-chief) (2003), *International Labor and Employment Laws*, Vol. 1, 2nd edn, Edition, Washington, DC: Bureau of National Affairs, 1–76 to 1–80.

Anti-discrimination

Around the world, countries are passing legislation to protect the rights of employees and job candidates to be free from discrimination and harassment based on their gender, race, color, religion, age, or disability. The laws in place, in some countries, such as the US and now in the EU, are pretty well developed, although within the EU, there has been a distinct lack of uniformity in many of these areas, with the possible exception of sex discrimination. Until the turn of the millennium, many EU countries had not yet even moved beyond approval of protections as put forth by the ILO. However, in 2003, directives went into effect in the EU requiring all member states to pass legislation prohibiting discrimination on the basis of race, gender, disability, age, sexual orientation, and religion or belief.

This is clearly an area of international labor standards to which every MNE must pay very close attention.[13] And because of national and regional cultures that in the past may have allowed practices which are now being prohibited, making sure that all managers and employees of the global firm abide by these new standards presents a major challenge to IHR. Although there is considerable convergence developing, there are still some significant variances. Since courts in some countries are beginning to refer to the laws of parent countries in cases involving MNEs in their jurisdictions, it certainly suggests that IHR and their MNEs must pay close attention to these differences.

Of particular interest is the issue and treatment of sexual harassment. Its cultural interpretation around the world as to what constitutes such harassment and the legal framework protecting employees from harassment and bullying vary extensively between countries. The EU, UN, and ILO all address sexual harassment in the workplace. Several industrialized countries have specific sexual harassment prohibitions (e.g., Australia, Canada, France, New Zealand, Spain, Sweden and the US).[14] In these countries, sexual harassment in the workplace is protected by four different types of constraints (equal employment opportunity law, union contracts, tort (contract) law, or criminal law). In the US, the sexual harassment prohibition is also applied extraterritorially. As this issue has received increased attention, an increasing number of countries have begun to consider sexual harassment issues in the workplace.[15] IHRM in Action 4.1 describes the situation of Toyota in the US that shows how different cultural perceptions and practices can affect the outcome of harassment issues and how non-US management can struggle with the notion of sexual harassment as it is applied in the US.

Termination and reduction in force

In most countries, employment is protected by a contract that defines the terms and conditions of employment, including that it cannot be ended unilaterally or arbitrarily by the employer. The concept of "employment at will," as practiced in the US (where the employer, with a few exceptions, has the right to terminate an employee at will —and the employee has the right to quit at any time for any reason), does not exist in most countries. In most countries, an employer's right to terminate, lay off, reduce, restructure, move, outsource, or subcontract work (and, therefore, workers) is highly constrained. In most countries, even the US, employees (or work) cannot be terminated on grounds of health and safety, pregnancy or maternity, asserting a statutory right, union activity, or the basis of one's gender, race, religion, or disability. In general, firms need to search for alternative employment (within the firm or externally, if nothing is available internally) and consult with their unions, works councils, and the individuals affected (typically, at least thirty days prior to taking action, if twenty to 100 people will be involved and ninety days prior if 100 or more people are to be made redundant).[16] This includes any outsourcing, work transfers to other countries, and subcontracting.

In terms of pure reductions in force, only three situations are seen as possible acceptable excuses:

SEXUAL HARASSMENT LAWSUIT AT TOYOTA NORTH AMERICA

On May 1, 2006, Sayaka Kobayashi, executive assistant to Hideaki Otaka, Chief Executive of Toyota Motor North America, alleged sexual harassment from her boss and filed a lawsuit in New York State court. She claimed that if matters had been handled differently, she would not have proceeded with the lawsuit. All she wanted was to be moved to another position.

In late November, 2005 about six months prior to filing her lawsuit, Kobayashi complained to Ko Takatsu (the executive dealing with HR issues at Toyota North America) that her boss (Otaka) was sexually harassing her. Although Takatsu listened and appeared sympathetic, she was not told of any plan to investigate the allegation of sexual harassment. After talking with Kobayashi, apparently Takatsu took no further action.

In December, 2005, she sent an email to Dennis C. Cuneo, Senior Vice-President of Toyota North America), detailing the accounts of alleged romantic and sexual advances that she had endured for three months at the hands of her boss. Her email stated: "Nowadays, I come to work with anxiety and pray that Mr. Otaka will not ask me to accompany with him to another lunch, another dinner, another business trip. (. . .) I would like to seek advice from you on the issues that I feel helpless." Cuneo responded that he would discuss her letter with Otaka—but that he didn't want to offend him. Instead, he planned to inform Otaka that it was Kobayashi's boyfriend who was upset, rather than Kobayashi herself. Cuneo e-mailed Kobayashi that he had met with Otaka but that he did not go into any details with him. He recommended in his email that Kobayashi meet privately with Otaka to air her concerns. Although uncomfortable with the suggestion, Kobayashi aired her concerns, one-on-one, with Otaka that same month.

In January, 2006, Kobayashi discussed the sexual harassment with Alain Cohen (General Counsel, Toyota Motor Company North America). Cohen suggested that in light of her problem, she might want to consider various options, including returning to school full-time and leaving the company. Kobayashi viewed this as if he wanted to get rid of her. In May, 2006, she filed her lawsuit. Although still employed, she was on medical leave awaiting the outcome of the lawsuit. In August, 2006, Toyota and Kobayashi agreed on a confidential settlement and Otaka was sent from New York to Japan to become an auditor at the Tokyo affiliate Daihatsu Motor Company

Source Orey, M. (2006), Trouble at Toyota, *Business Week*, May 22; Clark, H. (2006), Toyota's Otaka sued for sexual harassment. *Forbes*, May 2; www.card.wordpress.com/2006/08/09/toyota-settles-us-sexual-harassment-lawsuit (retrieved February 11 2007).

- Business closure
- Workplace closure
- Diminishing economic need for the work.

All of these situations involve the requirements for notice and consultation with employees and/or their representatives.

In addition to notice of work force redundancies, most countries also require payments to terminated employees. Indeed, in most countries it is very difficult to terminate any employee for any reason, even with notice and consultation. Particularly when the termination involves a number of employees (that is, it involves a downsizing, relocation, or significant layoff), notice and consultation are both necessary. However, even when terminations are possible and done, they usually still require significant severance payments to all individuals involved. Such payments are often required even when the termination is for disciplinary reasons or poor performance. Separation practices differ in a number of countries and illustrate both the legal requirements for dismissals and the severance payment formula.[17] In most countries, the amount of severance pay is pro-rated by the employee's age, years of service, and last rate of pay or salary. For example, as of a few years ago, a terminated thirty-nine-year-old sales manager earning €75,000 per annum who has been employed for eleven years in Belgium would have been owed 14.49 months' notice or 14.49 months' pay in lieu thereof.[18] A similar employee terminated in Ireland would have been owed at least six-and-a-half weeks' pay (up to a ceiling of one year's maximum pay of £20,800), in Japan thirty days' notice or thirty days' wages, and in Venezuela up to ten months' pay or, in this case, €62,500. It is not unusual for termination pay for longer-term and more senior employees to equal as much as eighteen months' pay.

In some countries, employers will find it difficult to terminate employees at all. In Portugal, for example, all terminations are legal actions defended in court, while in countries such as Germany, where there is a strong tradition of reliance on works councils, terminations are topics for mandatory consultation. Also, in many countries, all employer-paid benefits become what are referred to as acquired rights, that is, once offered, they cannot be taken away, even in the case of redundancies of any type, e.g., in acquisitions, employee transfers, work transfers, or closing of offices. Employers cannot move work or workers to new countries or locales and, in the process, create new compensation, benefits, or work designs that are less than in the previous location. In many countries, particularly in Europe, and in EU law, more specifically, the employee has "acquired rights" to his or her existing level of compensation and benefits and to the nature of his or her work that cannot be reduced by moving either the employee or the work to another location. After notification and consultation, often MNEs "buy" their way out of these liabilities by negotiating settlements with affected workers to compensate them for their acquired rights. But they cannot just unilaterally reduce the benefits. And the ultimate point is that redundancies of any type can be, at least in many countries, quite expensive and require close attention from IHR.

Intellectual property

Intellectual property includes property (sometimes referred to as industrial property) such as patented inventions, trade marks, geographic indications, and industrial designs as well as items that can be copyrighted such as literary and artistic works such as novels, poems and plays, films, musical works, artistic works such as drawings, paintings, photographs and sculptures, and architectural designs. Although it may not at first be obvious, there are several links between intellectual property and IHR. For example, inventions and intellectual contributions which are a result of an individual's employment are usually considered by the employer to be its property. As a consequence, employers take a number of steps to insure that such "property" as trade secrets (such as client and customer lists) and patents are either filed for legal protection or are protected through non-disclosure agreements with their employees (meaning the employees do not have the right to share or give the information to anyone else, particularly, of course, competitors). Also, publications such as the many training materials and product/service manuals that an employer develops for use by their employees and customers also are copyrighted in order to protect them from use by outside people.

The situation of protection of property rights is especially complicated when operating internationally, because different countries have different conceptions of what constitutes property and vary in their practices related to its protection. In addition, there is no international institution which has the capability to extend intellectual and copyright protection to the MNE worldwide.

With regard to industrial property, each country usually has an intellectual property office (IPO) or an administrative unit within a government that is in charge of administering the system of IP rights acquisition and maintenance. Depending on the country, theses offices have varying ranges of resources. Poorer countries tend to have fewer resources for screening and approving pending applications for new patents and for maintaining databases of protected patents. The World Industrial Property Organization (WIPO) is a specialized agency of the UN responsible for the promotion of the protection of IP worldwide. WIPO administers the multiple international treaties and develops conventions for its member states. The Patent Cooperation Treaty (PCT) dramatically reduces the duplication of effort with regard to patents (filing, researching and execution) in different countries and allows filing in a single national office. As an international procedural mechanism it offers a trade mark owner the possibility to have his trade mark protected in several countries by simply filing one application directly with his own national or regional trade mark office.

With regard to copyright, there is no single statute that extends copyright protection worldwide; rather, each country has its own copyright laws. There are, however, a number of bilateral agreements and international treaties among countries regarding copyright protection. Most countries abide by one of two international agreements: the Berne Convention (which provides national and automatic protection) and the Universal Copyright Convention (which provides only national protection). National treatment (minimal protection) means that local laws apply to all copyright infringements that take place within the country even if the original work was created elsewhere. Automatic protection means that local laws apply even to works that have not satisfied the country's required formalities (copyright notice and/or registration). To ensure full copyright protection, MNEs must investigate whether the country in question is a member of the Berne Convention or Universal Copyright Convention, or whether it has entered into any trade agreements with the country in which the original work was created. They must research the local laws of the countries that are *not* Berne Convention members as well as those for which any applicable trade agreements do not have an automatic protection provision and comply with any required formalities, such as registration with the national copyright office for these countries.

One additional consideration, particularly in firms with highly specialized technology or other forms of intellectual property that is critical to their ability to compete, involves different countries' attitudes about non-compete agreements. These agreements, signed by employees, restrict their going to work within some particular time period for a competitor, setting up on their own a new competing business, or taking competitive-critical information with them to their new (former competitor) employer.[19] MNEs must take care to write these non-compete agreements in understandable language (not legal jargon) and translate the agreements into the local languages of the countries in which they operate (often required by local law). This is not only the case because local law dictates translations, but also because of the need for true informed consent by the employee who signs the agreement (i.e., employees can read the agreement in their own language rather than the language of the parent company). As labor markets become global, and firms develop new forms of relations with workers in foreign locales (such as IT workers or call centers in overseas locations), it becomes increasingly difficult to control the movement of workers from one employer to another and their taking of intellectual property (such as, product or process technology or customer lists and preferences) from their current employer to their new one. Because the rules (and cultures) are so different from one country to another, it becomes very difficult to enforce any non-compete agreements in employment contracts.

IHR is usually the link between the legal department and the employee with regard to enforcing the protection of industrial property and copyright in the MNE. It is also IHR that ensures the signing of the non-compete agreements by new employees or employees engaged on new highly sensitive projects. IHR may also need to develop communication and training materials for employees, especially for those employees from countries that do not have the cultural practice of protecting the intellectual property of MNEs.

INTERNATIONAL LABOR RELATIONS

Domestic labor lawyers and HR practitioners are usually unfamiliar with most labor and employment policy laws, institutions, and labor relations practices in other countries. Because labor relations tend to be unique to each country, the practices of the MNE in its employee and labor relations should vary as well. Indeed, it is likely to face unfamiliar restrictions in its foreign operations. In this section we review a number of issues related to international labor relations, including international union membership, the evolution of international labor relations, works councils, co-determination, and the role of the MNE in labor relations.

International union membership

Just like with many international data, it is difficult to compare union membership data across countries. Data integrity and comparability issues with regard to union density relate to problems with and variances in the sources of information, definitions, statistical coverage, reporting errors, special groups who are outside the legal employment market, and the selection of the employment base for calculating union density. The strength of trade unions is usually measured by union membership (relative to the number of people eligible to join a union). Yet, this measure does not really reflect what unions do and how effective they are, but rather focuses on potential union bargaining pressure.[20] In some countries, unions represent all workers while only a small percentage actually are members, while in other countries unions represent only those who are actual members. In some countries managers and professionals like engineers and scientists belong to unions while in other countries they don't. And in some countries unions are seen as partners with management, while in other countries there is a long-standing antagonism between unions and firms. Thus, in some countries where unions are strong their actual membership is small (Germany), while in other countries where unions may not be so strong, their membership may actually be quite large (Mexico, Japan). Absolute union membership is largest in countries like Sweden while absolute membership is lowest in countries like the US.

Evolution of international labor relations and organizations[21]

Although initially some aspects of the union movement developed in the nineteenth century as a very international movement (after all, "l'Internationale" was the fight song of the union movement), it became more national and protectionist in nature as a result of national variances in industrialization and two twentieth-century world wars. However, partially as a result of the Cold War, the international federations divided into two factions: a Western-oriented group and a communist-supported group. Then, with the end of the Cold War and the rapid development of global trade, this East–West divide and the national focus of trade unions began to become once again more global![22] Now, largely due to the uncontrolled growth of the power of MNEs, there is a strong trend in the labor movement to cross borders and join together for the achievement of their common labor-related missions. The major institutions of the international trade union movements are now using the term "international" in their names. And, over the last fifty years or so, national trade unions have created the beginnings of an international trade union structure in an attempt to develop some international focus and capabilities to deal more effectively with MNEs and globalization. At the same time, employers have also created equivalent trade associations to provide a cross-border and cross-industry voice for global labor relations. International federations and labor union organizations include the following.

World Federation of Trade Unions (WFTU)

WFTU was established in 1945 to bring together trade unions around the world in a single organization modeled after the UN. After a split in 1949, when many Western trade unions formed the ICFTU (International Confederation of Free Trade Unions), it is now primarily a federation of state-run unions from communist countries. Despite the fall of communist régimes in the Soviet Union and Eastern Europe, and the defection of many of its national unions in several Central and Eastern European (CEE) countries, the WFTU has declined to join the ICFTU and subsequently formed the International Trade Union Confederation (ITUC).

The International Confederation of Free Trade Unions (ICFTU)

ICFTU is an international confederation of national trade unions established in 1949 after a split with the WFTU. It grouped the major unions in the Western world. The ICFTU was dissolved in 2006 to join the ITUC.

The International Trade Union Confederation (ITUC)

The ITUC is an umbrella organization of national trade union federations (154 countries and 168 million workers) to defend workers' rights in the era of globalization. The ITUC's primary mission is the promotion and defense of workers' rights and interests, through international cooperation between trade unions and through global campaigning and advocacy within the major global institutions.[23]

European Trade Union Confederation (ETUC)

The ETUC was established in 1973 to promote the interests of working people at the European level and to represent them in the EU institutions. Its prime objective is to promote the European Social Model by being actively involved in economic and social policy-making at the highest level, working with all the EU institutions.

World Confederation of Labour (WCL)

WCL is an international trade union confederation inspired by the basic values of Christian humanism. It unites autonomous and democratic trade unions from countries all over the world, but mainly from Third World countries. In the last few years the WCL has adopted a critical attitude toward the neo-liberal model of economic globalization (where global free trade is promoted as the highest and best value) and questions its legitimacy.

Trade Union Advisory Committee (TUAC) of the OECD

TUAC is an international trade union organization which has consultative status with the OECD. It is the interface for labor unions with the OECD and its various committees.

Global Union Federations (GUFs)

A GUF is an international federation of national and regional trade unions representing specific industrial sectors and occupational groups. Most major unions are members of one or more GUFs that represent the interests of their members. Currently there are ten specific industry sectors or occupation groups: education; building and woodworkers; journalists; metalworkers; textile, garment and leather workers; transport workers; food, agriculture, hotel, restaurant, catering, tobacco and allied workers; public services; chemical, energy, mine and general workers; and union networks.

In spite of the above developments in the labor movement, unions (and, therefore, labor relations) exist and operate mostly at the local and national level, even though a number of unions have the term *international* in their names. The increase in global trade and in the number of MNEs has led to concern by trade unions about this primarily local and national focus. Their major concern is that multinational firms can manipulate local unions in collective bargaining by having the ability to move work to areas of the world that either have no unions or where unions are weak or where, in general, wages and benefits are less and working conditions are less protected. And because unions are not organized on a global basis, and there are no international laws requiring bargaining on a cross-border basis, and because unions tend to be primarily focused on local and national concerns of their members (and thus sometimes find it difficult to work together with unions in other countries, which often have different concerns), they perceive that the power balance between unions and MNEs is totally skewed toward business. MNEs operate in many countries and often in many industries. In contrast, unions almost always have membership in only one country and normally in only one industry. And thus they can typically bring pressure to bear on only a small segment of an MNE—one industry (or even one firm within one industry) within one country.

In spite of what has been said above about the development of international confederations of unions, there has been very little cooperation between unions at the collective bargaining level across national borders, and there are no union structures similar to or parallel to that of MNEs, so that, for example, international unions have not been able to negotiate global agreements with MNEs that would apply to all of their operations around the world (although some collective bargaining agreements in the airline industry—which by its very nature is international—have moved in that direction).

In practical terms, what this means in terms of labor relations is that unions view MNEs as being able to:

- Locate work in countries with lower social protections and lower wages and benefits (often this means countries with no unions or very weak unions), staying away from countries with stronger unions and stronger protections and higher wages and benefits.
- Force workers in one country, faced by competition from workers in other countries, to "bid down" their wages and benefits in order to keep their jobs.
- Take advantage of differences in legally mandated benefits for workers by restructuring the operations in countries where the costs of work force adjustments are lowest and thus force excessive dislocation burdens on workers in these low-benefit countries.
- Outlast workers in the event of a labor dispute in one country because cash flows (and the ability to maintain business) are at least partially maintained by operations in countries where there are no disputes.

One result is that unions are beginning to look for ways to exercise influence over labor relations on a cross-border and multinational scale. National trade union federations and more recently established international federations and GUFs (as described above) are providing assistance to national unions in dealing with MNEs and have become closely involved with bodies like the ILO and the OECD, working with them to develop, enhance, and enforce their covenants and declarations on labor standards. Their ultimate goal is to develop transnational bargaining, although right now there are no laws or regulations that require it nor any international bodies that could enforce it. As described above, the ILO and OECD guidelines are trying to go beyond merely suggesting that MNEs abide by the industrial relations statutes in force in each of the countries in which they operate. And national courts are beginning to defer to or consider these international standards or a firm's parent country laws when adjudicating labor disputes. This has been accomplished at least partially because of the pressures of these international union federations. Nevertheless, these guidelines and standards are only as effective as individual firms and governments are willing to allow them to be as adherence to them is essentially voluntary.

Some interesting labor disputes in different parts of the world show the increasing pressure unions are putting on MNEs. When Renault closed its plant in Vilvoorde, Belgium, and laid off 3,100 people (1997), the Belgian labor court ruled that Renault broke the rules on worker consultation which requires consultation ahead of layoffs. When the British retailer Marks and Spencer (2001) announced that it was closing its eighteen French stores (and laid off 1,500 employees), the French employees obtained a court ruling that M&S had violated French labor law. Rather than closing, the stores were eventually sold to French retailer Galeries Lafayette. At Siemens in Germany (2004), although workers accepted a work week extension from four days to forty hours without extra pay, it demonstrated the role of the union as protector of employment by avoiding outsourcing over 4,000 jobs. In the UK, the unofficial strike of British Airways baggage handlers in sympathy for Gate Gourmet (2005) forced the caterer to settle the dispute and offer enhanced redundancy deals to its employees. In Mexico, the national mining union took on Grupo Mexico (2006) after sixty-five miners were killed in a mining accident. Wildcat strikes at over seventy Mexican companies paralyzed the mining and steel industry after government action failed to support labor. These strikes demonstrated the political power of organized employees.

There still remain a number of barriers to multinational bargaining. In addition to the global power of MNEs and the fractured nature of unions, and the unwillingness of nations to get involved under the existing lack of international governing covenants, other obstacles also will need to be overcome in order for progress to occur in movement toward multinational bargaining:[24]

- The widely varying industrial relations laws and practices among different countries.
- The lack of any central, international authority for labor relations or global labor law.
- Major economic and cultural differences among different countries.
- Employer opposition.
- Union reluctance at the national level, because the national leadership often fears that multinational bargaining will transfer power from them to an international leadership.
- Absence of a centralized decision-making authority for unions.
- Lack of coordination of activities by unions across national boundaries.
- Differing national priorities.
- Employee unwillingness to subordinate local concerns to the concerns of workers in other countries.

As MNEs become more global and more connected across borders they must deal with these international labor organizations. It is inevitable that multi-country, maybe even multi-employer and multi-union, negotiations involving employers and unions from multiple countries will develop. Business global issues are already part of the "relevant facts" for negotiations in many MNEs. And this will only increase in prevalence and importance. Before global labor relations evolve very far, however, the following types of questions will need to be addressed:

- What rules will apply to the resolution of disputes?
- What rules will apply to the process of negotiations?
- What law will cover the negotiations, e.g., between companies in two or more countries?

In spite of all of the above, unions have achieved a major impact on the protection of the individual rights of workers and their activities have resulted in the enactment of pro-labor and pro-employee legislation, especially in the EU. Many of the EU directives and agreements (e.g., parental leave directive, part-time work directive, fixed-term contracts directive, home working and teleworking framework agreement) are a result of union activity, and unions are strong social partners with government and management. In some EU countries, trades unions can invite the government to extend compulsory application of a collective agreement across geography and/or an entire industry sector. Even though the structure of unions in Japan is radically different than that present in Europe and the EU, Japanese unions can also claim major impact on employment relations and employee rights, such as lifetime employment practices and protection of seniority. Now the challenge is to develop global mechanisms to accommodate the reality of global commerce.

Multinational enterprises and labor relations

MNEs must share decision-making power with unions (and/or other representatives of employees, such as works councils) and, often, agencies of government, to greater or lesser degrees throughout the world but almost always to some degree. For many businesses, what they confront in their foreign operations is often quite different than what they deal with at home. So, responsibility for labor relations is frequently left to the HR (or labor relations) managers at the level of the local subsidiary or joint venture.

MNEs often develop worldwide approaches to issues such as executive compensation, but such a worldwide approach to labor and employee relations is quite rare. IHR departments within MNEs often follow one of these seven approaches to labor/employee relations in the global context:

- *Hands off* (by headquarters of the parent firm). In this approach, responsibility for labor/employee relations is left totally in the hands of local managers in the host countries.
- *Monitor.* In this approach, headquarters IHR managers will try to forestall major problems for the parent company by asking intelligent and insightful questions about labor and employment responsibilities at each of their foreign locations. But primary responsibility still stays in the hands of local managers.
- *Guide and advise.* This approach is a step beyond mere monitoring. Here IHR managers from headquarters will provide ongoing advice and guidance to subsidiary managers on how to conduct labor and employee relations, usually based on the policies of headquarters. Of course, this requires a higher degree of knowledge about local labor relations regulations and practices. Still, overall control stays in the hands of local staff.
- *Strategic planning.* At this level of involvement, international labor relations issues are fully incorporated into the MNE's strategic planning. Management of all aspects of the global firm, including labor and employee relations, is integrated into a centralized program, particularly for policy purposes. Local control may still exist, but all labor relations practices will follow this global strategy.
- *Set limits and approve exceptions.* MNEs that follow this approach to their international labor/employee relations provide even more specific centralized control over local practices. Subsidiaries are allowed freedom of action only within

quite narrowly defined limits, and any efforts to try different approaches must be approved by headquarters.

● *Manage totally from headquarters.* In this scenario, local subsidiary staffs have no freedom of policy or practice in their labor/employee relations activities. Indeed, all labor relations actions are directed by staff from headquarters.

● *Integration of headquarters IHR and line management in the field.* In this final approach, labor and employee relations in the field, as managed by local HR and management, are fully integrated with IHR assistance from headquarters.

American firms (and, sometimes, Asian) that have strong anti-union or, at least, very adversarial, approaches to labor relations tend to operate at the level of one of the last three options. These firms try to ensure that their approaches are followed as much as possible in their foreign operations. Of course, in many countries (e.g., where there are works councils and/or union negotiations are mandated), even these firms must deal with third parties, whether they want to or not. For example, although a US or Japanese MNE many basically be a non-union global enterprise, it may need to deal with unions in some of its worldwide operations. While in the US or Japan the enterprise may be union-free, in its French subsidiary, if even a single employee claims to belong to a union, the MNE must negotiate with that union. The French subsidiary of the MNE may even have its own company union and its employees may belong to one or more of the five national unions. As a consequence, under French labor law, this French subsidiary of the MNE will have to negotiate with six different unions plus it must comply with the EU's information and consultation directives, as well, with its French and/or European works councils.

Still, much autonomy is often possible, even when the law requires dealing with third parties, such as works councils or unions. And because each country is so different in its evolution of labor relations law and practice, leaving primary responsibility for labor and employee relations to the local level, usually with the assistance of employment law firms, is often the only workable approach. Usually, this is achieved with certain overlying strategic objectives providing some guidance.

The global economy places many stresses on industrial relations. MNEs must cope with very different labor relations systems in each of the countries in which they operate.[25] It is not the intention of this book to provide in-depth coverage of union relations in various countries. Rather, a very limited sampling of the variations of the law and practice of labor relations is provided to inform students and IHR managers with a sense of the importance of understanding the impact of those variations on MNE operations around the globe. IHRM in Action 4.2 describes some of the global labor relations scene for Ford Motor Company, a firm that has had global operations for almost 100 years.[26] Obviously, for an MNE like Ford, global labor relations are indeed quite complex.

One difficulty for IHR managers in assessing the power or importance of unions in various countries arises from the inconsistencies between countries in how they count membership and the differences in who is covered by union contracts. For example,

IHRM in Action 4.2

FORD MOTOR COMPANY'S GLOBAL INDUSTRIAL RELATIONS

Ford Motor Company manufactures cars, trucks, and parts in thirty countries, with 275,000 hourly employees worldwide. It negotiates contracts with fifty-six different unions in every country where it manufactures except six (where there are no unions). In some countries, such as Italy, it must also negotiate with salaried staff and managers, who are also unionized.

Because of this great variety of unions and countries, bargaining takes on as many different forms as there are countries. For example, in Australia, all major issues are first discussed by subcommittees at the local level which, after agreement is reached, are then taken to the full national bargaining committee for Ford Motor. In contrast, in Germany, negotiation is done through the national employers' association for all of the auto companies and the national metalworkers' union, which represents workers at all automotive companies.

Even with this complicated bargaining reality, or maybe because of it, bargaining is handled almost exclusively at the local level, with minimal coordination on a global level. As can be imagined, this not only causes coordination problems for the many unions involved, but also for Ford Motor Company itself. In spite of this, the office of the Director of International Labor Affairs Planning and Employee Relations in Ford's headquarters in Dearborn, Michigan, is literally only one person. As the Director of International Labor Affairs said, ". . . because I work in so many countries, one of my primary roles is to educate all the parts of the business in the US about what is going on around the world and how that affects the total business."

Source Excerpted from a presentation by David Killinger, Director, International Labor Affairs, on Ford Motor Company's global labor relations, delivered at the Faculty Development Seminar on International HRM at the University of Colorado, Denver, 8 June 2000.

even though a relatively low percentage of workers belong to unions in France (about 12 percent), the unions play a very important role in determining government policy and legislation concerning workers and toward general industrial policy, and employers are required by law to negotiate with any union present (represented by as few as one employee) and to implement national policies on wage rates, and so on.[27] In fact, about 85 percent of all workers in France are covered by the contracts negotiated by unions, even though their actual membership is quite low. In most Scandinavian countries, retired workers are still union members, although this is not usually the case elsewhere, and professionals such as teachers and members of professional associations, such as engineers, are sometimes included and sometimes not.

An additional problem is created by the rapid pace of change in labor relations so that data only a few years old can be out of date by significant amounts. Nevertheless, relative differences between countries remain quite obvious.[28] For example, fewer than 16 percent of the labor force are union members in Spain (yet 50 percent of the labor force are covered by union contracts) while in Japan about 25 percent belong to unions, with approximately 60 percent of the labor force covered by union contracts. As illustrated, some countries have quite low union membership (which doesn't necessarily indicate how many workers are covered by the contracts negotiated), while other countries have much higher union membership, such as Denmark with about 75 percent union membership and Sweden with about 85 percent membership and most employees, in both the private and public sectors, covered by union contracts.

In terms of the pattern of labor relations practices themselves, some countries have developed industrial relations systems patterned after the laws and traditions of other countries. And yet others have pursued relatively unique avenues to labor relations. Within this milieu, each country has developed a tradition and legal framework that reflect its own special history and political experience. As a consequence, firms that conduct business on a multinational or transnational basis must understand and cope with a great deal of diversity in the performance of industrial relations around the world. This typically leads to decentralizing the labor relations function (much as is also true of the general HRM function), providing subsidiaries with considerable autonomy in managing employee relations.

These next few paragraphs provide a very short glimpse at the evolution of labor relations around the world. In some countries (e.g., Canada, the US, Germany, and Japan), union activity is basically economic. That is, unions involve themselves primarily with economic issues of concern to their members, such as setting wage rates, determining hours of work, and ensuring job security. This is usually manifested through some form of union–management collective bargaining. In other countries, particularly England, France, Italy, and those in Latin America, unions tend to be very political and generally achieve their objectives through political action rather than through direct collective bargaining. This is not to say that "business-focused" unions don't try to influence government to achieve legislation favorable to their members and that "politically focused" unions don't participate in collective bargaining. But the historical pattern for business unions has been the former forms of activity, rather than the latter. And the opposite has been true for political unions. In addition, in some countries, union activity is focused on industry-wide or even nationwide bargaining while in other countries union relations are very decentralized, taking place almost exclusively at the level of the local firm. Thus, even in industrialized (and usually heavily unionized) countries, major differences in labor relations can be found relative to issues such as (1) the level at which bargaining takes place (national, regional, industry, or workplace); (2) the types of workers involved (craft, industrial, professional); (3) the degree of centralization of union–management relations; (4) the scope of bargaining, that is, the topics which are usually included in negotiations and contracts; (5) the degree to which the government is involved or can intervene; (6), the degree to which employment issues, such as wage rates and benefits, are determined by legislative action versus collective bargaining; and (7) the degree of unionization. In order to be effective in labor relations throughout the operations of an MNE, IHR managers need to understand these issues and differences in each of the countries in which they conduct business.

And, as a last general point, economic and political issues of concern to management and unions are not static. They are constantly changing. Globalization, technological and job changes, and changing demographics are heavily impacting the role and importance of unions (and companies, for that matter) in most countries, as well.[29]

Interestingly, American MNEs, in particular, may face even more difficult problems in understanding and coping with industrial relations around the world than is the case for many other MNEs, since American labor relations are quite different in many respects from those practiced in other countries. As a quick summary, the primary features of the American labor relations scene include the following:

- Only non-supervisory and non-managerial employees have the right to organize or join unions.
- Typically, professional and technical workers also do not form or join unions.
- The only employees who belong to unions (that can thus bargain with the employer) work for employers where a majority of those employees have voted in free but secret elections for union representation.
- Contracts between such unions and employers are negotiated primarily at the local level between a single union and a single employer.
- Such collectively bargained contracts are legally enforceable and typically last for three years.
- The only mandatory subjects for bargaining are wages, hours, and working conditions.
- Both unions and employers are restricted in their behaviors toward each other by a considerable amount of regulation.
- Disagreements over the meaning of contracts are handled through established grievance procedures (not by renegotiating the contract), settled by union and management acting together and settled in the case of impasse by a privately hired, neutral arbitrator.

This highly decentralized, "business" unionism (although extensively regulated) is significantly different from the form of unionism present in most other countries (which is often referred to as "political" unionism).[30] In most countries, labor relations practices are very different, even opposite, to these characteristics. Thus many American MNEs may have even more difficulty than MNEs from other countries coping with the diversity of labor relations practices, because their experiences and familiarity may well not provide adequate guidance in other countries. Of course, every MNE will experience differences in labor relations practices, although they may not be as great.

There are also a number of issues concerning the local union environment which MNEs—no matter which country they come from—must consider as well. MNEs will need to seek answers to the following types of questions regarding global labor relations practices wherever they operate:

- *Existing trade unions.* What is the nature of the unions in the particular country? Is recognition an entitlement or not?
- *Level of organization.* How are unions organized (by firm, region, industry, national, craft)? Is the union national, regional, or company-wide? Is there multi-unionism within firms, so that the MNE must negotiate with multiple, often competing unions, within the same subsidiary or organization?
- *Focus breadth.* Is the focus general or industry-specific? Is most bargaining being conducted on a national and/or industry-wide level, applying to all or most employers and employees?
- *Affiliations.* Are there political or religious affiliations? Are the unions associated with political parties and if so, which ones? Are they related to religious organizations? Which ones?
- *Type of workers.* Who belongs? Who is covered by the contracts? Is there white-collar unionization? Do managers belong to unions, such as the *dirigenti* in Italy? Are there closed-shop requirements or practices? That is, is the situation such that employees must belong to the union(s)?
- *Union density.* What is the percentage of employees covered by collective bargaining agreements?
- *Focus of labor relations.* Where does the focus of labor relations lie? Is it collective bargaining or individual representation or both? What is the nature of the plant or site-level role of unions? Are there shop stewards? Are there works councils? And are they independent or essentially arms of the unions?
- *Negotiation partner.* With whom does the firm have to negotiate? Who is the negotiation partner at company level? What is the role of government in bargaining?
- *Employer's associations.* What is the nature and role of the employers' associations in each country? Which associations exist? Should the MNE belong (why, why not)? What does membership entail, do most employers join, and can the firm avoid joining? Is there an obligation or recommendation to align with any of them?
- *Operation method.* What is the procedure for labor relations in the workplace? Is there a legal obligation to install employee representative bodies in the company and comply with information and consultation procedures? What are the information and consultation requirements? Are ballots compulsory? Are there specific rights and protections for employee representatives?
- *Issues typically covered by union agreements.* What topics are contained in the contracts? Are they specific or general in nature?
- *Binding force of union agreements.* Are agreements concluded at national, industry and company level? What is the nature of the contracts or agreements

with unions? Are the contracts enforceable? Are they breakable for any reasons? When and under what circumstances are contracts renegotiated?

● *Strikes and industrial action.* Under what circumstances can unions strike? For what reasons can and do unions go on strike? What forms of industrial action are common, theater by theater? If strikes occur are they legally regulated? Is "secondary" industrial action common and/or legal? What sanctions are available to employers who find themselves the subject of industrial action?

● *Union-free.* Is it possible to operate union-free? How can employee relations be fostered?

All of these questions illustrate potentially significant differences between labor relations practices in different countries. This is just one more area of complexity with which IHR managers and MNEs must learn to cope.

Works councils

Works councils are a critical component of worker relations in many countries, particularly in Europe.[31] In many countries in Europe, particularly the Netherlands, Germany, France, Hungary, and Italy, there is a long tradition of workers' right to participate in decision making relevant to the operations of their employers. These rights are in addition to rights of organization and collective bargaining. Many other countries, such as the US, Japan, China, Australia, Mexico, and the UK, do not have such a history and do not have built into their industrial relations systems the concept or practice of works councils. This makes it essential that IHR managers from such countries gain an understanding of what is involved in these works council requirements.

Essentially, works councils (which are made up of elected representatives of the firm's work force) have the right to receive information and consultation relative to many decisions a firm makes (particularly, to ease the social consequences of restructurings by companies and within industries). The extent to which the councils have authority to approve employment-related (or, even, more broadly, enterprise) decisions varies from country to country. For example, since many countries in Europe have long involvement with works councils, the EU has gradually been passing directives that require employers with more than fifty employees in all member countries (or twenty in any single country) to inform and consult with their work forces—through works councils or other, equivalent forums—on employment-related matters such as job security, work organization, and terms and conditions of employment.[32] Under a 2002 directive, member countries must pass legislation requiring works councils in every employer with more than fifty employees and establishing the obligation to inform and consult. Once the legislation is passed, employers—if they don't do it on their own—can be compelled to set up an "inform and consent" arrangement if workers request it.

In addition, an earlier EU directive required all employers with more than 1,000 employees throughout the EU, and with at least 150 employees in each of two countries, to establish a Europe-wide works council to receive information and consultation on all decisions that cut across country boundaries. Under this directive, larger employers not only need to establish country-required works councils (which, under the new directive, all countries must require), but must also establish a Europe-wide council. Firms that operate in Europe, but that come from countries where the concept of a works council does not exist, must learn to adapt to the EU requirements. This means that any decisions such as plant or office closings, work restructuring or movement from one country to another—including outsourcing and subcontracting, and employment downsizings—all require firms to inform and consult with their councils prior to implementation of such decisions. In some countries, such as Germany, the council must agree with the nature of the decision and its planned implementation; in other countries, such as the UK, extensive consultation about the impact, and planned efforts to mitigate them, are required.

In 2001 the EU adopted legislation giving companies operating in the EU the possibility of forming a central "European company," also known as a *societas europeae* (SE), instead of having to form a number of companies under the laws of each of the individual member countries. This way MNEs operating in Europe can form an SE to avoid the complexities of the different regulations in each of the countries in which they operate a business. The critical issue here is that, relative to employee involvement, the MNE does not need to establish an employee involvement mechanism where none already exists and this gives them, then, a way to establish a single, Europe-wide, employee involvement procedure. While most works councils are found in continental European countries, other countries (e.g., Argentina, Bangladesh, Japan, Thailand, and South Africa) also have them. These works councils can be composed of both management and employee representatives (e.g. Denmark, Belgium); composed of employee representatives and overseen by a member of management (e.g., Japan, France); or composed of employee representatives without management oversight (e.g. Austria).

It should be noted that the minimum firm or location size for installation of works councils differs from country to country and the number of works council members varies with the number of local employees. Although works councils are core instruments of industrial relations and representative bodies for information and consultation, the country-to-country variation is substantial. In some countries (e.g., Germany) they may even make joint decisions with management (co-determination) (see the next section).

Co-determination

Some countries, such as Germany, go a step further than consultation and works councils. They have *Mitbestimmung*, or co-determination. Co-determination is a legal requirement in which employees are represented on supervisory boards or boards of directors and participate in major strategic decisions (that is, employees are not just consulted but management must obtain their agreement).

It differs from works councils in the sense that co-determination includes a decision-making component. Most EU companies have some form of participation of employee representatives in the company's decision-making process. Only three countries have no national legislation regarding board level representation (Belgium, Italy, and the UK).

Employee involvement (in most EU countries) lies on a continuum, in terms of operational issues versus strategic decision making, from simple informing and consultation to works councils and co-determination. Employee involvement may range from pure attendance with an advisory role (e.g., France) to membership and co-decision powers (e.g., Germany).

There are three corresponding systems of co-decisions: (1) *dual* system, where the supervisory board (on which employee representatives have one-third of the members) supervises the board of directors (e.g., Austria, Germany, Denmark); (2) *single* tier system, where there is only one board of directors and the employees have one or two representatives; (3) *mixed* system, with obligatory participation but only an advisory role (e.g., France).

Litigation risks in global labor relations

One of the most important pressures for IHRM and MNEs to pay attention to in international employment law and industrial relations is the increased pressure of litigation risks. These risks focus on activities in foreign jurisdictions, and dealing with foreign employees and international assignees. In recent years there has been a significant trend toward holding MNEs accountable in various courts for their protections of employee and human rights in their foreign operations. Increasingly, MNEs are being sued in their home jurisdictions on the basis of allegations of breaches arising from the firm's activities in foreign jurisdictions. In the past, MNEs have been able to block such actions on the basis that the home courts were not the appropriate jurisdictions in which to litigate the dispute. However, recent cases are illustrating that this defense may not be sufficient, as courts are increasingly willing to hold parent firms accountable under both their parent country laws and those of the foreign country in which such litigations are initiated.

Development of a strategic global industrial relations policy

The implication of all of this complexity in global labor and employment law and regulation is that MNEs need to develop strategic policies for themselves that establish a code of conduct that defines acceptable behavior in terms of employee and labor relations for their far-reaching managerial and employee work forces.[33] These codes of conduct should be defended as the "company culture," a culture that insists on and supports abiding by all national and international employee relations regulations and, further, defines what is seen as legal and ethical behavior when dealing with these regulations. Without this, the firms and their managers and employees can face any or all of the following: criminal liability, damaged individual careers, damaged firm global reputations, lowered share prices, and even possible risk of total organizational disruption. The point is, senior management must insist that this support for organizational ethics is the "way they want to run their business," that, for example, sexual or racial discrimination (or harassment) is not wanted because it limits the firm's ability to work as a team, because such behavior is divisive, and it is just not wanted. Having such as policy removes the possibility of managers disagreeing with certain practices because they perceive them to go against local or national cultural practices that vary from those in an MNE's parent country. In this way, the decision to abide by certain labor standards is based on the defined company culture and policies, not on any given individual's biases or preferences nor on reference to any country's perceived cultural practices.

THE INTERNATIONAL FRAMEWORK OF ETHICS

The conduct of international business increasingly involves concerns about the values and practices of MNEs when they conduct business outside their countries of origin. International governing bodies, non-governmental organizations, labor organizations, and special interest groups increasingly raise questions about the "ethical" nature of the business practices of many MNEs, often particularly as they relate to employment-related practices. As businesses look outside their country borders for business opportunities, they claim many benefits for themselves and the countries in which they do business. Yet those who are opposed to globalization often charge these firms with worker exploitation and increasing inequities in the countries in which they do business, particularly in less developed countries. Because of this, confusion about business rules, ethics, and HR policies and practices has intensified.[34]

This last section in the chapter provides an overview of concerns about international business ethics, particularly as they relate to IHRM. International ethics looks at what's right and wrong in business conduct across borders and the impact of cultural (country and company) variances on ethical conduct of MNEs. International ethics also deals with issues of corruption and bribery, and the various ethical dilemmas that MNEs face in the conduct of their international activities. Because MNE ethics, particularly issues which relate directly to employee relations, are often relegated to the responsibility of IHR, the primary focus here is the impact of ethics on global HR practices. Because these concerns appear to be increasing, as more firms operate outside their countries of origin, and as more groups such as labor unions, groups of activists and college students, and the international media give attention to these issues, more firms are finding it in their best interests (both in terms of public and customer opinion and ultimately in terms of competitive advantage) to pay closer attention to the ethical conduct of their foreign operations.[35]

International ethics and culture

In this area of global ethics, even the best-informed, best-intentioned executives must often rethink their assumptions. What works in an enterprise's home country may be viewed very differently in another country, which may have very different standards or perceptions of what is ethical conduct.[36] Evidence even suggests that there is not only variance among countries and cultures, but even among different industries.[37] Often one's national perspective clouds one's view of another country or culture's way of doing things. For example, the traditional development of long-term business linkages, which are central to the conduct of business in certain countries—such as the *keiretsu* in Japan or *chaebol* in Korea—are often viewed as collusion from an American perspective. Difficulties in understanding and working with another country's often very different practices are unavoidable, especially for business people who live and work outside their home countries.

Even if there is relative agreement on basic human values and ethical principles around the world (a point which some would disagree with), clearly there is considerable variance in what might be referred to as the ethical climate in different countries.[38] That is, differing country cultures view various employment and business conduct issues, such as bribery, gifts or favors, tax evasion, or child labor, differently. Thomas Donaldson, one of the US's top experts on international ethics, tells the story of an expatriate manager of a large US company operating in China who fired an employee caught stealing and turned him over to the local authorities, according to company policy.[39] Later, the manager was horrified to learn that the employee had been summarily executed. Obviously, the cultural context in which the policy was formulated was vastly different from the cultural context in which the manager carried out the policy. In the US, no firm would expect an employee caught stealing from the company and turned over to local police for prosecution to be executed. And yet in the Chinese culture, such acts, that are seen as important enough to "turn in" the employee, are clearly viewed with a much greater degree of finality.

In order to understand ethical variances such as this, ethicists describe possible approaches as being on a continuum, from ethical relativism to ethical absolutism. On one end of the continuum lies *ethical relativism*, which suggests that what is right is whatever a society defines as right. This definition may be at the individual level (individual relativism) or at the societal level (cultural relativism). In the relativistic view, there are no absolute rights or wrongs; rather, the values of the individual or the society are sovereign in deciding what is right or wrong for that culture as long as no laws prohibit the behavior. In this perspective, if a society says that women shall not be paid the same as men for the same work or that child labor is all right, those rules would be seen as right for that society at that point in time. Under ethical relativism, there can be no external frame of reference for judging that one society's set of rules is better—or worse—than another's. So, under ethical relativism, IHR managers who try to impose their values on HR practices in a host country are guilty of what is often referred to as ethical imperialism, or ethical chauvinism. Under the philosophy of ethical relativism, it is entirely appropriate to follow local practices regarding the treatment of employees. Though appearing on the surface to be a liberal, open-minded approach, this view may result in actions that home country constituencies (at least from the Western industrialized countries) would find entirely unacceptable, such as child labor or gross inequality. This view of "when in Rome, do as the Romans do" is challenged when one considers whether someone from an outside culture can really have a local understanding of what's right or wrong in that particular culture. Ethical relativism takes a particularistic view of the culture, namely that there are no universal standards, rather differing evaluation rules are based on the context or the situation.

The opposite position is called *ethical absolutism.* This is the view that there is a single set of universal ethical principles, which apply at all times, in all circumstances, in all cultures. This universalistic approach views moral values and principles as eternal and that they should apply universally and equally in all places and times. This more standardized approach is often reflected in an MNE's global code of ethics (i.e., a set of universal principles that, under no circumstances, should ever be violated). This might be very useful to an IHR manager, as it would suggest which local practices—even though they may be quite different from those of the parent country—are morally acceptable because they do not violate universal principles and those which are not morally and must not be followed, because they do violate such universal principles. The problem with this view is specifying what the universal principles are and developing a logical case for why these, and only these, principles are truly universal. In adopting the values of a single culture or religion as universal one runs the risk of ethical imperialism. Thus both of these philosophies create potential problems for the IHR manager, for MNE employees around the world, and especially for international assignees who are posted to foreign subsidiaries. In order to deal with these extremes, some have suggested that situations often compel the MNE, through collaboration and/or imagination, to develop unique responses to cross-cultural ethical dilemmas, ones that try to find common ground among disparate moral views. This has been referred to as *cosmopolitanism.*[40] Such an approach calls for reconciling seemingly opposing differences in ethical choices and requires debate, effort, and compromise. But such solutions are far from easy for the diverse employees of the MNE and their international managers.

Bribery and corruption

In many cultures, giving "bribes" (facilitating payments) is an acceptable business practice. Bribes are given names such as *la mordida* in Mexico, "dash" in South Africa, "baksheesh" in the Middle East, India, and Pakistan, *Schimmengelt* in Germany, and *bustarella* in Italy. The level of corruption present in any culture (which often originates within government, itself) is one of the major factors that make consideration of solutions to ethical problems difficult.[41] This form of corruption may, in fact, be illegal. But that doesn't keep it from being present. One of the major reasons for the complexity in this area is due to this: what is called corruption in one country may be merely seen as actions to sustain relationships in another. Even so, there is typically agreement on at least the extremes. Most people will agree that payment of hundreds of thousands of dollars to line a military general's pockets is wrong; but payments to administrative people to expedite paperwork is often considered necessary as a grease payment and all right, given the level of pay for clerks and the prevailing cultural norms which see it as a normal way of conducting business. One is most likely to find this sort of bribery in poor and/or developing countries.

However, even in developed countries, there is considerable disagreement over what is acceptable behavior. US-headquartered firms often complain about the disadvantages they sustain, since their domestic legislation (e.g., the Foreign Corrupt Practices Act 1977, the FCPA) precludes them from being able to give bribes to government officials while some of their competitors for global business from countries such as Germany, France, and the Netherlands can take tax deductions for such bribes. The law was written with extraterritorial intent, meaning that it applies outside of the territory of the US. While the law allows small grease payments, to facilitate and expedite the administrative functions of low level government employees, such payments are still subject to being recorded in the firm's bookkeeping. For larger payments, US firms and their employees may be subject to criminal and civil liabilities. A few years ago, studies suggested that US firms lost at least $45 billion a year in foreign contracts due to their being unable to make such payments, under penalty of fine and jail time.[42] Indeed, it is estimated that 80 percent of the deals available for major government contracts in foreign countries are received by firms that pay bribes.

A number of organizations make estimates of the level of corruption present in various countries. The one that has received the most media attention, Transparency International (TI)[43] in Berlin, Germany, measures "bribery, graft, extortion, and all their slimy cousins" in over 160 countries, as perceived by business people. In this organization's annual rankings of the TI Corruption Perceptions Index (2006), countries that score over 9.0 (on a scale of 0 to 10, where high numbers mean least corrupt and low numbers most corrupt) include Finland, Iceland, New Zealand, Denmark, Singapore, and Sweden. Countries with the lowest scores (less than 2.0) are Congo, Sudan, Guinea, Iraq and Haiti. Emerging market countries like China and India have relatively low scores (3.3). Noteworthy, however, is that countries like the US (7.3), Belgium (7.3) and Japan (7.6) do not get extremely high ratings either. Since TI has been keeping track of the perception of corruption, the Scandinavian countries have always been among the top ten with Singapore as a close top contender.

The range of possible actions that might be undertaken by any particular country to combat its corruption is quite broad.[44] These actions could include changing everything from its civil service system and the country's laws and regulations governing procurement of goods and services to reform of the accounting and auditing requirements to reform of the country's criminal law and tax systems. But these types of reforms are long-term and require a level of political will and agreement that is rarely present. In order to address concerns about the levels of bribery and corruption on a global level, international groups have begun to try to develop guidelines for ethical conduct.[45] In 1999, the United Nations General Assembly finally passed (after a number of earlier unsuccessful attempts) a forceful Declaration against Corruption and Bribery in International Commercial Transactions which, in addition, called on several other UN organizations, such as the ILO, to take complementary action. Both the International Chamber of Commerce (ICC) and the Organization for Economic Cooperation and Development (OECD) have developed policies intended to end the practice of payment of bribes in order to gain foreign contracts by getting their member countries to stop allowing companies to deduct foreign bribe payments from tax payments.[46] The World Trade Organization (WTO), since its first summit meeting in Singapore in December, 1996, has had a working group on corruption. In addition, the World Bank, the International Monetary Fund (IMF), and most regional development banks have also adopted formal anti-corruption policies. In recent years, the World Bank and the IMF have withdrawn or postponed development projects because of the refusal of receiving countries to deal adequately with problems of corruption. And regional groups, such as the Organization of African Unity and the Organization of American States, have also adopted conventions against corruption. All of this suggests that the issue of corruption and bribery has finally reached the level of concern that most countries are now at least trying to take action to stop it and to change the circumstances that allow it to exist. But the efforts of most of these organizations are limited to raising awareness and increasing pressure, as their statements have the force of recommendations only and have no legal binding impact for countries and individuals.

The new rules of conduct being pursued under these arrangements include banning extortion, bribes, kickbacks, "off the books" and secret accounts, and ensuring that intermediary business agents be paid only "appropriate remuneration for legitimate services rendered." The measure adopted in 1997 by the ministers of the members of the OECD aims to make it illegal to bribe foreign public officials to obtain or maintain a contract, such as has been the case in the US since the passage of the FCPA. A particularly difficult question for ethical values as they relate, in particular, to corruption involves whether there are cultural differences in attitudes and values related to specific areas of behavior, such as the demand for or the payment of bribes in order to get contracts or to get things done.[47] In lists compiled of the most corrupt countries in the world, one variable stands out as common among the most corrupt: poverty. Even though the poorest and most corrupt countries typically have laws against bribery, it is still often a common practice of government and business officials. Besides being poor, economies perceived as relatively corrupt also tend to be over-regulated, that is, tangled in red tape, and less controlled by the rule of law. Bureaucrats usually are given much discretionary authority to arbitrarily determine issues for or against companies, particularly foreign firms, and this often leads to the request for bribes to expedite decisions and/or to acquire contracts for major work projects. IHRM in Action 4.3 illustrates how insidious bribery can be in some countries.

DOING BUSINESS IN CHINA

A creative way to bribe

Charles Patton's company sent him to China to oversee the building of a new manufacturing plant. The company originally considered building its plant in Guangzhou but, due to rising labor costs, determined that investing in Sichuan province would be more cost-effective. The government officials in Chengdu were eager to see the company invest in their region and had been very helpful in providing the initial permits. The company sponsored many dinners for their Chinese hosts and Charles made every effort to establish strong ties with local businessmen and government officials. As the project progressed, however, Charles had more and more difficulty obtaining approval from the necessary government agencies. Considerable time and money had been sunk into getting the plant built and Charles was feeling pressure from headquarters to get the plant up and running.

In a meeting with Liu Jing, his contact in the municipal government, Charles expressed his concern that the bureaucratic process to obtain the requisite permits was going more slowly than anticipated. Charles was eager to speed up the process and wondered if she had any advice. A few days later, Liu Jing came to Charles's hotel. She suggested that Charles had not been generous enough with the government officials, and that a few well placed gifts might help speed the permit process. Charles was taken aback and said that the laws in his country, not to mention company policy, prevented him from doing so.

Liu Jing smiled and handed Charles a piece of paper with the name of a local physician. She indicated that if Charles went to this doctor, the doctor would prescribe a costly medical procedure. As the cost would not be out of line with accepted international rates and the claim would be difficult to investigate, the insurance company would not likely question its validity. The insurance company would pay the fee to the doctor, who would take a small cut and turn the rest over to the appropriate government officials. For a quick doctor's visit and a few insurance forms to fill out, Charles would have his permits.

Source Claus, L. (2007), Global HR in Action Vignettes, Willamette University, www.willamette.edu/agsm/global_hr.

Ethical dilemmas in international business

One of the basic ethical dilemmas for IHR and MNEs involves what management should do when an employment practice that is illegal or viewed as wrong in the home country is legal or acceptable in the host country.[48] Examples might include sex or race discrimination in hiring, job placement, or compensation; use of child labor;

or providing unsafe working conditions. Thomas Donaldson has tried to provide a framework for decision making in a multinational environment that tries to resolve these possible ethical dilemmas.[49] Donaldson states that the task is to "tolerate cultural diversity while drawing the line at moral recklessness."[50] In some ways, his approach is absolutist because it relies on a statement of thirty fundamental international rights (which have been recognized by international bodies, such as the UN, in the Universal Declaration of Human Rights). Among these, maybe ten or so apply directly to issues of concern to IHRM. These include the rights to freedom of physical movement; ownership of property; freedom from torture; a fair trial; non-discriminatory treatment; physical security; freedom of speech and association; a minimal education; political participation; freedom to work in fair and safe conditions, and to earn a decent standard of living. Organizations need to avoid depriving individuals of these rights wherever they do business (even though, in some countries, some of these "rights" are not very well recognized or agreed to).

However, these rights alone do not always provide sufficient practical guidelines for operating in an international environment. When IHR managers and the management of MNEs are trying to decide if their organizations can follow a practice that is legal and morally acceptable in the host country but not in the parent country, Donaldson suggests they ask themselves a series of questions in the ethical decision-making process. First, ask *why* the practice is acceptable in the host country but not at home. Answers to this question fall into two categories: (1) because of the host country's relative level of economic development; or (2) for reasons unrelated to economic development. If the answer is (1), the next question is whether the parent country would have accepted the practice when (or if) it was at that same level of economic development. If it would have, the practice is permissible. An example might be the building of a fertilizer plant that provides a product necessary for the feeding of the population of the country, despite the fact that there is a risk of occupational disease for employees working in the plant. If the parent firm (or the parent country) were willing to accept this risk for itself under similar circumstances, then the building of such a plant would be all right within Donaldson's framework. The second answer, that the difference is not based on economic considerations, requires a more complicated decision process. The manager must ask two additional questions: (1) is it possible to conduct business successfully in the host country without undertaking the practice? And (2) is the practice a clear violation of a fundamental right?[51] The practice is permissible *only if* the answer to both questions is no. That is, the practice is acceptable if it is critical to doing business in the country *and* it does not violate a fundamental right. Otherwise, the organization should refuse to follow the local practice. For example, in Singapore it is common to see help-wanted ads for "Chinese women, age 21–28." This type of advertisement violates US (and other countries') laws and *mores* regarding age, sex, and ethnic discrimination. Would it be permissible from an ethical point of view for a US subsidiary in Singapore to run an ad like that? (Note that, legally, extraterritoriality of the US anti-discrimination legislation may apply to this US company operating abroad if the company meets the integrated enterprise test.) According to Donaldson, the answer is no because the discrimination is not tied to the level of economic development, is not necessary for doing business in Singapore, and violates fundamental international rights to non-discriminatory treatment (a right which is codified in the resolutions of a number of international bodies, such as the United Nations and the International Labour Organisation).

There can be many difficulties when discussing issues of ethical attitudes and practices in various countries. Obviously, the gap between policy and practice can often be quite wide. Solutions to the problem of child labor, for example, are not necessarily easy to develop in a way that benefits the parties involved.

Ethical issues have become a top concern to executives of MNEs as well as of governments and non-governmental organizations. There is a growing desire to find approaches to these issues that would both provide protection for the rights of employees worldwide as well as provide guidelines for organizations that enable them to conduct business in ways that benefit all of their constituencies: customers, employees, owners/shareholders, suppliers, and communities in which they conduct business. Many organizations and individuals have proposed guiding principles to balance the extremes.[52] IHR must proactively consider these global ethical issues, usually incorporated in a Global Code of Business Conduct, and entertain some of the solutions being suggested to these problems.

In the end, the assurance of ethical behavior and conduct of firms that conduct business outside their home borders depends on the attitudes and behaviors of their managers, at home and abroad. Accordingly, it is suggested that businesses can take three steps to help ensure that their employees (managers at home, expatriates abroad, and their foreign employees) behave not only appropriately, but also ethically:[53]

- Develop a clearly articulated set of core values as the basis for global policies and decision making.
- Train international employees to ask questions that will help them make business decisions that are both culturally sensitive and flexible within the context of those core values.
- Balance the need for policy with the need for flexibility or imagination.

Given these three points as general guidelines for an overall approach, the following list of steps provides some guidance on how an MNE might ensure the effective implementation of ethical standards for worldwide operations.[54]

- *Be clear about your reasons for developing a global ethics program.* Is it for compliance reasons (at home or abroad)? Or, is it an opportunity to build bridges across varying cultures and constituencies, a way to instill a common set of corporate principles and values in order to unite the firm and its customers and suppliers around the world? Within that purpose for an ethics code, design and implement conditions of engagement for suppliers and customers that fit it.
- *Treat corporate values and formal standards of conduct as absolutes.* That is, once the program is developed, do not allow local variations (except within the standards established in the program—see the rest of these guidelines).

- *Consult the stakeholders.* Consult broadly with people who are affected, including international personnel who will need to implement the program and junior-level managers who may be the people implementing the program in the future. Allow foreign business units to help formulate ethical standards and interpret ethical issues.
- *Choose your words carefully.* Many terms do not translate effectively into other languages. Even the term (or concept of) "ethics" does not translate well into many other languages and cultures. Alternatives, such as managerial responsibility, corporate integrity, or business practices are less culturally loaded and easier to translate.
- *Translate the code carefully.* When communicating the code to operations in other countries, the firm must be careful to translate the meanings and to screen for parent country biases, language, and examples.
- *Translate your "ethics code" training materials.* The same thing, of course, is true for training materials and practices. The training materials and activities also need to be carefully translated and carefully presented. For example, John Sweeney of the US AFL-CIO, says that even though Nike claims that its code of conduct is translated and distributed to all the employees in its foreign contractors, independent monitoring in countries such as China finds that employees say they have never seen it.[55]
- *Designate an ethics officer for your overseas operations.* For all regions where there are a large number of employees, a local ethics officer should be appointed, preferably a native who knows the language and customs of the region.
- *Speak of international law,* not just parent country law. Acceptance is greater when the reference is to "the law in many countries," or the codes of the UN, or the ILO, or even the OECD.
- *Recognize the business case.* In host countries, support efforts to decrease institutional corruption. And exercise moral imagination in dealing with cultural differences that conflict with your ethical standards. Be identified as the international firm with strong integrity but one that cares about local conditions. Companies with such reputations often gain a competitive edge both with consumers as well as with government agencies.
- *Recognize the common threads.* While it is important to understand and be aware of the significant cultural differences that do exist, fundamentally, people around the globe are more alike than they are different. They share many of the same priorities, interests, and basic ethical principles. Most of the time, the real challenge is how to communicate these principles effectively.

The preceding discussion has pointed out the difficulties for MNEs in both adopting a host country's ethics and in extending their home country's standards. Even the traditional test suggested in the US—what would people think of your actions if they were written on the front page of the newspaper—is an unreliable guide, since there is no set of agreed-to standards for business conduct. Kidder says,[56] "the very toughest choices people face [in international ethics situations] are not questions of right versus wrong, but questions of right versus right." Therefore, it might be suggested that companies need to help managers distinguish between practices that are merely different from those that are wrong. For relativists, nothing is sacred and, therefore, no practice is wrong. For absolutists, many things that are different are, because of that, wrong. Neither extreme provides much guidance in the real world of business decision making. Donaldson[57] suggests that the best solution to this dichotomy must lie somewhere in between. Donaldson[58] recommends that, when it comes to shaping ethical behavior in their international operations, companies should be guided by three principles:

- Respect for core human values, which determine the absolute moral threshold for all business activities,
- Respect for local traditions,
- The belief that context matters when deciding what is right and what is wrong.

The treatment of ethics in international context is very complex indeed. Yet, MNEs must confront the issue in their daily operations and resolve these difficult dilemmas that they encounter. IHR, through education, training, and problem solving, needs to play an integral role in raising the awareness of its firm's employees regarding ethical behavior. Today's stakeholders (including stockholders) demand that MNEs pay attention to even greater concerns, beyond ethical issues, in terms of corporate social responsibility (CSR) and governance. MNEs are adopting new ethics training programs in their organizations to ensure that employees do not only learn lofty principles but can apply them in their daily behaviors. These training efforts focus on group discussions of lists of do's and don'ts; they use case studies and have employees discuss them; they have line managers lead ethics training—as hearing it from the boss reinforces the importance of the message; they give employees multiple ways to seek ethics advice at the company; and they make sure top executives communicate that ethics training is a priority not just an exercise.

Corporate Social Responsibility, corporate governance, and sustainability

MNEs are increasingly paying attention to their role as corporate citizens. Corporate Social Responsibility (CSR), corporate governance and sustainability are taking on greater importance in the operation of MNEs and IHR is increasingly playing an important role in implementing these activities in their global organizations.

Corporate Social Responsibility

CSR is the continuing commitment by business, not only to behave ethically but also to contribute to the economic development of the communities in which they operate and to improve the quality of life of their work forces, their families, as well as society at large. CSR makes MNEs aware that they produce both benefits and harm simply by the fact that they operate globally. Therefore, they should be as concerned about their global ecological footprint, or the impact of their actions (and inactions) on the natural environment, as they are about generating growth and profits.

The social responsibility of MNEs can be viewed on a continuum of providing value from stockholder to external stakeholder. While past thinking emphasized that organizations were expected only to meet the needs of their shareholders, customers, and employees, current thinking implies that organizations must also be explicit about the economic and social benefits that they bring to society.[59] Putting environmental concerns and people equity issues on an equal footing with shareholder return (also called the triple bottom line) is now considered a CSR responsibility of large MNEs. To take it even one step further, the social responsibility of businesses and business people is commensurate with their social power (such as size, financial resources, visibility). This is referred to as the iron law of social responsibility. Responsible MNEs are expected by their external stakeholders to focus on sustainability management and make sure that, when they meet their present needs, they do so without compromising the ability of future generations to meet their needs.

CSR consists not only of a mind-set but also of a set of deliberate actions that MNEs take to fulfill their social responsibilities. Many different types of activities fall under the umbrella, as depicted in Figure 4.1.

There are several reasons why MNEs are increasingly paying attention to CSR. It enhances their reputation in the market place, may reduce business and legal risks, attracts customers and increases customer loyalty, averts pressure from investors and fund managers, and attracts and retains employees who desire to work for responsible

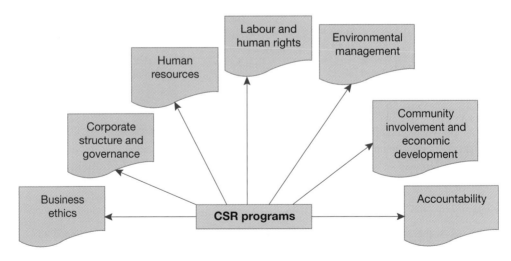

Figure 4.1 Umbrella of CSR programs

Source Phillips. R. & Claus, L. (2002). Corporate Social Responsibility and Global HR. Balancing the Needs of the Corporation and its Stakeholders. *International Focus.* SHRM.

companies. Many MNEs consult with other organizations (NGOs, consulting firms, etc.) to implement and improve their CSR programs. They also pay attention to social investment firms (who manage investment portfolios that only include companies considered to be socially and/or environmentally responsible), social entrepreneurs (who build business models around socially responsible or environmentally sustainable products that compete with them in the market place) and social venture capitalists (who seek out promising social entrepreneurs in whom to invest).

IHR managers are increasingly becoming the implementers of CSR programs in MNEs. Recommendations for the success of CSR programs include the following:

● *Develop a global CSR policy.* Such a policy must be as an integral part of the overall organizational strategy.
● *Obtain a high level of support.* CSR activities, such as any change activity, must clearly come with senior management support to enhance its implementation.
● *Communicate.* Increase awareness of CSR activities and clearly communicate the CSR policy.
● *Create a CSR culture.* Foster a culture that confronts difficult questions about ethics, the environment and social responsibility.
● *Provide adequate training.* Educate and train managers and employees on the MNE's code of conduct, the CSR activities, and the prescribed behaviors and activities.
● *Install reporting and advice mechanisms.* Encourage employees to report questionable conduct and ask for help with their own ethical dilemmas (without retaliation).
● *Include CSR in management's performance management.* Evaluate and reward employees for integrating company values in their daily work life.
● *Communicate.* Use ongoing communication to keep the message alive and share stories and lessons learned.
● *Lead by example.* As any managerial activity when actors are not leading by example but allowed to deviate from the principles without consequences, the CSR initiatives will not be taken seriously.

Corporate governance

Corporate governance refers to the basis upon which decisions are made in organizations. It also involves the structure and relationships that determine how corporate objectives are met and regulated by the different performance monitoring mechanisms (such as the management team, board of directors, investors, and shareholders). In light of many corporate scandals that have particularly plagued Western MNEs (Enron, WorldCom, Tyco International, Peregrine Systems, and Siemens) it is not surprising that this subject has received increased attention and is being regulated through legislation. The 2002 Sarbanes–Oxley Act is an extraterritorial federal US law which requires compliance with enhanced standards for all US public company boards, management, and public accounting firms. It is a direct result of these corporate scandals.

Sustainability

Sustainability is increasingly entering the parlance of MNEs. The Bruntland Commision defined sustainability "as meeting the needs of the present without compromising the ability of future generations to meet their own." Savitz and Weber in *The Triple Bottom Line* argue for the discovery of the sustainability sweet spot which they define as "the common ground shared by your business interests (those of your financial stakeholders) and the interests of the public (your non-financial stakeholders)."[60] For HR, the sustainability sweet spot is the place where the pursuit of organizational interests seamlessly blends with the pursuit of employee interests.

In the future, international HR practitioners will increasingly be called to defend management decisions made in MNEs in terms of the following factors:

- Is the decision *fair* to employees?
- Is the decision *sustainable* in the long run?
- Is the decision *green* in terms of the carbon footprint?
- Is the decision-making process *transparent* and open for scrutiny?

CONCLUSION

This chapter has examined the broad nature of international labor standards, global employment law and regulations, industrial relations around the world, and international ethics. Every MNE must work to understand this very complex regulatory, legal, social, and moral environment and to comply with all relevant codes, laws, and guidelines. Failure to do so can lead to significant liabilities.

First, this chapter looked at the institutional context of international business. International organizations have promulgated labor standards for MNEs. In addition, many international trade organizations and agreements (especially the EU) regulate industrial relations. Finally, commercial diplomacy activities of government (and to a certain extent MNEs) create regulations affecting the activities of the MNE.

Second, this chapter looked at the global legal environment in which the MNE operates. It focused on compliance with national and supranational. Through a variety of employment-related directives, the EU has imposed its social model on the activities of the MNEs. In addition, the US has created a number of extraterritorial laws (e.g., anti-discriminations laws, FCPA, SOX) that impact US companies and US citizens working abroad and that may, in some instances, also apply to non-US employees of these companies. We further discussed a number of comparative regulatory issues that affect the MNE such as immigration, data protection, anti-discrimination and harassment, termination and reduction in force, and intellectual property.

Third, this chapter looked at international labor relations as seen from the point of view of unions and from the point of view of the MNE. Special attention was paid to two forms of employee involvement through work councils and co-determination.

Finally, this chapter looked at international ethics, its relation to culture, the problems of bribery and corruption, and how ethical dilemmas must be solved. We broadened the discussion to corporate social responsibility, human rights, and corporate governance.

Global employment law, industrial relations, and international ethics are difficult topics IHR must deal with in the MNE. They often require IHR to challenge its "home grown" assumptions and take a more global view of the enterprise and its relations with internal and external stakeholders.

GUIDED DISCUSSION QUESTIONS

1 How do the various labor standards promulgated by international organizations affect the MNE?

2 How do EU directives (such as those developed in the area of HR) impact member states and MNEs?

3 How do US extraterritorial laws affect IHR?

4 How is the labor movement evolving as a response to increased globalization?

5 What is the role of IHR in ethics, CSR, corporate governance and sustainability?

VIGNETTE 4.1 PEOPLE AND PLANET MANAGEMENT AT NEW BELGIUM BREWING COMPANY

Sustainability in Action

Sustainability is increasingly becoming a business concern. The most often cited definition is the one created by the Bruntland Commission, which defined sustainability "as meeting the needs of the present without compromising the ability of future generations to meet their own." For many companies, sustainability is only skin-deep—this is hardly the case for New Belgium Brewing Company.

Founded in 1991 by electrical engineer and home brewer Jeff Lebesch and his wife Kim Jordan, a social worker, New Belgium Brewing Company in Fort Collins, Colorado, has always looked for ways to be environmentally, employee, and socially responsible. Embracing new technology, using alternative forms of energy, looking for means to reduce waste, being a good citizen in the community, and above all implementing sustainable employee practices all drive the basic business philosophy and daily decisions at New Belgium.

From the brewery's inception, Jeff and Kim knew it would require the support of committed employees to accomplish their vision. Their innovative employee owner business model began with their first hire and continues now that they have grown to more than 350 employees. It is this idea of employees sharing in both the benefits and the risks that inspires New Belgium's employees to seek out new ways to contribute to the overall success and long-term growth of the company. Kim and Jeff extend the employee owner mentality throughout the company and exemplify it through their practice of open book management and policy of fiscal transparency. Giving employees a sense of ownership and opening the books encourages a community of trust and mutual responsibility.

New Belgium's success does not merely lie in the employee owner business model but also in a company-wide commitment to energy efficiency and social responsibility. It is this ownership mentality that motivated their warehouse technician to spend a percentage of his time rebuilding wooden pallets. Even this small change makes it possible to reduce waste and reuse materials during the bottling/brewing process, and makes a positive net contribution to the bottom line. After an employee vote in 1998, New Belgium became the first brewery to subscribe to wind energy. With each expansion of its facility, New Belgium has incorporated new technologies and, in 2002, the company made two significant steps towards sustainability. That year, New Belgium participated in the US Green Building Council's "Leadership in Energy and Environmental Design for Existing Buildings" pilot program and installed its own water treatment facility. This cutting-edge technology allowed New Belgium to clean its process water without burdening the local Fort Collins municipal system. The methane gas emitted as by-product in this system is then used to fire a combined heat and power engine that produces both electrical and thermal energy; this energy powers roughly 10 percent of the brewery.

Environmental responsibility is, however, only one aspect of New Belgium's drive for sustainability. The sustainability link at New Belgium extends all the way from environmental to social and employee sustainability. Since its inception, New Belgium has donated millions of dollars and thousands of hours to organizations nationwide in the communities in which it does business. New Belgium employees work hard to support these local communities, and for every barrel of beer sold the prior year they donate $1 to a variety of philanthropic causes. New Belgium hires people for fit as well as competencies. Sustainable employee relationships are built through employee ownership, open book management, and a commitment to work–life balance. At the same time employees remain result-focused. And in line with the product line, each employee gets a cruiser bike after one year of work and a trip to Belgium after five. The philosophy is expressed on the side of New Belgium beer packaging and starts with "In this box is our labor of love." It best captures the spirit and commitment of New Belgium employees.

Questions

1 What are sustainable HR practices and how do they affect employees?

2 How can HR discover the sustainability sweet spot of an organization when it comes to employment relations?

Source Claus, L. and Benson, I. (2007), Global HR in Action Vignettes, Willamette University, www.willamette.edu/agsm/global_hr.

International human resource management in the multinational enterprise: policies and practices

5 Global talent management and staffing

LEARNING OBJECTIVES

This chapter will enable the reader to:

- Describe the process of global work force forecasting
- Explain the difficulties associated with global work force forecasting and planning
- Describe the globalization of talent management
- Outline a successful international assignee selection process
- Describe the characteristics of successful international assignees
- Describe the nature and causes of international assignee failure
- Identify and explain the many challenges that IHR confronts in global talent management

KEY TERMS

- Expatriate
- Global talent management
- Inpatriate
- International assignee
- Labor force
- Labor force participation rates
- Localization
- Parent company national (PCN), host company national (HCN), third country national (TCN)
- Repatriate
- Work force
- Work force planning

The first four chapters described the broad context and environment in which IHRM operates. This chapter begins the examination of IHR responsibilities within that context. Specifically, this chapter examines IHR staffing, describing how an MNE strategically manages the acquisition and retention of global talent and tactically decides on which staffing approaches and IHR policies and practice are most effective.

The quality of a firm's talent is central to its ability to learn and perform. Today this is a global issue for every enterprise.[1] So, the first chapter of this part discusses the nature of and problems associated with work force planning and staffing for global enterprises. The challenge of staffing the global enterprise is both complex and difficult. In addition to normal home country hiring responsibilities, MNE staffing includes staffing in all foreign operations plus the highly challenging responsibilities connected to relocation of employees from one country to another. In today's talent shortage environment, staffing MNEs has truly become a problem of global talent management.

Until quite recently, MNE staffing policies and practices were developed from the perspective of headquarters and the culture of the parent country, involving primarily concerns about employees sent on expatriate assignments to foreign subsidiaries and the staffing of local employees at home and in host country subsidiaries. But today, staffing policies and practices have become much more complex, involving a mobile, global work force, located in acquired enterprises in foreign locales, plus those located in traditional subsidiaries, joint ventures, and partnerships, and involving local hires, hires from countries around the world, and employees from any operation on assignment to any other operation. Partially as a result of this globalizing of staffing, one of the recent trends has included a shift in the numbers of workers in MNEs from Western countries to emerging markets. MNEs have even gone outside of the boundaries of their organizations in their search for talent by using outsourcing, offshoring and, sometimes, open source talent.[2]

This chapter, therefore, begins with a discussion of the process of planning the overall work force. It describes the great diversity of staff the typical MNE employs, and then it explains the process of recruiting, selecting, hiring, onboarding, and managing that staff. Subsequent chapters in this section then describe HR responsibilities in the managing of an MNE's global work force, including training and management development, compensation and benefits, performance management, and health and safety and HR information systems.

GLOBAL WORK FORCE PLANNING AND FORECASTING

The objective of global work force planning is to estimate employment needs of the MNE and to develop plans for meeting those needs. The term "work force" applies to an enterprise's employees. The term "labor force" applies to the pool of potential employees, the labor market, from which a firm attracts and hires its work force.

The size—and location—of the potential labor force from which a firm recruits employees varies according to many factors, such as the participation rates of men and women in various locations, whether only local people would be expected to apply for particular jobs, whether people with the necessary education or skills are available locally, etc.

As has been stated a number of times, one of the characteristics of today's global economy that add complexity to HR management is the broad scope of enterprises' operations—likely to be spread all over the world, in dozens if not hundreds of locations, using an equally large number of languages, dealing with a like number of cultures, and subject to various employment laws. The labor pool from which MNEs recruit staff is therefore also located in all those places, speaking all those languages, expressing all that diversity of cultural values and behaviors, and regulated by widely varying employment laws.

As a consequence, enterprises that develop international operations must find staff in whatever location(s) they operate (or relocate the staff they need—if unavailable locally—to those locations), learn to recruit and hire in multiple locations and cultures, and deploy staff where it makes most sense for the enterprise. In the best of circumstances, HR professionals will be asked to provide information about the adequacy of local labor markets prior to their firms' decisions about where to locate their global operations and/or whether to participate in any cross-border acquisitions, joint ventures, or alliances. But, if not prior to such decisions, at least after such decisions are made, HR will be tasked with ensuring the timely staffing of the new or existing international operations. Because of the shortage of skilled workers, the acquisition and deployment of talent are a key global HR imperative. In today's global environment, successful organizations of the future will be those which can attract the best global talent and nurture, develop, and retain it by having a compelling work environment and sophisticated succession management strategies.[3]

Availability of data

One of the major obstacles to MNE work force planning is the lack of accurate data about labor forces in many countries, particularly in less developed and emerging economies. Ideally, data about such labor force characteristics as participation rates (percentage of men and women of working age who work or look for work), levels and quality of education and literacy, availability of skill training, language skills, and unemployment rates, by country and metropolitan areas within countries, would be available to help IHR plan for their firms' local work forces. When available, these data are usually prepared by an agency of the government, or sometimes by international agencies, such as the International Labour Organisation (ILO) or the Organization for Economic Cooperation and Development (OECD). But in many emerging markets such government agencies don't always exist or the data they provide are inadequate, inaccurate, and/or politically motivated. In any case, they often do not provide data which is adequate for IHRM departments to be able to assess whether the people with the necessary skills and education are available or can be developed in any particular location in the numbers necessary to staff planned or acquired operations.

This usually implies that IHR professionals must develop such data from independent sources. Sometimes, such data are available from international or local consultancies. And, often, adequate information can be accessed from sources such as local chambers of commerce, embassies, firms that aid foreign companies in local employee sourcing, etc. In addition, IHR managers can often get some of the information they need from other firms that have prior experience in that particular foreign locale. The key point is that MNEs should not make the assumption that local labor forces will be adequate to provide the talent they need (although this is exactly what is typically done—leaving it up to HR to locate and hire the necessary work force). This adequacy should be one component of the executive decision-making process for where and with whom to do business. In any case, it is IHR that is expected to provide such information.

Population characteristics: shortages and surpluses[4]

Probably the most important labor force issue for developed economies is their aging populations and the resulting labor shortages, with more people retiring than entering the labor force to replace them. In contrast, the labor force issue of concern in most developing and emerging economies is their large young labor forces who often lack the skill sets that jobs in MNEs require.

To a significant extent, these characteristics determine the nature of the labor pool in various countries, although other issues also contribute. Male and female labor force participation rates vary so much from country to country that this factor alone has a major impact on the size of any country's labor pool. For example, female labor force participation rates (for the available data) range from a low of 24.3 percent (for Turkey) to a high of 73.4 percent (for Iceland). In other words, the employment of women in various countries ranges from one in four to three in four.[5] The Scandinavian countries all have female participation rates over 70 percent while Greece, Spain, Italy, Mexico, and Turkey all have female participation rates below 50 percent, with the cultural acceptance of women in the work force also being quite different in various countries.[6] Of course, today, technology makes it possible to use workers from almost any location without them having to relocate to where the employer is (see IHRM in Action 5.1, "Scouting at Google," for an example of a global firm's recruiting of employees around the world). And where people want to live may also influence MNEs in their decisions as to where to locate their work (see IHRM in Action 5.2, "Location, location, location").

In terms of aging, countries such as Japan, Germany, and the UK have 25–30 percent of their populations aged over 60 while countries such as India, Mexico and South Africa have only 7–8 percent of their populations aged over sixty, with much higher

IHRM in Action 5.1

GLOBAL RECRUITING IN ACTION

Scouting talent at Google

In the 1990s, Microsoft, Cisco, and Yahoo distinguished themselves as "hot" places to work in the global IT industry by developing comprehensive HR strategies and distinct workplace cultures to attract the best and the brightest talent from around the world. However, in the new millennium, suddenly Google became the new cool IT place to work.

Established in 1998 by Larry Page and Sergey Brin, Google grew rapidly to 10,000 employees worldwide by 2006. In 2004, at the time of Google's initial public offering (IPO), the company still only had about 2,700 employees, so it has experienced very rapid growth. In the early days, the recruitment process at Google consisted of a thorough, lengthy, almost legendary process in which:

- Candidates were initially given only sketchy information about what types of projects they would be working on or the positions to be filled.
- Every applicant was interviewed by six to ten Google employees.
- Interviews were lengthy and unpredictable, taking days to complete.
- Interviewers (Google staff members) had to submit detailed written assessments of the candidates they interviewed.
- There was a tremendous emphasis on academic credentials, élite school provenance, and high grade point average (GPA).
- Candidates were often required to submit "homework" assignments before being considered for a job.

Initially, almost all job candidates were interviewed by the co-founders before they were officially hired, and co-founder Sergey would often show up at interviews in rather unconventional dress code. As the company grew, at least one co-founder reviewed every job offer recommended by an internal hiring committee on a weekly basis. These early practices not only resulted in the recruiting process taking a lot of effort from both the company and the applicants but the lengthy time-to-hire also reduced the rate of acceptance from job candidates who, in the meantime, took other job offers. In order to capture the best available talent in a post-IPO era requiring massive hiring, Google was forced to streamline its recruiting procedures.

Thirty-three-year old Laszlo Block, Vice-President People Operations, joined the Google management group in March 2006 as the head of HR. According to Google's corporate information, he "leads Google's human resources functions globally, which includes all areas related to the attraction, development and retention of Googlers." Laszlo formerly worked for General Electric and McKinsey & Co. and brings valuable strategic compensation management expertise to the job. One of Laszlo's first job duties was to fine-tune the recruitment process and increase the standards by which Google selects and hires new people. According to Laszlo, Google's huge demand for talent (in the first quarter of 2006, Google hired sixteen new employees daily) forced the company to change the way it interfaced with job candidates. Accordingly, the following measures were put into place:

- Reduce the in-person interviews of candidates from between six to ten to five.
- Require staff members to submit their assessments of candidates within one week of the interview.
- Take into account professional track record as well as GPA.
- Focus on targeted feedback around four core attributes of successful Googlers.
- Use multiple scores to rate a candidate's competencies (knowledge, skills and abilities).

Laszlo also mapped thirty to forty job performance factors (out of 300 variables) based on a survey of current Google employees. This allowed him to identify clusters of variables to focus on in the selection process. These measures are intended to significantly reduce the time for Google to make a job offer without compromising the fit between the applicant, the job, and the company.

Google has taken its search for new talent global. It has opened R&D centers in South Korea, Japan, Britain, Switzerland, Norway, and Israel. The company utilizes creative "Google jams" to identify top software engineers around the world. Knowhow and innovation remain of the utmost importance in their search for the right talent. And it makes no difference what country that talent comes from. As Google expands from a startup to a global player, it must protect its brand as an employer of choice in the IT industry while retaining its pre-IPO Googlers who may have little financial incentive to remain with the company, since their stock options have made many of them quite wealthy.

Source Claus, L. (2007), Global HR in Action Vignettes, Willamette University, www.willamette.edu/agsm/global_hr. This vignette is also based on information contained in Kevin J. Delaney (2006), Google adjusts hiring process as it needs to grow, *Wall Street Journal*, October 23.

percentages of their populations under the age of twenty-five.[7] In some ways, these opposing profiles provide balance in the global labor force, with the surplus of young workers in the developing economies providing labor for the aging and shrinking labor forces in the developed countries. This happens in many ways, including the importing of workers and the exporting of jobs, through foreign direct investment, cross-border joint ventures and partnerships, outsourcing and subcontracting, and offshoring. IHRM in Action 5.3 illustrates two different ways that firms in developed

---

LOCATION, LOCATION, LOCATION

IHRM in Action 5.2

Today, for most firms, it is still important to be located near your customers. But in the war for talent, it may be equally important to be located in the best place to attract the high performers and specialists your business needs (see IHRM In Action 5.1. Over the last few years, specific locations have arisen as preferred places to live and work. High-talent employees can establish themselves in locales that enable them to create the work–life balance that meets their current needs and still be near to others like themselves. So, where are such places?

As it turns out, people don't look so much at countries as they do at cities, and often it is small cities that provide the lifestyles they are looking for. For example, it includes Groningen, a small town in the north of the Netherlands, and Eindhoven, another small town—but major business location—in the Netherlands. Of course, the traditional, popular cities continue to have appeal, but there are also new areas—in every region of the world—that are attracting the talent that today's MNEs need.

In Europe, this would include an area marked on the map by a gentle curve drawn from Barcelona, across southern France, northern Italy, Switzerland, and southern Germany, an area that already boasts the highest *per capita* income in the world. The big cities of interest in Europe still include Amsterdam, Brussels, London, Paris, Frankfurt, Munich, Nice, Berlin, Milan, Dublin, and Zurich. In Asia, these cities would include Sydney and Brisbane, Auckland, Singapore, Kuala Lumpur, Bangalore and Mumbai, Tokyo, Seoul, and Shanghai. If a global firm cannot find talent where its customers want them to locate, then maybe it needs to figure out where the talent is and go there.

Sources Adapted from Friedman, T. L. (2005), *The World is Flat*, New York: Farrar, Straus and Giroux; Howard, C. G. (1992), Profile of the twenty-first-century expatriate manager, *HR Magazine*, June: 93–100; Laabs, J. J. (1991), The global talent search, *Personnel Journal*, August: 38–43; Marsick, V. J. and Cederholm, L. (1988), Developing leadership in international managers: An urgent challenge! *Columbia Journal of World Business*, winter: 3–11.

---

countries are meeting their needs for employees. The first part of this showcases a major resort hotel in the US, which recruits employees from outside its country base, as do resorts around the world. And the second part of this showcases firms in the Netherlands that meet their needs through the hiring of retired Dutch citizens.

For firms that want to conduct business in emerging markets, IHRM's role in ensuring a good local work force can be critical. For example, when the Edinburgh-based marine service firm BUE Marine moved into Azerbaijan's capital Baku to take

WHAT SOME COUNTRIES DO TO FIND NEEDED TALENT

A US hotel finds a new way to fill jobs

At a time when workers are scarce and the Broadmoor Hotel in Colorado Springs in the US found its premier service and five-star resort ranking at risk, the hotel had to find a new way to fill jobs. Despite trying every conventional way to fill its jobs, the hotel still had at least 300 positions it couldn't fill.

The answer that the HR department came up with was to recruit staff from all over the world. Now, nearly a fourth of the Broadmoor's peak-of-season work force of 1,700 workers are foreign citizens on temporary visas through various government programs. Broadmoor president Steve Bartolin thinks every country in the world is represented (obviously an overstatement, but maybe not by much), but also says: "We are still understaffed—we still have 100 openings, but that compares favorably with 200 or 300 positions we had three or four years ago."

Because of a general labor shortage in the Colorado Springs area, many other employers, ranging from high-tech giants to restaurants and construction firms, are using foreign workers to fill their labor needs. No single strategy solves the worker shortages for individual employers, but the Broadmoor's example shows that recruiting foreign employees can help employers cope.

In the Netherlands, labor shortages are dealt with by hiring the retired

Frans Tuintjes, a retired former commercial airline pilot, who has flown all over the world, is now selling men's clothing and loving it. Recruiting the elderly—men and women who are either bored in retirement or need to supplement their pensions—is a new Dutch strategy to combat their labor shortage. In a program referred to as Sixty-five Plus the Dutch created an employment agency designed specifically for recruiting of the elderly.

Dutch companies find that their older employees are unusually motivated, experienced, and loyal. A short time ago, the Dutch welfare system was subsidizing retirement and encouraging people to retire early. Many people took advantage. But now, with a labor shortage due to low birth rates over the last forty-five years and fast economic growth, firms are finding the tight labor market is hampering further growth because they can no longer fill job vacancies.

Interestingly, the labor shortage is prompting a national debate (in the Netherlands as well as elsewhere) on some sensitive issues: How many more immigrants should be let into the country? Can the government force people to retrain? Should the government raise the retirement age and if so by how much?

At any rate, the retired Dutch who have gone back to work are finding it a rewarding experience. Frans Tuintjes, the retired pilot, says, for example: "I've sold airplanes, so I figured I could sell a suit." He says his part-time job at Marks & Spencer is a lot of fun because he gets to meet a lot of people and he can use his many skills, such as practicing his multiple languages.

Sources Broadmoar Hotel: Adapted from Springs cos. use foreign workers (2000), *Daily Camera* (Boulder, CO), September 6: 3B. *Netherlands*: Adapted from Amid shortage of workers, Dutch find reward in hiring the retired, *San Diego Union-Tribune*, April 23 2000: A-29.

advantage of its natural resources, it faced a large number of HR challenges, ranging from nepotism and theft to low skills and overstaffing and deceitful résumés. What it found was that when companies want a foothold in a developing country, they need to research labor costs, cultural differences, benefits, legal jurisdictions, and how to hire people locally, as well as the role that government plays in contracts and enforcement.[8] It falls upon IHRM to forestall labor problems and to provide information to senior executives on the costs of dealing with (or not) these kinds of such critical issues.

Increasing diversity of labor forces and work forces

One of the results of increased globalization, modern technology, and global communications on the global labor market is that people with the education and skills needed in today's global economy are increasingly available everywhere, making potential employees available from all racial and ethnic origins and nationalities.[9] This has the effect of dramatically increasing the level of employee diversity with which global firms must cope. In addition, employees in the global firm come from many groups that in the past and in many countries did not participate much in the labor market, including the young and/or old, male and/or female, disabled, married or single, people from various religious affiliations, etc.

Labor mobility

Emigration and immigration

The world is experiencing migration (emigration and immigration) on an unprecedented scale. Some of it is voluntary and some of it is forced. Some of it is legal and some of it is considered illegal. Some of it is planned and purposeful and some of it is unplanned and without direct purpose. However, in all cases, it is creating mobility of workers in such large numbers that formal and informal emigration has to be taken into consideration as MNEs examine their options for developing their global work forces.

Millions of people work outside their home countries, either as traditional expatriates (on assignment by their employers) or hired to emigrate to fill vacant jobs in other countries. Some countries like the Philippines purposely manage a percentage of their labor force to work in other countries every year. Others, such as Mexico, lose many workers with unofficial migration to their neighbors. And some, like Estonia, Romania, and Poland, lose many workers (legitimately) to other countries in their region, such as in this case to other countries in the EU. In addition, millions are forced from their homes because of civil unrest or natural disasters and become permanent refugees. And some trade treaties such as the one that creates the foundation for the EU (1957 Treaty of Rome) include provisions to facilitate movement of workers between countries. This allows people to seek the best possible work opportunities, facilitates EU firms in creating high-quality work forces by drawing on talent from throughout the EU membership, and eventually levels the wage and benefits "playing field" across the member states, so that firms do not gain advantages or disadvantages because of government practices. Other treaties such as NAFTA, Mercosur, and ASEAN do not yet include such labor mobility provisions, but if the EU is developing the model for such regional trade treaties, it may be only a matter of time before other regions begin to look at ways to facilitate labor mobility, as well.

Brain drain and job exporting

One of the major concerns created by the world's increasingly mobile labor force is what many countries, particularly emerging and developing countries, refer to as a brain drain, as their educated and skilled citizens leave for jobs with better pay in the developed countries. From the point of view of developing countries, it is often wrong for firms from the rich countries to recruit and relocate their citizens after the major resources that they have expended on educating and training their citizens. They feel they need these human resources for the development of their own economies.

An alternative to this brain drain, and one that is increasingly pursued by many global firms and is encouraged by the governments of developing economies, is to export the work and jobs from the developed economies to developing countries, through subsidiaries, joint ventures, outsourcing, and offshoring. Both sides can benefit from this arrangement: the firm gets top talent from the foreign countries in a period and location of labor shortage in their home country and at a lower cost and the developing country gets to hold on to its top talent and gets jobs and income from the MNEs.

In summary, today's typical MNE, with operations in multiple countries (from dozens to over 100 countries), has a work force that spans the globe. The task of IHR managers in these firms is to facilitate the hiring of competent, high-performing talent that enables sustainable, competitive advantage throughout the global marketplace. Planning for and hiring such a work force is a complex activity. It involves determining what education and skills are needed and figuring out where to find that talent and how to recruit it and hire it. This is difficult enough for local hires for local operations. It is much more difficult for global operations. The first part of this chapter has described some of the complexities in that process.

The labor market is different in every country—and often by regions within countries. The challenges for collecting or creating the information necessary for work force planning and forecasting are often difficult to overcome. And yet the health of today's MNE is a function of IHRM's ability to match their firms' work force forecasts with the supply of global talent. Indeed: "In a fast-changing global economy, world-class work force planning is the key to success."[10] With global work force forecasts and plans in place, MNEs' next moves are to fulfill those plans through recruiting and staffing, the subject of the rest of this chapter.

STAFFING THE MULTINATIONAL ENTERPRISE: AN INTRODUCTION

Staffing for the MNE involves hiring at the local level (in both the parent country and in all foreign locations where it does business or has operations of any kind) as well as management of the mobile work force, that is, the employees who are hired in one locale and are relocated for varying times and purposes to other locales. In staffing the MNE, firms have choices by using either ethnocentric, polycentric, geocentric, or regiocentric staffing options.[11] When using an ethnocentric staffing approach, MNEs tend to hire from the headquarters country and send employees on international assignment to the subsidiaries. In the case of polycentric staffing, MNEs prefer to use locals from the subsidiary country. When using a geocentric approach, MNEs source talent from anywhere in the world, while a regiocentric approach favors using people from the region. Thus IHR staffing practice is challenged by the problems associated with recruiting, hiring, training, compensating, managing performance and welfare, and retaining and deploying a global work force, sourced from multiple locations and managed under the constraints of multiple national cultures and legal systems.

International assignees and local nationals

Until quite recently, staffing of MNEs was simplistically described as involving only three types of international employees: parent country nationals (PCNs), host country nationals (HCNs), and third country nationals (TCNs).[12] Most of the IHR literature has concerned itself with PCNs, who are typically defined as citizens of the country of the headquarters of the MNE and employed by the firm in the country of its headquarters. When PCNs are transferred (posted/assigned/relocated) to another country, to work in a foreign subsidiary or other type of operation (such as a joint venture or alliance) of the MNE for more than one year, they are generally referred to as *expatriates* or international assignees (IAs). When they return home, they are referred to as *repatriates*. Administering the traditional expatriate has historically been the primary time-consuming responsibility of the IHR manager and staff (and the primary research focus of academics).

Most of the literature in IHRM that deals with expatriates or international assignees —individuals who are or have been on international assignments—has assumed that all employees who are on foreign assignments are traditional expatriates. Studies have invariably referred to "international assignment experience" or "expatriate" to simply refer to anyone who has been on an international assignment for more than one year. But, as with everything else in IHRM, international assignments have also become more complex. So, the next few paragraphs provide an introduction to the many different types of international assignees (IAs) before the chapter describes in more detail the many issues surrounding recruiting and staffing for international assignments.

Purpose(s) of assignments

There have been a number of approaches to describing the purposes for sending people on international assignments.[13] In general, these purposes can be combined into two broad categories: demand-driven and learning-driven. The demand-driven purposes include using international assignees as general managers or directors, for subsidiary startups and to roll out new products, for technology transfer, to solve problems, to perform functional tasks such as accounting, sales, and manufacturing, and for organizational control. The learning-driven purposes include management development (of both international business skills and general management skills for both PCNs and HCNs), transfer of knowledge, and the socialization of locals into the corporate culture and values. Except for the need for general managers, increasingly all of these purposes are being pursued with shorter-term assignments (less than a year, for sure less than three years), rather than the more common three- to five-year assignments found in years past.[14]

Types of assignees

The above paragraphs describe the traditional expatriates and repatriates, relocated primarily from the home country. In contrast, when HCNs are relocated to the headquarters of the parent firm, they are generally referred to as *inpatriates* (although they are probably viewed by themselves and their home country families, colleagues, and friends as expatriates from their home countries). And when an MNE hires a citizen of a country other than the parent country or the country of the subsidiary to work in one of its foreign subsidiaries, this person has been typically referred to as a TCN. In contrast to the literature on PCNs and expatriates, there has been only limited literature published on local nationals (HCNs) or TCNs.

As more firms globalize and develop more operations in an ever-increasing number of locations, they have begun to create additional options for staffing foreign work assignments. One consequence of this has been an effort to find a better term to describe the many types of international employees, as a replacement for "expatriate."

Thus terms such as "international assignee," "transpatriate," even "transnational" have been used by various companies in attempts to find a term that might describe anyone on a foreign assignment. None has been found, as will be shown in the next section, which covers all types of foreign employees. Yet, still, the term most often used, today, "international assignee," is generally used as a "catch-all" term but mostly refers to the traditional PCN on a typical expatriate assignment as well as to the inpatriate and other HCNs and TCNs who are moved from subsidiary to subsidiary.

Today's diversity of international employees

Even though the use of expatriates has seemed to be the logical choice for staffing international operations, at least for startups, technology transfer, and major managerial positions, such as director general and sales manager, several problems with the use of expatriates have led MNEs to seek other options for achieving their objectives in their foreign operations. Some of these issues include making mistakes in the choice of employees for international assignments, the high cost of these assignments, difficulties in providing adequate training and support for employees and their families on international assignments and the resulting problems with their adjustment to the foreign situation, too frequent failures of international assignments, local countries' desire for hiring of local employees and managers, problems encountered in managing repatriates, and a growing suspicion that local hires may actually perform better.[15]

One result of this is that many MNEs are finding that it no longer makes sense to give all attention and priority to expatriates. "This arrangement was adequate in yesterday's international organization because leadership, decision-making authority, and organizational power flowed from the parent site to the foreign subsidiaries. Today, however, new technologies, new markets, innovation, and new talent no longer solely emanate from headquarters but are found cross-nationally, making the expatriate model obsolete."[16] Indeed, international managers can and do come from just about everywhere, not just the headquarters of the traditional large MNE.[17]

The following is a summary of the many different types of international employees that MNEs draw on to staff their operations in the global marketplace.[18] There are many different options available to MNEs and there are probably even more examples that the authors have yet to come across.

- *Local hires or nationals:* employees who are hired locally (an HCN hired under a polycentric staffing approach).
- *Domestic internationalists:* employees who never leave home but conduct international business with customers, suppliers, and colleagues in other countries (via telephone, email, fax, or even snail mail).
- *International commuters:* employees who live in one country (home countries) but who work in another (host) country and regularly commute across borders to

perform aspects of their work. They may live at home in one country yet commute on a daily or weekly basis to another country to work.

- *Frequent business trips:* employees who, on a frequent basis, take international trips that last a few days, weeks or months at a time. These international trips usually include travel to a variety of countries or continents to visit MNE sites or customers.
- *Short-term international assignees:* employees on assignments that last less than one year but more than a few weeks (increasingly being used to substitute for longer-term international assignments and typically do not include the relocation of the employee's family).
- *International assignees:* This is an international assignment that lasts more than one year and includes full relocation. This is the traditional expatriate and the focus of most research and surveys about international employees. These international assignments may be intermediate-term assignments (twelve to twenty-four months) or long-term assignments (twenty-four to thirty-six months).
- *Localized employees:* Often referred to as localization, this normally refers to the situation where an employee is sent to work in a foreign country but hired as a local employee (with some allowances to get over there). This may be because they really want to work in that country, often because they marry a local spouse or for some other reason want to spend the rest of their careers in that location. It may also involve an international assignee who is converted to permanent local status once the assignment period is over.
- *Permanent cadre or globalists:* These are employees who spend essentially their whole careers in international assignments, moving from one locale to another.
- *Stealth assignees:* This is the term used to describe international assignees who are relocated by their managers without ever informing HR (that is, they "fly under the radar"), so that they do not show up in the records, benefits, and support systems used to manage such employees. Many short-term assignees fall under this category.
- *Immigrants:* (a) traditional TCNs, employees who are hired to work in a foreign subsidiary but whose home of citizenship is another country, thus they become immigrants to the country of the subsidiary; (b) people hired by the parent firm (either in-country or as new immigrants and brought into the country) to work in the parent country.
- *Internships* (temporary immigrants): These are workers brought into a firm's home country to work for short (six months to two years) periods as interns or trainees, used especially to fill in for labor shortages.
- *Returnees:* These are emigrants who are hired (or selected, if already employed by the firm) to return to their home countries to work for the firm there.
- *Boomerangs:* These are individuals who have emigrated and are hired by firms in their original home country to return home or are foreigners with experience in the country, who have returned home and are now hired to come back to the foreign country.
- *Second-generation expatriates:* These are naturalized citizens (immigrants who have become citizens) and are sent on foreign assignments to countries other than

their countries of birth. The assumption is that, since they have lived through the "expatriate" experience once, they should be better able (than those without this experience) to handle it the second time.

- *Just-in-time expatriates:* These are *ad hoc* or *contract* expatriates who are hired from outside the firm as they are needed and just for one assignment.
- *Reward or punishment assignees:* These are employees who are late in their careers and who are either given a desirable foreign assignment to enjoy and to pad their pensions for when they retire in a couple of years (pay is higher on foreign assignments) or are sent to a difficult locale or undesirable assignment as a way to sideline them to finish out their careers, rather than have to discipline or terminate them because of marginal performance.
- *Outsourced employees:* This is the situation that occurs when the MNE decides to pay someone else (in another country) for the services of an "employee" or group of employees. In recent years, global employment companies (GECs) have evolved, which provide a few employees or whole staffs for overseas locations. Some firms use their own GEC to house all of their globally mobile employees, simplifying pay and benefits, since everyone in the GEC gets the same pay and benefits, no matter where they work within the firm, possibly with cost-of-living adjustments.
- *Virtual IEs:* This is the situation where all or most of the work is performed across borders via electronic media: teleconferences, email, telephone, videoconferences, fax, etc.
- *Self-initiated foreign workers:* This term refers to individuals who travel abroad (usually as tourists or students) but who seek work as they travel and are hired in the foreign location, often by firms from their home countries.
- *Retirees:* This refers to the hiring of a firm's retirees for short-term foreign assignments.

Global staffing choices: implications for multinational enterprises

There are two issues that appear to have led to this use of so many different types of employees for foreign assignments. One has to do with increased needs that firms experience as they increase their level of international commerce. And the second has to do with the problems they experience as they cope with these increased needs.

As new firms become engaged in global commerce and experienced firms become engaged in new and unfamiliar countries, both seek help from employees who before might not have been closely considered for international assignments. In addition, technology has made it possible (even necessary) to conduct global business in new ways. Thus firms are more likely to use domestic internationalists, virtual assignments and cross-border teams, returnees and second generation expatriates, and outsourced, offshored, and just-in-time international employees.

When problems with the high cost of traditional expatriates, retention of repatriates, and increasing resistance from employees and their families to foreign assignments continue to go unresolved, firms rely more heavily on short-term assignments, extended business trips, commuters, local hires, returnees, and retirees. As firms recognize their need to internationalize their work forces and management ranks, they gradually place more emphasis on developmental assignments, such as shorter-term international assignments and international transferees. And problems with transfer of learning among units of global businesses (headquarters, subsidiaries, business units, joint ventures, partnerships) lead MNEs to pay more attention to the management of all their global staffs.

This increased variety of employees presents all sorts of new challenges for the planning, selection, preparation, deployment, and management of a global work force. Not the least of these is the increased need for all managers—and for IHR managers in particular—to increase their cross-cultural awareness, knowledge, and skills, their foreign language abilities, and their overall management competencies within this new international setting. And it is IHRM that should be tasked with providing the expertise and support to the rest of the firm to ensure that all these varieties of global managers and employees develop the necessary international competencies.

STAFFING WITH INTERNATIONAL ASSIGNEES

Typical employment practices for managerial and often marketing and technical positions in foreign subsidiaries often place heavy emphasis on the use of expatriates or intermediate and long-term international assignees.[19] As discussed above, there are many reasons that MNEs transfer personnel from one country to another. But the key reasons still appear to be for their technical or functional expertise, for control, to start new operations, and for managerial development purposes.[20] As the following quote suggests, however, at least large MNEs are increasingly recognizing the importance of international experience for higher-level managerial positions, making this an increasingly prominent focus of international assignments (although, as will be shown later in this chapter, the rhetoric may be stronger than the reality).

> What seems clearly true is that at many big companies . . . putting in time abroad is increasingly a required, and critical, step in an executive's progress up the ladder. To run a global enterprise, the reasoning goes, you need the ability to psych out the foreigner as a consumer, as well as a sense of how to get things done offshore. What better training for this than a tour of duty overseas?
>
> Another, more subtle consideration may also be at work. A number of companies report finding that the personal qualities that enable an executive to negotiate his way through a job over there—an ability to think himself into the shoes of someone else, a capacity to make decisions even in the face of thoroughgoing ambiguity—are precisely those qualities increasingly needed at the top back here.[21]

Historically, the term "expatriate," as used by companies, referred to employees who were relocated from the parent company or headquarters to foreign subsidiaries or "overseas" operations. Today, the term "international assignee" is more generally used to describe the process of moving any employee from one country to another for a period of more than one year while staying in the employment of the same firm.

Even though global enterprises are using multiple ways and multiple types of employees to conduct their international business, there is still major interest in and use of traditional international assignees. Many large multinationals, that have been international for a long time, such as Unilever, the large Anglo-Dutch consumer products firm, Royal Dutch Shell, and Ford Motor Company, move managers from subsidiary to subsidiary and country to country to help build global relationships and to develop a common corporate identity and business culture among their management ranks, as well as to ensure they have the necessary talent in the right location at the right time.

In the typical MNE of any size, there are divergent forces operating relative to the use of international assignees. Larger MNEs use a greater number and percentage of HCNs but also need international experience in their management team. So to develop this experience, they are increasingly likely to move managers from the parent company or regional headquarters, as well as their foreign managers, to assignments in countries other than their countries of origin. Firms which are newly developing their international businesses, of which there are a constantly increasing number, typically rely heavily on interntional assignees from the home office for the development of that business, both because they trust their existing managers more than unknown foreign managers and because they lack experience in working with foreign operations and it seems easier to establish their new foreign businesses with their existing managers.

Sometimes there is simply a shortage of qualified skills in local nationals, although, with global communications and hundreds of thousands—if not millions—of students from the developing world getting higher education in developed countries and many developing or emerging economies (such as the BRIC economies) providing world-class education to millions of their own citizens, this is rapidly becoming less of a concern. A more pressing concern is the lack of supervisory and managerial skills in these emerging markets.

As MNEs increasingly develop (or hire) local nationals to manage their local operations in countries around the world, it is often suggested that the numbers of international assignees would therefore be decreasing. Countering this possibility, though, is the increased use of expatriation for individual and organizational development coupled with the obvious increase in number of firms operating internationally. Although the relative number of international assignees may be decreasing (compared to the other staffing options), the absolute numbers are still growing as global business opportunities are expanding, especially in large markets like China and India. In addition, experience shows that firms that are early in the evolution of their international activity tend to use more PCN expatriates to manage and develop their international sales and operations than do more internationally mature firms.[22]

As would be expected, there are no counts of the numbers of international assignees. But there is large anecdotal evidence that most MNEs use international assignees. Some estimates can be made. The Internal Revenue Service in the US (the agency that collects taxes) reports increasing numbers of tax returns from US expatriates, while surveys by consulting firms (which mostly survey large multinational firms) report varying results: some find a reduction in reported numbers, some find an increase.[23] The explanation for the different findings, though, is probably found in the pattern of evolution of MNEs: the number of expatriates for the first few years after international start-up is high, grows for a short time, and then tapers off to the minimum number necessary to ensure effective continuity of the international business. As the number of headquarters international assignees decreases, local nationals increasingly receive regional assignments. Thus, survey results from most consulting firms which come primarily from larger, more experienced MNEs, show a declining use of international assignees.

In explanation of this, the use of international assignees (especially from headquarters) is high during the initial stages of foreign operations in order to accomplish technology transfer, including production and management technologies, product knowledge transfer, and staffing and implementing a startup. The number of international assignees will then decline as the firm's local managers and technical and functional staff assimilate this knowledge. The number may later expand, again, as local operations become increasingly integrated into a global operational framework. In addition, as the enterprise becomes more global, it develops a need for international managers with greater international experience as it develops its worldwide competitive advantages. However, at this stage, these global managers may well come from any country, not necessarily, or even primarily, from the country of the parent company.

Most of the rest of this chapter deals with the management of the expatriation process and of international assignees. This is then followed with a discussion of some of the issues associated with local and third-country nationals.

Developing a pool of international assignee candidates

One way that firms can develop more lead time to manage the international assignee selection process is to develop a pool of potential candidates.[24] This will involve early assessment, self-identification of interest and self-assessment for readiness, and possible early preparation, in terms of language training, cultural training, and other cultural awareness activities and training in international business. With such a pool of interested and qualified candidates available, when needs are recognized, IHR (and assigning managers) can refer to this pool of qualified candidates and can encourage (even insist?) line managers to rely on the pool for identifying candidates for their open positions. And over time this will encourage line managers to get involved with earlier planning and identification of potential candidates for the pool.

Selection

The selection decision for international assignees is critically important. Errors in selection can have major negative impact on the success of overseas operations as well as on the careers of relocated managers.

From the perspective of headquarters, it is most important that potential international assignees be seen as able to perform both the specific tasks to which they are assigned as well as to perform well in a different national culture. Thus, the first consideration for international firms is to fully understand the requirements in both technical and cultural terms of the jobs to which expatriates will be assigned as well as of the country of assignment (refer to Figure 5.1, "Successful international assignee experience").[25] As with all HRM activities, a thorough job analysis of the assignment (including an examination of the foreign work environment and culture) is necessary in order to make appropriate international assignment selections.

Because of the nature of most international assignments, selections for international transfer are most successful when based on factors such as the following:[26]

- The maturity of the candidate (i.e., being a self-starter, able to make independent decisions, having emotional stability, sensitive to others who are different, and having a well rounded knowledge of on- and off-the-job subjects to facilitate discussion with foreign colleagues and contacts who are often quite knowledgeable and interested in such topics).
- Ability to handle foreign language(s) (see discussion below).
- Possession of a favorable outlook on the international assignment and locale by the expatriate and his or her family (i.e., s/he wants to go overseas).
- Possessing appropriate personal characteristics (excellent health, desire for the assignment, this is an appropriate time in the individual's career and family life, individual resourcefulness, adaptability, desire to learn and experience new things and new people).

From the viewpoint of persons being considered for international assignment, studies suggest that two specific factors—in addition to a strong personal interest in getting a foreign experience, usually based on having previously enjoyed living overseas—are primary in their decisions to take on such an assignment: increased pay and perceived improved career opportunities.[27] This suggests the importance of paying close attention to these factors when making selections for international assignments.

From the company side, increasingly the problem of selection of international assignees involves finding employees with the necessary skills to function successfully in the new "global" environment and convincing them to take on the

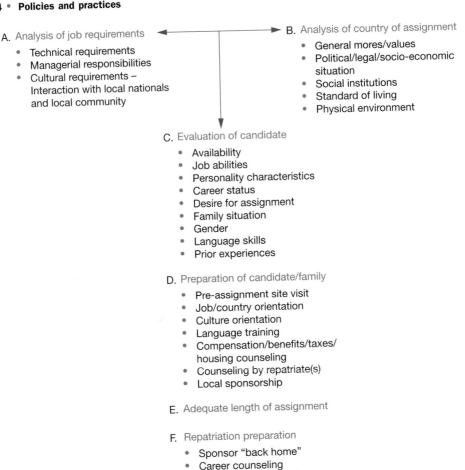

A. Analysis of job requirements

- Technical requirements
- Managerial responsibilities
- Cultural requirements –
  Interaction with local nationals
  and local community

B. Analysis of country of assignment

- General mores/values
- Political/legal/socio-economic
  situation
- Social institutions
- Standard of living
- Physical environment

C. Evaluation of candidate

- Availability
- Job abilities
- Personality characteristics
- Career status
- Desire for assignment
- Family situation
- Gender
- Language skills
- Prior experiences

D. Preparation of candidate/family

- Pre-assignment site visit
- Job/country orientation
- Culture orientation
- Language training
- Compensation/benefits/taxes/
  housing counseling
- Counseling by repatriate(s)
- Local sponsorship

E. Adequate length of assignment

F. Repatriation preparation

- Sponsor "back home"
- Career counseling
- Culture reorientation

G. Successful expatriate experience

Figure 5.1 Successful international assignee experience

Source Briscoe, D. R. and Gazda, G. M. (1989), The successful expatriate, *Proceedings*: Managing in the Global Economy, third biannual international conference, Eastern Academy of Management, Hong Kong, November

assignment. Because of dual career families, disruption of their lives, work–life balance issues, and the uncertainty about the impact of the assignment on their careers, employees are becoming increasingly reluctant to take on international assignments.

The competency profile of an assignee is an important aspect of the selection process. Box 5.1 lists the skills that are being cited as important for the twenty-first century expatriate manager. Even though this list was developed almost twenty years ago, these are the skills still being sought, today. In the words of two major MNE executives:[28]

BOX 5.1 TWENTY-FIRST-CENTURY EXPATRIATE MANAGER PROFILE

Skill	Managerial implications
Core skills	
Multidimensional perspective	Extensive multiproduct, multi-industry, multifunctional, multicompany, multicountry, and multi-environment experience
Proficiency in line management	Track record in successfully operating overseas strategic business units and/or a series of major overseas projects
Prudent decision-making skills	Competence and proven track record in making the right strategic decisions
Resourcefulness	Skillful in getting him/herself known and accepted in the host country's political hierarchy
Cultural adaptability	Quick and easy adaptability into the foreign culture—individual with as much cultural mix, diversity, and experience as possible
Cultural sensitivity	Effective people skills in dealing with variety of cultures, races, nationalities, genders, religions. Sensitive to cultural difference
Ability as a team builder	Adept in bringing a culturally diverse working group together to accomplish the major global mission and objectives of the enterprise
Physical fitness and mental maturity	Endurance for the rigorous demands of overseas assignments
Curiosity and learning	Constant interest in learning about all aspects of international cultures, foreign countries, and global business
Augmented skills	
Computer literacy	Comfortable exchanging strategic information electronically
Prudent negotiating skills	Proven track record in conducting successful strategic business negotiations in multicultural/multinational environments
Ability as a change agent	Proven track record in successfully initiating and implementing strategic and global organizational changes
Visionary skills	Quick to recognize and respond to strategic business opportunities and potential political and economic upheavals in the host country
Effective delegatory skills	Proven track record in participative management style and ability to delegate in cross-cultural environments
International business skills	Proven track record in conducting business in the global environment

Sources Black, J. S. (2006), The mindset of global leaders: Inquisitiveness and duality, in Mobley, W. H. and Weldon, E. (eds), *Advances in Global Leadership*, Vol. 4; Black, J. S., Morrison, A. and Gregersen, H. (1999), *Global Explorers: The Next Generation of Leaders*, New York: Routledge; Howard, C. G. (1992), Profile of the twenty-first-century expatriate manager, *HR Magazine*, June: 96; Marquardt, M. J. and Berger, N. O. (2000), *Global Leaders for the Twenty-first Century*, New York: State University of New York Press; and Rosen, R., Digh, P., Singer, M. and Philips, C. (2000) *Global Literacies: Lessons on Business Leadership and National Cultures*, New York: Simon and Schuster.

"The top twenty-first-century manager should have multi-environment, multi-country, multi-functional, multi-company, multi-industry experience," according to Ed Dunn, at the time corporate vice-president of HR at Whirlpool Corporation (now an independent consultant). Michael Angus, at the time chairman of Unilever, added: "Most people who rise toward the top of our business will have worked in at least two countries, probably three. They will probably speak another language and they most certainly will have worked in different product areas."

Placing high importance on the alignment of selection decisions with corporate strategy and goals is becoming more common.[29] Successful global firms link their global staffing decisions to their global business goals. The more important the international strategy and the more complex the structure developed to implement that strategy, the more critical are the international staffing decisions.

Selection decisions also need to consider the receiving (host country) managers and location. Successful international assignments make demands not only on the international assignee (IA) but on the receiving manager and company as well as the sending manager and company.[30] Often the sending manager has little (or no) international experience and, therefore, does not have a clear idea of what it takes to handle a foreign assignment—and may also downplay how important are the difficulties of the foreign assignment. And receiving managers may have the same problems—they have not worked at headquarters or elsewhere outside their home countries and they do not know what strengths it takes for a successful expatriate assignment. Thus, the sending company can have a negative impact on the success of the international assignee by relying on domestic experience for guidance on how to manage and evaluate the international assignee and not understanding the pressures of the foreign environment. And the receiving firm may compound the problems by not understanding the perspective of the parent company.

Criteria for selection

The specific criteria an MNE uses to select its international assignees has a lot to do with their future success in the international assignment. First this section takes a look at a number of criteria that are used by various global firms to select their international assignees. Then the section examines the consequences of making mistakes either in choosing international assignees or in preparing and supporting them in their assignments or in helping them make a successful return to home at the end of their international assignments. The most important selection criteria for international assignments include job suitability, cultural adaptability and desire for international assignment.

- *Job suitability.* Most firms base their choices for international assignments on candidates' technical expertise.[31] That is, the primary focus is on their ability to perform the target job requirements. Experience suggests, however, that all the other topics discussed in this book are at least as important as the individual's job competencies. Nevertheless, at least in smaller and medium-sized firms (and, regrettably, still too often in larger firms), the parent company supervisor usually makes the choice of individual to be sent on an international assignment and that choice is usually based on the individual's perceived ability to fill a perceived (and usually immediate) functional or technical need in the foreign operation.

- *Cultural adaptability.* Experience in MNEs suggests that cultural adaptability is at least as important to the successful completion of an overseas assignment as is the individual's technical ability. Expatriates must be able to adjust to their new and often alien environments while effectively delivering their technical and managerial expertise. They must graciously accept their new cultures but not at the expense of not getting their jobs done. While technical expertise is usually important (and the primary reason most firms send a particular expatriate to a foreign assignment), the principal difficulty faced by most expatriates lies in the inability of the managers and their families to adapt to the foreign cultures. Maybe not surprisingly, American firms tend to be more likely to place the most emphasis on the individual's work experience and expertise than is the case for many MNEs from other countries.
- *Desire for foreign assignment (candidate and family).* Since adaptation to the foreign culture is so important to an international assignees performance, his or her desire for that foreign assignment is critical to their willingness to make the necessary efforts to adjust. This needs to be assessed in the early stages of candidate review.

Several companies and consultants have compiled profiles of successful international assignees and, from these, developed international assignee selection tests. These profiles are then used to screen potential international assignee candidates, on the generally valid assumption that candidates with similar profiles are more likely to do well in international assignments. These profiles usually include factors such as experience, education, personal interests and activities, signs of flexibility, family situation, and desire for such assignment.

When an organization first begins to develop international business, it normally doesn't have the luxury of developing its own international managers in-house. And it may not have employees who already have the necessary knowledge and experience or cultural and language competencies. It will need to recruit such people from the outside or acquire the expertise from consulting firms. (Of course, many firms pursue international opportunities with inexperienced managers and sales people, but this inevitably leads to months, and often years, of frustration while these managers "learn the [international] business.") Such expertise can also sometimes be recruited from the overseas countries, themselves. And, over the long term, future foreign managers can often be recruited from local universities of either the country of the parent firm or the countries in which the firm is operating.

Selection methods

Different organizations rely on differing procedures in their selection of individuals for international assignments. They rely on varying criteria, as summarized above.

And they use one or more of the following in application of those criteria. This is just a short summary of selection methods and illustrates that methods used in selection for international assignments is probably not much different from the methods used in domestic staffing decisions. As with everything international, however, the differences lie in the impact of culture in how these procedures are applied and in the focus in each procedure.

- *Interviews (international assignee and spouse/partner)* may be best done with a representative of the home country (representing the technical requirements of the position), a representative of the host country (possibly the host manager), and an interculturalist, i. e., someone with the ability to assess the candidate's and family's ability to adjust to the foreign culture.
- *Formal assessment.* There are a number of formal assessment instruments designed by industrial psychologists that primarily evaluate a candidate's personal traits and competencies that have been found to be important to successful foreign cultural adjustment, such as adaptability, flexibility, openness to new experiences, and good interpersonal skills. Critical here is whether or not any such instruments are reliable and valid for predicting expatriate success. IHR or other managers who seek to use such instruments need to make sure they get evidence of their reliability and validity from any consultant or manager that is requesting their use.
- *Committee decision.* In many large MNEs, the process of selecting individuals for international assignments is a committee decision, a committee made up of someone from corporate HR, home country HR, host country manager, director of development, and the individual's functional manager, with a decision based on the individual's preferences, assessment of past performance and future potential, needs of the foreign assignment, and developmental needs of the individual candidate.
- *Career planning.* The choice of international assignee may be made as one step in the individual's career and succession plan with the MNE.
- *Self-selection.* Many MNEs use some combination of the above procedures but rely, in the end, on self-selection by the candidate (after being accepted through the above "screens"). In particular, the MNE is interested in candidates taking the time (and usually using some type of formal self-assessment instrument) to look at the issues involved with relocation to a foreign country and culture and assessing whether they think they are ready or have the necessary skills, experience, or attitudes to be successful in the overseas assignment. Such self-assessment may result in the individual realizing they aren't ready, now, for such a move, but that they would like to take such an assignment at some later time in their career. So, rather than relocating now, they begin a process to gain the skills and experiences necessary to be chosen for such an assignment at a later date. This self-assessment process then is part of a larger career planning process. Candidates may also self-opt out when they realize the importance of their family members (and their lack of desire to relocate to another country) in making the international assignment successful.

- *Internal job posting and individual bid,* usually then combined with interviews and/or other assessment activities.
- *Recommendations* from senior executives or line managers with overseas human resource needs.
- *Assessment centers.* A few organizations use assessment centers as a tool for evaluating candidates for suitability for foreign assignments.[32] But it is rare for MNEs to use assessment centers to adequately think through the impact of culture on everything from the nature of the exercises used to the cultural sensitivities of the evaluators used, in order to be able to assess an international assignee candidate for an international assignment.

The actual techniques used are probably an extension of procedures used for domestic staffing decisions. Thus, there may be an *ad hoc* nature to this, using whatever technique seems easiest and quickest given the circumstances surrounding any particular need for an international assignee. Smaller firms are likely to use less formal and more *ad hoc* procedures, while larger, more experienced firms are likely to have developed more formal and standardized procedures. The primary outcome of the selection process is to choose individuals who will stay for the duration of their global assignments and who will accomplish the tasks for which they were sent abroad. Executives who make these choices, should, therefore, consider both enterprise-based as well as individual- and family-based factors to enhance the probability that the international assignment will be successful.

Mistakes and failures

MNEs want to select managers who, with their families, will be most able to adapt to another country and who also possess the necessary expertise to get the job done. Many firms that lack experience in international operations often overlook the importance of cultural adaptation. Indeed, even more experienced firms may do this, as well. This attitude, combined with firms' inclination to choose employees for foreign relocation because of their technical competencies, generally leads to individuals being sent on international assignments without the benefit of training or help in acculturation.[33] This may—and all too often does—lead to failures in foreign assignments with individuals returning home early, or even being dismissed in the foreign locale.

Success or failure is a more complex issue than simply not completing the assignment.[34] Success or failure for international assignees is usually defined in terms of three types of failure: dropout, brownout, or turnover upon repatriation. An international assignee *dropout* returns early from the assignment but usually stays with company. Although this is considered a failure, in fact, it is better than not realizing at all that the assignment was a mistake. In a brownout failure, the international assignee does not return early but performs poorly and is ineffective in the assignment. As a result of this failure the international assignee may initiate projects that are costly and not effective, damage relation with the local employees, or drive out high-potential local nationals. A last type of failure is when the assignee leaves the company within one year upon repatriation. This is the most costly type of failure for the company.

These three forms of assignment failure are the traditional forms of failure that MNEs have focused on. However, international assignment failure can also be defined in terms of poor overall performance in the foreign assignment, personal dissatisfaction with the experience, lack of adjustment to local conditions, lack of acceptance by local nationals, or the inability to identify and train a local successor (see Box 5.2). In addition, a number of factors seem to influence the severity of expatriate failure rates (and help to explain why Japanese and European firms don't experience the high rates of expatriate failure experienced by many American firms). These include length of assignment (longer assignments appear to be based on the employer's willingness to provide the international assignee with more time to adjust and to "get up to speed" in job performance, which is more common among Japanese and European firms), receipt of training and orientation (with training and orientation about the new country and culture being associated with more successful adaptation), lack of participation by HR in the selection process, too much emphasis placed on expatriates' technical expertise to the exclusion of other attributes that might aid in adaptation, and lack of support provided by home office for international assignees and their families while on foreign assignment.

BOX 5.2 DEFINITION OF EXPATRIATE FAILURE

- Usually defined in terms of *early return home* or *termination*
- But could also be defined in terms of:
  - Poor quality of performance in foreign assignment
  - Employee not fully utilized during assignment
  - Personal dissatisfaction with experience (by expatriate or family)
  - Lack of adjustment to local conditions
  - No acceptance by local nationals
  - Damage to overseas business relationships
  - Not recognizing or missing overseas business opportunities
  - Inability to identify and/or train a local successor
  - Leave soon after repatriation
  - Not use foreign experience in assignment after repatriation
- Compounding factors
  - Length of assignment
  - Degree of concern about repatriation
  - Overemphasis in selection on technical competence to disregard of other necessary attributes
  - Degree of training for overseas assignment
  - Degree of support while on overseas assignment

A number of surveys and studies have found the most important factors in the early return of expatriates to lie in the inability of their families (and/or themselves) to adjust to the foreign assignment.[35] To the extent that preparation is provided, often the parent company will provide that preparation only for the new transferee, not for his or her family. In addition, after arrival in the foreign locale, international assignees have the advantage of personal contacts and involvement with their colleagues at work, while their spouses and families are often left on their own to "figure out" their new surroundings and to develop local relationships, often with little understanding of the culture and an inability to speak or read the language. Thus the individual expatriate often finds adjustment easier and less "lonely" than does his or her spouse and family. Box 5.3 lists the most common reasons for expatriate failure, when defined as early return or termination from the foreign assignment.

Of course, the international assignee's ability to adjust and/or difficulty in merging with the new culture can also be a major handicap. Too often, expatriates bring stereotypes and prejudices against the foreign culture—as well as strongly felt biases in favor of their own culture's ways of doing things—that keep them from feeling comfortable in their new foreign assignments. And, lastly, when the employer makes a mistake by assigning an employee who lacks the necessary technical abilities or motivation to perform the foreign job requirements, the expatriate is likely to be sent home early.

BOX 5.3 **REASONS FOR EXPATRIATE FAILURE**

- Inability of spouse/partner to adjust or spouse/partner dissatisfaction
- Inability of expatriate to adjust
- Other family-related problems
- Mistake in candidate/expatriate selection or just does not meet expectations
- Expatriate's personality or lack of emotional maturity
- Expatriate's inability to cope with larger responsibilities of overseas work
- Expatriate's lack of technical competence
- Expatriate's lack of motivation to work overseas
- Dissatisfaction with quality of life in foreign assignment
- Dissatisfaction with compensation and benefits
- Inadequate cultural and language preparation
- Inadequate support for IA and family while on overseas assignment

Sources adapted from National Foreign Trade Council (NFTC), Society for Human Resource Management (SHRM), and GMAC Global Relocation Services (GMAC GRS)/Windham International *Global Relocation Trends Annual Survey* Reports, 1993–2007; Stroh, L. K., Black, J. S., Mendenhall, M. E. and Gregersen, H. B. (2005), *International Assignments: An Integration of Strategy, Research, & Practice*, Mahwah, NJ/London: Erlbaum; and Tung, R. L. (1987), Expatriate assignments: Enhancing success and minimizing failure, *Academy of Management Executive*, 1 (2): 117–126.

As suggested earlier, the rates of early return for expatriates are different for different countries. The rates of early return appear to be highest for American firms, with rates reported from as low as 10 percent to as high as 80 percent, with a common failure rate in the 30–40 percent range, with the average cost per failure to the parent company ranging from US$500,000 to US$1,000,000 or more.[36] These costs only involve the lost costs of relocation and compensation and benefits, they don't include the costs to the overseas operation of the loss of such key personnel, or the costs associated with the other forms of failed assignments. On the other hand, European and Japanese multinationals rarely experience failure rates over 10 percent, which seems to have to do with, in the case of European international assignees, more exposure to differing cultures and languages, and in the case of the Japanese, the generally longer adjustment periods accommodated with their longer assignments (and, possibly, to the unwillingness in the Japanese culture to offend anyone—a "face" offense—by admitting failure and by cutting an international assignee's assignment short due to performance or adjustment problems).[37]

Mistakes in selecting international assignees

MNEs typically do a number of things that lead to problems with their international assignees.[38] These include:

- Decision to relocate people made with too little lead time.
- Assignees not provided with any or adequate cultural training and/or language training.
- Spouses or partners not included in the decision to relocate.
- Spouses/partners and kids not included on pre-assignment visits.
- Spouses/partners and kids not included in language lessons.
- Spouses/partners and kids not included in cultural training.
- Spouses/partners do not receive counseling on jobs and other opportunities.
- Spouses have no home office contact.

Challenges to successful staffing with international assignees

There are many challenges to MNEs in their quests to ensure that the best employees are selected for international assignments. The following paragraphs summarize eight issues: spouses and partners, language, family, female expatriates, lifestyle, localization (or "going native"), career development, and costs.

Trailing spouses or partners

It is not just the business situation that determines expatriate success. A number of personal and cultural issues are also important. For example, research by Organizational Resources Counselors (ORC) found that international HR managers believe that dual-career-couple overseas assignments are among the top five challenges they face.[39] According to a survey by Bennett Associates of accompanying career spouses, worldwide, active involvement in the career of the accompanying spouse is the type of assistance preferred by dual-career couples above all other possible interventions.[40]

According to surveys by Runzheimer International and ORC, nearly 50 percent of firms offer some form of spouse assistance for dual-career international assignees.[41] Of those firms, 87 percent provide *ad hoc* interventions (helping as and when in ways that seem necessary) but only 13 percent have formal policies. Support programs for spouses fall into three broad categories: personal adjustment, career maintenance, and offset of loss of income. These surveys find that support services by employers for trailing spouses were critical to their satisfaction with their foreign relocations. The types of interventions—as appropriate—found in these surveys included the following:

- Pre-acceptance assessment sessions and site visits.
- Career and life planning counseling.
- Pre-departure and re-entry job hunting trips.
- Couple/family counseling.
- Specially adapted cross-cultural/language training.
- Relocation assistance to help spouse settle in and network quickly.
- Search firm retained to help spouse find employment.
- Company employment or consulting opportunities.
- Intra- and inter-company networking and job search assistance.
- Visa and work permit assistance.
- Shorter-term assignments for expatriate employee.
- Commuter marriage support.
- Tuition and/or training reimbursement.
- Paying for professional development trips.
- Arranging and paying for child care provision.
- Partial compensation replacement for spouse.
- Increased employee compensation, bonus, and non-cash benefits.
- Re-entry outplacement services (to find job upon return to home country).
- Tax equalization for second income.
- Spouse "inconvenience" or incentive payment.
- Set allowance to be applied to a "cafeteria" selection of assistance programs.

Language

One of the continuing issues with both international assignees and foreign work forces concerns the issue of language. Do international assignees on foreign assignment need to learn the language of the country to which they are posted? And to what extent do local employees need to know or learn the language of the parent firm? These issues are discussed at some length in Chapter 3 on culture and in Chapter 6 on training and development. Like concern with cultural differences, concern with language differences also impacts most of international business. And it certainly is an issue with the selection of international assignees.

Even though English has become the international language of business, with most large MNEs using English among their top management around the world, it is just as important for international assignees to have a working knowledge of the language of the countries to which they are assigned as it is for the local management of subsidiaries to speak the language of the parent firm. International assignees need to speak their customers' languages—if their business relationships are going to flourish.[42] MNEs approach the need to provide language training in a variety of ways, but they typically find the increased numbers of employees who can speak foreign languages an asset in the development of their global businesses.

Language training, on a wide scale, can be quite expensive, in both employee time and in money. For example, Siemens, with over 400,000 employees around the world, spends millions of euros a year for language training.[43] It offers ten languages, with training divided into eight stages, all requiring eighty to 100 hours each. Lower-level executives are told that one and preferably two extra languages are necessary for continued success in the company. Siemens sees this as critical to its ongoing success as one of the most important electronics enterprises in the world.

In surveys of expatriates, language is often mentioned as the most important personal or professional challenge in their assignments.[44] An expatriate living in Germany says: "Speaking only English during an assignment is a big mistake. You can be a friend and a colleague speaking English, but to be 'one of them,' you must speak their language."[45] An expatriate living in Brazil offers the advice: "Persevere with the language at all costs."[46] Often, one major factor in the inability of MNEs to fill key expatriate assignments is the lack of language expertise and preparation. And as is discussed in this section, many firms do not provide any opportunities for language training. Interestingly, some countries seem to understand this problem better than others. For example, maybe only a third of American MNEs provide language training, while, in comparison, almost all Japanese MNEs offer both language and cultural training.[47]

English has become the international language of business for a number of reasons.[48] Even so, not all interactions are likely to take place in English, particularly within the host country. As stated above, dealing with customers, suppliers, and employees is often best done in the local language. Still, transnational exchanges are more and more expected to take place in English. When the top worldwide staff of Swiss-Swedish ABB Asea Brown Boveri meet, the one common language for their joint sessions is English. And when the Italian middle manager for the Milan, Italy, branch of Commerz Banc of Germany phones to headquarters in Frankfurt—which she must do many times a day—the conversation takes place in English. Of course, all the worldwide managers above a particular level for firms like Unilever (a Dutch–British firm), ABB Asea Brown Boveri, IBM, or Toyota Motor Car Company, all of which operate in seventy or more countries, must speak English.

It is in fact now estimated that English is spoken worldwide by more people than any other language, by at least one billion persons.[49] One result of this may be that employing local nationals that are fluent in English may be as important as requiring expatriates to be fluent in the local language(s). Even so, it is clear that an ability to speak the local language is still quite important—for international assignees to deal with local nationals and local customers and suppliers, as well as to adapt to the host culture (and be accepted into that culture), both of which are major keys to successful expatriate assignments.

Families

Many of the challenges presented by international assignees involve their families. Increasingly, the types of managers and specialists that either seek foreign assignments or are asked by their employers to relocate have spouses (or partners) and/or children. Often the spouses or partners are involved in their own careers (as discussed in the first topic of this section on challenges). If the international assignee candidate has an unmarried partner, it is likely to be quite difficult for the MNE to acquire a visa for the partner. The international assignees may have problems with their adolescent children, health problems with family members, dependent parents whom they have responsibility for, marital conflicts, or mental health problems of their own, such as depression—or, even, something like a flying phobia, or special education requirements for their children (such as children with disabilities or learning problems or gifted children—or even children getting ready for college). In addition, candidates for expatriation (or members of their families) with medical problems like AIDS, substance or alcohol abuse, or problems like multiple sclerosis, can cause what may seem like insurmountable problems for IHRM and the firm in being able to get overseas work visas. These types of individual or family problems are both a problem in expatriate selection as well as posing problems for acceptance into and adaptation to foreign cultures. And yet firms, in order to find the numbers of expatriates they need and stay away from possible charges of illegal discrimination in staffing decisions, must accept and find ways to accommodate international assignee candidates with these types of problems.

Many of these concerns make a health screening of the international assignee and her or his spouse and family members advisable, both to determine if a health problem exists that might either preclude relocation or be aggravated by a relocation or need special support services. Often even minor health problems are not treatable in the foreign country because qualified health professionals or facilities are not available.

Probably the most important of the family challenges, today, revolve around the dual-career couple and problems with relocating non-married partners. In both cases, an international assignee candidate's partner can pose difficult-to-resolve challenges for IHR.

Women expatriates

Most international assignees are men. Gradually, over the last twenty-five years or so, the percentage of women on international assignments, as determined by surveys, has increased from about 5–6 percent to 20–22 percent today.[50] This low percentage may have as much to do with stereotypes about foreign acceptance of women in professional or managerial roles as to the realities in the host countries.[51] Early research showed that one of the key factors in women not receiving overseas assignments was that selecting executives generally assumed that women would not be accepted in the foreign culture.[52] Other barriers to women receiving international assignments include their dual-career marriages, domestic managers not choosing them, perceptions that women were not interested in such assignments, etc.[53] In recent years the number of women who have successfully taken on foreign assignments, even to countries such as Japan, Brazil, and China, has risen considerably, although it still is a relatively small proportion of the total international assignee population, except in some industries, such as banking.[54] Of course the assignment of women international assignees, except in very specialized professional positions, is likely to remain limited to some countries such as Saudi Arabia.[55]

The evidence, though, suggests that the fact that there are only a comparatively few women working abroad for MNEs may be due more to bias and stereotyping in the home country and company than to prejudicial treatment or limitations in the host country or foreign subsidiary.[56] Women are not only as likely to welcome such opportunities as are their male colleagues (for the same reasons their male counterparts seek them), but they often perform better than their male colleagues, even in traditionally male-dominated cultures, such as in Asia and the Middle East.[57] As an American professional woman on assignment in China put it:

> I feel more respected as a manager in China than I do in the United States. The Chinese value two qualities in their leaders: competence and *ren* [warmheartedness, benevolence, and readiness to care for others]. If a leader is *ren*, he or she will receive subordinates' loyalty in turn. Adopting *ren* behavior is more common by American female assignees than by American males.[58]

Typically, female expatriates are treated first as representatives of their firms or as professionals, and rarely experience the bias that the stereotypes from their home firms presume. This isn't meant to imply that women never experience stereotyping and treatment in line with cultural norms that may not accept women in the workplace, except in very menial tasks. This does happen.[59] But the evidence suggests that women are frequently quite successful in international assignments.[60]

In addition, women expatriates also have trailing spouses and unmarried partners and families to consider, and thus need to be given the same consideration received by their male counterparts. Women are clearly interested in international positions and have demonstrated that they can perform well in global assignments.[61] Increased global competition pressures MNEs to make the best use of all of their resources, including their women employees.[62]

Lifestyle
Increasingly MNEs are having to deal with employees who either seek foreign assignments or who are eligible for such postings who live what might be referred to as "alternative" lifestyles that may not be acceptable in target foreign locations. This might involve "gay" or unmarried couples or single parents or employees who live with their parents or who are taking care of elderly parents. Or it just might concern employees who are involved in outside-of-work activities that are very important to

the individual and they may not be able to pursue them in the host location. All of these situations create challenges for IHR to overcome.

Localization, or "going native"

One challenge that has been confronted by many MNEs involves expatriates that stay for an extended period (usually at the firm's request, but sometimes at the international assignee's request) in a foreign assignment (beyond their original assignments).[63] This becomes an issue because international assignees in this situation continue to draw their expatriate allowances and incentives, even though they have learned to live "like locals." These particular international assignees may be critical to the success of the foreign operations, which may make it difficult to change their status. Often they have married a local and are raising a family in the foreign locale. To deal with this issue, many firms have developed policies, such as requiring that all international assignees convert to a local compensation package if they stay on their assignment for longer than the assignment contract period. Even with such a policy, it still creates problems for dealing with this particular situation. Without such a policy, this can be an especially challenging problem.

Career development

Since it is often expected that an international assignment is highly developmental, and since many firms now expect managers above some level in the organization to have international assignment experience, it is becoming more common to make a posting to a foreign assignment a critical part of an individual's career plan.[64] The challenge is to manage this process, both from the standpoint of the organization (where key managers may have their own ideas as to who they want to fill open foreign positions) and the individual, who may not see the career advantages. The firm may state the importance to one's career advancement, but observation suggests that international assignees on return to the parent firm are not always given assignments that use or take advantage of the foreign experience.

Costs of international assignments

From the firm's perspective, a major international assignee challenge is to contain costs. Moving employees from country to country is expensive, both in direct remuneration (compensation and benefits), and in the administration of their relocation expenses. Consequently, many MNEs are searching for ways to reduce the costs.[65] For example, MNEs are dealing with these high costs by replacing international assignees with more short-term assignments and extended business trips, outsourcing the administrative aspects of managing international assignees, and looking for ways to reduce the compensation incentives and add-ons that make international assignments so expensive. And at least some MNEs are recognizing they can minimize the costs of failed assignments through developing better selection processes, better preparation and orientation, better destination support services for both international assignees and their families, and improved repatriation processes. But, even though firms say international assignees are too expensive, some surveys find that many firms are not doing much to counter the high costs.[66]

Repatriation

At the end of the assignment, the international assignee either repatriates to the home country, is redeployed to another country, or becomes localized in the host country. Repatriation involves the move of the international assignee and family back "home" from the foreign assignment. For many expatriates and their families, the move "back home" is even more difficult than the original move abroad. Even so, it is often overlooked or minimized in the management of the total expatriation process.[67]

The international experience is generally challenging, exciting, highly developmental, and full of visibility and exposure for the assignee. The international assignee is the representative of the parent company, of headquarters, and is therefore looked to for perspective, help, and favors. In addition, because the compensation practices of most MNEs reward their international assignees quite well, the international assignee and family typically live quite well in the foreign location, often better than they did "at home." Thus expatriates usually return from such experience quite "charged"—and with high expectations that their employers will use their new experiences and excitement and family and friends back home will share their enthusiasm.

But if an MNE is to reap the benefits of its international assignees' learning while on foreign assignments, it is imperative that these valuable employees stay with the organization long enough to share their experience. This should encourage MNEs to place a strong emphasis on the repatriation experience of their international assignees.

But the reality is more likely to be "out of sight, out of mind." Firms often fail to use the experience or knowledge gained internationally and most likely have not thought much about the career implications of this experience. Typically, the repatriate is reassigned to a position similar to the one he or she left two or three years before, while their colleagues may have been promoted. Repatriates often find it difficult to relate the value of their global experience to managers with a domestic focus.[68] Domestic managers, themselves usually without any international experience, cannot relate. (This is also likely to be true for the expatriate's friends and colleagues.) For the repatriate, this makes re-entry and the job search within the company quite challenging. The global experience may be viewed as helpful to the specific foreign situation; but the domestic manager usually views domestic experience as more important. To many domestic line managers, developing international experience and a global mind-set to operate internationally is the CEO's problem. Globalization is often not a concern to the line manager trying to achieve a specific set of local objectives.

For these reasons, career planning for expatriates needs to begin prior to an international assignment and to be updated regularly during the assignment. The assignment needs to be part of a larger plan for the firm so that the repatriate returns to a specific position that uses the international learning and experience. One of the programs used by some firms is a back-home mentor or sponsor, who is both a contact in the home office for the expatriate and who is at least partially responsible for looking after the interests and prospects of the expatriate while he or she is on assignment, but who also provides an avenue for keeping the international assignee informed about what is going on back home.

The readjustment is challenging not only for the international assignee but for the family members as well. Repatriates and their families often have trouble adjusting to the lifestyle back home. Reverse cultural shock (readjustment to the home culture) is often experienced by the international assignee (and accompanying family). Most people are changed by the foreign experience and not only must relearn their original culture and lifestyle, but probably view it quite differently than when they left. Indeed, time does not stand still while the expatriate is abroad. While changes at home may be all but invisible to those who experience them gradually (those at home), to the returnees they can be overwhelming.[69] Just as MNEs need to provide their expatriates with preparation for the move abroad, so must they prepare their expatriates for the move back home and prepare themselves to use these individuals' overseas experiences in their home assignments. This preparation can make the difference between an overall favorable attitude by the repatriates about the whole experience and a failed expatriate experience. Ultimately, an unfavorable attitude will likely lead to the individual returnee's turnover. A dissatisfied repatriated employee is more likely to resign and seek a position with another employer which will utilize that individual's foreign experiences and skills.

Inpatriation

The term "inpatriate" was developed to describe particular employees (HCNs or TCNs) who are relocated from a foreign subsidiary or joint venture to the parent company in the headquarters country. This posting is usually for a relatively short period of time (from a few months to one or two years) and is for the purpose of teaching the "subsidiary" employee about the products and culture of the parent firm and to introduce the employee to the operations, ways of thinking, and corporate culture of the headquarters.[70] Increasingly, these assignees are also used to fill functional or technical needs in the parent company for a limited period of time or to serve on multinational teams for a specified period of time. The challenges of selecting and managing inpatriates are basically the same as those for expatriates. From the standpoint of the foreign subsidiary, the inpatriate is an "expatriate," going on a foreign assignment. From the standpoint of headquarters, the individual is an inpatriate. In this situation, the issues for IHRM are to consider the experience of headquarters in receiving relocated employees—in addition to the "normal" issues related to the experiences of any relocated employees.

Successful expatriation and "best practice"

Expatriation success is the flip side of the issue of expatriate failure. Typically, expatriate success is defined as: (1) completion of the foreign assignment (achieving the original goals and objectives); (2) cross-cultural adjustment while on assignment;

and (3) good performance on the job while on the foreign assignment.[71] Sometimes these factors are viewed as a unitary construct, that is, they are seen as a package of issues that go together to define a successful assignment. But research shows them to be separate constructs, meaning that each needs attention.[72] And this demonstrates that the foreign environment (company and national culture and practices), local management, technical skills, and expatriate personal characteristics all ultimately play a role in expatriate success.

A number of IHR consulting practices, surveys, and research projects have identified what might be considered "exemplary practices" in the selection of international assignees.[73] A summary of these findings can be found in Box 5.4. Following these suggestions will go a long way toward helping IHR to be successful in its management of international assignees.

HOST COUNTRY NATIONALS

In general, MNEs staff their subsidiaries—at least below the top management levels—with local nationals (a.k.a. host country nationals, HCNs). At times, these workers may be supplanted by TCNs, described in the next section, and international assignees from the home office or region. Of course, whether or not there are enough potential employees with adequate training, education, and technical, business, managerial and language skills is always of utmost importance to an MNE strategy of staffing with HCNs. In the case where the decision is made to locate a subsidiary or business unit in a country where the local population lacks the necessary education or training (or there is a shortage of the types of workers the MNE needs, as is increasingly the case, for example, in China[74]), then IHR must find other ways to staff the necessary work force, for example by training locals, hiring TCNs, or bringing in parent company international assignees.

Relying on local managerial talent

The expensive international assignee and their not infrequent failure in assignment, combined with a general trend toward local staffing (using and developing local talent), regiocentrism (using regional talent), and geocentrism (a truly global approach to resources, markets, and staffing), have led in recent years to a greater reliance on local managers in foreign operations.[75] Foreign nationals already know the language and culture and do not require huge relocation expenditures. In addition, host country governments tend to look favorably on a greater degree of local control and the development and use of local personnel and may have legislation that requires the use of local workers or foreign enterprises and JVs. Indeed, some countries require that most staff come from the local labor force. On the negative side, however, local managers may have an inadequate knowledge of home office goals and procedures and may have difficulty with the parent company language. Thus the staffing of

BOX 5.4 **BEST PRACTICE IN INTERNATIONAL ASSIGNEE SELECTION**

- Involve HR in global strategic planning
- Link each assignment to corporate strategies
- Involve HR in assignment decisions and support services
- Help assignees and their families make the smoothest transition into, during, and out of assignments
- Utilize an assessment process that promotes the selection of the best employees for international positions
- Administer consistent international assignments through comprehensive programs that cover each step from design of the assignment to return of the employee and family

More specifically, these reports suggest:

- Periodically review relocation policies and practices to ensure fit with the current business and strategic situation
- Train home office staff in dealing with international assignees
- Be honest about the job and location when recruiting candidates for foreign assignments
- Provide adequate lead time for relocation
- Involve spouse/partner/family at the outset of the expatriation process (i.e., at the beginning of the selection process)
- Provide language and cultural training for international assignee and family
- Recognize the importance of dual-career and trailing spouse/partner issues, financially and otherwise (pre-departure job counseling, networking contacts, education and training, job hunting assistance, legal assistance for work permits, career assistance upon repatriation, etc.)
- Provide pre-assignment site visit for whole family
- Don't neglect repatriation issues

Sources GMAC Global Relocation Services/Windham International, National Foreign Trade Council, and SHRM Global Forum (2007 and previous years), *Global Relocation Trends Annual Survey Report*, New York: GMAC GRS/Windham International; Lomax, S. (2001), *Best Practices for Managers and Expatriates*, New York: Wiley; Stroh, L. K., Black, J. S., Mendenhall, M. E. and Gregersen, H. B. (2005), *International Assignments: An Integration of Strategy, Research, and Practice*, Mahwah, NJ/London: Erlbaum; Vance, C. M. and Paik, Y. (2006), *Managing a Global Workforce*, Armonk, NY: Sharpe.

foreign positions—particularly key managerial and technical ones—is necessarily decided on a case-by-case basis. Firms that are new to international business may feel more comfortable having home country managers in control in the firm's new foreign locales, while MNEs that have been global for many years and have operations around the world may find it easier to operate with fewer parent country nationals on international assignments. It is also likely that these global MNEs will be more likely to move managers and functional specialists from country to country for developmental purposes as well as for control and coordination reasons, rather than using traditional expatriates. Lastly, the need for large numbers of highly qualified personnel has also made it increasingly necessary to use larger numbers of foreign (host country/local) nationals.[76]

Most MNEs favor hiring local nationals for foreign subsidiaries, home country nationals at headquarters and, where a regional organization exists, a mix of foreign and home country managers for regional positions. Within this general approach, however, the nationality mix will vary with the nature of the firm's business and its product strategy. Where area expertise plays a major role, as in the case of consumer goods and/or a limited product line, the use of home country personnel for overseas assignments will be minimal. Where product expertise is highly important and/or industrial markets are being served, home country personnel will be used more extensively for foreign assignments because they generally have quick access to the home country sources of supply and technical information. Service industries also tend to have more home country personnel in foreign posts, particularly where the firm is serving home country multinationals in foreign areas, as has been the case in banking.[77]

THIRD COUNTRY NATIONALS

TCNs tend to be used particularly in areas where there is either a shortage of people with the skills the firm needs or where there is relatively free movement of people from one country to another. In recent years, with the global shortage of, for example, IT and computer specialists and engineers, many firms have relied on the hiring of people from third countries who have these skills to fill positions in their foreign subsidiaries, just as they do at home. And, increasingly, TCNs are being used if parent company managers and technicians are not readily available or not available in the numbers needed, for example, to make major staffing commitments to new operations in China and India.[78]

While much of the world's skilled and unskilled human resources are being produced in the developing world, most of the well paid jobs are being generated in the cities of the industrialized world (or their enterprises)—although this is changing as more developed country firms subcontract to firms in developing countries, hire employees offshore to work via telecommunications, invest directly in operations in the developing world, and entrepreneurs and business leaders in developing countries develop their own successful global enterprises. This increasing equality of jobs and talent between where the potential employees are and where the jobs are has several implications:

- It will trigger massive relocations of people, including immigrants, temporary workers, retirees, and visitors. The greatest relocations will involve young, well educated workers flocking to jobs, wherever they are located.
- It will lead some industrialized nations to reconsider their protectionist immigration policies as they come to rely on and compete for foreign-born talent.
- It may boost the fortunes of nations with "surplus" human capital. Specifically, it could help well educated but economically underdeveloped countries such as China, the Philippines, India, Egypt, Cuba, Poland, Hungary, Brazil, Argentina, South Africa and, maybe, Mexico.
- It will compel labor-short, immigrant-poor nations like Japan to improve labor productivity dramatically to avoid slower economic growth. They will use more technology and transfer more work to labor-surplus and cheaper-labor locales.
- It will lead to a gradual standardization of labor practices among industrialized countries. Within fifty years or so, European standards of vacation time (five to six weeks) will likely be common in the US. The forty-hour work week will have been accepted in Japan. And world standards governing workplace safety and employee rights will emerge.[79]

Much attention has focused on the current or looming labor shortages in the industrialized world, particularly in the US, Europe, and Japan, due to their aging populations.[80] Yet the overall world labor supply continues to grow (primarily in the developing world). In addition, the growth in the labor force in the developing world is magnified by the entry of women into the labor force, a phenomenon which has pretty well worked itself out in most of the developed world (although not all of it, as participation rates for women are still quite low in some developed countries, such as Germany and Japan). When these demographic differences are combined with the different rates of economic growth between the developing and developing world, it becomes more likely that firms in the developed world will increasingly seek workers among the developing countries and will move jobs to those countries, as well. Just as product and service markets have become or are becoming global, such is also happening to labor markets. In one sense, this may alleviate the pressures created by labor surpluses in developing countries; but in another sense it may also exacerbate the economic differences between the countries of the developing world and those of the developed world as MNEs hire the educated and trained citizens of developing countries, lessening those countries' available human resources for their own developmental needs.

An extension of the focus on local managers and technical specialists, as described at the end of the previous section on HCNs, involves the increasing willingness to look for management and technical expertise from all countries for assignment to any country. These TCNs are often the solution to overseas staffing problems.

IMMIGRATION LAW

One last topic of concern to IHRM staffing concerns the nature and application of immigration law. This topic was introduced in Chapter 4, but needs consideration here, because it is central to staffing the global firm, as new immigrants are hired, visas are acquired for international assignees, and HR managers work with officials in other countries as they arrange work visas for the managers and technicians they send abroad as expatriates. It is beyond the scope of this book to examine the wide variety of immigration regulations found in varying countries. Suffice it to say that every country controls immigration quite closely and now, with increased concern over global terrorism, most countries are even more concerned about the level and nature of immigration into their countries. It is necessary for IHR managers to either manage all the forms of visas and immigration issues their firms confront or to know where to get the necessary expertise to ensure that the firm adheres to every nation's laws and policies.

CONCLUSION

This chapter focused on the IHRM responsibility for staffing. It explained issues related to global work force planning, recruiting, and selection in multinational enterprises, but primarily it focused on expatriation and repatriation, the movement of employees from country to country, and the employment of host country and third country nationals. Because the use of parent country nationals is so important to IHR in MNEs, much of this chapter discussed the selection and management of PCNs, including their failures and adaptation to foreign assignments, and their repatriation at the end of their assignments.

The chapter examined the difficulties experienced in the selection and management of international assignees and suggested some of the approaches successful MNEs use to ensure positive experiences with those expatriates and repatriates. In addition, the chapter discussed problems that MNEs experience with non-traditional international assignees, such as women.

The biggest issue for most MNEs in the management of their international assignee system is the alignment of the competing interests of the firm, IHRM, and international assignees and their families. The business is concerned about its globalization and needs quick action, to generate new revenues, and to manage the costs and risks involved with doing that. IHR need adequate lead time to find and select effective international assignees; they need a low enough case load of international assignees to be able to provide good service; they want to be able to apply an effective process for selecting and developing quality international assignee candidates; and they desire to be able to apply a consistent policy of treatment of international assignees. And international assignees themselves, and their families, desire adequate compensation for their personal and career sacrifices in relocating; they want their family concerns to be given central priority; and they expect to be able to come back to a career promotion that will take advantage of their overseas experience.

MNE experience suggest a number of steps that can be taken to ensure the success of international assignments. And when the steps are followed, experience suggests that MNEs will enjoy greater success in the global operations.

GUIDED DISCUSSION QUESTIONS

1 Why are planning and forecasting a global work force so difficult?

2 Why are so many countries bothered by their "brain drain"?

3 If you are given the opportunity in your next job to go on an extended foreign assignment, what types of support programs would you expect or ask for?

4 If you ever have the responsibility to select an associate for a foreign assignment, how would you go about doing that and what characteristics would you look for to ensure success?

5 What do you think is the most significant challenge for IHR in managing international assignees? Why?

VIGNETTE 5.1   TALENT MANAGEMENT IN EMERGING MARKETS

Global talent management at Standard Chartered Bank

Standard Chartered Bank has turned the emerging talent and skills shortage challenge around. They have created a "talent factory" that makes it capable of growing its own talent from within instead of raiding them from other organizations. Standard Chartered, an international retail and corporate bank with headquarters in London, derives 90 percent of its profits from emerging markets in Asia, Africa and the Middle East. Operating in fifty-seven countries, it has 64,000 employees with over 100 different nationalities. With Standard Chartered's declared goal of measurably increasing leadership capacity by 2011, the bank faces major global HR challenges. It must add 65,000 new jobs over five years—which roughly represents 2 million applications and a half million interviews! An additional challenge is that it must recruit people from countries where there is a limited, often non-existent, pool of banking talent with the requisite financial skills and experience. There simply are none or few experienced bankers in these parts of the world.

Aware of the enormous talent management challenge, HR understands that the bank needs to create its own talent factory and do a number of critical things right. First, it needs the endorsement and emotional commitment of the CEO, regional business teams, and country CEOs. The talent management processes of acquiring, developing, and retaining people must become core strategic objectives of the bank and part of everything that managers do in every market in the world.

Second, building a talent pool is a long-haul journey. For Standard Chartered, that translates into simple core processes, minimum standards, and reliable data so that managers can have acceptable "country conversations" on how to best manage talent in their part of the world. While introducing global standards and tools, managers in the emerging markets are given some latitude to decide how to how implement HR practices around talent. With 9,000 line managers, who tend to be rational and data-based bankers rather than touchy-feely types of people, an HR decision to focus on hard data as the source of action is a good fit. The result is a Human Capacity Scorecard, introduced in 2005. It has now grown to an extensive database that contains detailed work force information regarding the effectiveness of people processes and their impact on business performance for each business unit and country. The data are managed through a Shared Service Center in India. Employees are classified into one of four categories, ranging from high-potentials to underperformers. This helps manager better understand what they need to do to support their local talent and plan for the future talent needs of the bank.

Third, because of the absence of skilled talent in the emerging markets in which they operate, Standard Chartered made the decision to focus on the strengths of its people (whether potential recruits or employees) rather than on traditional HR competency models. Since people perform best when they play to their strengths, it matches the strengths of its employees with the appropriate competency requirements of the positions to be filled. They select people for strength and aptitude, and train them on the necessary skills so that they can hit the ground running as bank employees.

Finally, with the proposed aggressive growth pattern, Standard Chartered understands that it must massively multiply leaders, not only in the top management layer, but also throughout the organization. Standard Chartered uses a structured interview process to get leaders to play to their best skills, creates profiles to increase self-awareness, and offers coaching and self-help tools for improvement. Because leadership development is imperative for sustainability, growth and a satisfied work force, they focus on the creation of an internal pipeline of people who can accelerate their personal development and assume leadership roles at a rapid pace.

Combining executive commitment, standard processes, a data-driven Human Capital Scorecard, a focus on the strengths of its labor pool and an ongoing development of the leadership pipeline, HR is strategically managing the talent factory essential for the bank's future success. As a result, Standard Chartered is focusing on managing people capability and getting early warning signals of areas that need to be improved before they become major challenges.

But there is no guarantee for success. As Geraldine Haley, group head of talent management and leadership development, said: "You don't know whether you are doing the right thing. It takes three to five years to see if your talent management strategy works."

Questions

1 How does an organization design, deliver and evaluate a global talent management strategy?

2 Which talent management indicators would you include in the Standard Chartered's human capital scorecard?

3 How does the practice of "playing to one's strengths" work for Standard Chartered Bank?

Source Claus, L. and Thalsgård, C. (2007), "Global HR in Action Vignettes," Willamette University, www.willamette.edu/agsm/global_hr.

Training and management development in the multinational enterprise

6

LEARNING OBJECTIVES

This chapter will enable the reader to:

- Advocate training and development (T&D) programs for the MNE's global managers and work force
- Identify the challenges of training an international work force
- Explain key learning objectives that drive training programs aimed at enabling a productive global work force
- Design cross-cultural training programs that enable international assignees to successfully complete their assignments and develop an effective global management team
- Develop a global mind-set, global competencies, and global leadership in the international organization
- Improve the effectiveness of global and virtual teams

KEY TERMS

- Cross-cultural adjustment
- Cross-cultural training
- Cultural shock
- Global competencies
- Global mind-set
- Global leadership
- Glue technology
- Knowledge management
- Virtual/global teams

Firms that operate in the global arena confront a number of special problems related to the T&D of their global work forces and managers. Responsibility for T&D is traditionally one of HR's core functions. So when an enterprise's international business reaches a significant level, when it is involved with multiple subsidiaries and partnerships in other countries, with the transfer of its technology to other countries, with developing and pursuing a global strategy, and with the assignment of a number of employees to international positions, the T&D development function takes on a new and more complex nature.

In this chapter, T&D is examined from the perspective of the MNE, including instructional design issues that arise when T&D programs are used in the MNE, the preparation of employees to work effectively in virtual and global teams, the sharing of knowledge and best practices across the MNE, the design and delivery of global management/leadership development programs, the development of a global mind-set for management and employees, and the special training needs of people on international assignments. All of these issues, critical to the success of the MNE, relate to the development of "glue technology"[1] or the application of human resource management processes that produce coordination and cohesion for the organization. These informal mechanisms for coordination include lateral relationships, best practice transfer, project management, shared frameworks, and the socialization of recruits into shared values. IHR needs to be prepared to analyze the MNE's global T&D needs, design, develop and implement T&D programs, and evaluate whether these T&D initiatives ultimately help the MNE achieve a competitive advantage in its global operations. It is the objective of this chapter to provide the basics for that IHR responsibility.

TRAINING IN THE MULTINATIONAL ENTERPRISE

Since an MNE's human capital may be its most important source of competitive advantage, a well trained and educated global work force is critical to success in the global marketplace. Therefore, the following seven imperatives have been suggested as key to global organizational learning and T&D.[2] Further, these imperatives provide a statement of the values which underlie this chapter's discussion of training and management development for the successful MNE.

- *Think and act globally.* That is, a global enterprise must think about and prepare for a presence in all the critical markets in the world, not just its home region.
- *Become an equidistant global learning organization.* That is, learning from all cultures, anytime, in any manner possible, must be facilitated.[3] In Kenichi Ohmae's words: "It may be unfamiliar and awkward, but the primary rule of equidistance is to see—and to think—global first. Honda, for example, has manufacturing divisions in Japan, North America, and Europe—all three legs of the [major markets of the world]—but its managers do not think or act as if the company were divided between Japanese and overseas operations. In fact, the very

word overseas has no place in Honda's vocabulary, because the corporation sees itself as equidistant from all its key customers."[4]

● Focus on the global system, not its parts. That is, development programs need to focus on breaking down the silos of departments and even the boundaries between countries and those that separate customers and suppliers and focus on the "big picture" global organizational system.

● *Develop global leadership skills.* That is, global leadership requires competencies different from those needed in the domestic marketplace. These should be the focus of global training and development programs.

● *Empower teams to create a global future.* That is, cross-border and virtual teams should be increasingly used and empowered to perform critical organizational projects and problem-solving activities. In addition, these global teams can, themselves, be a major tool in the development of cross-cultural competencies.

● *Make learning a core competence for the global organization.* That is, the global organization needs to become a global learning organization, where learning and development permeate all that the organization does.[5] As Arie de Geus, former head of strategic planning at Royal/Dutch Shell, puts it: "Over the long term, the only sustainable competitive advantage may be an organization's ability to learn faster than its competitors."[6]

● *Regularly reinvent yourself and the global organization.* That is, constant self-development must become the cornerstone of strategies for success for both individuals and organizations in today's highly competitive global economy.

The challenge of mastering the ever and rapidly changing and expanding global needs of individuals and organizations may be overwhelming. But it is exactly this challenge for IHRM which is addressed in this chapter on global training and management development.

ISSUES RELATED TO GLOBAL TRAINING AND DEVELOPMENT

The instructional ADDIE[7] (analysis, design, development, implementation, evaluation) model, commonly used by instructional designers, focuses on the various stages of T&D. Many of the decisions that are made during these stages are impacted by the fact that T&D programs in the MNE are used by employees in various locations, cultures, and languages. When enterprises operate subsidiaries and partnerships around the world, the training of the members of their global work force takes on special importance and difficulty. The major issues related to global training and development center around the design, development and implementation of the communication and training programs, including both technical and non-technical training. It is risky to roll these out without localization as it reduces the acceptance and effectiveness of the training interventions. Localization of training programs includes localized translation, adaptation to the local cultural practices, and compliance with local laws affecting training. Too often, corporate T&D simply tries to apply successful training programs from headquarters. But this simply doesn't always work. The types of problems confronting the MNE when it begins to discuss the need for training of its local work forces around the world include the following:[8]

- Who should deliver training in the foreign subsidiaries and joint ventures? Trainers from headquarters? Local trainers? Independent trainers?
- How should the training be delivered? Are there local cultural differences and learning preferences that need to be considered?
- What are the effects of language differences? Will there be translation problems (for both written and orally presented materials)? Are there differences in the meanings of words? Are there terms and phrases that don't exist in the "foreign" language(s)? Who should take responsibility (headquarters personnel, host country specialists, or third-party vendors) for translation? Should training programs be exported from headquarters or should overseas employees be brought to centralized or regional training facilities? How effective is e-learning in the MNE? Can training programs be developed in various locations and made available to everyone? What are the effects of the various options?
- Should courses for management development be handled differently than training for host country and third country employees?
- To ensure respect for each host country's culture, should each subsidiary or joint venture develop its own training? Does it have the capability? Or are there strong reasons to insist on centrally developed training programs?
- How does an MNE adapt a training program (in terms of both the content and the process of the training) to different countries and cultures?

Of course, part of the challenge for MNE trainers and IHR is that there are no easy answers to these questions. Because of that, many firms develop international training practices to fit their particular needs, resources, and make assumptions about what should work best. The approaches taken by differing MNEs to training of local work forces in their foreign subsidiaries and joint ventures range from total localization, with all training designed and managed at the subsidiary level, to total integration, with all training directed from headquarters and with the goal of full integration with the culture and perspectives of the parent firm.

Localized approach to global training and development

Cross-cultural differences play an important role in the design, development and implementation of T&D for the MNE. In addition, structural components (such as legal obligations to train, educational levels, and different approaches to education and educational systems) may impact the effectiveness of T&D. For example, an American MNE spent several million dollars on upgrading its IT systems in all of its plants around the world, as well as on training initiatives to make sure that everyone understood the new system.[9] Yet its HR director couldn't understand why, months after the training had taken place, some subsidiaries were still using the old procedures. Although the Scandinavians and the British welcomed the new ideas, the French, Italians, and Latin Americans were reluctant to accept another *Diktat* from US headquarters. And although the Asians didn't complain during the training sessions, they, too, failed to implement the new system. It's a common scenario, says Richard Harlow, senior development consultant at global training consultancy TMA in the UK:[10]

> Time and time again, I hear similar stories of global training initiatives not having the desired effect. And it boils down to a number of reasons. Sometimes badly interpreted material is to blame, other times internal politics may be at play, or perhaps employees in a particular location are just not accustomed to the way the briefing/training is delivered. And companies end up digging deeper in their pockets to retrain or troubleshoot.

Sometimes, firms face such disappointments because they simply transfer a program devised at headquarters straight to another country, without taking cultural norms into account. It goes much deeper than just translating the training material into another language; trainers have to work around the cultural nuances as well. In many cases, the "global" training falls flat because it is just completely inappropriate for the particular culture. Although there is no general road map for adjusting T&D programs to local conditions and cultures, at a minimum, IHR professionals must make the effort to understand local laws, practice, and employer obligations in order to improve the probability of achieving the required learning and development objectives of the MNE. The next sections deal with T&D localization issues in terms of culture, language, learning styles, education levels and forms, language, local T&D laws, and transfer of learning.

Culture

National (and even professional and organizational) culture influences training in a number of ways. Before they set up a training program in a foreign subsidiary, IHR professionals must understand how that culture views the educational process. For instance, in many Asian cultures, education is considered to be a very authoritarian phenomenon. The teacher is seen as the expert, and someone students should respect. Teachers impart knowledge through one-way conversation: The teacher tells and students listen respectfully. In such a context, students do not ask questions, and teachers do not solicit students' opinions. In such high-power distance cultures, the atmosphere is formal and respectful toward authority. US educational techniques, for example, which are less formal, and which focus on interactivity and encourage student participation, can be ineffective in such an Asian environment. The degree of deference to instructors influences the extent to which a participative style can be used and the extent to which participants will ask questions or offer opinions and become involved in open discussion. Culture will influence adherence to a hierarchy among students, such as deference to the most senior member of a training group in discussion and the stating of opinions. Culture influences all forms of interactions with instructors and influences what a training group will accept in terms of the behavior of instructors, e.g., degree of formality and appearance. Culture influences the roles of students, e.g., based on their gender and positions, in ways that may be different from that which is familiar to the trainer or to those who developed the training. Training which is delivered to employees from cultures which are foreign to that of the people who designed the training or delivered by people from different cultures must take into account these and other issues related to culture or the success of the training may be limited.

Box 6.1 illustrates one attempt to match training pedagogies with the cultural characteristics of a number of countries, particularly the degree of power distance and uncertainty avoidance, since they impact trainees' experiences with participation in the learning process.[11] As Box 6.1 suggests, people from high power distance (acceptance of status differences between students and instructors) and strong uncertainty avoidance (unwillingness to take risks and to try new things) cultures are likely to desire and perform better in training programs that rely more heavily on structured and passive learning techniques, such as reading assignments and lectures versus those who come from weak uncertainty avoidance and low power distance, who will probably do better with experiential training techniques. Of course, individuals within a culture may vary from these guidelines and any particular country subsidiary may have developed a company culture that supports the use of training techniques that are different from the norm for the particular culture.

Learning styles

This issue is also related to culture. It is clear that, in additional to personal learning styles, people from differing cultures and countries are used to differing training and teaching styles. And thus their most comfortable learning approach needs to be considered in the design and delivery of training. IHRM in Action 6.1 illustrates how culture and learning styles issues impact the effectiveness of training programs in subsidiaries in Malawi, a Southeast African country and a former British colony.[12]

Education levels and forms

One of the reasons that the provision of training to multiple subsidiaries around the world is so complex is because the basic educational infrastructure varies so much from country to country. The basic level of literacy varies dramatically; the nature of the educational system and the type of education it provides vary significantly (e.g., whether theoretical or practical in orientation); the level, nature, and availability of higher education varies; the availability of vocational education varies considerably; and teaching and, therefore, learning styles, used in any country's school system, vary

BOX 6.1 **THE MATCH OF TRAINING TECHNIQUES TO COUNTRY CULTURE**

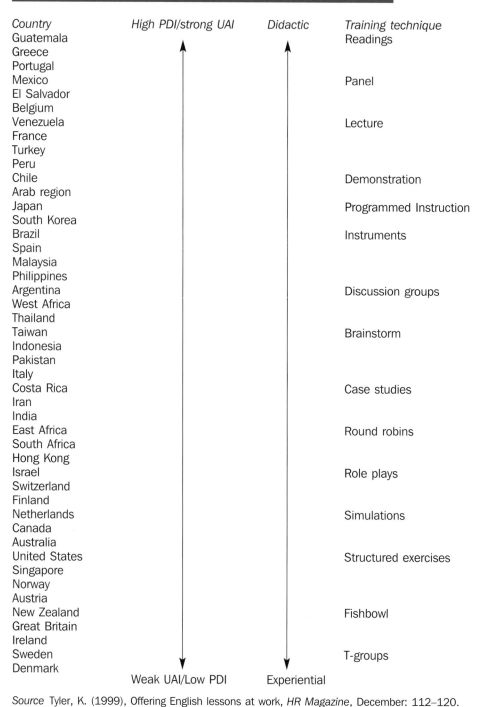

Country	High PDI/strong UAI	Didactic	Training technique
Guatemala			Readings
Greece			
Portugal			
Mexico			Panel
El Salvador			
Belgium			
Venezuela			Lecture
France			
Turkey			
Peru			
Chile			Demonstration
Arab region			
Japan			Programmed Instruction
South Korea			
Brazil			Instruments
Spain			
Malaysia			
Philippines			
Argentina			Discussion groups
West Africa			
Thailand			
Taiwan			Brainstorm
Indonesia			
Pakistan			
Italy			
Costa Rica			Case studies
Iran			
India			
East Africa			Round robins
South Africa			
Hong Kong			
Israel			Role plays
Switzerland			
Finland			
Netherlands			Simulations
Canada			
Australia			
United States			Structured exercises
Singapore			
Norway			
Austria			
New Zealand			Fishbowl
Great Britain			
Ireland			
Sweden			T-groups
Denmark			
	Weak UAI/Low PDI	Experiential	

Source Tyler, K. (1999), Offering English lessons at work, *HR Magazine*, December: 112–120.

TRAINING MANAGERS IN MALAWI

Malawi was once a British colony. Thus it inherited a British administrative tradition, which is very Western and very bureaucratic. However, traditional Malawi cultural values, which emphasize family membership and attention to status, are also superimposed on to business administrative systems, mostly imported from Europe and the US. In the Malawian culture, workers view employers as an extension of their families. They expect to be provided with a broad array of benefits from their employer, such as housing and transportation. Malawi society also places great importance on status differences. The relationship between managers and subordinates is viewed as authoritative; workers give deference and expect managers to act paternally. Malawians view proper protocol as very important. Managers often resist accepting individual blame for their own mistakes and do not directly criticize their subordinates. Malawian managers rarely delegate authority because the culture believes that delegation strips managers of their authority and thus lowers their status in the eyes of their subordinates. How do these cultural practices influence the development of T&D programs by MNEs in Malawi? MNEs setting up local operations in Malawi must consider the following three realities when developing training programs:

- American and Western models of innovation, motivation, leadership, etc., will not work well in Malawi. For example, most US management experts believe that proper leader behavior depends on the situation: There is no one right way to lead. However, the Malawian culture believes that leaders should always be authoritative. Consequently, HR professionals must first learn how these issues apply in a Malawian culture and then train the Malawian workers accordingly.
- Status-conscious Malawian managers will resent being ordered to attend a training program. They will interpret this gesture as an indication that they are considered "below average" performers. A company must thus carefully prepare a strategy to solicit trainee attendance in a way that will not cause managers to "lose face" with their peers or subordinates.
- Training methods must be congruent with employee learning styles. Malawians learn best in "process-oriented" educational settings. Consequently, training methods that use small-group techniques and other "supportive learning" techniques should be used in lieu of those that focus on lectures and rote learning.

Source Adapted from Jones, M. L. (1989), Management development: An African focus, *International Studies of Management and Organization*, 19 (1), 74–90.

from culture to culture as well. In addition, familiarity with various teaching techniques and media as well as relationships between students and instructors also vary so much that it is often impossible to transfer directly either the content or the method of instruction from one place to another.

Language

There are a number of issues in global T&D that involve language. One has to do with whether to provide training for the global work force in a single, common language, or to translate training programs into varying languages for the global work force. If the training is provided in a single language, that language will likely be the language of the headquarters or English. Another has to do with providing language classes, themselves, in order to enable employees to be able to interact more effectively both within the enterprise as well as to interact effectively with external constituencies, such as suppliers, subcontractors, and customers. In today's shrinking world, the ability to communicate accurately and effectively takes on increasing importance. Even though "business" English has become the primary language in which global business is conducted, it is clear that being able to sell, negotiate, discuss, and manage in the language of one's neighbors, customers, and employees can improve the probabilities of successful communication and, therefore, successful business transactions. MNEs have learned how important foreign-language skills are. The ability to speak another language is seen as so important it has become a major plus when recruiting new employees. Language acquisition opens the door to deeper cultural understanding—speech patterns, thought patterns, and behavior patterns (for example, of customers) are interlinked. And, therefore, language study is a link to better understanding (and interacting with) the customer (as well as employees). Increasingly within MNEs, internationalists having multilingual and multicultural capabilities are becoming the norm. As a specific example, Chinese (particularly Mandarin) has become more popular as firms send increasing numbers of employees on assignment to China.

Teaching everyone to speak a common language, usually English, has also become popular, at least in some firms. Such programs (usually referred to as ESL—English as a Second Language—or ESOL—English for Speakers of Other Languages—programs) not only help new employees adapt (in the case of recent immigrants into an English-speaking country, for example) but also help others do their jobs better and increase worker loyalty and improve customer relations.[13] To the extent possible, language lessons should be presented in terms of workplace situations, which enhance the training's immediate usefulness.

Another area of primary concern relates to the language of the training itself. Global enterprises must make difficult decisions about whether to translate training materials into the languages of the local (foreign) work forces and whether to provide the training itself in the language of the local work force (either through the use of local trainers or through translators, if the trainers come from regional or corporate headquarters training groups and they don't speak the local language). If the decision is taken to provide the training through translators, then the selection of interpreters and translators needs to be given special attention, since being good at interpretation and translation requires more than training in the original and the foreign language. It also requires close familiarity with the nature of the business and any technical and special managerial terminology that may not translate easily into the foreign language or back into the original language. Of course, MNEs may be obligated by local law to provide the training in the language(s) of the country in which they operate. National pride also plays a major role. Although, for example, Chinese employees may understand the training in English, they may want to receive the training in Mandarin as a matter of pride.

Training and development laws

MNEs must also take account of the national laws and regulations affecting T&D in the countries of operation. These laws may focus on the requirement to spend a certain percent of payroll expenses on training (or, alternatively pay a percent in taxes to a government-sponsored training program), to train on certain subjects (i.e., safety, sexual harassment, cross train, reduction in force, etc.), to translate material into the local language, to provide financial resources for employees to receive training, or to comply with labor contracts.

Transfer of learning

Finally, transfer of learning issues is especially critical in cross-border T&D. Not only do they need to be understood by the MNE providing training, but as firms go to more and more countries, this is just one more reason for training itself becoming an increasingly complex responsibility. There are many reasons why training may not transfer smoothly to other cultures or countries. In addition, there are also a number of practical problems with achieving what is referred to as "transfer of learning." This issue has to do with the extent to which people on training programs are able to (and/or actually do) apply what they learn in training programs to their day-to-day jobs. Many of the problems are related to the types of cultural issues that have been discussed throughout this book. Trainers have to consider not only the nature of cross-border training (as discussed above) but also must pay close attention to who needs to receive training. For example, even well educated work forces, say in developing countries, may still need training in things like new technologies. In the end, transfer of learning concerns (in the traditional sense of transfer from training program to job performance as well as in the sense of transfer from one country to another) arise in a number of special situations for the MNE, including in the merging of various company and national cultures in cross-border acquisitions and joint ventures, when coping with increased cross-national diversity due to the development of global work forces, and when dealing with the many problems of cross-cultural work teams. All of this makes the management of international T&D programs a very complex responsibility, indeed.

Standardized approach to global training and development

While there are many cultural reasons to localize training, MNEs also must integrate their T&D activities, not only to achieve economies of scale and scope, but to ensure that the same T&D is available for all of their worldwide employees on a just-in-time basis. In a globally integrated enterprise there will always be a need to develop T&D interventions around common processes, practices and organizational principles. This is especially the case in non-technical training (e.g., around management and leadership development issues). With the advance of communication and IT technologies barriers to information and knowledge being readily accessible to everyone have been quasi-eliminated. MNEs are now taking advantage of the development opportunities provided through IT by making training programs on virtually every conceivable topic available through company-sponsored web sites. MNEs are developing learning portals and making technical information and a wide array of T&D courses available to their employees online and accessible through personal computers, laptops, personal digital assistants (PDAs) and downloadable to hand-held devices. The once very expensive development of computer-based training (CBT) is being democratized and put at the fingertips of everyone through e-learning tools.

E-learning issues, however, remain and should not be overlooked. Although e-learning may be an efficient and cost-effective means of delivering training, there may still be implementation and cultural acceptance issues. These may include issues such as the following: Is the training standardized (reflecting home country management and regulations only) or is it localized to reflect local management practices and laws? Does everyone have access to the technology and is familiar with its use? How acceptable is the type of training being offered and the form of communication in which it is delivered in different cultures? Even though there may be good reasons to pursue standardization of T&D programs, some localization will always be necessary and desirable.

VIRTUAL AND GLOBAL TEAMS

The changing nature of organizations (and the type of work and the manner in which it is performed) requires that employees work increasingly in teams. The global interconnectedness, especially as a result of delocalization, disassembly of work in manufacturing and services, and the development of new technologies, have made the use and nature of teams increasingly more global, virtual, and common. And, now, where a team was usually thought of as consisting of five to fifteen people, larger teams (more like 100 or more) are increasingly becoming the norm in MNEs.[14] These teams, in turn, must now organize themselves in subteams to achieve their goals. This has made it increasingly necessary for MNEs to organize training programs and curricula around the formation and management of teams.

Teamwork and team effectiveness have been a subject of research in organizational behavior for many decades. Critical success factors for effective teamwork include trust, commitment, accountability, conflict management, and expertise.[15] All of these factors are, obviously, heavily influenced by culture, making training in their achievement difficult. For example, how does one build and earn trust in different societies? How do team members from different cultures manage conflict on the team? And how do team members from different cultures deal with confrontation when there is a problem on the team? Networks have also been found to play important roles in the success of teams. The forms of networks that benefit teams the most include friendships and personal networks that are formed with people outside of the group; business-centered relationships that are developed with people in other parts of the organization; and relationships that extend into the social sphere (often referred to as social capital).[16] Indeed, team members from cultures that are relationship- rather than task-oriented may be more effective in utilizing their networks to benefit the team than are people who come from cultures where the nature of the deal is most important. The point is that the cultural norms of the people who are members of a team have a lot to do with how—and how well—the team will function. And this makes training for team members quite important, to ensure smooth interaction between team members.

While virtually unknown in the US, but extensively used by MNEs in Europe and the rest of the world, is the research over many years on team effectiveness by Meredith Belbin. According to Belbin,[17] a team role is "a tendency to behave, contribute and interrelate with others in a particular way" and relates to how well one takes on "tasks" on the team (i.e., a range of behaviors and contributions). According to Belbin, in a perfect team, there are nine complementary team roles and all roles are necessary for team success. Each team role has strengths (the major contribution to the team) and allowable weaknesses (or the price paid for the particular strength). The better the "mix" of team members, the better the team will perform. Although people have "preferred" team roles, most people can play only one to three team roles effectively. While it is possible to change natural behavior, it is not desirable to train team members in multiple roles (beyond three roles), as team members usually will play the extra roles inadequately.

While Belbin's research has shown that an individual's preferred team role tendency impacts the overall effectiveness of the team, team roles do not adequately take into account the global and cultural context in which teams now increasingly must operate and their seemingly increased size. These contextual variables present additional challenges in making global and virtual teams work. First, team members are increasingly geographically dispersed and work in different time zones. Second, they are more likely than domestic teams to be very heterogeneous in terms of national cultural backgrounds. Third, they tend to be larger than co-located teams because they often work on issues related to the global enterprise and must have geographic representation. Fourth, they communicate in English, which is unlikely to be the native language of many or most of the global team members. No matter how challenging effective team work may be in co-located teams, the problems are compounded in dispersed teams due to the fact that team members are (usually) not working face-to-face. Hence, virtual teams present some unique leadership and training challenges. Who else but IHR is responsible for making sure that global team members receive the necessary training to work effectively with one another?

Long before the current discussion on virtual global and far-flung teams, researchers have been interested in assessing whether culturally homogeneous teams are more or less effective than heterogeneous teams.[18] The results indicate that diverse teams that are well managed perform better than homogeneous teams, but poorly managed diverse teams do not perform with the same effectiveness as homogeneous teams. The reason for the increased performance of heterogeneous teams is due to the synergy that comes from their diversity. The reason for their ineffectiveness is because they have problems overcoming the management of the complexity of their teams (see Figure 6.1). If heterogeneous teams can overcome the difficulties of managing their diversity, they will be able to capture the benefits of their synergy and be more effective than homogeneous teams. Thus, a major topic for team training becomes diversity training, whether the teams are co-located or dispersed, cross-border, and virtual.

Since MNEs are increasingly using these cross-border and virtual teams, ensuring their effectiveness is paramount. Therefore, creating training programs that help create such productivity is a high priority for IHR. Several sets of best practices with regard to the effectiveness of virtual teams are currently being proposed. Tips for virtual teams include: start with a face-to-face meeting; keep the team as small as practical; have a code of practice for communicating; communicate regularly, but don't overdo it; ensure everyone understands each other's role; have a supportive sponsor; keep strong links with the parent organization; and reward results—not how people work.[19] Best practices related to virtual team leadership include:

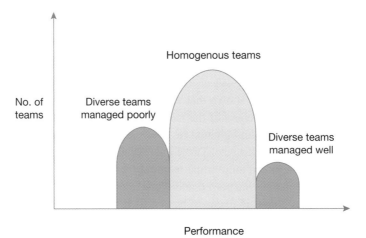

Figure 6.1 Effectiveness of homogeneous and heterogeneous teams

Source DiStefano, J. J. & Maznevski, M. L. (2000) Creating value with diverse teams in global management. *Organizational Dynamics*, 29 (1), 45-63

- Establish and maintain trust through the use of communication technology.
- Ensure that distributed diversity is understood and appreciated,
- Manage virtual work–life cycle meetings.
- Monitor team progress using technology.
- Enhance the visibility of virtual members within the team and outside the organization.
- Enable individual members of the virtual team to benefit from the team.[20]

Lynda Gratton[21] in her book, *Hot Spots*, looks at how to develop exceptionally successful teamwork in large organizations and proposes eight ways to build collaboration among large, diverse, and virtual teams.[22] Best practices include:

- Invest in *signature relationships*—practices that demonstrate executive commitment to collaboration and build bonds among the staff.
- Have executives *model collaboration among themselves.*
- Establish a "gift culture" in which managers support employees through daily mentoring.
- Ensure that the needed *relationship skills*, especially communication and conflict resolution, are fostered through training.
- Support a strong *sense of community* through HR-sponsored activities.
- Assign *ambidextrous leaders* (who are both task and relationship-oriented) to teams.
- Build on *heritage relationships* by assigning some people who know each other on teams.
- Understand *role clarity* (know what is expected) while allowing for *task ambiguity* (give team members latitude in how to achieve a task).

As more MNEs are using virtual and global teams, the knowledge on how to make these teams more effective and how to prepare employees for such team experiences can be expected to grow in the future. And one could predict that the need for and delivery of training programs (on a global basis) to improve team effectiveness can also be expected to grow.

GLOBAL LEADERSHIP DEVELOPMENT

Another important area of T&D is the development of managers and global leaders for the MNE. Most contemporary management and leadership development theories originated in the Western world. At the turn of the twenty-first century, and with rapid globalization, a number of leadership books[23] questioned whether the characteristics that made Western leaders effective were universal. Assuming that leadership theories are context-specific (time and place bound), it became legitimate to question whether US- and Western-centric leadership theories are as effective in multicultural and international environments as they have been in the Western contexts. Hence, a number of new "global leadership" theories emerged as a parallel to the emerging "global company" model.

Global leadership theories

The GLOBE study is the largest academic research on leadership from a global perspective. GLOBE (an acronym for Global Leadership and Organizational Behavioral Effectiveness) is a study on culture and leadership in sixty-two societies and has now been in process for almost a decade and a half.[24] The primary objective of the research was to identify global leadership characteristics that are universally accepted and effective across cultures. The main finding of GLOBE is that charismatic/transformational leadership styles are strongly endorsed across cultures. Transformational leadership—according to Bruce Avolio[25]—is a process whereby leaders develop followers into leaders. Transformational leaders are moral agents who focus themselves and their followers on achieving higher-level missions (get commitment, trust, loyalty, performance). They take the time to get to know the people they work with, what these people need to know to perform at their best, how far they can be stretched, challenged, and supported. They are respected for taking a stand on important issues (causes and concerns), encourage people to question and use their intelligence, and tap into the full potential of those being led.

The European contribution to global leadership theory has been heavily imbedded in cultural discussion. In their book *Twenty-one leaders for the Twenty-first Century*, Fons Trompenaars and Charles Hampden-Turner[26] argued that effective global leaders must deal with the seemingly opposing objectives that they continually seek to reconcile. Effective global leaders exercise "through-thinking" in their synthesizing of seemingly opposed values. Manfred Kets de Vries in his book, *The Leadership Mystique*, identified leadership styles that differ in their effectiveness depending upon the culture in which they are most likely found: consensus, charismatic, technocratic, political process, and democratic centralism.[27] Effective global leaders build on traditional leadership competencies and exhibit the ability to create a cohesive and globe-spanning organizational culture by tapping into the deeper, universal layers of human motivation. The development of global leaders is the result of personal development (cultural background, family influence for character building, early schooling, continuing education, support of parents), work experience, and professional development within organizations.

The identification of high-potential individuals, the development of their leadership skills, and the acceleration processes geared at key talent in the global organization for succession planning purposes are considered crucial competitive advantages, especially in an era of increased war for talent. The following provides a short summary of these processes that are so critical to global management development.

Identification of high potential leaders

The way organizations identify their leaders is influenced by cultural practices and different leadership identification approaches that can be traced according to culture.[28] The "élite cohort" approach is a model for identifying talent at the time of entry when cohorts are recruited from top universities, carefully selected, screened, trained and developed for a number of years. It is most typical of the Japanese model of leadership identification. The "élite political" approach is a model for identifying talent at the time of entry when individuals are recruited from élite schools (such as the *grandes écoles*). The top graduates are given managerial positions without a trial period. This model is most typical of Latin European countries, particularly France. In the "functional" approach, leaders are identified for their functional excellence. This is quite typical in German companies. In the "managed development" approach, the decentralized responsibility for functional development lies at the local level while the overall process of management development is centralized at the corporate level. This is most typically found in large multinational companies. Each of these culture-based models of leadership identification follows a somewhat different leadership development plan.

Development of leaders

In their book, *Global Explorers*, Stewart Black, Allen Morrison, and Hal Gregersen[29] argued that leadership is not a function of position but of action. They conducted in-depth interviews of 130 global executives from some fifty companies throughout North America, Europe, and Asia. They concluded that two-thirds of the global leadership capabilities are driven by global dynamics and one-third by business-specific dynamics. Every global leader requires a certain set of unique skills and abilities that arise from country affiliation, and from industry, company, and functional dynamics. Global leadership is a function of being competent and interested in global business. In their study, every global leader had a core set of global attributes and was consistently competent in four important areas:

- *Inquisitiveness* (curiosity). The characteristic of inquisitiveness and curiosity was the glue that held the other characteristics together. Effective global leaders are unceasingly curious. Far from being overwhelmed by all the differences in language, culture, government regulations, and so on that exist from one country to another, they are invigorated by the diversity. They love to learn and are driven to understand and master the complexities of the global business environment.
- *Perspective* (how leaders look at the world). Global leaders also have a unique perspective on the world. While most managers have learned to avoid uncertainty and structure their environments to get rid of it, global leaders view uncertainty as an invigorating and natural aspect of international business.
- *Character* (emotional connection and unwavering integrity). The leader's ability to connect emotionally with people of different backgrounds and cultures through the consistent demonstration of personal integrity. This is essential for engendering trust and goodwill in a global work force and with a global firm's many partners.
- *Savvy* (exceptional business and organizational savvy). Demonstrated by the ability to recognize global business opportunities and then to mobilize organizational

global resources in order to capitalize on them. Global leaders are highly skilled at both identifying market opportunities and applying organizational resources to make the most of those opportunities.

MNEs are not only interested in developing leadership throughout their organizations, they also want their leaders to have global competencies and experiences. It is almost unheard of today that the CEO, or senior leader, of an MNE could occupy such a position without prior international experience. Therefore, many MNEs are insisting on the development of a set of global competencies in the job descriptions of their key leaders and managers. The interesting question then becomes, "What are these global leadership competencies?" According to Michael Marquard's[30] global business competencies framework, global leaders should seek to develop a variety of "globe-able" competencies, such as the abilities to:

- Describe clearly the forces behind the globalization of business.
- Recognize and connect global market trends, technological innovation, and business strategy.
- Outline issues essential to effective strategic alliances.
- Frame day-to-day management issues, problems, and goals in a global context.
- Think and plan beyond historical, cultural, and political boundaries, structures, systems, and processes.
- Create and effectively lead worldwide business teams.
- Help one's company adopt a functional global organization structure.

Nancy Adler[31] also focused on the skills and competencies required by managers working for transnational firms. As she indicates, managers who are transnationally competent require a broader range of skills than traditional international managers. First, transnational managers must understand the worldwide business environment from a global perspective. And they must develop a series of skills for working with businesses and people from multiple countries and cultures. Box 6.2 summarizes the skills of a transnational manager and contrasts them to those required of the traditional international manager.

DEVELOPMENT OF A GLOBAL MIND-SET

The development of a global mind-set is at the core of global leadership development. First, this section takes a look at the concept of a global mind-set.[32] One of the goals of many management development programs in the global arena is to develop a cadre of managers who have what is referred to as a global mind-set.[33] As will be discussed, an international management development program alone may not achieve this objective. This global perspective includes sensitivity to multiple cultures and their differences, work experience in more than one country, and knowledge about how and willingness to seek customers, financial resources and supplies, technology, innovations, and employees throughout the world.

BOX 6.2 SKILLS OF THE TRANSNATIONAL COMPETENT MANAGER VERSUS THOSE OF THE TRADITIONAL INTERNATIONAL MANAGER

Transnational skills	Transnationally competent managers	Traditional international managers
Global perspective	Understand worldwide business environment from a global perspective	Focus on a single foreign country and on managing relation between HQs and that country
Local responsiveness	Learn about many cultures	Become an expert on one culture
Synergistic learning	Work with and learn from people of many cultures simultaneously	Work with and coach people in each foreign culture separately or sequentially
	Create a culturally synergistic environment	Integrate foreigners into the organizational headquarters' national organizational culture
Transition and adaptation	Adapt to living in many foreign cultures	Adapt to living in a foreign culture
Cross-cultural interaction	Use cross-cultural interaction skills on a daily basis throughout assignments	Use cross-cultural interaction skills primarily on foreign assignments
Collaboration	Interact with foreign colleagues as equals	Interact within clearly defined hierarchies of structural and cultural dominance
Foreign experience	Transpatriation for career and organization development	Expatriation or inpatriation primarily to get the job done

Source Adler, N. J. and Bartholomew, S. (1992), Managing globally competent people, *Academy of Management Executive*, 6 (2): 52–65.

The internationalization of jobs, companies, technology, products, money, and neighborhoods has caught many people and firms off guard. Peoples' domestic thinking has not caught up with the global reality of a flat world: business and life, in general, have been and are being globalized at a fast pace. Few people have much long-term experience working or living with people from other cultures. The result is that few people are familiar with the rules to follow when engaging in business across international borders. And most people assume that the rules they are familiar with and that work well "at home" should be adequate when they work abroad. But, as has been emphasized throughout this book, this is seldom the case. Thus, the opportunities for being embarrassed and making mistakes are ever present. Often, the reaction of managers and employees, in their interactions with colleagues, customers, and suppliers from other countries is "Why can't they be like us?" But they aren't and their ways of behaving and conducting business too often seem strange and difficult. Because of this, businesses are increasingly concerned about how to develop managers and employees that exhibit a global mind-set, that is, an ability to think and function effectively in a multiculture world.

Given the globalization of business, the success of employees' and managers' interactions with global customers, suppliers, and colleagues often is dependent on their abilities to think and act with a global frame of mind and reference, even though they work and live at a time when national pride and focus are as strong as ever. Indeed, the ability to cope with this conflict between a global focus and a local/national focus is one of the critical competencies in today's business world.[34] This global mind-set predisposes people to cope constructively with these competing priorities (global versus local), rather than advocating one set of cultural values (most likely to be the individual's home country values) at the expense of all others. This mind-set involves being able to form and sustain a holistic global outlook; a completely different way of looking at the world and being able to synthesize the many complex and conflicting forces.[35]

People try to make sense out of the confusing effects of globalization with their existing mind-sets. Essentially people's mind-sets are the interpretive frameworks that come from their experiences and cultures and that guide how they classify and discriminate events and people in ways that help them to understand what they observe and perceive. These mind-sets determine people's perceptions of and reactions to international experiences and observations of people from other countries and cultures. But their lack of international experience and exposure often limits their abilities to be successful in their international experiences (except maybe as travelers, although a domestic mind-set can cause problems even while traveling). In the words of Catherine Scherer, who has studied those whom she calls *internationalists*, a global mind-set is characterized by tolerance, flexibility, curiosity (inquisitiveness), and the ability to deal with ambiguity.[36] Everyone seems to agree that a global mind-set is crucial to effective global management. Yet, because of the rather elusive nature of the concept global mind-set, we will first define what it is, identify its major characteristics, identify patterns of organizations with a global mind-set, and discuss how people can develop a global mind-set.

Definition of a global mind-set

Knowing how to live and work across cultures is the essential competency of people with a global mind-set. For most people, developing this mind-set is both an emotional education as well as an intellectual one. The lessons are professional and personal—yet often profoundly personal.[37] It is the complexity of the professional lessons and the transformational quality of the personal lessons that leads to the broader perspective of those with a global mind-set. It is in fact this unique perspective that underlies this quality called a *global mind-set*. One author with extensive international business experience, writing for the American Society for Training and Development, says this global mind-set:

> is a way of being rather than a set of skills. It is an orientation to the world that allows one to see certain things that others do not. A global mind-set means the ability to scan the world from a broad perspective, always looking for unexpected trends and opportunities that may constitute a threat or an opportunity to achieve personal, professional, or organizational objectives.[38]

Another set of authors, who are European academics and consultants, define the global mind-set in terms of both its psychological (personal) and its strategic (professional) perspectives.[39] That is, they see it as "the ability to accept and work with cultural diversity" as well as involving "a set of attitudes that predispose individuals to balance competing business, country, and functional priorities which emerge in international [situations] rather than to advocate any of these dimensions at the expense of the others."

Ultimately, the global manager must become the facilitator of personal and organizational change and development on a global scale. To achieve this, the global manager must not only be attentive to a developer of organizational cultures, values, and beliefs that reach well beyond the manager's own cultural, technical, and managerial background, but s/he must also be a consummate reframer of the boundaries of the world in which s/he works.[40] This global mind-set is about balancing perspectives, not just about being global. The global manager needs to continue to understand, appreciate, and accommodate local, cross-cultural differences and variations while at the same time maintaining a global view. As a precaution, however:

> academics and others writing from a normative perspective sometimes have the tendency to see global or cosmopolitan as superior to local, calling for a "universal way that transcends the particular of places." What is "local" is seen as parochial and narrow-minded. However, in our view, global mind-set requires an approach that may be seen as the opposite to such one-dimensional universalism—it calls for a dualistic perspective, an immersion in the local "particulars" while at the same time retaining a wider cross-border orientation.[41]

Characteristics of a global mind-set

Learning a global mind-set requires the developing of a new set of competencies. Even though there is much disagreement over exactly what are the characteristics of those who possess this global mind-set, the following is a synthesis of the efforts to describe these characteristics.[42] In the end, there is considerable agreement over the following. Those with a global mind-set exhibit the ability to:

- *Manage global competitiveness.* They have broader business skills, exhibiting the ability to conduct business on a global scale as well as to design and manage complex international structures and strategies.[43] They demonstrate awareness of national differences, global trends and options, and the global impact of their decisions and choices. These technical and business skills provide them with credibility in their various international assignments.
- *Work and communicate with multiple cultures.* They show the ability to interact with people (employees, customers, suppliers, colleagues) from many cultures with sensitivity to their cultural and language differences. They understand differing cultural contexts and incorporate that understanding in their work and communication styles. And they understand the impact of cultural factors on communication and work relationships and are willing to revise and expand their understanding as part of their personal and professional growth and development.
- *Manage global complexity, contradiction, and conflict.* They show the ability to manage the complexity, contradictions, and conflict which are experienced when dealing with multiple countries and cultures. They develop a sensitivity to different cultures and cultural values; they function effectively in different cultural environments;[44] and they show the ability to handle more complexity and uncertainty than is experienced by their domestic counterparts.[45] They consider more variables when solving problems and are not discouraged by adversity.
- *Manage organizational adaptability.* They demonstrate the ability to manage organizational change in response to new situations (that is, they are able to manage the global corporate culture and adapt it to multiple cultural environments). They show the ability to reframe their fields of reference, to be flexible, changing their organizational culture when necessary.[46] And they possess extensive curiosity and openness toward other ways of living and speaking, from which they draw ideas for organizational adaptation.
- *Manage multicultural teams.* They are able to effectively manage (and manage effective) cross-border and multicultural teams. They value the diversity present in such teams and are able to be a cross-border coach, coordinator, and mediator of conflict for such teams.[47] They relate well with diverse groups of people and are able to develop the necessary cross-border trust and teamwork that are important to the effective performance of such teams.[48]
- *Manage uncertainty and chaos.* They are comfortable with ambiguity and patient with evolving issues which are so characteristic of global experience. They can make decisions in the face of uncertainty and can see patterns and connections within the chaos of global events. They show extensive curiosity about other cultures and the people who live in them.
- *Manage personal and organizational global learning.* Both for themselves and for others with whom they work.

Characteristics of organizations with a global mind-set

An organization with a global mind-set is often referred to as geocentric. That is, its ultimate goal is to create an organization with a globally integrated business system with a leadership team and work force that have a worldwide perspective and approach. They recruit employees for their global and expatriate potential, because their perspective is that all employees must contribute to the global success of the firm. The whole work force needs to be globally aware and support the enterprise's global strategy. The concept of the globally integrated enterprise has best been described by IBM's CEO, Sam Palmisano, who has reinvented IBM's organization in that way.[49] It is a fundamentally new architecture where IBM is locating work and operations anywhere in the world based on the combination of best locations for economics, employee expertise, and the right business environment and then integrating their operations horizontally and globally. One of the key challenges of this model is that it needs to create a pool of truly global leaders. In Palmisano's own words the challenge is: "How do we develop people who can lead truly global teams and operations and understand cultural and societal norms and expectations all around the world? Where will this new generation of leaders come from?"

Acquiring a global mind-set

The four Ts (travel, training, team, and transfer) [50] have been described as effective ways to develop a global mind-set. However, the bottom-line experience that is required for developing a global mind-set is living in another culture and going through the culture shock that is necessary to learning how to accept and to enjoy living in the foreign culture. Although frequent international business travel and short-term international assignments (defined as less than one year) help broaden a person's perspective, they do not develop the cultural and leadership skills that are required for acquiring a global mind-set. Reasons given for this are that short-term travel and assignments do not require acculturation and assimilation into a foreign culture. Hence, they are not as effective at developing a global mind-set because they do not really require the person to acquire the coping skills to overcome cultural shock.[51]

A number of people have argued that, in the end, people who seem able to operate effectively in a global environment are not just described by a list of attributes that are largely extensions of the knowledge, skills, and abilities needed by those who are effective in a purely domestic environment. Indeed, the evidence is accumulating that at some point a fundamental transformation takes place for globally successful people—a transformation that can be described in shorthand as the acquisition of a global mind-set.[52] Such transformed people become more cosmopolitan, they extend their perspectives, and they change their cognitive maps of the world. Out of this deep change the individual develops a *new perspective* or *mind-set*. This is not just a new view of oneself but also a new view of one's organizational and professional role. This change goes far beyond a change in the skill-set—it is a change in the *person.* It is known that these deep changes in personal identity occur as a result of being confronted with a higher level of complexity in the environment—and that is precisely what happens in an international assignment. Not only does the person develop new perspectives, but he or she also *develops skills in the taking of new perspectives, and developing and holding multiple perspectives.* This ability to acquire and hold multiple, perhaps competing, perspectives (i.e., the ability to see a situation through another person's eyes) is a quality of a more "evolved" identity.[53] As studies are now finding, the lessons of cultural adaptability are pretty much learned *only* with expatriation, that is, through living in another culture.[54]

As with most learning experiences, global executives report learning from challenging assignments, significant other people, perspective-changing events, etc. But, when these experiences take place in different cultures, they take on a decidedly different tone; they are decidedly more complex. Functioning in a country significantly different than one's own is an experience for which there is no substitute. And then doing it a second time, in a substantially different culture, again, is transformational. However, people don't necessarily learn about others or develop this global mind-set purely through being in close proximity or through osmosis. Proximity doesn't necessarily lead to better communication or understanding. Nor do common sense and goodwill take the place of deliberate education. That is, one must work at it, one must want to learn from the new cultural experiences and must let go of the attitude that what is familiar is necessarily best.[55] To develop cultural literacy or competency, one must take deliberate steps to learn about another country's or culture's practices and values. One must make a concerted effort to learn about the deep values that motivate people and provide the context for their actions. One must experience the culture shock of coping with a new culture in order to begin to fully understand it so as to function effectively within it. And it is this that IHRM and MNEs must facilitate and encourage.

Many MNEs, learning from both their own and others' experience, now make overseas experience a necessity for the development of executives.[56] Indeed, all high-potential managers in these firms are required to have significant international experience as part of their career development. These international assignments, of course, work best when the expectations of the organization and the individual are aligned. That is, the real (and psychological) contract between the firm and the individual assignee need to be in agreement and both sides need to live up to their obligations and to the other side's expectations.[57] And this requires constant vigilance by both sides as well as regular discussions about both expected consequences from the assignment and how the assignment is to unfold and how it actually does unfold.

CROSS-CULTURAL PREPARATION FOR INTERNATIONAL ASSIGNEES

The first international training responsibility for an HR manager usually involves the training and preparation of international assignees and their families. Indeed, for many enterprises that have recently "gone international," this may well be the only international training issue looked at for some time after the enterprise begins developing its international operations. Management development programs will typically not involve any international considerations and the training of local work forces stays primarily the concern of local-national HR managers. Yet, at some point, the global enterprise usually comes to recognize the importance of training and preparing its expatriates. That is the subject of this section of the chapter.

The preparation of international assignees prior to going abroad (and after arrival) is at least as important to their successful performance as selecting the right candidate and family in the first place. A lot of evidence suggests that firms still do not do a very good job of selecting or preparing their international assignees. Indeed, surveys find that only about 35 percent of US firms offer any pre-departure cross-cultural or language training for their expatriate managers.[58] The percentage is not much different for Asian or European firms.[59] And yet the inability to adjust or to perform the expected role—both of which can be improved through training and orientation—generally provide the major reasons for "failure" in an overseas assignment. When international executive relocations fail, they generally fail either because expatriates can't fathom the customs of the new country or because their families can't deal with the emotional stress that accompanies relocation.[60] In both cases, orientation to the "culture shock" they will experience in their new environments seems particularly important.

Cross-cultural adjustment

Many international assignees and their families experience difficulties adjusting to their new, foreign situations.[61] Most of the time, the spouse or significant other (usually a woman, since most international assignees are men, although this is slowly changing) has to give up a job, house, friends, and family to accompany her spouse on his foreign assignment. The husband may also give up house, friends, and family, but he still has his job and relationships from work at the new assignment. Consequently, the wife typically has more difficulty adapting to the foreign environment. Some of the adjustment problems faced by people, men and women, as they move to a new, unfamiliar, foreign assignment include changing routines, cultural shock. Many of life's established routines have to change in a foreign locale. This includes everything from eating habits and favorite foods to initiating and developing relationships. This disruption takes significant energy and time to combat. And the greater the scope, magnitude, and criticality of the disruptions the more draining and, depending on one's success in dealing with them, the more depressing they can be. Culture shock is the set of psychological and emotional responses people experience when they are overwhelmed by their lack of knowledge and understanding of the new, foreign culture and the negative consequences that often accompany their inadequate and inexperienced behavior. The psychological and emotional symptoms of culture shock include frustration, anxiety, anger, and depression. Disruption of one's routines leads to these consequences.

But culture shock often leads to reactions that go beyond even this. Most people don't experience culture shock at the beginning. There is usually a form of euphoria and excitement about the new experiences in the early stages of the assignment. The international assignee and family usually don't even know enough at this stage to understand they are breaking local cultural taboos. But after a while, the international assignee and her/his family will begin to realize they don't know or understand many of the basic cultural ground rules, and this creates a major blow to their egos. The more significant the ground rules being broken, the more significant the blow to one's ego, and the greater the subsequent feelings of culture shock and depression. Some never recover from this culture shock and many of them return home early. Yet others stay and eventually work their way through culture shock, learn to understand and accept the local culture, and gradually adjust to living and working in the foreign locale. The pain of mistakes is the primary cause of culture shock but it is the learning to which these mistakes lead that shows the way out of it. Once a cultural mistake is made and, more important, recognized, it is less likely to be repeated or to become an ongoing source of frustration, anger, or embarrassment. Gradually, by making mistakes, recognizing them, and observing how others in the culture behave (and putting forth the effort to understand the deeper values that underlie local cultural behavior), people learn what to do and say and what not to do and say.[62]

Preparation for the international assignment

Experienced IHR managers think it is absolutely essential for success in international assignments to first, provide both an international assignee and his or her family enough accurate information about the assignment and location for them to be able to make informed decisions about the desirability of such an assignment (beyond the self-assessment discussed in the prior chapter).[63] This needs to be more than a short familiarization trip to the proposed location, even though this is important and should be seen as a necessary part of the preparation and orientation process. Both the employee and spouse should be well briefed on the new assignment's responsibilities, as well as on the firm's policies regarding international assignee compensation, benefits, taxes, security procedures, and repatriation. In addition, the employee and family need to be provided with all the information, skills, and attitudes which they will need to be comfortable, effective, and productive in the overseas assignment. Much of this orientation and training must be focused on the cultural values and norms of the new country and the contrast with those of their home country. Box 6.3 illustrates how many of these concerns might be sequenced and delivered in the preparation of an international assignee for an overseas assignment.[64] Given a number of different types of problems that international assignees and their families might face, plus a number of possible development objectives, the particular methods chosen for training and orientation should vary as well.

First, in the development of such an international assignee preparation and training program, IHR must recognize the various types of problems that exist for

BOX 6.3 **PREPARATION AND TRAINING FOR INTERNATIONAL ASSIGNEES**

1 Establishing and maintaining relationships
- (a)   Internal within the firm
- (b)   External with the community
- (c)   Family
- (d)   Host government
- (e)   Home government
- (f)   Headquarters

2 Preparation objectives
- (a)   Review terms and conditions of assignment
- (b)   Increase cultural awareness
- (c)   Increase knowledge of host country
- (d)   Impart working knowledge of the foreign language
- (e)   Increase conflict management skills
- (f)   Minimize re-entry problems

3 Forms of training
- (a)   Predeparture
  - (i)   Cultural orientation
  - (ii)   Area study
  - (iii)   Language instruction
  - (iv)   Cross-cultural T-group
- (b)   Behavioral simulations
- (c)   Case studies
- (d)   Post-arrival training
  - (i)   Cultural orientation and training
  - (ii)   Intergroup problem solving
  - (iii)   Assignment of a local "buddy" and/or culture mentor
- (e)   Re-entry training and orientation

4 Training outcomes
- (a)   Knowledge about cultural, political, economic, business, legal, and social factors of the host country
- (b)   Awareness of the needs and expectations of the different parties interested in the international operation
- (c)   Awareness of the problems of family relationships in the host country

Source Based on Rahim, A. (1983), A model for developing key expatriate executives, *Personnel Journal*, April: 23–28.

international assignees. These range from difficulties with business relationships (either within or external to the firm or with headquarters), difficulties within the international assignee's family, or difficulties with either the host or home country governments. Each of these potential sources of difficulty has its own particular solutions with its own specific objectives that will help overcome the problems. For example, developing a working knowledge of the host country language can lead to improvements in a number of the possible relationship concerns. And the particular development methods chosen should be matched to specific development needs. As the differences between the culture of the international assignee and his or her family become greater relative to that of the new foreign location, the length and rigor of the training should also become greater.[65] Ultimately, the objective is for the international assignee to be successful in his or her assignment, to remain in the foreign locale for the duration of that assignment, and to return to the parent firm to an assignment that effectively uses the international assignee's new skills and motivation.

In terms of design for training for international assignees, research and writing about training, in general, have suggested a number of guidelines that seem appropriate, here.[66] For example, training needs to take into account the influence of the environment, which seems particularly relevant in cross-cultural training. And it ought to progress in terms of content and pedagogy in relation to the knowledge, experience, and competencies of the trainees. Lastly, it has been suggested that international assignee training most comprehensively should focus on all of these competencies:[67]

- *Cognitive competency.* The acquisition of knowledge and facts about cultures, including such factors as history, economics, politics, business practices, sensitive areas, and family relations.
- *Behavioral competency.* The ability to adapt to diverse conditions, to communicate in other cultures, to scan the country environment capably, to show skill at human relations in another culture, learn the appropriate etiquette and protocol, and to manage stress effectively.
- *Performance competency.* The ability to perform well in the assigned business or organizational tasks in another culture, including the appropriate technical and managerial skills, the ability to be creative at adaptation while engaging in critical thinking, positional understanding and learning on the job, and the ability to develop networks and support systems for accomplishing the tasks at hand.

At a minimum, training and preparing international assignees for international assignments should cover the following *topics* to facilitate the ever-crucial adjustment process:[68]

- *Intercultural business skills*, e.g., negotiation styles in different countries and cultures.
- *Culture shock management*, e.g., what to expect and how to deal with the stress of adaptation.

- *Life-style adjustment*, e.g., how to deal with different shopping and transport systems and the different availability of familiar foods and entertainment.
- *Host country daily living issues*, e.g., any unfamiliar problems with water or electricity.
- *Local customs and etiquette*, e.g., what to wear and different behavior patterns and gestures for men and women.
- *Area studies*, e.g., the political and religious environment and the local geography.
- *Repatriation planning*, e.g., how to stay in touch with the home office and how to identify an appropriate assignment prior to repatriating back home).
- *Language learning strategies*, both before leaving for the new assignment as well as after arrival.

In the broader picture, many firms divide their preparation of international assignees into two categories: counseling and training. The counseling component deals primarily with the mechanics of a move abroad while the training tries to develop skills and sensitivities to national and cultural issues that will better enable the international assignee and family to adapt to and enjoy their new situation. Increasingly, firms are realizing how important such preparation is to the international business success of their international assignees.

The types of topics covered by their normal counseling and training sessions for people going on a foreign assignment include the following:[69]

Counseling

- Compensation, benefits, and taxes.
- Travel.
- Shipping and storage of household goods.
- Housing and property management.
- Local transportation.
- Allowances.
- Vacations and home leaves.
- Language training and orientation.
- Children's educational expenses and options.

Training

- Local customs, politics, religions, attitudes.
- Local laws.
- Safety, health, and security.
- Cultural sensitivity, food, water, and so on.
- Background briefing on company: history, policies, individuals.

And lastly, another firm recommends that a thorough preparation program should include all of the following:[70]

- A pre-visit to the new site.
- Language training.

- Intensive area study.
- Country-specific handbooks that include both country and company facts and where to get additional information.
- In-company counseling on issues such as taxes, legal matters, compensation, the move, and the like.
- Meetings with repatriates who have recently returned home from the location to which the international assignee is moving.
- Local sponsorship and assistance for arrival and orientation to the new locale and assignment.

Such an extensive program of preparation can minimize the high level of premature returns and bad experiences due to maladjustment to foreign assignments by international assignees and their families and the consequent inadequate levels of performance in the foreign assignment.

Even though there is much controversy as to the ability of people to learn about other cultures through training programs (some authors suggest one must experience a culture first-hand in order to gain a real understanding and/or adaptation to it—this is discussed in more detail in the section on developing global executives), at least some evidence suggests that these sorts of training programs do help.[71] Indeed, the experience of the American University-based Business Council for International Understanding in its work with Shell Oil Company in the US shows that pre-departure training can reduce dramatically the international assignee failure rate).[72] For example, prior to providing any training to its employees being sent to Saudi Arabia, Shell was experiencing a 60 percent early return rate. With three days of training, that rate dropped to 5 percent. With a six-day pre-departure program, the figure dropped to 1.5 percent! It is estimated that, without any pre-departure cross-cultural training, only about 20 percent of Americans sent overseas do well.[73]

As stated in the discussion of culture shock, international assignees and their families must learn to cope with—depending on the country—a varying number, importance, and criticality of disruptions to their normal routines and ways of living. Accordingly, effective pre-departure training must vary its content and intensity according to the distance between what is normal and familiar and what will be experienced in the new assignment. The greater the distance between the home culture and the host culture (i.e., cultural distance), the more extensive and lengthy the training should be. And, whenever possible, both pre-departure and post-arrival training should be provided, with the post-arrival training focusing on the more complicated aspects of the new culture, since the typical international assignee and family are not ready for the more detailed cultural training—until they have experienced the culture first-hand.[74]

The design and delivery of cross-cultural training

Training for cross-cultural adjustment should focus on helping international assignees and their families do three things: (1) become aware that behaviors vary across cultures, including being different than what they are used to, and work at observing these differences quite carefully; (2) build a mental map of the new culture so they can understand why the local people value certain behaviors and ideas and how those behaviors and ideas may be appropriately reproduced; and (3) practice the behaviors they will need to be effective in their overseas assignments. Without training of this sort, most people will not be successful in learning how to adapt to their new culture.[75]

When the training and preparation of international assignees and their families are done well, the IHR department will have completed a checklist that looks something like this for each international assignee and his or her family:

- Develop an overseas compensation and benefits plan, taking into account cost-of-living differences and any special needs.
- Provide tax advice and financial counselling.
- Supervise the sometimes extensive paperwork involved with making an international move, such as arranging work visas.
- Assist with housing and the selection of good schools for any children.
- Help the international assignee set up banking accounts and make cash transfers.
- Transfer medical, dental, and school records, and assist with inoculations.
- Help with absentee ballots and international drivers' licenses.
- Organize and provide cross-cultural training to be delivered both pre-departure and post-arrival to both the international assignee and the family.
- Provide language training, often through "immersion" courses;
- Assist with moves of household furniture and goods abroad and living arrangements in the foreign locale.
- Helping the trailing spouse get work permit and/or job abroad, if possible.

The more effort and time both trainers and trainees put into such training and preparation, that is, the more rigorous is the training, the more likely the international assignee and family members will be to learn the behaviors and attitudes they will need for success in the foreign assignment. And matching rigor to the needs of the international assignee and family and to the degree of "differentness" of the new country and culture is the key to the design of a valid cross-culture training and preparation program.

The previous paragraphs in this section have focused on the training and preparation of international assignees and their families. But some form of training and/or orientation would also seem appropriate for other employees of the MNE, especially those working internationally, managing diverse work forces or international parts of the organizations. This would include domestic internationalists, international commuters, business travelers, and virtual internationalists, as well as traditional short-term and long-term international assignees. If the global enterprise really wants to expand its work force's global business capabilities, then it seems essential that it provide cross-cultural training and orientation to everyone

Global executives: developing managers in the global enterprise

There also comes a time in the development of global enterprises when they begin to examine the development of their managers from an international perspective. At this point, they will not only begin to realize that international experience is necessary for their parent-country managers, but they will also begin to realize the importance of developing managerial talent from throughout their global enterprise. Indeed, probably the most formidable task in the human resource area facing many global firms today is the development of a cadre of team members, managers and executives who have a deep understanding of the global marketplace, have the ability to transfer this knowledge into resolute global action, and who expect to see their rewards and personal and professional growth linked to opportunities for global careers in which to exercise this understanding.[76] Global companies need executives (and, probably, other employees as well) who can easily switch from one culture to another, people who are fluent in several cultures and languages, and who can work effectively as part of an international team, keeping misunderstandings to a minimum.[77] They are the keys to global business success. But it's not easy. Too many companies have been slow to become truly culturally aware simply because their key decision makers lack the necessary international experience and exposure and, therefore, global vision.

Many global firms have invested well in the development of their local staffs (in both their parent country and host country operations) and can thus identify competent managers who are well qualified to handle local operations in most of their principal markets. At the same time, though, they are short of seasoned executives with broad international skills who are closely attuned to the firm's global strategy. Too much localization has often resulted in insufficient globalization of the managerial ranks. But reversing this reality is not easy, in terms of both the cost and complexity of developing a new breed of global executives and the challenge this creates for the established process of management development.

Often, the business environments that international firms experience are radically different than what they are used to. In such situations, IHR must tailor its policies and practices to local conditions while at the same time modifying the mind-set and technical skills of local managers and employees to accept and match world-class standards. To facilitate and manage this globalization, it becomes critical for firms to identify and develop leaders who are capable of functioning effectively on a global scale and with a global perspective. In a global economy, this strategic preparation of global leaders has become a major component of IHR's contribution. In essence, IHR must design HR processes, including global training and management development programs, which encourage and facilitate the organization so as to ensure that its "global whole" is greater than the sum of its domestic parts.

Patterns of global management development

As important as management development with an international focus is for today's MNEs, the reality is that there has not been much research into patterns or methods employed by major firms. Nevertheless, the following few paragraphs summarize what has been identified.[78]

The most important of these common elements for the major MNEs is the priority placed on identifying and developing management talent. At firms such as IBM, Shell, Philips, and Unilever, responsibility for international executive development is so important that it is specifically a board concern and the executive in charge of this activity reports direct to the CEO. These firms have found that the lack of globally savvy management talent has been a major inhibitor in setting up overseas businesses or developing new global projects, even in some cases preventing them from staffing projects which have been technically feasible. Even smaller firms have come to understand the importance of having a cadre of global managers. In the words of Graham Corbett who, a few years ago was senior partner for KPMG's continental European practice: "We are on a fast growth track, and our major task is to attract and develop enough professional talent to enable us to support the [global] growth rates we are experiencing."[79]

Firms from different countries appear to have evolved varying approaches to management development. Yet there are some common elements among them. These include practices such as:

- The early identification of individuals with executive potential, either through early-in-career assessment procedures and close monitoring of job performance or recruiting at only élite universities and *grandes écoles* or the use of in-house apprenticeships that lead to increasing levels of management responsibility.
- The use of close monitoring of those individuals identified through whichever procedure(s) to be candidates for positions of executive leadership.[80]

The primary purpose of the close monitoring is to manage the careers and job assignments of these high-potential employees. The movement (or mobility) of these individuals is controlled so as to ensure that they experience job assignments, including overseas assignments, of adequate variety, challenge, and appropriate responsibility (to include multiple functional, product, and country experiences, and important developmental content, often away from the individual's area of proven expertise) and length, so as to ensure the individuals learn how to achieve results in new settings and through new associates, particularly colleagues from other countries and cultures. A number of observers have also noticed that this mobility among international locations creates informal networks that enable information and problem solving to be shared worldwide in a more effective way than the formal, traditional, hierarchical structures appear to provide.

Senior executives from Europe, Asia, and the US indicate that their firms have a shortage of managers with the necessary competencies to operate effectively in a global marketplace.[81] They indicate that this is a major constraint on their abilities to expand their operations and to compete well in that global marketplace. In this context, then, IHR managers must ask themselves the following questions:

If global enterprises do indeed have such shortages, then what does a global executive "look like"? That is, what are their characteristics? And how can an MNE develop them? Or is it possible to just copy in the international arena that which is done on the domestic front? This section of the chapter addresses these types of questions.

KNOWLEDGE MANAGEMENT IN THE MULTINATIONAL ENTERPRISE

A true transnational company is globally integrated through standardized processes, locally responsive to adapt to cultural practices and legal compliance, and is able to share knowledge across the enterprise.[82] Although the benefits of knowledge management are well known, effectively sharing knowledge and best practice across the MNE is much harder to achieve. Many barriers to knowledge sharing in domestic environment are exaggerated when the firm gets larger, more complex, and global. Common barriers to knowledge management include:

- Ignorance and lack of relationships.
- Lack of a system for sharing.
- Belief that knowledge is power (so one doesn't want to share it).
- People are insecure about the value of their knowledge.
- Lack of trust.
- People are afraid of negative consequences related to sharing what they know.
- The belief that best practices do not move across borders and cultures.
- Language and translation issues.
- Superiority and/or condescending attitudes.
- Intra-organizational competition.

IHRM in Action 6.2 describes how disaster relief organizations often are forced to "reinvent the wheel" rather than relying on previous expertise.

CONCLUSION

This chapter on T&D in the MNE has focused on one of the key assets of successful MNEs, namely the development of competent work forces, ones which are capable of operating in global teams, equipped with global mind-sets, and able to provide leadership in the global arena. It also has emphasized the importance of cross-cultural preparation, especially for international assignees. While many of these elements are considered to be the "soft" part of global management, an MNE's ability to build these competencies in its work force is considered a key competitive advantage.

BUILDING ON FIELD EXPERIENCE

The International Federation of Red Cross and Crescent Societies

In the world of humanitarian non-governmental organizations (NGOs), few voluntary organizations are as recognized as the Red Cross. The International Federation of Red Cross and Crescent Societies (IFRC) directs and coordinates international assistance to some of the world's most vulnerable people. Although this large relief organization may be a household name and thought of as one entity, in reality its organizational structure is highly fragmented. How, then, does such a global federation of organizations expand its informational network and share knowledge across efforts and field employees?

IFRC is the world's largest humanitarian organization, with 185 member national societies. Together they have 97 million members and volunteers and 300,000 employees, assisting around 233 million beneficiaries every year. All work is guided by seven fundamental humanitarian principles: humanity, impartiality, neutrality, independence, voluntary service, unity, and universality. The idea for the Red Cross emerged in 1859 with Henri Dunant. In 1863, five Geneva men (including Dunant) set up the International Committee for Relief to the Wounded. This was the foundation of the Red Cross. The following year twelve governments adopted the first Geneva Convention, a milestone in the history of humanity. The International Federation was founded in 1919 in the aftermath of the First World War with five national societies as founding members. Today, that number has grown to 185 recognized national societies, one in almost every country in the world.

The "added value" of the IFRC lies in both direct disaster response and its efforts in sustaining developing countries. In disaster situations, time is almost always of the essence, since every passing day may entail the loss of lives. The logistic apparatus rolled out for any given response relies heavily on information available about the affected region and its implicated stakeholders. In order for a response to be effective, a large amount of information must be processed, analyzed, validated, and distributed to the right people—all this without losing the neutrality of the organization and thereby eroding its mandate or "license to operate."

When responding to a disaster, the IFRC usually deploys two different units: the Field Assessment Coordination Team (FACT) as first responders who have to hit the ground running, and the Emergency Response Units (ERUs) who follow up on the emergency response, addressing logistics, basic health, water treatment, medical services and telecommunication needs. Experienced IFRC staff employees and highly trained field delegates are likely to hold a large amount of tacit knowledge about disaster response. When responding to an emergency or disaster the FACT and ERUs work closely together with any relevant national society in serving the beneficiaries in the affected area or region. Each engagement has different phases where effective management and sharing of knowledge are of the utmost importance. A standard approach entails a "ramp-up phase" where appeals for funds and goods will take place alongside initiating early assessments and immediate help. The typically longer-lasting "sustaining phase" then follows with a focus on the logistic layout and aiding affected beneficiaries. Finally a "ramp-down" phase is initiated, entailing an exit strategy and possibly handing over relief work to the local national society or any other engaged stakeholders.

Each IFRC deployment represents a scenario where knowledge is of the essence. It also offers the opportunity to harvest imperative information. This information is presumably best collected when "hot" and preferably debriefing sessions should be held with delegates after completion of any field session. As can be expected, this is not always feasible due to the nature of the work and the sometimes very hectic work lives of globally based IFRC delegates. This is really the Achilles heel of effective knowledge management regarding disaster relief in this organization. After a deployment, it is a best practice to produce an After Action Report (AAR) building on consolidated information. This allows the harvesting of valuable lessons learned or best practices that can be used in forthcoming actions.

To assist with knowledge sharing, a virtually based Disaster Management Information System (DMIS) was started in 2001. One of the key objectives of the system is to respond to the need for information so that fast and informed decisions can be made efficient operational readiness deployed when a disaster occurs. The creation of the DMIS system sought to address these hurdles by ensuring that existing knowledge within the IFRC and the network of national societies is captured, codified and made accessible to the staff at large. The DMIS provides real-time information on disaster trends, online internal and external resources, and valuable tools and databases. It is accessible only to Red Cross and Red Crescent staff, including delegates and national societies. The advantage of such a system becomes apparent when mitigating the fallout of cyclical disasters. Knowing that some parts of the world suffer from these disasters with regular intervals, the DMIS can be used to carry out early risk assessments, initiate procurement, and develop high levels of preparedness. AARs and the DMIS are two concrete ways by which the IFRC makes the tacit knowledge gained from disasters explicit and codifies it in order to share it within the larger worldwide organizations. Interestingly enough, it seems that difficulties in fieldwork are not always caused by lack of information or imperfect knowledge, but may also be the result from information overload fueled by a chaotic situation. The problem with too much information is how to validate and distribute it effectively as well as sorting the relevant from the irrelevant.

The IFRC is not constantly reinventing the wheel when it comes to disaster relief. To the contrary, it shares knowledge from one disaster to another and formally captures lessons learned for subsequent use around the globe.

Source Claus, L. & Schjotz-Christensen, M. (2007) Global HR in Action Vignettes, Willamette University, www.willamette.edu/agsm/global_hr.

GUIDED DISCUSSION QUESTIONS

1 What are the major issues related to global T&D?

2 How can the effectiveness of global virtual teams be improved?

3 How can global leadership be developed?

4 How does one acquire a global mind-set?

5 What is the role of cross-cultural preparation in international assignment management?

6 How can MNEs overcome barriers for knowledge sharing across borders?

VIGNETTE 6.1   NORDIC AND SCANDINAVIAN MANAGEMENT CULTURES IN ACTION

Globalization at TietoEnator

How does a Nordic and Scandinavian startup in the IT services and software industries become a global provider and employer without losing its Nordic and Scandinavian roots? This is TietoEnator's challenge!

TietoEnator, one of the largest IT services providers and software companies in Europe, supports clients in selected vertical markets, mainly in the banking, telecom, health care, energy and forest industries. Founded in 1999 in Espoo, Finland, where its corporate headquarters are still located, it has rapidly grown to become a global company with €1.6 billion in revenues and over 16,000 employees worldwide (2006). As a young start-up, its business was mainly focused in the northern European countries in terms of customers and employees. Befitting its industry, the company made a strategic decision to go global through well chosen acquisitions in selected vertical areas. While it originally had a decentralized approach, it quickly realized that it must become more globally integrated by leveraging its people through a well executed strategy and processes.

TietoEnator has a strong Nordic and Scandinavian background and one of its key objectives, besides growth and profit, is to be a preferred employer by IT professionals around the world. Its Nordic and Scandinavian management culture is characterized by:

- An emphasis on the high value of people.
- A highly participative management style.

- A culture of communication and dialogue.
- A fast decision-making process, yet forward-looking at the impact of the decisions on employees, leadership, and the organization.
- Strong emphasis on building technical, business and leadership competencies.
- Reliance on metrics.
- A business philosophy that it is "one" global company.

As the company globalizes very rapidly it understands the need to leverage its knowledge base around the world by insuring that current and future leaders obtain the skills needed to lead a very dynamic and growing global organization. As a result, a number of targeted HR interventions have been implemented, including promoting international assignments, creating global development opportunities, promoting employees internally, and delivering HR programs and policies that are global yet consider local country differences.

In the high-tech industry, it is very important for TietoEnator to maintain its competitive edge by ensuring that employees build technical, business, and leadership competencies for their current and future needs. Operating in twenty-five countries, the company offers a variety of training programs worldwide. It does not necessarily limit employee participation based on work geography but a variety of different country employees may be attending any one training session anywhere in the world. For example, the company offered a leadership course in India and the attendees were a mixture of management employees from India and European countries. As a global company, TietoEnator understands the benefits of having employees from a variety of cultures participate in the same training sessions. The training results for both the company and the employees provide a richer global experience, breaking down any national barriers, which keeps contributing to the company's global business philosophy of being a "one TietoEnator."

To address the need for competencies, TietoEnator created an integrated performance management and development system. It is called Bridge because it focuses on "bridging" the current employee competencies with what will be needed within the next one to five years. Senior HR managers throughout the world worked together to create this truly global HR program. Extensive Bridge training has been conducted for managers and employees worldwide to obtain the best employee and organizational results. Each year, senior managers establish targets for their groups based on the company's vision, mission, strategy, and objectives. Together with their employees, they establish at least three performance targets for the next period through the Bridge development discussion process. The success of the Bridge process relies on managers regularly following up with their employees by coaching, developing, and supporting them to reach their targets, which ultimately results in the employee and organization obtaining higher performance levels. Through this program employees are encouraged to grow and develop, and they understand that the company is investing in them for the longterm.

Even HR has been expected to create global synergies while responding to local differences. The VP of HR developed an Employment Management Services (EMS) international organization made up of senior HR representatives from around the world. This group works closely with the domestic HR organizations to create a "one TietoEnator" by prioritizing and creating global HR programs and policies. According to Carol Olsby, Seattle-based HR director, Americas and Asia, and member of EMS: "Working within HR at TietoEnator has been very exciting and a much richer and more global experience than I have had in the past. The company has gone to great lengths to ensure that the HR programs and policies that we are creating consider both global and local HR perspectives."

TietoEnator also relies heavily on HR centers of expertise to leverage subsidiary knowledge when developing global HR programs and policies. For example, Nordic and Scandinavian countries are known for their expertise in developing employee competencies and India leads in employment branding knowledge. By focusing on participative management style and leveraging the HR knowledge throughout the world, TietoEnator creates "best practices" HR programs and policies which truly represent global perspectives. TietoEnator understands that the most important thing it can do is leverage its own employee knowledge base around the world in support of its strategic globalization efforts.

Questions

1 What are the characteristics of the Nordic and Scandinavian management culture at TietoEnator?

2 What ways can a company use to leverage its knowledge resources globally?

3 How does a rapidly growing startup maintain its organizational culture when it becomes global?

Source Claus, L. (2007), Global HR in Action Vignettes, Willamette University, www.willamette.edu/agsm/global_hr.

Global compensation, benefits, and taxes

LEARNING OBJECTIVES

This chapter will enable the reader to:

- Outline the basic objectives of global compensation and benefits (C&B)
- Distinguish between global remuneration and international assignment C&B
- Identify critical issues in C&B of the global work force of the MNE
- Describe the types of compensation systems available for international assignees
- Explain the balance sheet approach, as well as other approaches, to designing international assignment C&B packages
- Identify the challenges of dealing with various tax structures and methods affecting international assignment C&B

KEY TERMS

- Balance sheet
- "Cafeteria" plan
- Cost of living allowance (COLA)
- Differential index
- Efficient purchaser index
- Expatriate compensation
- Global remuneration
- Hardship allowance
- Home country spendable
- Host country spendable
- Housing norm

- ▪ Hypothetical tax
- ▪ Incentives and premiums
- ▪ International assignment compensation
- ▪ *Laissez-faire*
- ▪ Localization
- ▪ Lump sum
- ▪ Reserves
- ▪ Split payroll
- ▪ Stock options
- ▪ Tax equalization
- ▪ Tax protection

The design and maintenance of an enterprise's total reward system are always a critical responsibility for HR managers. International business makes this responsibility more complex and difficult and requires additional HR competencies in global remuneration and international assignment compensation and even closer collaboration with business partners in the accounting, finance, tax, and legal divisions, and the line managers of the MNE. The determination of pay and benefits on an international basis becomes extremely complicated because of new considerations such as C&B for subsidiary work forces in multiple countries, for employees from many different countries (such as inpatriates, host country nationals, and third country nationals), varying country approaches to and levels of pay and benefits, international assignees who move across borders for differing periods of time, and problems such as dealing with differing standards and costs of living, multiple currencies, exchange rates, inflation rates, tax systems, and tax rates. In addition, international HR managers also spend a lot of time and effort creating and managing compensation packages for expatriates.[1] When the development of compensation systems for subsidiaries and determining pay and benefits for a global work force are added to these IHRM responsibilities, it is easy to see why this area of concern is so important.

In global C&B, a distinction is made between global remuneration and IA compensation. *Global remuneration* deals with the C&B structure for employees of the MNE in various locations/subsidiaries around the world. Global remuneration is more complex than domestic compensation because salary levels and benefit provisions invariably differ significantly among the various countries in which an MNE operates.[2] Employees performing essentially similar jobs in different countries may have different titles and will receive varying amounts and forms of compensation. This is due to differing costs of living and general pay levels throughout these economies and varying traditions and values for particular jobs. *International assignment compensation* deals with the compensation and benefits of globally mobile employees—or those who cross borders as part of their employment with the MNE, either as short-term international assignees or as long-term expatriates.

International assignment compensation is also complex because it deals with people relocating to different countries and are, thus, subject to different laws and regulations, cost-of living adjustments, taxation systems, exchange rate fluctuations, and varying inflation/deflation rates. In addition, the cost of attracting and maintaining expatriates and an international cadre of managers and technicians in the traditional ways has become so expensive that MNEs are now looking for new ways to handle international compensation.[3]

The effective design of a global C&B philosophy is absolutely necessary for successful HR management in the MNE. How an MNE copes with these C&B issues tends to, at least partially, be a function of the company's overall rewards strategy, its level of international development, its corporate culture, and the other talent management elements in the HR (such as competency management, performance management, training and development, and deployment). A well designed global C&B system will balance the cost and benefits for the company and yet make the total reward system attractive for the recruitment and retention of employees. Therefore, the main objectives for the typical MNE global C&B program include:

- Attraction and retention of the best qualified talent to staff the MNE.
- Attraction and retention of employees who are qualified for international assignments.
- Facilitation of transfers between the various employment locations within the MNE.
- Establishment and maintenance of a consistent and reasonable relationship between the compensation of employees of all affiliates, both at home and abroad.
- Maintenance of compensation that is reasonable in relation to the practices of competitors yet minimizes costs to the extent possible.

If these objectives of a well designed reward system are achieved, the MNE will be able to attract the best possible talent, design a compensation system that will be externally competitive and internally equitable, and will be able to remove financial obstacles to the geographic mobility of employees. To address the issues related to the design of a global C&B system, this chapter first looks at the design of a this system and examines the problems associated with the design of worldwide C&B programs and policies. Second, this chapter looks at the problems associated with C&B for international assignees and reviews the different expatriate compensation approaches used by MNEs. Because of the extreme complexity of this subject (MNEs usually contract with specialists to design and administer the details of compensation, benefits, and taxes of international assignees), this chapter can only provide an overview of and introduction to the many issues related to global C&B.

GLOBAL REMUNERATION IN THE MULTINATIONAL ENTERPRISE

Global remuneration involves partly the philosophy of how an MNE pays its employees (a common set of principles on which the organization bases its reward system) and is partly the result of the external contextual constraints of the countries in which the MNE operates (i.e., cultural practices, laws, and tax systems). Because the pervasive centralization–localization dilemma also impacts C&B, the rewards strategy in MNEs is generally standardized (in order to be aligned with overall strategic objectives) while the specific C&B practices tend to be localized (to fit the cultural, legal, and taxation context of each specific country). The firm's compensation approach can be to lead, lag, or be at market equivalency compared with the competition in the same industry and/or geographic location. This decision will mainly depend on its corporate culture and values regarding employee rewards. Yet, the specific national context in which the employee works will determine a number of compensation issues such as comparability, cultural factors, salary–benefit ratio, tax laws, sunshine rules, and salary expression, to name a few. In best HR practice, a compensation approach starts with a job analysis (job description and job specification), and job evaluation. This determines what the job entails (job description), what kind of people to hire for the job (job specifications), and how much the job is worth (job evaluation).

Global remuneration issues and challenges

C&B specialists encounter a number of new challenges when developing a total reward system for the MNE compared to those experienced in a purely domestic company. Especially important in global remuneration is the issue of *comparability* or determining who is a peer for a job in the various countries and subsidiaries. For example, the term "manager" may have different meanings and connotations in different countries. In one country the job of "manager" may be a job exempt from overtime compensation (such as is usually the case in the US), while in another country it may be a unionized job (such as is sometimes the case in certain Western European countries). In some countries, a car and fuel credit card may be a standard benefit for a manager, while in others a car may be provided only if needed as part of the job requirement.

Obviously, national and organizational *cultures* also influence how people perceive the value of the various rewards available in the compensation system. For example, the culture may be performance-driven (and pay for performance is a well established norm) or it may be entitlement-oriented (with longevity of service rewarded). In some cultures people are more willing to accept risk in their compensation while in others people are quite risk-averse. In addition, the level of uncertainty avoidance in a culture may determine the amount of fixed versus variable pay that people will accept.

The *salary–benefit ratio*, or the amount of compensation that is salary versus benefit, may also differ by country as a result of cultural practices, laws, or regulations. And *tax laws* have, probably, the biggest impact on how MNEs structure their C&B systems. Not only are people taxed differently on their incomes and their benefits are treated in differing ways across national tax systems, but C&B expenses of companies are treated differently in different countries in terms of corporate tax expense deductions. Therefore, a benefit that, in principle, may seem to have general appeal from, say, headquarters' perspective, may very well be viewed as unacceptable, depending on how it is taxed locally. Countries also differ in terms of "sunshine rules" and how they *express salaries*. Whether or not employees' salary information is confidential or disclosed is generally dictated by local cultural practice and law. In some countries and some occupations, everybody knows what everyone else makes (openly disclosing salary information to the public is called a sunshine rule); in others salary information is strictly confidential. In some countries salaries are quoted in net amounts while in others they are stated in gross amounts, or in weekly, monthly, or annual terms. In some countries, thirteenth and fourteenth month payments (usually end-of-year and vacation/holiday stipends) are part of the annual compensation package, no matter the performance of employees, while in other countries they are part of a bonus plan for only certain groups of employees. So, knowing how base salary is expressed (net or gross, weekly, monthly, or annual) and what is included in the amount is important to reduce misperceptions and errors in judgment about appropriate levels of C&B based purely on home practices. Understanding these issues is highly important for IHRM as it attempts to design C&B programs and practices for the global operations of the MNE. IHR practitioners should never assume, especially with regard to C&B, that things are done in other parts of the world the same way as they know it.

In addition to these challenges, other factors such as economics, labor relations, laws and regulations, and the level of government-provided and mandated benefits play a role. A global staffing approach within the MNE implies that the right people are hired, with the right skills, and are located at the right place, at the right time, at the right cost. Yet the *global law of economics* with regard to staffing must be considered, with work needing to be located where the quality and cost of the production of goods and services are optimized. Important variables in determining the best locations for MNE operations include employee C&B expenses, operational logistics, and proximity to raw materials and the customer base. Labor costs differ considerably around the world. Table 7.1 presents international comparisons of hourly compensation costs for production workers in manufacturing industries in selected countries. Hourly compensation costs include (1) hourly direct pay and (2) employer social insurance expenditures and other labor taxes. They are appropriate measures for comparing levels of employer labor costs. Using the US as the index (=100), labor costs in Scandinavia, Western Europe and Australia are higher than the US and lower in Southern Europe, Central and Eastern Europe and the rest of the world. Considering $ equivalency, the hourly labor costs in manufacturing range from $2.5 in Mexico to $4.64 in Norway (2004).

International HR practitioners—in order to make effective decisions about the best locations for MNE operations—must develop metrics of the fully loaded cost of labor and productivity by employee groups in different parts of the MNE so as to be able to balance staffing decisions based on the strategic priorities of their organization.

Table 7.1 Hourly compensation costs for production workers in manufacturing, 2004

Country	Index (US = 100)	Hourly $
Australia	101	23.09
Austria	124	28.29
Belgium	131	30.10
Brazil	13	3.03
Canada	94	21.42
Czech Republic	24	5.43
Denmark	148	33.75
Finland	134	30.67
France	149	23.89
Germany	142	32.53
Hong Kong SAR	24	5.51
Hungary	25	5.72
Ireland	96	21.94
Israel	53	12.18
Italy	90	20.48
Japan	96	21.90
Luxembourg	116	26.57
Mexico	11	2.50
Netherlands	134	30.76
New Zealand	56	12.89
Norway	151	34.64
Portugal	31	7.02
Singapore	33	7.44
South Korea	50	11.52
Spain	75	17.10
Sweden	124	28.41
Switzerland	132	30.26
Taiwan	26	5.97
United Kingdom	108	24.71
United States	100	22.87

Source ftp://ftp.bls.gov/pub/special.requests/ForeignLabor/industrynaics.txt.

Labor relations, collective bargaining, and employee representation also differ greatly from country to country. Job security, compensation, benefits, and worker entitlements tend to be the major concerns of labor unions. Therefore, relations with unions are bound to impact the MNE's local C&B plans.

In addition, countries around the world have passed various extensive *laws and regulations* impacting remuneration of employees such as minimum wage, overtime, compulsory bonuses and other entitlements, severance payments, employee contract requirements, and taxation of employee and corporate incomes. This includes great variance from country to country in *government-provided and mandated benefits*. HR must know which benefits are government-provided and mandated in each country in which they operate, especially in terms of the severance-related benefits, paid time off, social welfare benefits (such as health care and retirement) and various leave requirements.

Finally, the global C&B specialist plays a critical role in the due diligence and post-merger integration phases of a merger/acquisition. Critical in the due diligence phase (prior to the acquisitions) are reviews of C&B practices, funding regarding future pension obligations, potential severance liabilities, equity and stock option plans, vacation accruals, and any other unwritten but established reward practices. In the post-merger integration phase, the redesign of the new global C&B system is critical.

IHR C&B specialists must examine the MNE's C&B programs for their employees at each and all of its subsidiaries and foreign operations. The greater the number of foreign subsidiaries and joint ventures and the greater the number of countries within which the MNE operates, the greater will be the problems associated with establishing, monitoring, and controlling C&B programs on a worldwide basis. The stage of the MNE's evolution or development (as described in Chapter 2) makes a big difference in how it handles C&B for all of its global employees. If it is still in stage one (export) or two (sales subsidiaries), it will differentiate between parent country (PCN), host country (HCN), and third country (TCN) employees and most IHRM attention from headquarters will be given to C&B packages for expatriates (PCNs). Later, when in stages three (international), four (multinational), five (global), six (transnational), or seven (born global), i.e., becoming more global in emphasis and attention, the C&B package will be more likely to be designed for all employees worldwide based on the same reward strategy, yet with local implementation tactics. Global remuneration must achieve a delicate balance between standardization and adaptation. Advanced MNEs usually have a consistent strategic approach to compensation of their employees in different locations around the world emanating from their corporate culture, headquarters mandate, and overall strategy. Yet, they also develop local C&B tactics for each country in which they operate because of differing cultural practices, legal requirements, and tax systems. A critical step in this is for global C&B specialists to determine the specific compensation model in each country in which they operate so they can appropriately localize their C&B packages.

A last major challenge of global remuneration is the issue of equity and comparability: are comparable employees in different parts of the organization treated equitably—or fairly? When dealing with a global company, this perceived equity is of the utmost importance to maintain employee engagement. Fairness is a culturally laden concept: what is considered fair in one culture may not be so in another and a seemingly universally fair procedure may even appear unfair in some cultures solely because of the fact that it is standardized.[4] The MNE's efforts to design a global C&B program, therefore, have to address these types of questions:[5]

- Under which country's C&B programs should employees be covered—parent country, host country, or some specially designed program for everyone?
- How should potential gaps or inequities in pension and health care coverage be bridged? Can employees be covered under a single plan throughout their careers, particularly if they move around during those careers?
- Is benefits coverage adequate for all employees? What's more, is the benefits package equitable when compared with benefits of peers in other countries, both within and without the parent firm? Should employees be covered under the provisions of selected home *and* foreign programs?
- How can the cost of providing social benefits be minimized? Can coverage under employees' home country social programs be maintained, even as they move around? Should there be a global umbrella program to provide equitable coverage for everyone?
- What are the tax effects to employers and employees of special benefit arrangements for all global employees?

To better understand the complexity of global remuneration, the next two sections examine issues that apply specifically to global compensation and to global benefits.

Global compensation

A number of different options (for establishing a worldwide compensation system) have been used by various MNEs. One option is the use of a headquarters scale. In this approach worldwide salary levels are established at headquarters with differentials for each affiliate subsidiary according to their differing costs of living. This option is usually reserved for managerial and executive-level positions. A second option is to base the salary scale on local geography (i.e., the country where the work is performed). In this option, employees are basically paid on a local scale (i.e., Indian employees working in India are paid according to Indian norms and Brazilian employees working in Brazil are paid according to Brazilian norms). This option tends to be used for the broader employee base (usually excluding executives and globally mobile employees). Another option is to determine a global base per position for everyone, possibly with affiliate differentials. This, then, becomes a form of equal pay for equal work on a worldwide basis. The global approach is usually followed when there is a global labor market for the type of talent sought (e.g., software engineers, nurses, designers, etc.) and therefore is of high value because of specific competencies and shortages. This approach also tends to be reserved for employees above a particular job or salary classification.

MNEs often create two classifications—local and international with regard to compensation. All local nationals above a certain level are placed on the headquarters scale, with salaries that are performance-based. The rest of the employees are paid on a local scale. Practices can vary enough so as to make this strategy difficult to implement and may lead to two common problems for host country nationals in the subsidiaries.[6] The first problem relates to a possible in-country gap in compensation between the highest and lowest-paid employee. In most Western countries, there is typically a fairly constant differential between job classifications (e.g., there is typically about a 15 percent increase in salary from job class to job class, and this tends to be the case across all job classifications). In many developing countries and emerging markets, where there tends to be more unskilled labor, it is common to have low pay at all of the lower job classifications, with very little differential between them and then a major jump in compensation only at the upper few classifications. This creates a situation where there can be a much greater ratio between top management and lower-level employees than would be the case for the typical Western, or other developed country, MNE work force. The second problem relates to the gap in executive compensation of the senior managers of the MNE between countries. Comparing the total compensation of CEOs in twelve different OECD countries, US executive compensation is the highest, followed by the UK. Japan has the lowest executive compensation and continental Europe is somewhere in between. In addition, the proportions of base (plus bonus) compensation, long-term compensation, and all benefits/perquisites of executives are also wide-ranging, indicating that executive compensation practices are contextual in terms of practices and taxation.[7]

Not only is there great disparity between wage rates and salary levels in different countries, but it is also difficult to get reliable data on what those rates and levels are so that MNEs can establish competitive pay scales for themselves. Nevertheless, there are a few organizations that publish comparative wage rate data for at least some common locations for MNEs, such as international banks (e.g., the Union Bank of Switzerland), consulting firms (e.g., Hay International), and the US Department of Labor.[8]

However, even the best global compensation program will not eliminate future claims by employees of perceived continued inequity. That is because variations in local labor laws, tax systems, and the cost of living will ensure that dissimilar programs and varying gross pay levels will continue to be a fact of life in a global organization. The goal, though, of a global compensation system is not to eliminate employees' questions about compensation, but rather to remove the de-motivational impact of inexplicable variations in compensation across borders. Designing a global compensation program in this way can enable IHR to create a working environment that hopefully will attract and retain good employees and keep them focused on performance.

Global benefits

However, salary is only one aspect of total remuneration. A second critical component involves the benefits package that employees receive as part of their employment relationship. The design of a comprehensive C&B program for all worldwide employees must, of course, include these non-salary benefits. As is the case with salaries, the development of benefit programs from a global perspective has its own challenges.

The major concern that MNEs face in designing their benefit packages is the widely varying approaches to employee benefits as approached by each country.[9] These include differences in government-provided and mandated benefits, and taxation of these benefits (at the individual and corporate level). In addition, benefits make up a significant (yet varying) portion of the cost of payroll (averaging about 40 percent of payroll expenses in the US). The problems this creates cannot be overstated. Many benefits that are provided by the employer in one country may be provided or mandated by the government (and paid for through employer taxes) in another. Benefits include such offerings as health care, retirement programs/pensions, vacations, and holidays. If they are provided by the government in a particular country, then there is no need for a firm to offer them on a private and voluntary basis. A prime example involves the handling of health care. In some countries, such as the US, health care is basically a private system paid for either by individuals and/or their employers. In most other developed countries, though, health care is provided by a tax-supported system of government-subsidized and/or managed medicine. In yet other countries, such as Great Britain and Mexico, in addition to the government-sponsored, tax-supported system of health care, there is also a competing private medical system, mostly paid for by insurance, with premiums paid by some employers, particularly for higher-level managers and professionals. This makes the provision of many benefits, such as health care, by necessity very localized to the particular country of operation.

In every area of benefits, the variance from country to country in terms of what is normally provided, what is paid by the government from tax revenues, and what employees expect of their employers is quite wide. The global benefits manager in the MNE is faced with such tremendous complexity that it is very difficult for any such manager to be knowledgeable about benefits administration in more than a few countries. As with taxes, the MNE must typically seek advice and assistance from specialized, international accounting and HR consulting firms. The following illustrates this country-by-country variation for a number of common benefits and incentives such as holidays and vacations, pension plans, insurance, leave, flexible benefits, and equity-based compensation.

Working hours

The number of hours worked per year varies considerably from country to country (see Table 7.2). In general, there has been a decline in the number of working hours per year around the world. South Korea remains the only country with more than 2,000 working hours per year. Annual working hours are much higher in the Central and Eastern European countries as compared to Western Europe.

Table 7.2 Hours per year per person in employment, 1994 and 2004

Country	1994	2004	Δ Decade
Australia	1,875	1,816	−59
Belgium	1,551	1,522	−29
Canada	1,749	1,751	2
Czech Republic	2,043	1,986	−57
Denmark	1,494	1 540	46
Finland	1,777	1,736	−40
France	1,650	1,520	−130
Germany	1,536	1,443	−93
Greece	1,935	1,925	−10
Hungary	1,895	1,925	30
Iceland	1,813	1,810	−4
Ireland	1,824	1,642	−182
Italy	1,607	1,585	−22
Japan	1,898	1,789	−109
Korea	2,651	2,423	−228
Mexico	–	1,848	–
Netherlands	1,362	1,357	−5
New Zealand	1,849	1,826	−22
Norway	1,432	1,363	−68
Poland	–	1,983	–
Portugal	1,744	1,694	−50
Slovak Republic	1,975	1,958	−17
Spain	1,816	1,799	−17
Sweden	1,621	1,585	−36
Switzerland	1,671	–	–
United Kingdom	1,736	1,669	−67
United States	1,864	1,824	−39

Source Economic, Environmental and Social Statistics, *OECD Factbook 2006*: OECD, 2006.

Holiday and vacation benefits

There are wide variances among countries in holiday and vacation requirements. National (e.g., the country's national holiday) and religious holidays (the religious holidays of the major faith groups and their observances) are part of the cultural fabric of a society and the religious groups within that society. While in most Western Christian societies no one would consider calling an important company meeting on Christmas day, yet they seem ignorant or oblivious to major religious holidays celebrated by other faiths of their non-Christian employees.

Table 7.3 illustrates how vacation and holiday benefits are mandated in some countries and provided voluntarily in others. It shows the vacation requirements, holidays, and hours of work (weekly) in a number of different countries.[10] Among the countries listed, vacation provisions range from six days for employees with one year of service in Mexico to thirty days for such employees in Austria and Denmark. A US worker must often stay at a job for thirty years to match (and most never reach that level, even in thirty years) the level of paid vacation time that is commonly provided to beginning workers in many European countries. The US, Canada, New Zealand, and Japan are the developed countries that provide the shortest paid vacation time for employees—each granting an average of only ten to fifteen days a year. In the US, paid vacation time is left to the discretion of each company, a situation which is true for most benefits. Most firms base the amount of time provided to employees on the employee's length of service. The average received by American employees in their first years at a firm is eleven days. After five years of service, they earn fifteen days, on the average. Ten years of service result in seventeen days, and thirty years earn employees twenty-four days of paid vacation. In contrast, most European countries (and, others, as well), mandate paid vacation for workers. Denmark mandates thirty-one days of paid vacation while Austria requires companies to give their employees thirty days of vacation; France requires five weeks; and Germany mandates twenty-four days. In addition, most European employers actually extend employee vacation time to six weeks. In the U. K., employees average twenty-two days off with pay.

Pension plans

Retirement benefits create their own special complexities for MNEs.[11] Some countries have defined benefit plans (pays a fixed periodic benefit upon retirement) while others have defined contribution plans (distributes retirement benefit based on contributions to the plan); some have government social security systems (albeit with varying retirement payouts) while others have different (e.g., Providence Funds in some Asian countries) or no retirement plans at all. This makes it difficult for an MNE to streamline the pension plan benefits. For example, when Johnson & Johnson examined its pension system a few years ago, it "discovered" that it not only had a US defined-benefit pension plan covering some 20,000 participants with $1.2 billion in assets, but that it also had another fifteen plans with 15,000 participants worldwide and another $700 million in assets.[12] And this is only one of the many benefit programs with which MNEs must concern themselves.

Table 7.3 Vacations, holidays, and working hours, 2000

Country	Mandated vacation days	Holidays	Work week
Mexico	6–12+	7–10	–
Russia	–	10	40
China	–	No mandatory	37.5
Singapore	7–14	11	44
Hong Kong	7–14	12–18	48
United States[a]	10	10	40
Japan	10–20	12–14	40
Canada	10–15	9+	40
New Zealand	15	11	40
United Kingdom	20	10	40
Switzerland	20	variable	40
Netherlands	20–24	10	40
Ireland	20	–	–
Belgium	20	–	39
Australia	0	9+	38
Spain[b]	22	10	40
Brazil[b]	22	13	–
Germany	24	Up to 15	40
Sweden	25	13	40
Norway	21	11	40
France[c]	25–30	11	35
Austria	30	–	–
Denmark	31	–	37

Notes
[a] No statutory minimum; 82% of companies provide from two weeks (ten days) to fourteen days.
[b] Thirty total calendar days.
[c] Based on six-day work week.

Sources Adapted from Kaplan, C. Y. and Bernstein, Z. S. (2000), "Other benefits", in Reynolds, C. (ed.), *Guide to Global Compensation Benefits*, New York: Harcourt (2000); and "Working practices around the world" *HR World*, November/December (2000), 18–19.

Insurance

Another area of benefits that can add complexity to the design of benefits programs, especially for international assignees, is insurance benefits (such as life, disability, and long-term care insurance). Most large MNEs provide their managers and senior technicians with different insurances as part of their employees' benefit packages. But many insurance policies have territorial and null and void clauses (for example, in case of declared or undeclared war). As a result, the firm may need to purchase special coverage while international assignees and their families are in foreign locations. Depending on the location, the firm may also have to provide special "work risk" insurance, for more dangerous or remote locations and, possibly, other forms of special insurance, e.g., kidnapping insurance.

Leave

An area of employee benefits that has been receiving increasing attention involves the provision of leave for a variety of reasons (e.g., maternity, paternity, parental, family, sabbatical, military, etc.) with or without pay, often with a guarantee of getting one's job back at the end of the leave. This is a benefit provided by most Western countries. Most Western countries tend to be further advanced on the provision of family leave benefits than the US. Approximately two-thirds of all nations, including most industrialized countries, have provision for paid and job-protected maternity leave of four to twelve months prenatal and three to twenty-nine months postnatal.[13] Many countries have parity in terms of maternal and paternal leave. The leave may be paid for by the employer, by the government, or both. Leave of absence management differs greatly among countries. Even though the EU is trying to develop common practices on these types of social policies, there exists diversity even within these close-proximity countries. The IHR practitioner will often need to rely on country-based leave of absence specialists to comply with national regulations.

Flexible benefits

Flexible benefits are offered by an increasing number of US domestic and multinational companies. In essence, employees are typically given choices, up to a certain dollar limit, among a series of options for their benefits (including such things as pension contributions, health insurance options, dental insurance, life insurance, etc.). They may choose not to get certain benefits because they are provided to them by other means (e.g., a spouse or partner) or are not attractive to them in their particular family situation (e.g., child care assistance). MNEs are beginning to examine flex-benefits for their global operations, designing global flex-benefit plans similar to what has been tried within the US[14] This is happening because:

- Flex benefits have been successful in the US, so employers in other countries are beginning to take a look at the idea.
- MNEs have a need to attract and retain more diversified work forces (in terms of age, marital status, family situation), thus they are looking at flex-benefits as a way to attract workers with diverse benefit needs.
- Foreign firms are investing in American health care companies and are thus being exposed to how important flex benefits are in the US for controlling rising health care costs.

● The increased aging of the labor force around the world is leading MNEs to look at flex-benefits as a way to provide diverse benefits to all workers with a single benefits program.

Issues such as the tax treatment of benefits, private versus state health care, employee expectations and culture, non-standardized social benefits from country to country, and varying company structures all need to be addressed in order to design flexible benefit packages that might be used throughout an MNE. Nevertheless, such an approach may help simplify worldwide comprehensive compensation systems for multinational firms.

Equity compensation

In recent years there has been a trend in global firms to look for ways to internationalize their employee equity participation schemes.[15] In particular, this has included experimenting with ways to grant stock options and restricted stock to their overseas employees.[16] Equity compensation programs are being used by MNEs (especially in young, growth-oriented companies and high-tech/telecommunication industries) to attract, motivate, reward, and retain key employees. When employees have a stake in the business by which they are employed, it creates an ownership culture and better aligns individual employee objectives with organizational objectives. Equity compensation programs are generally seen as a powerful and competitive talent management tools for attracting talent, providing an incentive for higher productivity, and reducing turnover.

Major types of equity programs used by MNEs to reward talent on an international scale include employee stock ownership plans (ESOP), employee stock purchase plans (ESPP), stock option plans, stock appreciation rights (SAR), and phantom stock. (Note that phantom stock is not really equity-based.)[17] An overview of these different types of equity compensation plans is presented in Box 7.1. Note that these different plans affect performance and retention in different ways. Equity-based compensation plans may be qualified or non-qualified. A qualified plan provides a favorable tax provision for the employee (at least in the US) but has more qualification rules than a non-qualified plan where the employee does not benefit from the favorable tax rule. For example, US non-qualified stock option plans are generally taxed at exercise tax rates. Equity-based compensation gives young companies an effective way to attract talent, at little cost, and the opportunity of sharing prospective wealth with critical employees, which is often viewed as a very desirable incentive. Yet, using equity-based, long-term incentive compensation has ramifications for the MNE. Varying national accounting tax rules, exchange and currency controls, and tax-withholding requirements make managing equity-based compensation at a global level quite complex.

Earlier accounting rules in the US allowed companies to treat stock options as an expense (i.e., companies were able to deduct that taxable employee income from their own taxable corporate income—even though they didn't really have to spend actual

BOX 7.1 TYPES OF EQUITY COMPENSATION

ESOP

Gives employees shares of company stock (in a bonus or profit-sharing plan) for individual and overall company performance. The benefit is usually redeemable by employees when they leave the company. Awarding employees with stocks is a practice known as "non-restrictive" stock bonus

ESPP

Gives employees an opportunity to purchase company stock, usually through payroll deduction and at discounted price, during a certain period

Stock or call options

Grants certain employees the right to receive or purchase company shares at a specific price called a "strike" or "exercise" price. In other words, it gives employees an option or the right to buy stock in the future at today's price. These grants may be offered "at the money" (the exercise price matches the stock price at the time of the grant), "out of the money" (the exercise price is higher than the stock price at the time of the grant—premium option), or "in the money" (the exercise price is lower than the stock price—discount option). The MNE may choose to grant stock options only to executives or to many employees to create broad-based ownership by its work force. Stock options may be restricted or non-restricted. Common restrictions are that the stock cannot be sold to a third party, that it must be vested (usually after one to five years after the options are granted), that they must be exercised before a defined maturity date (usually ten years), and that they do not qualify for dividends

SAR

Awards a grant to the employee, subject to a vesting schedule, but he/she receives no benefit unless the underlying stock value appreciates. This gives the holder an incentive to improve the financial performance of the company and subsequent stock value appreciation. Obviously, this type of grant is an incentive for the employee only if the stock value increases

Phantom stock

A simulated equity plan that grants the employees a number of fictitious (pretend) stock units whose value corresponds to the price fluctuations of a given number of shares. On maturity the employee is paid a cash bonus based on how much the stock grew by vesting time. Phantom stocks, if structured properly, have certain advantages for the employee and the company. There are no tax consequences to either the company or the employee when a phantom stock unit is granted. It merely gives employees the economic benefits of owning stock without any actual transfer of stock and it doesn't dilute the ownership rights of existing shareholders. Phantom stocks, although not actual equity, are tied to the value of the company's stock.

money to provide the options, with the exception of administrative expenses). However, the Securities and Exchange Commission (SEC) in the US has added new requirements for the disclosure to shareholders of option grants and the reporting of income from options. Stock options have an impact on shareholder value, primarily in terms of earnings dilution. Corporate-fraud scandals, especially backdating of stock options (i. e., pretending that options had been issued earlier than they really were at more favorable prices) are being investigated in several MNEs.

Because of the various tax rules and currency exchange restrictions, an MNE must adapt its stock options offering to employees in its subsidiaries to deal with the complexity of operating in different countries. Different countries treat stock options differently in terms of employee taxation. In some countries, employees pay tax when they exercise their stock options (even if they may not get any future value for them). This highly reduces the incentive of the award. In other countries, employees pay taxes on the capital gains when they redeem their options. Still, other countries tax their employees both at the issuance and redemption of stock options. When giving stock options to employees worldwide, MNEs must consider the often detrimental effect of local tax implications, foreign exchange controls, and the overall after-tax income effect. They must also comply with the different payroll withholding requirements that are in effect in different countries. Rules become even more complex when dealing with international assignees and the cross-border tax implications of stock option taxation and currency exchange. For example, the tax code of the host country (where the employee is located) may have a considerable impact as the stock options may be seen as compensation for employment services performed outside that country even for shares that were granted to them prior to their departure from their home countries.

Global stock option plans must be designed and adapted to local laws and regulations and the prevailing tax systems in each country where the MNE operates. Adaptation must focus on ensuring local compliance and reducing the negative consequences of taxation. Therefore, MNEs must give out options judiciously and hire compensation specialists (Global Stock Plan Administrator) who have specific competencies to manage equity-based compensation plans in terms of compliance and effectiveness. MNEs must evaluate the local and cross-border implications of their global stock option plans and make appropriate adjustments country by country while trying to maintain internal equity among employees. Changing market conditions and expected changes in national tax regulations and international accounting rules will continue to increase the complexity and cost of effectively using and managing stock option plans.

Global firms with equity compensation plans for their worldwide employees are affected by the accepted accounting and tax rules that govern the MNE's balance sheet and its employee and corporate tax treatments. Today, stock options for employees throughout the company are very popular for incentive compensation, particularly in the US and the information technology industry. More and more, non-US multinational companies are adopting widespread stock option programs.

For example, Canon, a Japanese MNE, has adopted decidedly non-Japanese incentive schemes to support its global competitiveness.[18] Yet, some American MNEs have experienced difficulties as they have tried to extend their employee stock ownership plans overseas.[19] IHR needs to work collaboratively with the Global Stock Plan Administrator (who usually resides in the Accounting and Finance Department) to structure effective global compensation plans, customize these plans to local operations, communicate them to managers and employees, and respond to equity-based compensation inquiries. Ultimately, equity-based compensation must remain cost-effective for the company and motivational for employees to be used as a competitive talent management tool for attracting, motivating, and retaining key employees.

Global benefits in practice

Because of these widely varying benefit practices in different countries where the MNE operates, corporate policy on establishing and changing benefits must be monitored in such a way as to minimize unnecessary differences among subsidiaries while maintaining parent company concern for costs, competitiveness, and comparability from locale to locale.[20] Since a foreign subsidiary's benefits program may be more difficult to monitor or control than the parent company's domestic counterpart, it often makes sense to appoint an effective local manager in each country to act as that country's benefits coordinator, responsible for coordination and liaison with headquarters. And yet there must also be global or, at least, regional co-ordination as well. When managers transfer from one country to another, they will expect to at least retain benefits, such as vacation time comparable to that from their home country. For international assignees moving from countries with relatively low levels of such benefits, this will not create a problem. But for managers moving in the other direction, it can be the source of significant concern.

MNEs should develop both qualitative parity and quantitative parity in terms of benefits.[21] Qualitative parity is a commitment to offer something from each core category of benefit to every employee worldwide. This would include:

- *Core benefits*, a basic item that the company commits to making available to all employees worldwide, such as a certain level of health care.
- *Required benefits*, a compensation item or non-cash benefit required by local law.
- *Recommended benefits*, a less essential compensation or benefit program to be made available wherever cost considerations permit, such as life insurance.
- *Optional benefits*, a non-essential compensation item to be made available if it is a competitive practice in the local marketplace, such as local transportation or meal support.

The use of qualitative parity is one component of a firm's global compensation approach that provides a way to make a commitment to the entire work force while still preserving local variations in pay for the less skilled and less mobile employees.

COMPENSATION AND BENEFITS FOR INTERNATIONAL ASSIGNEES

Determining the C&B package of international assignees (or employees who are relocated as part of their employment for a certain period of time to another country) is a major component of the IHRM practitioner's role. While, in general, MNEs favor hiring locally in the countries in which they operate (for cost, cultural, and social responsibility reasons), they still often need to relocate some employees, for short- or long-term durations, across borders because of the need for operation startups, management control, and talent deployment in specific locations of the MNE.

To consider international assignment C&B, this chapter reviews the evolution of expatriate compensation, its specific purposes, the different types of international assignees who may require different packages, the various approaches to IA C&B (with a major focus on the balance sheet approach), and some special issues inherent to IA C&B, such as payment methods, inflation, exchange rate fluctuations and taxation.

The evolution of expatriate compensation

In the early stages of internationalization, a firm's primary international involvement usually consists of supporting a limited number of international assignees sent abroad to market its products, transfer its technology, and manage relatively small operations. At this stage of development, remuneration concerns are largely limited to providing adequate compensation and incentives for these expatriates. But as the firm's international involvement develops further, concerns about C&B packages for employees from multiple countries moving around the world as well as equity among work forces in many different global locations present many new challenges.

One of the most important considerations for MNEs in the design of their IA C&B programs is the problem of comparability (although cost is probably a very close additional and critical consideration). Indeed, in at least one survey, 77 percent of the expatriates surveyed were dissatisfied with their salaries and benefits and their international compensation packages in general.[22] (Not all surveys show this level of dissatisfaction, but these results suggest that at least some samples of expatriates are unhappy with their compensation.) And a significant portion of this dissatisfaction was due to feelings of inequity in their salaries and benefits. This problem of comparability has at least two significant components: (1) maintaining comparability in salaries and benefits (to similar employees in other firms and to peers within the firm) for employees who transfer from one country to another (either from the parent company to foreign subsidiaries or from one subsidiary to another or to headquarters); and (2) maintaining competitive and equitable salaries and benefits among the various operations of the organization.

Until recently, most MNEs felt it was necessary for expatriates to receive a salary and benefit package at least comparable to what they were receiving in their countries of origin.[23] Because of the high cost of expatriates and because of changing attitudes about and approaches to international assignments—such as the use of alternative assignments (short-tem assignments, frequent business trips, international commuting) and localized transfers—this view about expatriate compensation is being questioned. But comparisons between local nationals and expatriates (and between local nationals in different locales of the MNE) are inevitably made. As IHRM in Action 7.1 illustrates, salary differences between different employees working in the same location in perceived similar jobs (that may or may not be comparable) is especially problematic in the case of MNEs operating in the People's Republic of China (PRC) where there is a shortage of experienced managerial talent.

In a globally competitive economy (or, even, a regionally competitive one, such as within Europe, and Asia), attracting and retaining the best employees and motivating them to take on international assignments requires developing a compensation strategy and policy that will minimize problems associated with such comparisons.

Compensation and benefit strategy and policy for international assignees

Determining a cross-border compensation philosophy and establishing an overall international assignment policy should be starting point for firms that are newly developing their international presence. The compensation component of the international assignment policy (note that there are other components dealing with the multiple aspects of the international assignment process) usually describes whether something is paid for by the company or considered for payment. The purpose of developing an international assignment policy is to ensure greater consistency and equity among international assignees and reduce barriers to global mobility. In other words, C&B differences should not be an obstacle or primary incentive to refuse or take on an international assignees. The international assignment policy educates employees on the important issue in the international assignment and sets realistic expectations in terms of what the company will and will not provide as part of the assignment package. With the international assignment policy (and its exceptions) companies determine the extent to which they want to set a precedent for their future presence in the international arena; whether they want any particular practice or policy to be its program for all future situations; or whether they want to customize compensation packages for each international assignee and subsidiary. In general, a well thought out policy should not be subject to many exceptions. It is one of the IHR roles to educate (sending and receiving) managers and employees on the content of the international assignment policy and the importance of policy adherence.

The compensation package of international assignees must meet certain objectives in order to be effective. These include (1) providing an incentive to leave the home country for a foreign assignment; (2) maintaining a given standard of living; (3) taking into consideration career and family needs; and (4) facilitating re-entry into the

SALARY DISPARITY BETWEEN CHINESE LOCALS AND INTERNATIONAL ASSIGNEES

When an MNE enters a country like the People's Republic of China (PRC) it uses international assignees who work side by side with local Chinese employees. In working jointly, Chinese locals with similar levels of education and job responsibilities tend to compare themselves with these international assignees and such comparisons crystallize the salary inequity and raise fairness problems.

The structural disparity between international assignees and Chinese locals is caused by different living standards and welfare and taxation systems, and is further complicated by currency valuation problems. The Chinese labor market is divided into two submarkets that respectively accommodate international assignees and locals. Although compensation comparisons are usually made between individuals with similar levels of education and job responsibilities, no matter the submarket the individuals are in, the comparability of the salary disparity also differs across the groups of international assignees (short-term international assignees, long-term expatriates, and localized international assignees), within the same submarket. Despite the fact that Chinese locals in MNEs work jointly with international assignees who have similar job responsibility and educational background, locals and expatriates compete only within each group, not across the group. Each market reaches its own equilibrium, resulting in the establishment of the structural salary disparity.

The existence of the huge salary disparity between locals and international assignees has many causes:

- Current models of determining expatriate compensation packages (such as *ad hoc* packages for each assignee).
- Local acceptance mitigates the problems of salary disparity.
- The lack of cost consciousness because of the initial privacy of the assignee contracts.
- Historical needs of expatriates, justifying higher compensation packages.

The salary inequity between Chinese locals and international assignees is under increasing criticism in China and results in several problems:

- Morale and loyalty of the locals continue to suffer from the disparity.
- Government preferential treatment will eventually be discontinued.
- Rising pressure from local competition, as comparisons by locals extend across firms.
- Challenges from highly qualified local employees, who find the differentials unfair.

It is unrealistic and, probably unfair, to totally eliminate structural disparity. However, the efforts of MNEs should be committed to rationalizing the existing salary disparity. Possible solutions to mitigate this salary disparity are:

- Increase inpatriation of local Chinese managers.
- Establish common standards for locals and international assignees in similar positions with similar responsibilities.
- Use expert HR agents to streamline the selection process of locals and international assignees.
- Reduce uncertainty during the international assignment by ensuring clarity about assignees, roles and the purposes of their assignments.

While some salary disparities between locals and international assignees are inevitable, several practical solutions can be implemented to reduce consequences of this type of compensation equity.

Source Lisbeth Claus and research associates Shengxin "Allen" Xiao and Yunxing "Eric" Peng, Willamette University, 2007.

home country at the end of the foreign assignment.[24] To achieve these objectives, MNEs typically pay a high premium over and beyond base salaries to induce potential international assignees to accept international assignments. The costs to firms often range from two to two-and-a-half times to four or four-and-a-half times the cost of maintaining the manager in a comparable position at home.[25]

Determinants of the international assignee compensation approach

When determining the most suitable type of IA compensation approach, IHR must consider a number of questions.

- *What is the type of employee population being relocated abroad?* Is the international assignee an executive who needs an international posting for additional global leadership experience, an experienced employee relocated for technical or managerial skills, or a young, and relatively inexperienced, employee? Is the international assignee part of an international cadre of expatriates who move from one foreign assignment to another or is the international assignee someone who seeks to become established abroad permanently? Each of these types of international assignees has different needs with regard to international assignment compensation.
- *What is the purpose or reason for the international assignment?* Is the assignment demand-driven (i.e., the international assignee is sent because the MNE wants control and consistency in the foreign operations or the employee has the

necessary competencies to solve a particular problem for the company) or learning-driven (the assignment is for the purpose of employee competency development and career enhancement)? Demand-driven assignments may require a better compensation package than learning-driven assignments, as the international assignee will derive additional developmental benefits from the latter and should not be provided as many additional incentives to do so.

- *What is the anticipated duration of the international assignment?* Is it a short-term assignment (usually less than one year and probably within the same calendar/tax year) or long-term expatriation (usually one to three years)? Duration (and especially the number of days out of the home country in a particular tax year) usually has important tax ramifications for the employee (and for the employer, if it is taking responsibility for part of the tax obligation).
- *What happens with the international assignee at the end of the assignment?* What are the repatriation plans for the international assignee upon completion of the assignment? Is the employee returning to the home country, continuing in the same country with an extended contract, or moving on to a third country?
- *Where is the international assignee leaving from and going to?* What are the home and host countries involved in the assignment and what is the context of these countries with regard to C&B (especially taxation) laws, regulations, and practices?
- *Who is the peer of the international assignee?* What typical employee will the international assignee compare him/herself to in terms of equity with regard to this assignment? The IHR manager should know who the peer group is of the particular employee considered for assignment so that they can justify the elements of the C&B package.
- *What is the overall cost of the international assignment?* Based on the answers to the above questions, what is the overall cost of the assignment and will the various decision makers (management and the international assignee) consider the benefits derived from the assignment to balance the costs?

MNEs are realizing that not all international assignees, types of assignment, and locations are alike. Therefore, they should not be treated as though they were the same. Rather, different compensation approaches may provide better solutions. This has led to the development of a number of different IA C&B approaches and even greater administrative complexity (although computer programs have made administration less cumbersome than it used to be in the earlier pre-personal computer IHR days) for different groups of employees within the MNE. Many MNEs are beginning to recognize these options and are looking for more flexible and cost-effective international assignee compensation systems. The next section describes the most common approaches now being used by MNEs.

Approaches to international assignee compensation

There are a number of basic approaches followed by MNEs to compensate their international assignees. These include negotiation, balance sheet, localization, lump sum, "cafeteria", regional, and global plans. Although we will discuss these approaches separately, MNE often use multiple compensation systems to suit their type of international assignee and global/local contextual needs. Our discussion revolves around what each compensation approach is and when it is most appropriate to use that type of system.

Negotiation/ad hoc

When firms first start sending employees on international assignments and while their number of international assignees is still relatively low, the common approach to determining pay and benefits is *ad hoc*, or negotiation of a separate (and usually unique) C&B package for each individual considered for a foreign posting. At the early stages of "going international" the firm sends its best expert abroad and pays the price it must to make it happen. There usually isn't much of a search; and the firm does whatever it takes to get the person relocated and pays whatever costs arise. Because the person and the assignment are so important, the firm tends to take care of all of their concerns. This approach may appear quite simple initially, and, given the inexperience of HR managers at this stage, the limited amount of information available about how to design a C&B system for international assignees, and the many complexities in such a package compared to domestic C&B, it is easy to see why IHR managers follow this approach. Yet, according to international assignment compensation experts, this approach is fraught with complications and, therefore, not recommended. In negotiation, the best negotiator (whether it is the IHR practitioner, the manager, or the employee) wins and the bar gets set for what future international assignees will want in their international C&B package. Such an approach is also difficult for systematic tracking of IA C&B packages and complicates effective tax planning. It is recommended that, even when a company only has a few international assignees, IHR put an international assignment policy together to set a framework for what the company is likely to provide.

Balance sheet

This approach is followed by most MNEs in the US when their international business expands to the point where the firm has a larger number of international assignees (a dozen or so). At this stage, the negotiation, or *ad hoc*, approach will have led to too many inconsistencies between the compensation packages of its many international assignees and the firm will realize it needs to develop policy and practice that will apply to all expatriates. In addition, the *ad hoc* approach will now be viewed as taking too much time—and cost—to negotiate, develop, and manage such a unique package for each international assignee. The firm will seek a more standard approach and will begin to make policy about what will and what will not be covered in the expatriate C&B package.

In essence, the balance sheet approach involves an effort by the MNE to ensure that it is easier for the IA to leave for an assignment and return home. The "old" balance sheet terminology emphasized keeping the employee "whole." That is, at a minimum, the international assignee should be no worse off in terms of compensation, benefits, and life style for accepting an international assignment (usually in a country with a lower standard of living than their own). It was common to assume that the C&B package not only should make the expatriate "whole" but also should provide incentives to take the foreign assignment, remove any worry about compensation issues while on that assignment, and ensure that the individual and his or her family felt good about having been on the assignment. Today, in an environment that increasingly asks IHRM to control all employment costs, including the costs of expatriation, the balance sheet approach minimizes total compensation losses or gains as a result of the assignment and the terminology does no longer imply that the employee will be kept "whole" and that the "home" lifestyle will be replicated in the "host" environment. To the contrary, international assignees are counseled to be flexible and urged to make some adaptation to the local culture as part of their own acculturation and assimilation process.

The use of the balance sheet approach is particularly favored in the US for experienced senior and mid-level assignees who will return home at the end of their assignments. However, the balance sheet (also called the build-up system in the UK) is rather complex to explain to all parties involved. Some international assignees have complained that this approach to determining their international assignment compensation (especially determining normalized spending patterns to calculate the differentials) is much more intrusive into their personal lives than is true for the traditional domestic compensation package. Theoretically, the balance sheet approach "balances" out the differences between costs in the home and host country. It ensures that the international assignee can maintain purchasing power parity when on assignment. As a result, taking the assigment on should result in only minimal changes to their life style. However, nowadays, the IA (and family) will be required to make some adjustments.

The balance sheet approach customizes the C&B approach for each international assignee by starting with the employee's existing compensation (salary, benefits, and any other forms of monetary or non-monetary remuneration) at home. To this are added two other components: a series of equalization components that ensure the international assignee does not suffer from foreign-country differences in salary or benefits and a series of incentives to accept (and enjoy) the foreign posting. Interestingly, today, even with pressure to reduce the high cost of IA compensation, most MNEs still find it necessary to provide significant incentives to encourage potential assignees to accept foreign postings. This is because there are many more pressures today for an employee to refuse an international assignment because of the disruption of family, increasing numbers of dual-career couples, lifestyle choices, career insecurity, and a general reluctance to live abroad.

One of the key complications in this balance sheet approach is the determination of the base upon which to add adjustments and incentives.[26] A number of possibilities exist, including basing the IA's salary on:

- Home country salaries (this is the primary base for the home country-based balance sheet approach).
- Headquarters salaries (an international standard based on headquarters).
- Regional salary standard (e.g., "old" and "new" EU countries, US and Canada, Latin America, Southeast Asia).
- Host country salaries. (This uses destination salaries in the host location).
- Better of home or host approach.

The choice of base to use may be best related to the nature of the firm and its international business strategy.[27] It is also based on the salary rates of the particular home and host countries (is the assignee going from a developed country to an emerging market, or vice versa?), and the length of the assigment. If the assignment is long (two to three years) and international assignees often go from one foreign country assignment to another, then an international standard (headquarters-based balance sheet) is probably most appropriate (but it will still probably be based on the parent country/company base, particularly if the MNE is from a high-wage, developed country). If international assignees go to foreign postings for relatively short and alternative types of assignments and then return to the parent country, then a home country base makes more sense. For some truly global firms or firms that operate within a specific region of the world it may make sense to use regional bases.

To date, most companies compensate their international assignees based on either a home or host country philosophy (or some combination).[28] The home-based, balance sheet approach is used by most firms, particularly in situations where the international assignee is opening new markets and new operations, transferring technology, and training local staff.[29] These are clearly not jobs similar to those performed by locals. Thus the need to maintain equity is greatly lessened. But where the operations are ongoing, and in developed countries, the international assigment is likely to be alongside locals performing similar jobs and the need for equity is high and a host-country base makes more sense. In addition, an MNE with operations in many foreign countries may opt for a home country or headquarters (international) approach because of the sheer scale of the administrative complexity involved handling multiple international assignment packages. On the other hand, if the firm operates in only one or two countries, a host country approach may be necessary because of local legal or cultural differences.

An alternative is to use the better of home or host approach (also called net-to-net). It compares the net pay under the home country compensation system to a local (location of assignment) net salary. The international assignee then receives the higher of the two. The philosophy underlying this system is that an international assignee will never have to live at a lower standard than a local counterpart, but that the international assignee will also be protected when the home country package requires a higher standard than the local counterpart receives.

Interestingly, in contrast to the earlier survey referred to, with all the attention given to designing these IA C&B packages, other surveys show that expatriates tend to be pretty satisfied with their financial packages but dissatisfied with the limited career planning, lifestyle support, and cultural training that are provided.[30] This suggests that more attention ought to be paid to these non-compensation factors. There are, however, two issues in the balance sheet approach that MNEs need to decide, namely (1) what type of adjustment (differential) will they need to pay to make up for the differences in home and host country living and (2) what additional incentives and premiums will be required to motivate the employee to take on the assignment?

Determining the type and amount of adjustments

Because of home–host countries' differences, MNEs must provide a number of equalization adjustments. These are payments whose purpose is to adjust for differences (generally in a higher direction), hence the name differentials, in mandated payments that the international assignees have no control over—some which are paid by the international assignee and some of which are paid to the international assignee. These have included adjustments for differences in (higher) costs of living; fluctuations in exchange rates between the international assignee's parent country currency and that of the foreign assignment location; all locally mandated payments, such as payment of salary for additional days or weeks per year (in many countries, firms must pay employees for thirteen to fourteen months every year, or as in Saudi Arabia, must pay for seven days' work per week, i.e., must pay for rest days as well as work days); an agreement to adjust for decreases in the value of the expatriate's compensation due to high inflation in the foreign country; similarly, reimbursement for any mandatory payments into the host country's welfare plans, such as health insurance or social security; and ensuring that the expatriate will not have to pay more in income taxes while on the foreign assignment than he or she would have to pay while at home.

To understand how adjustments are calculated under the balance sheet approach, an understanding of the different balance sheet components is necessary. The balance sheet is made up of different components: reserves or savings, goods and services, housing, and income taxes (see Figure 7.1, the balance sheet). These will be different in the home and host countries. To understand how these will vary some additional terminology (such as housing norm, home and host country spendables) is useful. Note that these definitions all assume a certain level of income and family size of the international assignee.

The *housing norm* is a normative expense for housing in the home country (i.e., what an employee with a certain income and family size is likely to pay for housing in the home country). Note that this is *not* the actual housing expense but a normative amount that the international assignee is likely to spend in the home country based on his/her situation. Depending on the firm, these housing norms may be the average in the home country or the average in specific regions or cities of the home country. The employee will be expected to contribute that portion as a share in the housing expenses while on assignment since they would have paid for it at home anyway if they had not left on assignment.

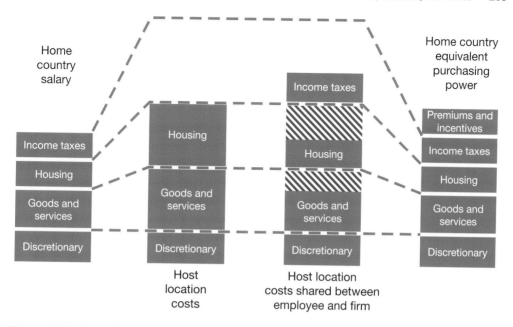

Figure 7.1 Balance sheet

Source Understanding the balance sheet approach to expatriate compensation. (2004), ORC Worldwide, International Compensation Services.

The *home country spendable* is the norm for goods and services or the portion of salary spent on goods and services in the home country according to salary and family size of the international assignee. The *host country spendable* is the amount for goods and services that the international assignee is expected to spend in the host country as an international assignee or the amount needed for the spendables in the assignment location. The *differential* is the difference between the home and host country spending for the international assignee and accounts for the cost-of-living adjustment (COLA) between home and host countries. It is usually calculated as a goods and services index. A number of international consulting firms provide data to help companies determine the local cost of living around the world. Such data are available for most countries as base countries to most other countries as receiving countries. Most companies use average country data and do not differentiate by area within the country. The purpose of the COLA is to enable international assignees to maintain as closely as possible the same standard of living in the foreign assignment that they would have had at home (or better, if coming from a low-cost-of-living city or country). Since the typical international assignee resides in a major city in the host country where costs of living tends to be quite high (particularly the cost of transport and housing, which may not be available—except at very high cost—in forms comparable to what the expatriate family experienced at home), COLAs of 50 percent or more are relatively common. The ratios vary according to family size and income, and the consulting firms that provide this type of data will alter the estimates based on these factors. These adjustments also vary according to the technology that the consulting firm uses to determine the cost of living in various foreign locations.[31] An example of variations in cost-of-living indices, as a result of the calculation method used, is reflected in Table 7.4 ranking the ten most expensive cities in the world.

There are at least two common techniques used. One of these uses staff of the consulting firm that are located in the particular foreign cities to estimate the cost of living in those locations based on their surveys of costs in a standardized (typical expenditures from the home location) market-basket of goods and services. A second technique involves the surveying of existing and former expatriates of the clients of the particular consulting firm for their typical spending in the particular foreign locale. Often this second technique—which arguably assesses the actual items that international assignees typically buy, as opposed to a theoretical market-basket of goods and services—results in a lower cost of living than that arrived at by the first technique. This second technique implies the concept of the international assignee becoming a more efficient purchaser in the host country as times goes by. The Efficient Purchaser Index (EPI) implies that the assignee, after some accommodation to the host country, has learned to purchase better because of increased familiarity with the location. Nowadays, the EPI is usually built in the differential calculations immediately, as phasing in lower host spendable (the longer the international assignee lives in the foreign location) is much more difficult and may be demotivational.

Table 7.4 The ten most expensive cities in the world, 2007

Rank (most expensive)*	EIU survey	Mercer survey	USB survey
1	Oslo	Moscow	London
2	Paris	Seoul	New York
3	Copenhagen	Tokyo	Oslo
4	London	Hong Kong	Tokyo
5	Tokyo	London	Zurich
6	Reykjavik	Osaka	Copenhagen
7	Zurich	Geneva	Geneva
8	Osaka	Copenhagen	Dublin
9	Frankfurt	Zurich	Chicago
=10	Helsinki	Oslo	Los Angeles
=10		New York	

Note * Index based on cost of living expressed in US dollars.
Source http://www.citymayors.com/economics/expensive_cities2.html.

In addition, companies often offer *destination services,* which help the international assignee and family to be more efficient from the start. Obviously, MNEs have an interest in trying to minimize the level of the differential which, as shown above, can often be a significant amount of money.

Due to the complexity of costing out an international assignment, IHRM will usually rely on an international C&B tax consultant to develop an international assignee compensation worksheet. At the end of this chapter, an example of an international assignment compensation worksheet is included as a way of illustration. Based on the balance sheet approach, it shows the different components and estimated costs associated with a relocation from San Francisco, California, to Amsterdam, Netherlands. While this worksheet will usually be prepared by an external international assignment C&B consultant, IHR will need to be able to explain the worksheet to a potential international assignee and his or her manager and respond to inquiries. Note that a number of additional elements contained in the worksheet (such as taxes and exchange rate fluctuations) will be discussed later in this chapter.

Determining the type and amount of allowances and incentives

Once the base salary has been determined, and the needed adjustments calculated, the firm must decide which incentives it feels are necessary to convince its employees that it will be to their financial advantage (or at least, as is being increasingly maintained, not to their disadvantage)[32] to take the foreign assignment. In the past (and still normally for less developed multinational firms), many incentives were offered, often with sizable monetary benefit to the expatriate. One of the current issues, however, is the high cost of expatriation (at least for more experienced MNEs) and the subsequent need to contain costs.

One of the most common incentives has been an additional "foreign premium," used to compensate the international assignee and her/his family for the "dislocation" of having to move to an unfamiliar country and to live in what might be seen as an uncomfortable (i.e., different) environment; provide an incentive to take the foreign assignment; and keep up with the practices of other MNEs. These premiums used to average about 25 percent of the expatriate's base pay. Today, it is more common for this premium to be about 15 percent of base pay. Increasingly, firms are questioning whether it is necessary to pay this premium for an international assignment (or, at least, for most foreign assignments).[33] Critics argue that in a truly global economy with improved communication and transport, general availability of global consumer products, and accepted international business norms, there is no longer as much trauma and dislocation associated with an overseas transfer. Still, a large (although declining) number of MNEs continue to pay such premiums.[34]

Additional forms of incentive include premiums for "hardship" postings and dangerous postings, which could include many assignments to developing countries, locations where the threat of kidnapping or terrorist activity is high, or to remote locations (such as the outback in Indonesia or on an ocean oil drilling platform) or locations with less modern or more restrictive living or environmental conditions.

The three broad areas typically considered in evaluating the extent of hardship include physical threat, level of discomfort, and inconvenience.[35] The physical threat category includes potential or actual violence, hostility to foreigners from the local population, prevalence of disease, and the adequacy of local medical facilities and services. The discomfort category evaluates the physical environment, climate, and pollution as well as geographical, cultural, and psychological isolation. And the inconvenience category rates the local education system, the availability and quality of local housing, access to recreational and community facilities, and the availability, quality, and variety of consumer goods and services. Hardship allowances typically range from 5 percent to 25 percent of base pay with danger pay may be adding another 15–20 percent to base pay. Depending on the location (such as Kuwait City, Kuwait), hardship and danger pay incentives could add as much as 30 percent to an expatriate's income. An example of what corporations provide for hardship pay is provided by these results of a survey of MNEs from a few years ago in the Middle East for the percentages of base pay added to expatriate compensation for assignments to the area:[36] United Arab Emirates 12.5 percent, Bahrain 20 percent, Egypt 20 percent, Saudi Arabia 25 percent, and Israel 42.5 percent. Given recent events in the Middle East, these percentages are probably even higher today.

Additional incentives usually (or may) include *housing allowances*, either to ensure the expatriate lives as well as her/his foreign peers or to make her/his housing comparable to what s/he had "back at home"—and to take care of her/his home in the parent country and the storage of household goods; settling-in allowances; *education allowances* for the expatriate (e.g., for language courses), her/his spouse, and any other dependants (e.g., for private schools for the expatriate's school-age children); all travel and *relocation expenses* necessary to go to and return from the foreign assignment; local *transport* in the foreign locale; any *language and cultural training* expenses prior to leaving for the assignment; and special *perquisites*, such as club memberships in the foreign assignment and special R&R (rest and relaxation) and home leave, for the expatriate and her/his family. Depending on the location, these incentives and adjustments typically cost the MNE more than US$150,000 per expatriate relocation. Indeed, for some locations, where the cost of living and cost of housing are particularly high, the figure can reach US$500,000 or more annually. This is in addition to base salary and benefits. For example, in Tokyo, the rent for an expatriate family often exceeds US$300,000 per year.[37] It is no wonder that the cost of expatriate failure is so high (often figured to be in the neighborhood of US$1 million). And it is no wonder that large MNEs are beginning to reconsider their approaches to IA compensation.

One of the consequences of these increasing costs is that firms are increasingly looking to provide the higher IA salaries through various forms of incentive pay based on performance (either individual or organizational) for at least part of the pay package for international assignee, just as they are using such programs in their domestic operations.[38] In order to minimize costs, firms are designing bonus deferrals (paid at the end of the assignment), in-kind benefits, and equity-based plans for international assignee (as well as HCN and TCN executives) tied to achievement of long-term strategic objectives in the subsidiaries (such as growth in subsidiary revenues and profits or return on capital employed at the subsidiary level). Another way to remedy the high cost of long-term expatriation is to use more alternative types of international assignments (usually shorter-term assignments that do not require families to accompany the assignee).[39]

Localization

A relatively new approach to IA compensation is referred to as localization. This approach is being used to address problems of high cost and perceived inequity among staff in foreign subsidiaries. Under localization, international assignees are paid comparably to local nationals and no equalizers are provided except for some additional allowances. These employees usually are early in their careers, eager for learning-driven international assignments, they are seeking employment abroad for a relatively long-term or indefinite period of time, they will not be repatriated after their assignment is over or desire to stay in the host location, or they are TCNs, or returnees (people who have studied/worked abroad and return to their home country). Localization tends to be relatively simple to communicate and administer (if done locally). Yet localization is seldom pure, especially when it involves moving from developed to developing country, and medical benefits, taxes, and housing may be an issue. Since these international assignees may come from different standards of living than that experienced by local nationals, special supplements are usually provided (local plus).

Lump sum

Another approach that some MNEs are trying, particularly in response to concern over the perception that the balance sheet intrudes too heavily into expatriates' lifestyle decisions, is the lump sum approach.[40] In this approach the firm determines a lump sum to cover all the major incentives and adjustments, and then lets the IA determine how to spend it (for example, on housing, transport, travel, home visits, education, life style, and so forth). In essence, lump sum is more of a payment method than a compensation approach, as the amount of the lump sum is usually calculated the same way as the balance sheet (housing and goods and services) but allowances are not paid out for each component. This lump sum allowance is a single payment, made at the start of the relocation process, to the transferring IA to cover all of the above, or only the costs associated with the relocation itself. Or, sometimes, the lump sum payment is split between payment at the outset of the assignment and the remainder paid upon successful completion of the assignment (as an incentive to perform successfully and to stay with the firm until the end of the assignment and to avoid tax hits). It should be noted that how the lump sum allowance is paid has an impact on taxes whether in the host or home country. Also, according to IA C&B experts, lump sum should be avoided for items that are currency sensitive.

Cafeteria

An approach which is increasingly being used for very high-salaried executives is to provide a set of "cafeteria" choices of benefits, up to a predetermined monetary limit in value. The advantages accrue both to the firm and to the individual and are primarily related to the tax coverage of benefits and perquisites as compared to cash income (paycheck). Since the individual doesn't need as much cash (most expenses are paid by the firm), this approach enables the international assignee to gain benefits such as a company car, insurance, company-provided housing, and the like that may not increase the assignee's income for tax purposes. The cafeteria approach is usually not used for things that are fundamental to the assignment (such as goods and services), but the company gives choices on things that are not really critical to the success of the assignment (for example, loss on the sale of an automobile). It should be noted that IHR and management usually decide whether an item is essential or not and a cafeteria item, not the international assignee.

Regional systems

For international assignees who make a commitment to job assignments within a particular region of the world, some firms are developing a regional C&B system to maintain equity within that region. This is usually seen as a complement to the other approaches. And if such individuals are later moved to another region, their pay will be transferred to one of the other regional systems, depending on what is used there, such as the balance sheet approach.

Global systems

A final approach being followed, at least for international assignee above a certain pay level (i.e., therefore, for professional/technical/managerial employees), is to implement a common global pay and benefits package for each covered job classification applied to everyone in that classification, worldwide. This is often done in recognition of the fact that for many specialized occupations (such as for example software engineers and programmers) and executives there is in fact a global labor market, with qualified specialists from anywhere and everywhere in the world all applying for the same jobs. In this approach, MNEs will have two general pay classifications: local employees below a defined level and international. The international level will almost always include a performance-based variable pay component. The standard used is usually the level paid for those occupations at the firm's headquarters.

MNEs that have employees from many different countries will usually have multiple IA C&B systems at work. While they may have a global philosophy and IA policy, the need for multiple systems is often dictated by the type of assignee, the intricacies of the country/region of operation (and the corresponding tax systems), and the cultural practice of providing certain C&B components. Not using multiple systems, or making adjustments, may result in failure to meet the needs of the international assignee and increased cost due to taxation.

Current methods for determining the C&B package of international assignees are being criticized for many different reasons. There is concern that all of these approaches don't adequately take into account the nature of the IA or the country of assignment and often actually discourage expatriates from assimilating into the local culture.[41] The housing differentials, for example, frequently serve to provide host country housing which is likely to be better than that enjoyed by their host country counterparts, although, as mentioned above, whether or not that is appropriate will depend on the nature of the international assignee's assignment. Even the continuation of home-based consumption patterns for goods and services does not encourage the cultural awareness so critical to the international assignee's success in the host country. In addition, critics argue, it seems as though IA C&B systems ought to pay more attention to the differences in perceptions by international assignees and by host country nationals about issues like the value of money compensation versus other types of perquisites or forms of motivation.[42] A flexible menu of perquisites, traditional incentives and adjustments, and tax reimbursement schedules might well meet some of the criticisms while actually reducing overall costs to the firm. Such an approach might even enable an MNE to replace the traditional cost-of-living concerns with a quality of life or a quality of career opportunity focus.

Additional important international assignment compensation issues

A number of additional compensation issues, such as payment method, inflation, exchange rate fluctuations, and social security are inherent to any IA C&B approach.

Method of payment

Once the amount of the international assignee's C&B package has been determined, the firm must decide whether the expatriate will be paid in local host country currency, in home country currency, or a split pay combination. Where there is limited convertibility between the home country currency and that of the foreign host locale, or there is rapid inflation, it is probably better for the firm to take care of providing the international assignee's salary in local currency (of course, with more frequent re-evaluation that guarantees against loss of purchasing power if there is rampant inflation). However, when the international assignee maintains home country financial obligations while on assignment, there will be a need for partial payment in home country currency to meet these obligations. It is typical for US MNEs to pay the international assignee's base salary and differential partly in local currency (with the amount in local currency pegged to ordinary living expenses) and the remaining amount in dollars (usually left in a US savings account). Bonuses tend to also be paid in dollars and typically left in the US, as well. This is referred to as a split payroll or split currency approach. This payment method helps the international assignee cover daily living expenses and maintains purchasing power in the host country while covering remaining financial obligations in the home country. It also, partially, protects against currency exchange rate fluctuations and the impact of differential inflation (more about that later). For international assignees from other than parent country homes, similar arrangements are made, using their home country and home currency as the base.

Impact of exchange rate fluctuations

While the differential home and host calculations in the balance sheet approach are made at the beginning of the international assignment, there are bound to be fluctuations in the home and host currencies during the course of the assignment. Fluctuating exchange rates (Fx) will alter the figures in the balance sheet for the international assignee. As exchange rates fluctuate up and down, they impact the index and the differential (between the host and home country spendables) as the comparative prices in the host and home locations change.

Let's illustrate this with an example and see the effect of the weakening and strengthening of a currency. (See Table 7.5.) For simplicity purposes, we make the assumption that only the exchange rate is fluctuating and that there is no inflation (i.e., home and host country spendables remain the same). In our example, at the start of the assignment the international assignee gets five units of the host currency for one unit of the home currency. The differential between home and host spendables is 1,500 in home currency units. One year later, the home currency weakens and the international assignee now gets only two units of the host currency (instead of five) for one unit of the home currency. As a result, the differential has gone up to 4,500 home currency units. Still one year later, the home currency has strengthened and the international assignee now gets ten units of the host currency for one unit of the home currency. Therefore, the differential has gone down to 500 home currency units.

The general rule is that, as the exchange rate goes up, the differential the company pays to the international assignee goes down. Similarly, as the exchange rate goes down, the differential goes up. In other words, the exchange rate and differential are indirectly related. The IHR C&B specialist will have to be able to explain to the international assignee why the differential that the firm pays changed as a result of the currency fluctuation and how an adjustment to the differential is in reality balanced out. If the international assignee is paid in both currencies (split pay), there is not really a concern about exchange rate fluctuations, as they may cancel each other out. MNEs will usually adjust for currency fluctuations when it reaches a certain percentage and indicate this in the assignment letter of the international assignee.

Impact of inflation

Inflation/deflation can occur in either the home or host country or in both. (If occurring in both, they could possibly cancel each other out.) What happens with the balance sheet differential when there is inflation? In our example, we will focus on inflation up and down (deflation) in the host country. We assume that the exchange rate between home and host country does not fluctuate. In Table 7.6, we see that

Table 7.5 Impact of exchange rate fluctuations on the differential in the balance sheet

Country A: home spendable	Country B: host spendable	Date	Exchange rate (Fx)	Home currency	Differential	Impact on differential
500	10,000	1 Jan. 2008	5B/1A	At start of international assignment: the international assignee gets five units of the host currency for one unit of the home currency	$\frac{(B)10,000}{(Fx)\ 5} - (A)\ 500 = (A)\ 1,500$	
500	10,000	1 Jan. 2009	2B/1A	One year later, the home currency *weakens*: the international assignee gets only two units of the host currency for one unit of the home currency	$\frac{(B)10,000}{(Fx)\ 2} - (A)\ 500 = (A)\ 4,500$	Goes up
500	10,000	1 Jan. 2010	10B/1A	One year later, the home currency *strengthens*: the international assignee now gets ten units of the host currency for one unit of the home currency	$\frac{(B)10,000}{(Fx)\ 10} - (A)\ 500 = (A)\ 500$	Goes down

Source Example provided by Carolyn Gould, SPHR, GPHR, PwC, 2006.

Table 7.6 Impact of inflation on the differential in the balance sheet

Country A: home spendable	Country B: host spendable	Date	Country B: host spendable after inflation/deflation	Net inflation	Differential (assume Fx of 5A/1B)	Impact on differential
500	10,000	Jan 1, 2008	(B)10,000		$\dfrac{(B)10,000}{(Fx)\ 5}$ – (A) 500 = (A) 1,500	
500	10,000	1 Jan. 2009	(B)12,000	Goes up	$\dfrac{(B)12,000}{(Fx)\ 5}$ – (A) 500 = (A) 1,900	Goes up
500	10,000	1 Jan. 2010	(B) 8,000	Goes down	$\dfrac{(B)8,000}{(Fx)\ 5}$ – (A) 500 = (A) 1,100	Goes down

Source Example provided by Carolyn Gould, SPHR, GPHR, PricewaterhouseCoopers, 2006.

when net inflation goes up, host country spendables increase. As a result, the differential goes up. In case of deflation, host country spendables are less and the differential goes down.

As a general rule, net inflation is directly related to the differential (goes up when inflation goes up, and goes down when inflation goes down). Obviously, in reality the differential is impact simultaneously by currency fluctuation and inflation.

Social security

An additional factor involves the varying country-specific practices related to social security taxes and government-provided or mandated social services, ranging from health care to retirement programs. These can add considerably to the foreign taxation burden. Countries that have established social security systems have negotiated bilateral social security treaties with each other in order to eliminate double taxation—referred to as *totalization agreements*. For example, since the 1970s, the US has totalization agreements for social security taxes with twenty-one countries (Australia, Austria, Belgium, Canada, Chile, Finland, France, Germany, Greece, the Republic of Ireland, Italy, Japan, Luxembourg, the Netherlands, Norway, Portugal, South Korea, Spain, Sweden, Switzerland, and the UK).[43] The purpose of these agreements is to eliminate dual social security taxation (when a worker from one country works in another country and is required to pay Social Security taxes to both countries on the same earnings) and to help fill gaps in benefit protection for workers who divide their careers between the US and another country. These treaties generally provide tax exemption to residents of one treaty country on short-term assignment—typically 183 days' presence in a year—to the other country. Under the "territoriality" rule, an employee remains subject exclusively to the coverage laws of the country in which he or she is working. Under the "detached worker" rule, an employee who is temporarily transferred to work for the same employer in another country remains covered only by the country from which he or she has been sent. Under these totalization agreements, the IHR department files for a *certificate of coverage* in the home country (i.e., for the international assignee to remain in the home social security system and be exempt from host social security taxes) prior to departure. Note that these totalization agreements are bilateral between countries and may differ in their stipulations. Some countries that do not have social security system may have funds (e.g., the Provident Retirement Fund in Singapore, Australia, and Hong Kong) that require payment by the international assignee into the fund. Sometimes, these retirement contributions may be recovered when the international assignee leaves the host country. The IHR department must be knowledgeable of these terms in the different countries where they deploy international assignees so that they can file on behalf of the employee.

Taxes on expatriate income

A major determinant of an international assignee's lifestyle abroad can be the amount of money the expatriate must pay in personal income taxes. Employees who move from one country to another are confronted with widely disparate tax systems, philosophies, and rates and may be required to pay taxes in both home and host countries, depending on the combination of countries. And to make things even more difficult, tax systems and rates are constantly changing, often every year. Thus, taxes not only create one of the most complicated compensation issues for IHRM, it is also the largest expense of an IA. This includes both income taxes and social security taxes (for those countries that have a social security system). Table 7.7 shows the widely varying total tax wedge (as a percent of average wage) for a number of countries.

Of course, social insurance rates and benefits also vary dramatically from country to country, even more than income tax rates. International assignees (or their firms) may be responsible for taxes on the international assignee's income independently of where it is earned. (This can mean in both their home countries and their host countries.) Typically MNE policies will protect incremental cost as a result of dual and increased taxation. The firm will cover these differential costs for their international assignees, i.e., over the tax amount the assignee would pay if he or she had stayed in the home country. This is called *hypothetical tax* or the tax that the international assignee would have paid if he/she had remained in the home country. The MNE must determine a strategy for dealing with these variances and potentially heavy costs. In general, MNEs follow one of four alternative tax strategies: *laissez-faire*, tax equalization, tax protection, or an *ad hoc* policy.[44]

Laissez-faire

This approach is uncommon, but smaller employers and those employers just beginning to conduct international business may fall into this category with their taxation policies. In essence, under this approach the international assignee is expected to take care of his or her own taxation, even if it means tax obligations in both home and host countries. One of the dangers is that the employee may not be in compliance with tax payments owed to the home and host countries, intentionally and/or due do to lack of knowledge.

Tax equalization

This is the most common approach, since it supports the home country system of the balance sheet approach. Because tax rates and obligations vary so much from country to country, tax equalization provides equitable treatment for all international assignees regardless of IA location. Under this strategy, the firm withholds a hypothetical tax from the IA's income (the tax obligation in the home country that they would otherwise have to pay anyway) and then pays all actual taxes in the home and host countries. In essence, the taxes that the international assignee must pay are equalized between home and host countries. This can, obviously, be quite expensive if the international assignee is posted to a high-tax country, such as many European countries. However, tax equalization facilitates tax planning for the MNE and reduces non-compliance. The company provides these tax services to the international assignee.

Table 7.7 Taxation of wage income, 2006

Country	Total tax wedge[a] as percent of average wage[b]	
	Lowest (67)	Highest (167)
Australia	35.3	51.4
Austria	57.3	41.8
Belgium	71.2	68.3
Canada	34.5	35.9
Czech Republic	44.9	51.3
Denmark	42.8	62.9
Finland	50.7	59.5
France	66.7	59.6
Germany	60.3	44.3
Greece	44.2	60.6
Hungary	51.8	63.2
Iceland	39.6	41.5
Ireland	31.3	49.8
Italy	52.7	59.1
Japan	28.1	31.0
Korea	17.6	23.3
Luxembourg	41.3	53.9
Mexico	14.4	30.9
Netherlands	57.3	51.9
New Zealand	21.0	38.9
Norway	43.2	53.8
Poland	45.8	53.2
Portugal	38.5	55.5
Slovak Republic	44.4	42.7
Spain	49.4	27.9
Sweden	51.1	67.2
Switzerland	33.9	42.8
Turkey	44.5	48.0
United Kingdom	40.6	47.6
United States	33.9	43.2

Notes: [a] *Total tax wedge.* The combined central and sub-central government income tax plus employee and employer social security contribution taxes, as a percentage of labor costs defined as gross wage earnings plus employer social security contributions.

[b] *Average wage.* The average annual gross wage earnings (in national currency) of adult, full-time manual and non manual workers in the industry (International Standard Industrial Classification C–K).

Source http://www.oecd.org/dataoecd/43/63/1942474.xls.

Tax protection

Under the tax protection strategy, the international assignee pays both the home and host taxes, but the hypothetical tax is compared to the actual taxes. If the actual taxes are greater than the hypothetical tax, the employer pays the difference to the international assignee. If the tax rate is less in the foreign assignment, then the employee receives the difference as a windfall. In essence, the employer protects the international assignee against higher taxes. Although this method used to be popular, it is less commonly used today. Rather than giving the tax windfall to the international assignee, MNEs use tax equalization to reduce their costs and control tax compliance. Note than when an international assignee is out of compliance when working abroad, it may have repercussions for the MNE in addition to the employee.

Ad hoc

Under this strategy, each international assignee is handled differently, depending on the individual package she or he received or negotiated with her or his employer. The *ad hoc* method usually goes hand in hand with the negotiation approach. In addition, the typical allowances paid to international assignees are often viewed as taxable income in certain countries. So the resulting tax bill—in both the home and the host country—can negate the financial incentives provided the international assignee.

To compensate, companies usually reimburse their international assignees for the global tax costs in excess of the tax they would have been responsible for if they had remained at home. The purpose is—as with other components in the IA compensation package—not to penalize the employee for taking on the IA. Indeed, surveys find that at least 75 percent of responding firms provide the following benefits tax-free to their employees on foreign assignment (usually by adding to the pay check the costs of the taxes for these items—referred to as "grossing up" the salary):[45]

- Tax reimbursement payments
- International premium
- Cost-of-living adjustment
- Housing allowances
- Automobile reimbursements (for business use)
- Emergency leave
- Moving expenses
- Dependent education

In addition, many firms provide tax-free (if deductible in the host country) a car for personal use (48.3 percent) or club memberships (62 percent). MNEs that operate in many countries are subject to widely disparate tax rates. Because of this and the complex systems of taxation, with differing attitudes toward what is and what is not taxed in various countries (i.e., what is counted as income), MNEs must use international accounting firms for advice and for preparation of the international assignee's tax returns.

Tax experts provide some practical advice to MNEs for saving money in their complicated tax obligations around the world.[46] Some of these ideas will work in some countries. But, there are really no approaches that will work uniformly everywhere. Nevertheless, the following precautions and advice make good general sense:[47]

- Get professional tax advice for all international assignees.
- Don't leave tax affairs to the responsibility of international assignee. Mistakes can impact an organization's corporate reputation and relations with the host government (and potentially create legal liabilities).
- Tax agreements between most developed nations mean that, with openness and good planning, employees should not lose.
- Tax havens are a great way to avoid paying tax only so long as that is where the firm or the individual is doing business and nowhere else. In other words, it is best to stay away from suggested ways to dodge taxes.

Special US issues in international assignment compensation

There are a number of international assignment C&B issues that are specific to US citizens regarding the taxation of US international assignees, the compensation by foreign multinationals operating in the US, and the compensation and taxation of foreign nationals working in the US.

Taxation of US international assignees

US citizens are taxed on their income, regardless of where it is earned or where they live.[48] Fortunately, special rules can limit the US tax liability of US international assignees during their employment abroad. As of the time of this writing, the Internal Revenue Service's Foreign Earned Income Inclusions allow US employees to exclude from income up to $82,400 of their foreign earnings (and certain foreign housing costs above a particular amount) provided the international assignee meets one of two tests: (1) 330 full days of presence in foreign countries in any consecutive twelve-month period or (2) foreign residence for any period that includes an entire taxable year. The income and foreign housing exclusions are both pro-rated on the basis of the number of days in the year in which the international assignee qualified under one of the tests (Form 2555–EZ). In addition, US tax laws provide a "foreign tax credit" that US citizens may use to reduce their US tax liability (limited to 90 percent of minimum tax, and applicable only to US income tax on foreign earned income). This is a dollar-for-dollar reduction against US taxes. The bottom line in terms of the amount of tax owed, however, is dependent on the level of tax rate in the foreign country compared to the tax rates in the US.[49]

Compensation by foreign multinationals in the United States

Just as US firms have recognized the need to pay their international assignees at least as well as their local colleagues (in countries where the locals make more than their US counterparts) such is also true for foreign firms that operate in the US. Foreign owners of US companies—and of US subsidiaries—are realizing that they must match US executive compensation practices to stay competitive and to retain their top US executives.[50] In most countries, executive compensation is not a subject that receives much attention, either outside firms or within them. This is clearly not the case in the US. Besides, overall executive salaries tend to be much higher (with maybe fewer perquisites) in the US.[51] Thus, foreign firms with operations in the US, particularly those that have acquired US firms, have had to adapt their policies and practices to fit US practices. For example, foreign firms have relied more heavily on base salaries and less on annual bonuses and long-term incentives than is common in the US.[52] Since this can lead to problems with retention of their US executives, foreign-owned firms in the US are increasingly adapting their compensation practices.

The same issues are present when enterprises from any country operate in any other country. The end result is that there is increasing conversion of compensation practices, at least at the top executive level (although there is also a countervailing pressure to localize practice, as well).[53]

Compensation and taxation of foreign nationals working in the United States

A last issue of concern is compensation and taxation for foreign nationals on assignment to the US. Foreign employees assigned to headquarters are usually referred to as inpatriates. This issue, of course, has a counterpart in foreign nationals who move from a subsidiary in any country to the country of the parent headquarters, no matter the country of ownership of the enterprise. These inpatriates are brought to headquarters for a relatively short period of time—usually two years or less—for the purposes of learning about the firm.

First, US MNEs that bring inpatriates into the US are increasingly realizing that they need to adapt these employees' compensation programs just as they must do for their expats that are sent abroad.[54] At a minimum, trying to keep inpatriates in as many of their home country benefit programs as possible and pegging their compensation to their home country structures appear to help minimize many of the C&B issues discussed in this chapter. Similar to US international assignees, such foreign employees in the US can typically be removed from extra premiums and adjustments and be localized if they wish to remain in the US after their assignment contract is up.

For US tax purposes, foreign individuals living and working in the US may be considered either "resident aliens" or "nonresident aliens." The general rule is that US resident alien is subject to US tax on all worldwide income, in the same manner as a US citizen, while the non-resident generally is taxed only on certain income connected with a US business or from US sources. Other variables adding complexity to the classification of foreign nationals concerns whether they are entering the US on immigrant or non-immigrant visas and whether their country of origin has negotiated a tax equalization treaty with the US. As US-based MNEs (US or foreign-owned) expand their use of foreign staff in their US operations, considerations such as tax treatment of these employees become just as important as the tax treatment of US international assignees sent abroad.

GLOBAL COMPENSATION AND BENEFITS MANAGEMENT IN THE MULTINATIONAL ENTERPRISE

It should be obvious by now that global C&B management is more complex than its domestic counterpart. This is at least partially due to the following problem areas not confronted in domestic HRM. First, the collection of data about pay rates, benefit packages, government practices, and taxation systems in different countries, and in different languages and cultures, from unfamiliar sources, makes it very difficult to design comparable pay packages for international assignees or for consistency among various overseas operations. Second, pay systems (particularly for international assignees) must contend with government currency controls (for instance limiting amounts that can be taken out of the country) and constantly changing exchange and inflation rates, making it necessary to constantly adjust the incomes of international assignees in local currencies. A third issue that adds to the complexity are the varying rates of inflation encountered in foreign locations, that may also require frequent re-establishment of international assignees' pay rates to counteract the effects of sometimes high inflation rates. Add to this the desire to export Western compensation concepts such as incentive pay, pay for performance, equity compensation, and the desire to create a common global data base to keep track of all the variances, and global C&B gets complicated indeed. When all of this combines with variances in legal systems and in country practices in C&B, it may be a miracle that MNEs ever satisfy either international assignee or local work forces with their reward structures. Additional practical C&B problems relate to getting valid salary data, payroll maintenance, data privacy, cost concerns, and benchmarking.

Salary data

It is often very difficult for MNEs to get country-specific compensation data that have much reliability. Very few governments (at least in developing countries) collect or publish adequate data. And there exist in only a few locations local trade associations that collect and publish such information (as is available in most developed countries). Therefore, MNEs must rely on the information provided by accounting firms with international practices, consulting firms that specialize in developing such data (local governments and international organizations, specialized consulting firms, or developing their own data through local MNE "compensation clubs" that share such information). None of these options provides necessarily reliable data, particularly in less developed countries, illustrating the difficulties encountered by IHR managers as they try to develop cost-effective and managerially effective compensation packages for their international assignees and equitable compensation programs for their employees in subsidiaries around the world.

Payroll maintenance

An additional problem with global C&B programs involves the maintenance of payroll files on international personnel (international HRIS), systems for handling payroll and benefits.[55] Domestic HRIS is usually not designed to handle all the additional pieces of information that are common to multiple locations and multiple currencies. In particular for international assignees, C&B items such as premiums, language training expenses, education allowances for dependants, storage of household goods, currency conversion, etc., are usually not available in standard payroll systems. Compounding the problems associated with maintaining these files is that typically MNEs use multiple IA C&B approaches. And, of course, tax and withholding requirements are different in every country, as well. Therefore, consulting firms have developed separate IA tracking systems for their customers. But even these systems do not always allow the tracking of short-term and alternative types of assignees.

Data privacy

Keeping these files up to date and using the information in them for employee decision making, such as pay increases or adjustments or career and job assignment decisions, get even more difficult, as many countries maintain laws against the transfer of "private" employee information out of country or region (e.g., EU Data Protection Directive). There are no easy answers to these problems, short of designing a computer program specifically to handle the problems of your international employees or hiring a firm to handle them for you, but for sure they must be considered when tackling the issue of creating and managing a compensation program for an international work force.[56]

Cost concerns

Another concern for the development of global C&B systems involves efforts by MNEs to include IHR issues in the strategic management of the enterprise. Global C&B systems are affected at a number of points, including the following. Decisions to downsize often include expatriates because of their high expense, but then it becomes more difficult to convince new people to accept foreign postings; pressuring IHRM to control costs; fitting IHR compensation systems into the firm's efforts to localize while globalizing; merging compensation systems in cross-border acquisitions; designing or negotiating new compensation systems in international joint ventures and cross-border partnerships and alliances; trying to simplify the design and administration of the international compensation system; coping with the new types of international assignees, including dual-career couples; and figuring out how to apply US extraterritorial anti-discrimination laws in the global context to compensation issues, such as those that "protect" the disabled, employees over forty years of age, and employees on the basis of their religion, gender, race, or national origin.

Benchmarking

Many firms are now trying to determine what successful MNEs are doing in terms of design and implementation of their international compensation systems.[57] Often this attempt to benchmark the best practices seems like an exercise in the "codification of ignorance," since there is so little research to identify what works best when.[58] Surveys of practices of MNEs may be doing nothing more than identifying what is currently being done. But as the above discussion indicates, many practices have evolved over time, without much knowledge or research to indicate which practices are best and under which circumstances. Over time this may result in many firms following what are totally wrong, costly, or inappropriate practices. There is clearly a need for more and better research on international C&B practices.

CONCLUSION

This chapter has presented IHRM practices related to the development of C&B plans in MNEs and discussed the many problems that firms confront as they try to design and implement C&B programs throughout their global operations. The discussion followed a dual focus: first we discussed global remuneration in the MNE among the various locations of their work forces, and then we focused on C&B programs for international assignees.

Country differences in laws (especially tax laws) and cultural practices complicate the design of effective C&B programs and make a global standardized approach ineffective. But pressures for equity and ease of administration provide the motivation to IHR to work on the development of such globally integrated programs. For MNEs that operate in multiple countries with local subsidiary work forces, having an understanding of these country-specific variances becomes critical to designing rational HRM practices for the total firm.

The chapter also described the special case of C&B for international assignees and reviewed several alternative approaches to IA compensation, with extensive discussion of the balance sheet approach. This method of IA compensation adds numerous allowances and incentives to a parent country base and is the most commonly used method for paying US international assignees. But the complexity of the balance sheet approach and the necessity for firms to get deeply involved in the personal lives of their international assignees when using this approach (as well as the high cost of international assignments compensation and administration of the balance sheet) have led many firms to begin experimenting with one of the other possible approaches. The issue which adds most of the complexity to the compensation of international assignees involves taxation practices and taxation rates in different countries. In an effort to ensure that their international assignees don't need to pay double taxation (for both their countries of origin and their countries of residence while on foreign assignment), MNEs use one of four methods: *laissez-faire*, tax equalization, tax protection, or *ad hoc* methods. In all cases, the purpose is to limit the tax liabilities of the international assignee. In this chapter, we also discussed several compensation and taxation issues specific to US MNEs. Finally, we reviewed other C&B concerns of a more practical nature that result from the global operations of an MNE.

The design and management of global remuneration programs around the world and IA compensation packages in particular are indeed a complex and difficult function. This chapter has made it clear why it absorbs the bulk of the typical IHR manager's time and energy. To deal with these complex issues, the C&B specialists working in this global environment have acquired additional global C&B competencies.

GUIDED DISCUSSION QUESTIONS

1 What is the difference between global remuneration and international assignment compensation?

2 What are the major issues related to the effectiveness of global remuneration plans?

3 How are equity compensation plans affected when used as incentive compensation with employees from different countries in the MNEs?

4 What are the common international assignment management compensation systems? What are the advantages and disadvantages of each system? When are they used most appropriately?

5 What different tax approaches can be used by MNEs for international assignment compensation?

VIGNETTE 7.1   EXPLAINING THE WORKSHEET TO POTENTIAL ASSIGNEES

International assignment compensation worksheet

Assignee name: John Doe   No. of pay periods per year: 26

	Previous period	*Current period*
Home location	San Francisco	San Francisco
Host location	Amsterdam	Amsterdam
Business unit	Marketing	Marketing
Policy	Long-term	Long-term
Effective date	September 26, 2003	October 10, 2003
Table date	June 13, 2003	September 12, 2003
Index	149.7412	140.4226
Fx rate (host per one home currency unit)	€0.8502: U$1	€0.9066: U$1
Location premium (%)	0	0
Family size at location	1	1
Family size for taxes	1	1

Balance sheet   *Per pay period amounts*

		Previous period		Current period		%
		U$	€	U$	€	change
1	Base salary plus bonus/ commission (lines 22 plus 23)	3,230.77		3,230.77		0
2	Total hypothetical tax (see details)	−792.77		−792.77		0
3	Goods and services differential (line 12)	564.00		458.35		−19
4	Housing differential (line 17)	−251.81		−256.19		−2
5	Location premium (line 27)	0.00		0.00		0
6	Other allowances and additions to income (see details)	467.96		438.85		−6
7	Net compensation (lines 1 through 6)	3,218.15		3,079.01		−4
8	Actual paid in home currency	**3,218.15**		**3,079.01**		0
9	Actual paid in host currency		0.00		0.00	0

Calculations

	A Calculations of G&S differential					
10	Host location G&S spendable	1,697.88	1,443.54	1,592.23	1,443.50	0
11	*Less* Home location G&S spendable	−1,133.88		−1,133.88		0
12	G&S differential	564.00		458.35		−19

B   Calculation of housing differential

13	Host location housing	0.00	0.00	0.00	0.00 0
14	Host utilities allowance	70.58	60.00	66.19	60.00 0
15	Total host/housing/utilities	70.58	60.00	66.19	60.00 0
16	*Less* home housing norm	–322.38		–322.38	0
17	Housing differential	–251.81		–256.19	–2

C   Protected in host currency

18	Host location G&S spendable (line 10)	1,697.88	1,443.54	1,592.23	1,443.50 0
19	Host location housing/utilities allowance (lines 13+ 14)	70.58	60.00	66.19	60.00 0
20	Other host allowances/ deductions (see details)	467.96	397.85	438.85	397.85 0
21	Amount protected in host currency (lines 18 through 20)	2,236.42	1,901.35	2,097.27	1,901.35 0

D   Protected in home currency

22	Base salary	3,230.77	3,230.77	0
23	Bonus (guaranteed)/commission	0.00	0.00	0
24	Total hypothetical tax (see details)	–792.77	–792.77	0
25	Home G&S spendable (line 11)	–1,133.88	–1,133.88	0
26	Home housing norm (line 16)	–322.38	–322.38	0
27	Location premium	0.00	0.00	0
28	Amount protected in home currency (lines 22 through 27)	981.74	981.74	0

Details

Details for total hypothetical tax

Hypothetical tax (State/local)	0.0	0.0
Hypothetical tax (Social	0.0	0.0
Hypothetical tax (FICA)	0.0	0.0
Hypothetical tax (Medicare)	0.0	0.0
Hypothetical tax (Federal/ national)	–792.77	–792.77
Total hypothetical tax	–792.77	–792.77

Other host allowances/deductions

Host transportation allowance	467.96	397.85	438.85	397.85
Total host allowance/deduction	467.96	397.85	438.85	397.85

Other home allowances/deductions

Total home allowance/deductions	0.0	0.0

Source International Assignment Compensation Worksheet courtesy of Carolyn Gould, SPHR, GPHR, PricewaterhouseCoopers, 2007.

Questions

1 What is the base salary of the international assignee?

2 How much is the G&S differential and how was it calculated?

3 How much is the housing differential and how was it calculated?

4 What type of allowance did the international assignee get and how much was it?

———————————

International employee performance management

LEARNING OBJECTIVES

This chapter will enable the reader to:

- Describe the importance of developing an IPM system
- Explain the characteristics of a successful IPM system
- Identify and overcome the major challenges to IPM
- Describe the role of cultural value dimensions in the design, implementation, and evaluation of an IPM system
- Formulate evaluation criteria and practices that meet parent company requirements while addressing the host culture's norms and expectations
- Identify and overcome the major challenges related to the performance management of international assignees

KEY TERMS

- International assignee (IA)
- International assignment
- International performance management (IPM)
- Global integration (GI)
- Local responsiveness (LR)
- Performance appraisal (PA)
- Performance management (PM)
- Rater competence
- Rater bias

High-performance organizations—such as MNEs—care a great deal about the performance of their employees, teams, projects, business units, as well as of the overall organization. They work hard to align job expectations with the strategic intent of the organization and rely on highly competent and engaged employees and teams to achieve their objectives. Measuring the performance of individuals and teams becomes an important tool to ensure organizational performance and identify possible gaps to be closed. Hence, the establishment of an employee performance management (PM) system is an integral component of managing the talent of an MNE. In addition, employee PM is linked to other HR activities such as job analysis, total rewards, learning and development, and talent deployment. It is the design and management of this employee PM system as practiced in MNEs around the world that is the focus of this chapter.

As with everything in the global arena, managing employee performance in an international enterprise is a lot more complex than is the case with solely domestic operations. There are a number of reasons for the complexity of an international PM system. First, culture heavily impacts management practice in terms of issues such as the meaning of performance management, employee acceptance of the review process, and the cultural value dimensions that affect performance appraisal (PA). Second, designers of PM systems in MNEs face a major dilemma in terms of reconciling whether PM should be a single, standardized practice throughout the organization or whether divergent systems can be used to reflect local culture and local management practices. And third, the PM of international assignees (IAs) presents particular challenges for managers and employees alike.

THE CONCEPT OF PERFORMANCE MANAGEMENT

There is a widely accepted body of knowledge within HR related to PM.[1] Yet, in the international context, issues arise for MNEs because most of the knowledge base has been developed from a purely Western perspective and in a largely domestic context. A number of particular characteristics are associated in the Western context with the concept of PM. For example, it is seen as a human resource activity or process that includes a number of necessary steps: setting employee performance expectations that are aligned with organizational objectives; regularly monitoring performance; providing ongoing feedback to employees; conducting periodic (annual or semi-annual) face-to-face performance appraisals; giving employees a chance to provide input; providing developmental and career guidance opportunities based on the results of the PA; and linking the reward system with individual and group appraisal results. This PM process is commonly described by practitioners in Western enterprises as the "performance wheel."

Yet, in recent years, a notable shift has occurred related to the practice of PM in these predominantly large, Western companies. The trend is towards greater accountability of employee performance, use of more objective measures and metrics, involvement of multiple raters, and ongoing coaching and development of employees as critical components of the PM system (see Box 8.1).

BOX 8.1 **SHIFTS IN WESTERN PERFORMANCE MEASUREMENT**

From	*To*
Focus on past performance	Focus on future performance
Subjective judgmental measures	Objective behavioral measures
Periodic (annual or semi-annual) PA interviews	Ongoing evaluation and coaching
Defensive and control-oriented	Development-oriented
Single rater	Multiple raters
Linked to negative employment decisions	Linked to positive employee development and rewards
Individual performance	Individual and multilevel organizational performance
Distinct (PM) HR activity	PM activity aligned with other elements in HR portfolio (talent management)
Complex to administer	Simple to administer
Individual results	Organizational metrics
Service and entitlement culture (experience, equality)	High-performance culture (accountability, equity, output measurement)
Hard paper process documentation	Use of software tools for process documentation and interactive employee communication
Domestic focus	International and global focus

In this chapter, we review especially the challenges that confront international PM as opposed to the practice of domestic PM. We start by looking at employee PM for MNEs and review the purposes of international PM systems, the impact of culture on the PM process, and the design choices (standardization versus adaptation) the MNE must make to integrate the PM system into its global operations. Then, we focus on the PM of a special group of employees, namely IAs, who are on short-term or long-term assignments to foreign locales of the MNE.

PERFORMANCE MEASUREMENT IN THE MULTINATIONAL ENTERPRISE

When discussing PM in the MNE, the term "international PM [IPM] system" is used to distinguish this process from the practice of PM in the domestic operations of the firm. In our view, an international employee PM system is a designed, implemented and evaluated intervention of an MNE for the purpose of managing the performance of its global work force so that performance (at the individual, team, and organizational level) contributes to the attainment of strategic global objectives and results in overall MNE desired performance.

A firm's performance appraisal system can greatly impact the performance of its workers. Yet conducting valid performance appraisals, even in the domestic environment, is quite a difficult task. But, PA is just one activity of the global PM system, the one that refers to the periodic formal evaluation of employees' performance, usually by supervisors. Appraising performance and conducting effective performance appraisals is even more challenging in the IHR arena.[2] It is this international context of PM that is described in this chapter.

Purposes of international performance management

Organizations develop PM systems for a number of reasons, but primarily for evaluation and development.[3] As the purposes of PM intervention differ, they are likely to impact the satisfaction of employees with the system. These purposes, however, are much the same for domestic and international operations. The major difference is, as mentioned before, that the implementation of these goals is much more complex in the global arena. Typically, most attention is paid specifically to the purposes of the PA process. The following describes these two broad purposes for PA: evaluation and development.

Evaluation goals for performance appraisals in the international environment include:

- Provide feedback to employees so they will know where they stand.
- Develop valid data for pay, promotion, and job assignment decisions, and to provide a means of communicating these decisions.
- Identify high-potential employees and manage their talent for optimal performance and retention.
- Help management in making discharge and retention decisions, and to provide a means of warning employees about unsatisfactory performance.

Development goals for performance appraisals in the international environment include:

- Help managers improve their performance and develop future potential.
- Develop commitment to the company through discussion of career opportunities and career planning with the manager.
- Motivate employees via recognition of their efforts.
- Diagnose individual and organizational problems.
- Identify individual training and development needs.

Of course, the national cultures of the countries where the MNE operates, the design choices the MNE makes with regard to its IPM system, and the nature of international assignments all impact the ability of any global organization to achieve these objectives.[4]

Culture and performance management

With increased globalization, particularly by developed-country MNEs, Western HR practices (such as PM) are being applied around the world, even in non-Western cultural contexts. Thus, an important question is raised as to the robustness of these practices in different national and cultural environments. Although the PM body of knowledge is highly US-centric, a number of researchers are increasingly turning their attention to the application of the concept to other countries and situations.[5]

As discussed in Chapter 3, the application of culture to management practices has focused largely on differences in *value dimensions* reflective of national cultures.[6] Using these dimensions, a number of empirical studies have identified cultural differences in several aspects of PA implementation. Many of these comparisons have involved Western and Asian cultures and have focused on the need to adapt PM practices to the cultural environment. Cultural value dimensions such as power distance, collectivism, harmony, and face have been shown to influence the way in which performance is evaluated.[7] For example, in collectivistic, high-power distance cultures, PM is culturally more compatible with a focus on broad performance targets than with specific performance criteria, with group-oriented appraisal accountability rather than individual accountability, maintaining harmonious relationships, saving face (*mianzi*) and connections (*guanxi*) rather than using direct confrontation, greater acceptance of ambiguity in feedback versus direct constructive feedback, avoiding conflict versus direct confrontation, focus on personal obligations of loyalty to the organization versus the self, and reliance on hierarchical judgments versus employee involvement. Considering these differences in cultural value dimensions, the PM process has to be adapted to align with the cultural characteristics of host countries in order to be effective.

Researchers have also looked at whether PM practices are becoming more convergent and easily transferred from the West or if they remain divergent and require cultural localization. As mentioned in Chapter 3, this line of thinking within cultural management theory is referred to as the convergence–divergence hypothesis. Similar to other areas of management research, the empirical evidence is divided. Proponents of *convergence* have shown that there are only small differences between, for example, American and Japanese managers of MNEs in terms of control processes like responsibility, rewards, and monitoring.[8] They have also shown that there were more similarities than dissimilarities in PA practices, for example in Ghana and Nigeria, than reported in the US literature.[9] In spite of cultural differences in HRM practices, some empirical studies suggest that there are considerable signs of convergence towards accepted best practices,[10] that differences in PA practices are gradually declining, and that Western and non-Western management approaches are moving closer together.[11]

Proponents of *divergence* have received somewhat greater support in the PM literature. This literature suggests that differences in cultural practices remain important,[12] that observed differences in PA link directly to known cultural differences,[13] that the assumptions of convergence should be rejected even in countries belonging to the same culture cluster and region,[14] that a one-size-fits-all approach without making allowance for local adjustment can produce desired results,[15] and that there is a high need to localize the methods used in performance appraisal to fit local cultural values and norms.[16] They generally accept that best PA practices do not exist independently of cultural context.[17] And they also accept the notion of "crossvergence" in PM, namely applying a relatively similar appraisal concept but adapting the process to align with cultural characteristics.[18] The argument supports the notion that while many of the PA practices in the West are easily transferred to another country with a different culture, tradition, and economic, legal, and political system, some of the local uniqueness must be maintained. Practices are more likely to transfer when the HR department enjoys a high status and can promote convergence of HRM practices at the firm level.[19]

The theoretical framework of *cultural fit* focuses on the influence of the socio-cultural context on HRM practices and the transferability of the Western practice of PM to another culture with a fundamentally different socio-cultural environment.[20] The impact of culture is particularly evident in three areas of PA, namely performance criteria, method of appraisal, and performance feedback. With regard to performance criteria, it is suggested that narrowly defined, task-related competencies and result orientation fit cultures with higher performance orientation, universalism, and lower power distance, while broadly defined, interpersonal competencies, and process orientation fit high power distance, high collectivism, low performance orientation, and fatalism-oriented cultures. With regard to methods of performance appraisal, multiple assessors, formal, systematic, objective, and periodical assessments are characteristics of low power distance and high performance orientation cultures while single assessor, top-down, informal and subjective assessment are characteristics of low performance orientation, high power distance and high collectivism cultures. With regard to performance feedback, individual or group-based, explicit and direct confrontational feedback are characteristic of specific, low context and high performance-oriented cultures while individual or group-based, subtle, indirect and non-confrontational feedback are characteristic of diffuse, high context and high collectivism cultures.[21]

In addition to the external context of national culture, the cultural fit theory also explores how the fit can be mediated by internal *organizational culture.* Organizations with strong performance cultures and socialization mechanisms offer somewhat of a buffer for the impact of local national culture. Companies with strong corporate cultures and centralized decision making may be inclined to favor a more standardized PM system aligned with their organizational goals and other management practices than those organizations that are highly decentralized.

Yet, the challenge for MNEs remains to design and implement PM systems that fit the global as well as the local context of their operations.

Standardization versus localization of international performance management systems

As an HR management activity, PM can be expected to be time and place-specific. MNEs, because of their predominantly Western country-of-origin headquarters, are likely to use a Western and standardized approach to PM across their subsidiaries. MNEs often use an "exportative" approach to PM.[22] In other words, the Western concept of PM is transferred from headquarters to the subsidiaries and applied, in a standardized manner, across the worldwide operations of the MNE.[23] Yet many managers and academics express concern with the implementation of a management process developed and tested in the West and applied to a different context—largely because of differences in national cultures, laws, and emerging market practices. For example, there is concern about the implications this might have for the operating Western paradigm of PM. Further, there are questions about whether or not a well established Western practice, such as PM, can be transferred to another external context and retain its intended value. Such questions have not yet been answered and pose challenges for both researchers and practitioners.

There are some valid reasons that suggest such a standardized approach may be warranted for the sake of global integration, uniformity, organizational culture cohesiveness, fairness, mobility of global employees, and as a control mechanism. An important question becomes how this Western concept of PM is impacted when used throughout the international operations of MNEs, particularly in non-Western cultures and emerging economies with different external contexts. In addition, MNEs are likely to have globally mobile employees and international assignees requiring expatriate PM. MNEs are also often involved in international mergers, acquisitions, joint ventures, and alliances where varying PM practices may have to be modified or integrated.

Companies, basically, have a choice of three different strategic options when it comes to IPM: an "exportative" strategy which develops the PM system in the home country and transfers it to foreign units, an "adaptive" strategy which develops unique PM and practices in each foreign unit, and an "integrative" strategy which combines local PM practices with those within the region and around the world. Each of these strategies has obvious advantages and disadvantages for the MNE.[24] The key strategic decision that MNEs must make with regard to the design of their PM is whether to standardize or localize their system, that is, whether to truly incorporate both global integration (GI) and local responsiveness (LR) in the design, implementation and evaluation of their PM system and achieve a truly "glocal" system. PM resides at the focal point of the global/local dilemma because it represents the enactment of upstream company strategy at the downstream local individual level. Upstream refers to company-wide strategy-type decision making at the headquarters level favoring convergence and standardization. Downstream refers to the flow of these decisions to the local level and favors divergence and localization. There are major upstream and downstream considerations with regard to global PM.[25] Upstream considerations include strategic integration and coordination; work force alignment; and organizational leaning and knowledge management. Downstream considerations include responsiveness to local conditions; sensitivity to cross-cultural differences; establishment of PM relationship, and comprehensive training.

A model of international performance management in multinational enterprises

In practical terms, the MNE can look at its IPM system in terms of three distinct phases: design, implementation, and evaluation. The major issues affecting IPM and its three phases are described in Figure 8.1.[26]

The *design* phase deals with the choices that management of an MNE must make with regard to its PM system. These decisions relate to identifying the purpose(s) of PM (why), performance criteria (what), method of evaluation and instrumentation (how), frequency of evaluation (how often), and rater identification (who) and whether a standardized or localized approach will be used. The outcome of these decisions will depend on a host of factors, including the internal organizational environment (i.e., corporate culture) and the external global context (or the socio-cultural environment). The *implementation* phase relates to communicating job-position performance expectations, identifying cognitive processes that affect

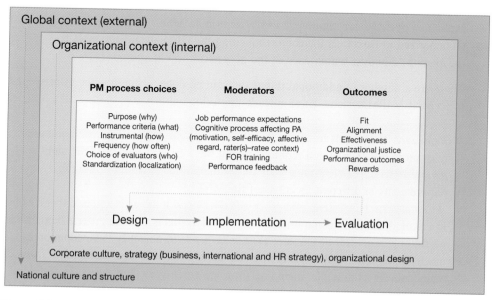

Figure 8.1 Model of international performance management in a multinational enterprise

the PA, frame of reference training for the PM process, and performance feedback to evaluated employees. In the implementation phase, cognitive processes related to the conduct of PA (such as ratee self-efficacy and affective regard, motivation, and rater(s)–ratee context) play a dominant role. Many of these factors are impacted by cultural practices. Finally, the *evaluation* phase consists of identifying and evaluating outcomes of the PM process. Fit, alignment, effectiveness, fairness, and performance outcomes play a dominant role in the evaluation phase. Again, many of these factors are subject to cultural interpretations.

The above discussion indicates that such an IPM system is complex for an MNE due to cultural differences associated with a global enterprise and the dilemma of reconciling standardization versus local adaptation. Therefore, an IPM system should be carefully designed, implemented and evaluated in the MNE, in order to achieve its stated objectives.

Guidelines for international performance management in a multinational enterprise

MNEs can do a number of things to ensure that valid performance evaluations are made in their global operations, or at least, to increase the likelihood of good results from the PM system. The most important concern for the MNE with regard to an effective IPM system is to find the right balance between standardization (for control, administrative ease, and employee global mobility purposes) and localization (for cultural fit purposes). How to achieve such a "glocal" strategy and reconcile such seeming opposing dimensions is not an easy task. The research evidence on PM in an international perspective, although limited, permits us only to provide a number of preliminary, yet practical, recommendations for the design, implementation, and evaluation of a "glocal" employee PM system in an MNE. These recommendations (summarized in Box 8. 2) focus on reconciling the GI (standardization)–LR (adaptation) dilemma within each of the phases of the PM system.[27]

There are a number of additional things that can be done to improve the effectiveness of an MNE's IPM system. These include the following:

- *Relevance.* IHR needs to ensure that the criteria and process for evaluation are relevant to the content and requirements of the job. This involves IHR and reviewers having a clear understanding of the unique situation of the job requirements in different locations of the MNE.
- *Acceptability.* The criteria and processes used need to be acceptable to those using it, i.e., both evaluators and ratees. One aspect of this is that the criteria being rated need to be in control of the ratee. The rater needs to objectify the evaluation as much as possible, while considering the "contextual" realities, using input from as many sources as possible, including from the employees themselves. In addition, the rater needs to follow standard procedures and the appraisal results need to be seen, particularly by the ratee, as fair and accurate. The appraisal form itself needs

BOX 8.2 **GLOCALIZATION OF KEY ELEMENTS IN THE DESIGN, IMPLEMENTATION, AND EVALUATION OF THE PERFORMANCE MANAGEMENT SYSTEM OF A MULTINATIONAL ENTERPRISE**

Design	*Standardization (global)/adaptation (local) reconciliation recommendations:*
Purpose of PM (why)	Determine multiple purposes of the PM system so that they meet global and local needs. Explicitly state and communicate throughout the organization the global and local intended purposes to be achieved.
Performance criteria (what)	Analyze performance dimensions and criteria in terms of their cultural neutrality and/or bias. Analyze performance dimensions and criteria in terms of perceived importance by diverse groups of employees, business units, and the company overall. Use a combination of soft and hard performance criteria and weigh them accordingly.
Method of evaluation and instrument (how)	Use a combination of quantitative and qualitative measurements in the instrument and weigh them accordingly.
Frequency of evaluation (how often)	Have ongoing informal feedback for developmental purposes. Have discreet (annual) feedback session for reward purposes.
Rater identification (who)	Determine the cultural acceptability of different types of raters. Use multiple raters to reduce rater bias.
Implementation	*Standardization (global)/adaptation (local) reconciliation recommendations:*
Job/position performance expectations	Clarify the global and local performance expectations for each job (some jobs may have only global or local expectations, others may have both).

Cognitive processes that affect PA:

- Motivation — Assess the manager's motivation in conducting PA and providing feedback to subordinates. Reinforce the importance of the manager in PM training.

- Self-efficacy — Focus the PM training at the individual/collective level based on the individual/collective cultural background of supervisor/subordinate.

● Affective regard	Provide means for managers/subordinates to maintain trust relationships when conducting PAs and adapt those means to the cultural background.
● Rater(s)–ratee context	Understand the importance of the nationality of rater/ratee (in self-rating, upward and downward evaluations). Use multiple raters.
Frame of reference training	Provide training on the PM process. Provide FOR training on how to rate performance from both local and global perspectives. Emphasize the impact of culture and the cognitive processes that may affect the PM process. Customize the training to reflect individual/collective value dimensions of participants.
Performance feedback	Distinguish between ongoing and discreet (annual) feedback. Identify different culturally appropriate ways to provide ongoing and discreet performance feedback. Increase the frequency of the ongoing feedback.
Evaluation	*Standardization (global)/adaptation (local) reconciliation recommendations:*
Fairness	Determine the different levels of organizational justice for the organization's PM system in terms of cultural differences and expectations: ● Procedural justice: fairness of the methods used in organizations. ● Interactional justice: the quality of the treatment. ● Distributive justice: the perception of due process and fairness of the outcomes.
Performance outcomes	Use a combination of individual and collective performance outcomes and weigh them accordingly.
Rewards	Use of combination of individual and collective rewards and weigh them accordingly.

Source Claus, L. Employee performance management in MNCs: Reconciling the need for global integration and local responsiveness. *European Journal of Management* 2(2): 132–152.

to accommodate special or unique circumstances; the ratee needs to receive timely feedback, the rater should suggest how the ratee can improve, and the ratee should get the necessary resources to improve, such as training programs. All of this is to say that the process needs to be seen as having "face" validity, i.e., it needs to be seen as fair, reasonable, and accurate.

- *Sensitivity.* An effective IPM system takes into consideration cultural and international business realities. It will include input from people with experience in the particular foreign setting (such as local employees and former expatriates). It needs to take into account issues like the operational language of the foreign organization, the cultural distance between the foreign firm and the parent, and the importance of contextual issues (such as, for example, the power of local unions, exchange rate fluctuations, local circumstances). IHR can build into the evaluation process a numerical factor based on the unique difficulty of the foreign location, freeing the home evaluator from having to directly assess this him or herself.
- *Practicality.* Finally, the performance evaluation system needs to be easy to use. If it is either too complex or too difficult to administer, managers will not use it. Or they will give it only surface attention, shortcutting a serious evaluation and thus abrogating any potential value from the assessment process and making it impossible to achieve the objectives set out for an effective IPM system.

All of these characteristics illustrate how important it is for evaluators (usually managers) to be trained in the use of international evaluation systems. The effectiveness of an IPM system can be improved, but it requires IHR to get involved and to work on implementing the types of characteristics described here. As stated by Cascio: "Performance appraisal has many facets. It is an exercise in observation and judgment, it is a feedback process, it is an organizational intervention. It is a measurement process as well as an intensely emotional process. Above all, it is an inexact, human process."[28] And when an organization has to add cultural and international dimensions to the process, it is even more difficult on every one of these characteristics. It is up to IHRM in the MNE to ensure that the IPM process makes the important contribution that it can and should.

PERFORMANCE MANAGEMENT OF INTERNATIONAL ASSIGNEES

An additional complexity in IPM is the PA of international assignees. The remainder of this chapter focuses on the special case of expatriate PM. The performance of international assignees, whether on short or long-term expatriate assignments, is critical to the success of the MNE. PA of international assignees is especially important because expatriates are very expensive (in terms of total international compensation) and many international assignments are not successful due to premature repatriation of expatriates, brownout while on assignment, or higher than average turnover of repatriated assignees upon their return from assignment. However, one of the most serious stumbling blocks to the effective management and development of these assignees is the frequent lack of recognition of the value of their foreign experience and expatriation, in general, and the informality with which firms often evaluate the performance of these employees. Indeed, large MNEs with many international assignees and many foreign subsidiaries report that most

(83 percent) do not use PM to measure the success of their international assignees. And many (35 percent) don't use any type of measurement at all.[29]

Appraising performance and conducting effective PAs of international assignees presents major challenges. One of these challenges for global organizations is that the types of skills developed and used in an international job are different from those developed and used in the domestic environment. The international assignee (as well as other foreign managers) must, of course, develop and use the competencies necessary for any managerial assignment. But, in addition to these capabilities, they must also develop the following abilities:[30]

- To manage an international business and all the complexities that entails.
- To manage a work force with cultural and subcultural differences.
- To conceptualize, and plan for, the dynamics of a complex, multinational environment.
- To be more open-minded about alternative methods for solving problems.
- To be more flexible in dealing with people and systems.
- To understand and manage the interdependences among the firm's domestic and foreign operations.

These skills are a natural outgrowth of the increased autonomy that international assignees and their foreign manager colleagues experience in the international environment. In addition, this autonomy results in a greater impact on the subsidiary's performance than would be possible at that same level in the home country situation. With increased decision-making responsibilities in the foreign environment, international assignees are typically subjected to a more intense working environment to which they have to adjust fairly completely and quickly. But the often distant evaluators seldom understand these difficulties and tend to not take them into consideration when evaluating the international assignee's performance. In order for the individual contributor and his/her organization to benefit, however, from this enhanced learning and performance, the organization must have a way to track and evaluate it. The reality usually is, though—as stated above—that this doesn't happen, either very well or not at all. There are many reasons that the international performance evaluation system doesn't work very well for international assignees, including:

- Problems with the choice of evaluator (e.g., local or parent company).
- Inadequate contact between home country rater and subsidiary rater.
- Difficulties with long-distance and virtual communication with home or headquarters management.
- Differences in host and host country management's perceptions of what is valued in terms of performance and in terms of perceptions of the actual behavior.[31]
- Inadequate establishment of performance objectives for the foreign operations (unclear and/or contradictory) and means for recording levels of individual and organizational performance.

- Home country ethnocentrism and lack of understanding of the foreign environment and culture.
- Frequent indifference to the foreign experience of the expatriate and to the importance of the international business, in general.

Given these major differences between the domestic and international PM environments and because the job context of an international assignee is different from that encountered in the traditional domestic assignment, experts agree that the PA system requires modifications for expatriates[32] and inpatriates.[33]

The central themes in the expatriate PM literature relate mainly to the tactical issues (What? Who? When? How?) inherent in managing the performance of an employee who is sent abroad on assignment. That is, they focus on what criteria are appraised, who does the PA, when (and how often) an appraisal is done, and how the appraisal is carried out (i.e., what format is used). In addition, they focus on the cultural and structural contexts of managing the performance of international assignees as well as the repercussions of failing to do so effectively.[34]

What should be evaluated?

The answer to this question—that is, what criteria should be used to evaluate the performance of IAs—is, indeed, complex. They need to meet parent company standards and they need to do it within the international and local cultural contexts. So the evaluation system needs to take both sets of standards into account. The problem is, criteria, roles, and performance expectations are typically defined in the home country but performed in the host country and the cultural norms that define performance in the parent country may not be the same as those considered appropriate in the foreign locale. This can cause significant role conflict for the international assignee.[35] If the international assignee adapts his or her behavior according to the role behavior expected in the host environment, it may well conflict with that predetermined by and expected at headquarters. This type of role conflict is likely to result in situations where the assignee has an understanding of the host country culture and realizes that the use of headquarters procedures or actions may lead to ineffective management. Evidently, the higher the degree of intercultural interaction and cultural distance, the more problems the IA is likely to have with role conflict. Such role conflict is also compounded by the lack of autonomy sometimes experienced in foreign assignments (where headquarters may impose more structure and defined protocols), allowing less space to deal with the conflicting expectations.[36] And this concern over conflicting role expectations is even more pronounced for third country nationals than it is for host country nationals or parent country nationals.[37]

Each performance criterion is composed of a number of sub-categories. One attempt to suggest a set of criteria and sub-categories for international appraisals is found in Box 8.3.[38] The first category refers to *qualifications*, meaning the criteria used to

BOX 8.3 **CRITERIA FOR APPRAISAL OF INTERNATIONAL ASSIGNEES**

Qualifications
Training
Experience
Technical skills
Social and language skills
Education

Targets
Directly derived from the parent company's objectives
Directly derived from the subsidiary's objectives
Directly derived from local objectives
Individually dictated, e.g., developmental goals

Attitude for
Flexibility
Interpersonal understanding and communication skills
Ability to cope with the stress (culture shock) of the assignment
Openness to change

Job performance
Result areas
Development of local team
Communication and decision making
Personal growth and development
Application of (newly gained) expertise

select the IA for the foreign assignment. These are included under the understanding that the performance of the international assignees should be a function of the original assessment of their qualifications for the assignments and their ongoing evaluations should continue to assess whether the original qualifications were accurate. The other categories take into account the variety and complexity of criteria that have been suggested as being so necessary in this environment. Normally, a variety of factors are applied, depending on the international assignee's job description and local circumstances. However, observation of common IPM practices of international assignees suggests that use of detailed criteria (such as listed in Box 8.3) may not really be so common but that the broader standards and more general evaluations are probably more the norm.

Obviously, business strategy largely dictates the overall expectations for IA's performance in any specific country. For example, it might not make sense to focus heavily on profits as a standard of success for a global manager in the early years of a subsidiary in the People's Republic of China. Efforts in the early years are most likely to be concentrated on the development of relationships and on building a base of customers. To expect the international assignee to produce profits equal to those generated in a similar kind of operation at home is unrealistic and will cause heavy frustration and possibly lead to wrongly destroying a manager's career. There needs to be alignment between parent company strategy and the realities of the local situation. In order to ensure this type of alignment, the home office will have to spend adequate time and attention to understand the local/foreign situation. Executives must travel to the foreign locale to observe and ask a lot of questions in order to gain understanding and insight into the local culture and operating situation. At the home office, outside experts from universities and consulting firms, as well as former expatriates (i.e., repatriates) from that country should be brought in to help provide the information upon which executives can best judge the factors for success in the foreign locations in question. Interestingly, research finds that transnational corporations are more likely to use the same basic performance criteria throughout their operations, with some variance in criteria importance depending on country situations.[39]

Ideally, a manager who has returned to the home office from an overseas site should be a permanent part of the team that updates performance criteria for overseas assignments. Re-evaluating the criteria and their prioritization periodically will ensure that the performance criteria will remain current with the reality of the overseas situation.[40] One way to deal with this important performance evaluation issue is to include both soft and hard criteria in the performance review of international assignees.

Who should do the evaluation of the international assignee?

Given all the problems in implementing an effective IPM, the issue of who should conduct performance appraisals of expatriates also becomes quite complex. How can the MNE and IHRM compensate for the many problems described above? The answer developed by most MNEs is found in the use of multiple reviewers.[41] These additional reviewers may not all be as directly familiar with the work of the international assignee (although some may actually be more familiar, given the problems of time and distance), but they may be able to add necessary perspective: peers, subordinates, customers or clients. This is an application of what is referred to as the 360° review process, i.e., using reviews from above, below, and beside the candidate reviewee, and even using self-review. In the domestic context, the 360° review process is relatively complex (certainly more complex and messy, at least, than the traditional superior-only review process). In the international context, it is even messier. In the case of an international assignment, the different raters of the performance of the international assignee may be located many miles and time zones away from the ratee. They may not come into contact with the work of the international assignee so that it is difficult for them to render a valuable evaluation of the individual's performance. In their expatriate jobs, most international assignees have some type of direct supervision from someone in the home country plus usually a direct supervisor in the host country, as well. In addition, the international assignee will entertain regular visits from home country staff and line employees, people on missions to check in on the foreign operation, and will also have frequent direct contacts in the foreign location with local customers, suppliers, banks, and government and community officials. The nature and complexity of all the international assignee's job activities will be much more difficult to assess from the home country. Table 8.1 illustrates the results of a survey of MNEs in terms of the percentages of usage of various types of potential evaluators.[42] Clearly home country and host country supervisors are the most common, although other home country and host country and regional executives also get involved frequently. Interestingly, a high percentage of firms also use self-evaluation. But some typical raters in 360° evaluation systems, such as customers and peers, turned out to not be used very much, at all.

Conducting 360° reviews for an international assignee is also logistically complicated. Let's take, for example, a list of potential reviewers for an international assignee, in this case a sales and marketing manager sent from The Hague, Netherlands, to Bucharest, Romania, for an American firm headquartered in Philadephia, Pennsylvania:

- Her immediate manager (home country) sending her on assignment, located in The Hague, Netherlands.
- The director of sales and marketing, located at product headquarters in Chicago, Illinois.
- The country manager in Romania.

Table 8.1 Raters of international assignee performance

Inside host country		*Outside host country*	
Customers	1	Sponsor	7
Subordinates	7	Corporate HR professional	17
Peers	10	Regional executive	23
HR professionals	12	Supervisor	41
Self	39		
Supervisor	75		

Note: Percentages refer to average percent, in which each type of rater is involved in evaluations across sample MNEs.

- The regional HR director in the shared service center for Central and Eastern Europe (CEE), located in Budapest, Hungary.
- The marketing director, European region, located in the European regional headquarters in Brussels.
- The corporate head of marketing, located at corporate headquarters in Philadelphia, Pennsylvania.
- Her expatriate and CEE sales and marketing peers, including the manager of sales of Romania, located in Romania and various other CEE capitals (Warsaw, Poland; Zagreb, Croatia; Bratislava, Slovenia; Prague, Czech Republic).
- The entire team of subordinates in the Bucharest operation working for her.
- And selected clients and customers in the CEE market.

Granted, the use of such multiple ratings is complicated; but the many difficulties involved with the PA of international assignees in international operations indicates the need to collect multiple perspectives to enhance the accuracy and validity of an expatriate's performance evaluation.

Multinational firms, participating in a survey by a large global consulting firm (see Table 8.2), gave the following responses to their use of various types of raters in the PAs of their international assignees.[43]

Obviously, as was suggested earlier, often the expatriate evaluation process is a pretty informal process. The survey also found that companies with fewer than 100 expatriates favored home country reviews, while companies with more than 100 expatriates favored host country appraisals. Apparently, once the foreign operations reach a certain size, the preference is to delegate the appraisal process to the local level where, presumably, managers with a more direct contact with the international assignee are able to provide more accurate and complete evaluations, although there is no direct research to verify that local managers do any better job at the PA of international assignees than do home country or regional office managers. Indeed, given the many perceptual issues stemming from differences in cultural values and norms and from problems with cultural adaptation, there is some reason to question the assumption that local managers are better equipped to

Table 8.2 Use of different types of rater in the performance assessment of expatriates

Type of review	%
Performance review in host country	71
Performance review in home country	56
Regular expatriate visits to home office	44
Regular manager visits to host office	39
Annual expatriate surveys (self-reports)	19

perform these evaluations than are home country managers (provided, of course, that these distant home country managers have been able to observe the performance of the international assignee and understand the context under which they perform their jobs). One additional result of the previous survey that relates to who does the assessments is that firms reported that international assignees are, on the average, evaluated by three individuals, while the same firms reported an average of six raters for their home country positions.[44] So even here in the admittedly more complex and difficult situation, international assignees do not receive the same level of management attention and involvement as occurs in the purely domestic environment.

Here are some of the advantages and disadvantages of using home versus host country managers as raters:

- *Home country managers.* In many cases, the final appraisal is done in the parent country, where the appraisers typically have little knowledge of local circumstances or of local culture and their impacts on the overall unit performance or on the expatriate or local manager's performance. Achieving results equivalent to a comparable unit or manager in the home country may well require larger efforts in terms of flexibility and creativity, to say nothing of interpersonal and managerial skills, all of which are difficult to quantify or measure and, therefore, aren't taken into consideration.
- *Host country managers.* In view of the geographical, communicative, and cultural, distance between the foreign subsidiary or joint venture and the home country appraiser, local management is often called in to give their opinion. In the case of the international assignee, the immediate supervisor responsible for the evaluation is probably a local manager. The assumption is that they are familiar with the international assignee's performance and are, therefore, in the best position to evaluate and explain it within the local situation and environmental factors. However, their perceptions and, therefore, their evaluations will be governed by their own cultural backgrounds and biases. Thus, for example, a parent company manager, who is used to guiding and managing with a high degree of involvement and participation, might at least initially find resistance from local team members, who expect strong leadership and ideas and initiative from their bosses, and thus not get the desired level of team performance, resulting in a negative (or lower than expected) evaluation.[45]

How should the evaluation of the international assignee be done?

There are a number of issues presented in answering the question of how international performance evaluations should be done. These include concerns about the specific form of the appraisal, the frequency of the appraisal, and the nature of feedback provided to the IA/FM as a part of the evaluation process.

Form

There continues much controversy over the specific form or instrument to be used in any performance review process, although this is not an area that has received any attention specifically focused on the international setting. So, presumably, all of the concerns over evaluation based on achievement of objectives versus trait-based reviews, or other approaches, such as critical incident methods, that have been researched in the domestic context would also apply to the international context. In addition, however, the international context must also take into account issues over language and translation or interpretation of terms and phrasing as well as the cultural context, such as the nature of relationships between subordinates and superiors, etc.

It is typical for firms to develop standard forms for their appraisal processes.[46] And there are valid reasons to retain such forms, including the importance of experience, comparative data for extended use, costs, etc. These reasons remain valid, as long as the context of the performance doesn't change. However, for international assignees, the context most obviously does change. Thus, using standard forms, developed for the domestic situation, can be problematic. Despite this, surveys find that US firms, at least, tend to use the same standardized forms developed for the home country environment for their expatratiates and, presumably, their foreign manager populations.[47] This makes the problems associated with consideration of cultural context in the actual assessment of performance that much more important, but probably results in even less attention being paid to these contextual issues.

Frequency

This is one area where, at least in terms of general performance appraisals, some basic guidelines can be established. According to Wayne Cascio, a major contributor to knowledge about the Western PA process:

> Research over the past twenty years has indicated that once or twice a year is too infrequent. Considerable difficulties face a rater who is asked to remember what several employees did over the previous six to twelve months . . . People often forget the details of what they have observed and they reconstruct the details on the basis of their existing mental categories.[48]

Supervisors tend to evaluate what they remember from the last few weeks or days, rather than over the six to twelve-month period. Even if they have maintained good records of events and performance, they are likely to be most persuaded and influenced by recent events (called recency bias). Ultimately, of course, to the extent the purpose of the evaluation is to provide feedback to the ratee for development purposes, the more frequent the evaluation and feedback the better.

The frequency of evaluation should also vary according to the role of the evaluator.[49] On-site superiors should rate their subordinate international assignee after the completion of significant projects, tasks, or milestones. This helps the superior to focus clearly on the specific context of the particular performance being assessed. These can then be reviewed at the time of the annual or semi-annual official reviews. It is probably best to ask other reviewers, such as peers, subordinates, and customers, for reviews that fit the schedule of the formal review.

Feedback

Usually, an important component of any effective IPM system would include the provision of timely feedback of the results of the evaluation. This may, however, prove to be problematic in many cultural settings. And, in addition, given time and distance issues separating many raters and their ratees, provision of this feedback is also likely to not take place in a timely manner, if at all. And evaluation by a distant manager probably has only face validity. IHRM in Action 8.1 illustrates how Nokia has developed an effective performance appraisal system for its expatriates that utilizes many of the approaches described in this chapter.[50] This system uses multiple raters, multiple criteria for evaluation, and multiple ratings in terms of types of ratings, forms for ratings, and frequency of ratings.

Guidelines for the performance management of international asignees

These recommendations for the PM of IAs, based on the limited research related to the PM of international assignees, are preliminary, but consistent with what has been reported:

- Put the specifics of the PA into the expatriate's international assignment plan and discuss the process prior to departure.
- Set clear performance expectations for the international assignee and the home and host country managers.
- Specify what successful performance in the host country entails;
- Use soft and hard performance criteria.
- Conduct frame-of-reference training for both the raters and the ratee.
- Modify the frequency of evaluations in terms of giving the international assignee more frequent evaluations yet also more time to obtain results.

As Oddou and Mendenhall indicate:

Regardless of the effectiveness or availability of performance management tools, expatriate performance management success depends largely on the manager and expatriate in question: how well they both understand, internalize, and accept performance management, and how skillful they are in its implementation. To this end, appropriate PM training should be available for all expatriates, including their superiors.[51]

NOKIA TACKLES EXPATRIATE PERFORMANCE MANAGEMENT

Nokia, the Finnish-based world leader in the telecommunications industry, has extensive experience with sending and receiving people on foreign assignments, with about 1,200 expatriates on foreign assignment at any one time. Because of this, Nokia has had to learn how to manage the performance of this large group of employees who are so key to the success of the firm's global business. Nokia has developed a comprehensive performance management program that includes goal setting, performance appraisal and feedback, continuous training and development, and performance-related compensation. One thing that Nokia has learned is that the performance of its various types of expatriates, who are in varying types of assignments and situations, should be managed dissimilarly, even within the context of trying to apply a standard approach throughout its global operations. Nokia has put in place what looks, on the surface, like a global, standardized performance management system, with the objective that all employees' performance is managed (to a great extent) the same. In terms of expatriates, however, it turns out that there are at least five different types of expatriates, including top managers, middle managers, business establishers, customer project employees, and R&D project personnel. For each of these groups, there are some common practices. For example, all expatriates know what is expected of them, how well they are performing, and what the opportunities are for them to develop new competencies in order to meet present and future job requirements.

However, the various expatriate groups also experience some differences in how their performance is managed. These differences revolve around the following:

- Whether and how performance goals are set, who sets them, and what types of goals are set.
- How performance is evaluated and who conducts the evaluation.
- Whether training and development plans are agreed upon with the expatriate.
- Whether expatriates have the opportunity to attend training while on their foreign assignments.
- What type and how clear the linkage is between expatriate performance and pay.

For example, as might be expected, the higher the expatriate's level, the more independent their position and the more distant their performance management will be. In addition, they and their bosses are more likely to have a longer-term focus, both for their present international position and in terms of their careers and developmental concerns.

Middle manager expatriates reported typically to a local manager and had local, relatively short-term, goals and focus. Feedback was given by the local manager, and the local manager determined financial incentive rewards. Performance goals for business-establisher expatriates and for customer-project expatriates were tied to the nature of their assignments, more so than the earlier two categories, with startup objectives for the former and deadlines for network operation common in the latter. Indeed, in all four areas tracked (goal setting, performance evaluation, training and development, and performance-related pay), performance management criteria were implemented differently for the five different groups of expatriates, even though all expatriates were managed in some form or another on all four areas.

This major global firm illustrates the high degree of importance that contingency factors play when managing expatriate performance. Even though Nokia has put in place a standard performance management system intended for global use, the reality is that expatriate performance was managed differently in the five categories of expatriate assignments. Evidently, off-the-shelf solutions may not produce the desired improvements in expatriate and company performance.

Source Adapted from Tahvanainen, M. (2000), Expatriate performance management: The case of Nokia Telecommunications, *Human Resource Management*, 39 (2–3): 267–275.

CONCLUSION

This chapter has addressed the crucial issue of performance evaluation and performance management for MNEs and their employees (whether local, global, or mobile international assignees) and managers. It has described the many difficulties encountered in trying to implement an effective IPM system in the international arena, not the least of which is figuring out how to accommodate in the evaluation process factors stemming from the nature of the local cultural environment. It is clear that it is inadequate to simply apply a PM process designed at the home country level for domestic use to the international setting. It is necessary to make some accommodations for problems with cultural adaptation and associated with the complexities of conducting international business. The chapter also focused on the design, implementation, and evaluation of effective IPM systems for employees of MNEs and then looked at the special issues related to the PA of international assignees. Each section ended with a discussion of a number of suggestions and guidelines for improving the process of implementing an effective IPM system.

Appropriately assessing employee performance is a question of fairness to the employee; but it is also a question of ensuring that the MNE receives full value from its managers, employees, and international assignees and the best subsidiary or joint venture performance possible. Ultimately, an MNE's objectives relative to a workable IPM system are to effectively manage employee talent to the benefits of the employee, the manager, and the overall organization. An effective talent management strategy not only focuses on attraction (recruiting and selecting) the best employees but also on evaluating and developing them and position them within the organization so that the firm's global business strategy will be increasingly guided by those who have experienced and understand the firm's worldwide operations and markets.[52]

GUIDED DISCUSSION QUESTIONS

1 What are the tensions between standardization and localization of the PM system of the MNE?

2 How does the international character of the MNE impact the *design* of the PM system?

3 How does the international character of the MNE impact the *implementation* of the PM system?

4 How does the international character of the MNE impact the *evaluation* of the PM system?

5 What are the major issues involved in PM of international assignees?

VIGNETTE 8.1   GLOBAL PERFORMANCE MANAGEMENT IN ACTION

"Open exchange" at dmg world media

dmg world media, an international exhibitions company leader in home and consumer shows, is a relatively small (fewer than 1,000 employees) yet international company. Developed mainly through acquisitions of other small businesses, dmg world media is not an asset-based company, but an intermediary that rents exhibit space and creates exhibits marketed and sold by its teams of employees. Employees are based in the UK, the US, Canada, Dubai, Australia, New Zealand, and Beijing. dmg world media's success is heavily dependent upon high levels of employee performance.

According to Warren Girling, executive vice-president of HR: "We have a culture of how we manage our people to get that high performance. We select groups of highly motivated and developed people who understand their customers and the business. And, we have an ongoing discussion on how we perform."

The company's previous HR-driven PM system was similar to that of many others in that it utilized a rating scale from 1 to 5 that was linked to a percent merit increase. This traditional system, particularly its once-a-year reference point performance appraisal, no longer fit the needs of the business or its organizational culture. The merit increase was highly distorted because market forces in this business have a greater impact on salary increases than merit. Additionally, managers considered the system too time-consuming and wanted more of a report card type of approach. Moreover, some of the newly acquired companies were often so small that they had no formal experience with PM.

The new PM system, Open Exchange, was developed by a small group within the company, including the three most senior executive vice-presidents, HR, and selected employees from around the world. The group started with only a blank sheet and a vision that had previously been defined by the company. This vision, or business statement, was developed in the form of a constitution because constitutions are the broad foundation documents of modern societies. Yet, much like a standard constitution, not every single word of dmg world media's business statement applies to every day-to-day activity. The core elements of dmg world media's constitution are that it is the leader in its field, getting things done in a very unbureaucratic and decentralized way by understanding the customer's business. Performance is the common purpose behind which the company unites as it reviews every set of results regularly, exhibit by exhibit.

Essential performance dimensions were identified by looking at its own high performers and asking: "If we think about our best/most successful people and customers we love to work with, what are their essential characteristics?" These essential qualities are sought in the people who join the company, and major features of the new PM system were based on checking performance against these "essentials."

Rather than an annual affair, performance review is now done by managers, event by event. As employees work in small teams, they know when someone on the team is not performing and inform the manager. Not only do underperforming people feel peer pressure, but they are required to sit down with the manager, who is held accountable for solving the problem. It is dmg world media's strong belief that when someone has a performance problem, the appraisal is not the right place to discuss it. Performance problems cannot wait for a period review.

In the new performance reviews, employee performance is regularly reviewed by the manager and categorized into one of three groups. Employees are either (1) exceptional performers; (2) great but not exceptional performers; or (3) great people but not trainable or right for the job. Exceptional performers are the role models. Great employees may have the essential skills but also some blind spots that can be improved upon. That's where training is an option. The manager completes a grid of training analysis needs and coaches the employee to work on areas needing improvement. Employees who struggle with job knowhow and perform poorly on more than one of the essentials must complete a face-to-face action plan. For those below expected level, training is rarely an option. Most of the time, there are multiple reasons for unacceptable performance: lack of skills, competency, motivation, or simply the wrong person in the wrong job. Sometimes there are bad hires, bad promotions, and bad placements. At dmg world media, heavy focus is on bringing in the right people and putting them in the right jobs.

Managers document performance because the company recognizes that some of the best performers need management confirmation of their accomplishments and stroking. Documentation is the recording of a positive. Negatives are handled outside of the performance appraisal process.

Although dmg world media does not have a common single workplace and is dispersed throughout different countries, it successfully uses a standardized PM system. This is possible because the employees from different national cultures are held together by a single common product (the exhibitor business), common personalities (the type of people that work in the exhibitor business), and a similar organizational culture (their constitution). In addition, they are flexible, adaptable, and willing to be elastic, based on these common principles.

Questions

1 How is performance management at dmg world media different from traditional performance management systems at other companies?

2 What was the impetus for developing a different performance management system at dmg world media?

3 Can a standardized performance management system be used effectively with managers and employees from different cultures in an international company?

Source Claus, L. (2007), Global HR in Action Vignettes, Willamette University, www.willamette.edu/agsm/global_hr.

_____

The well-being of the global work force, global human resource information systems, and the structure of today's international human resource management

9

LEARNING OBJECTIVES

This chapter will enable the reader to:

- Explain the importance of global health and safety
- Describe IHRM's role in managing a global health, well-being, safety, and security program
- Describe an effective crisis management program
- Describe the various support services delivered by IHR
- Explain IHRM's role in global HR research
- Describe the problems associated with implementing an effective global HR information system
- Describe the new IHR competencies
- Explain the professionalization of IHR
- Describe the new structure for IHR in today's MNEs

KEY TERMS

- Employee health and safety
- Crisis management
- Family-friendly policies
- Work–life balance
- International relocation

- e-HR
- Global Human Resource Information Systems (GHRIS)
- Shared service centers
- Professionalization of IHR

This last chapter deals with three critical yet seldom reported on aspects of IHRM strategy and structure: concern for the well-being of the MNE's global work force, development and maintenance of the global HR information system, and the structure and delivery of today's IHR programs in the MNE. All three of these areas of concern are central to IHR's ability to deliver on its vision of making a major contribution to the MNE's competitive advantage in the global marketplace. And taken together they provide an important conclusion for the themes of this book, with a look at both the practical side of IHRM and a focus on the way that MNEs are struggling to find ways to deliver strategic support while delivering the necessary IHRM services within acceptable metrics.

THE WELL-BEING OF THE GLOBAL WORK FORCE

This continues to be one of the more challenging (yet important) topics to write about in IHRM. There has been relatively little written about the general topic or any of the specific aspects of it, in either the "popular" press or the academic and practitioner presses. Periodically, events occur that put certain aspects of the topic on the front page, such as the kidnapping of a well known executive of an MNE, an exposé about worker exploitation at a foreign subcontractor, a workplace accident that kills and/or injures scores of employees in a foreign plant, or the total lack of concern for the work–life balance of employees around the world, especially in rapidly developing emerging markets. Thank goodness, catastrophies are fairly rare. Even so, employee health, well-being and safety are increasingly important topics for MNEs, for the following reasons:

- Increasing attention to employee well-being around the world.
- Increasing numbers of employees at potential risk because of increased global trade:
  - Increasing number of workers in a growing number of locales in "at risk" jobs in manufacturing, chemical, mining, and affiliated activities, such as transport and construction.
  - Increasing number of offices and plants in a growing number of locations and forms (subsidiaries, licensees, joint ventures, alliances, subcontractors).
  - Increasing number of business travelers, in general.
  - Increasing number of people on short and longer-term international assignments to an increasing number of countries, often with their families.

○ Growing problems with civil unrest and global terrorism.
● Increase in risk factors.

All of these factors create increasing concerns for the health, well-being and safety of an MNE's global work force—and potentially for the safe and continuing operation of the global business. Although it is not always the case, in most countries the health and safety of workers are one of the responsibilities of HR and, therefore, in the global enterprise, of IHR.

Even though not much has been written about this subject, a number of specific aspects can be identified and discussed. These include (1) coping with health and safety practices and regulations that vary from country to country; (2) the establishment of health and safety policies on a global basis for all employees of the MNE; (3) dealing with specific health and safety concerns of business travelers and international assignees and their families as they travel on business trips around the world or are posted to foreign assignments; (4) the very specific threat of issues like kidnapping and/or terrorist acts against foreign operations and international assignees and their families; (5) dealing with real and potential, natural and man-made, threats and disasters; and (6) the work–life balance of workers in markets with differing levels of economic development.

The following provides an introduction to at least some of the factors that an IHR manager might need to consider when dealing with international health, well-being, and safety issues. First, general issues for the MNE at the country or regional level are discussed. Then issues related to business travelers and international assignees are addressed. This section ends with a discussion of how MNEs might develop crisis management programs for preparing for and dealing with various health and safety contingencies.

Employee health and safety around the world

In most large firms, headquarters-located HR managers responsible for IHR do not often deal with health and safety issues among their firms' foreign subsidiaries or joint ventures. Responsibility for these issues is normally left to local managers and their HR staffs to manage within the constraints of local custom, culture, and regulation. Clearly, attention to these concerns varies dramatically from country to country.[1]

Health and safety statistics

From a strategic point of view, it would be helpful if firms (and their IHR staffs) could compare occupational health and safety regulations and experience between countries, for example to help assess the problems and potential costs that might be associated with locating operations in any given country. Yet, this remains quite difficult to do. Different countries follow different reporting standards regarding what constitutes an injury and whether it must be reported. Even for workplace fatalities, variation in methods makes cross-national comparisons difficult. Some countries (but not all) include deaths that occur when an employee is traveling to or from work, whereas others exclude deaths that result from occupational diseases. It is also the case that developing countries, in general, report significantly higher occupational accident and fatality rates than do more developed countries.[2]

For IHR planning and decision-making purposes, the most important point is that accident and fatality rates vary widely for a number of reasons, only some of which are related to variances in record-keeping standards and practices. What may be more significant are factors such as the mix of industries present in each country, the percentage of service jobs, and the level of education and training among the general labor force. Some industries and jobs are inherently more dangerous than others. For instance, logging, mining, and quarrying tend to have the highest fatality rates in most countries, while construction, transport, utilities, and agriculture have moderately high rates. World Health Organization data suggest that, worldwide, approximately half the world's workers are employed in hazardous jobs, both from risk of injury or illness and from death.[3] Retail trade, banking, and social service industries generally have many fewer injuries and illnesses, and fewer fatalities. Thus those countries which have a mix of industries that favor those with lower fatalities will have more favorable country-wide occupational health and safety statistics. Yet they still may have dangerous working conditions within their normally high-risk industries.

Health and safety laws and standards

A country's occupational safety and health laws and enforcement may also influence its statistics. Although not much research of this sort has been done, a 1986 study comparing five European countries with the US concluded that the US was the weakest in terms of law and enforcement mechanisms.[4] Sweden, the former East Germany, and Finland were the highest ranked (although with what is now known about the levels of pollution, the age and lack of maintenance of industrial equipment, and the poor quality of labor and health statistics in many former East German factories and towns, these conclusions about the former East Germany might well be called into question), followed by the former West Germany and the UK. Of importance to IHR planning, the study concluded that a strong national union movement facilitated the passage and active enforcement of effective health and safety measures. In Sweden, union-run safety committees can order production stopped if they believe that a hazard exists, and keep it stopped until the hazard is remedied. These committees also have a great deal of control over the hiring and firing of industrial physicians and safety engineers.

In countries with strong industrial democracy, such as most of those within the EU and Australia, MNEs are more likely to find regulations empowering employees or their representatives in unions and works councils in the monitoring and enforcing of workplace safety. Indeed, the EU has adopted a common framework for occupational health and safety which now applies to more than twenty-five countries. Pursuant to this framework, member nations are modifying their workplace safety laws to achieve common standards. The intent is to retain the highest safety standards set in the more progressive countries, while minimizing the competitive cost advantages that might otherwise flow to nations with less stringent standards.

At the opposite end of the spectrum, the setting and enforcement of occupational safety (and, even more so, health) standards in developing countries often leave much to be desired. Most developing countries have only rudimentary employment safety laws and very limited funds for enforcing such laws. Often the efforts by developing countries to attract foreign investment are often enhanced by offering a business environment relatively free of government regulation. Typically, unions are weak or are primarily focused only on issues such as politics, wages, and fair treatment of employees, not on workplace safety concerns. In addition, the tendency to rely on labor-intensive enterprises, dated equipment, pressure to create and preserve jobs, and the lack of safety training for specialists as well as for workers, themselves, all contribute to the poor safety records in many developing countries.[5]

An additional area of concern for MNEs (and IHR) involves the differences in the nature and quality of medical systems in different countries, the coverage of the health care system, and who pays for health care, and the form and level of support systems for various forms of disabilities.

All of these issues impact employment practices for both IAs and for local nationals. Attention to fitness, employee stress, use of drugs, awareness of problems with major health issues such as AIDS, and problems with inadequate nutrition are all issues which can influence IHR planning and practices in global operations.

Family-friendly policies and work–life balance[6]

Family-friendly policies and work–life balance raise a whole new set of issues and opportunities for IHR, issues and opportunities which need to be taken into account when planning the nature of and locale for foreign operations. They have become central issues over the last decade, particularly in the EU and in other developed countries, reflecting a growing concern over quality of work life, lengthening work hours and stress, growing support by governments for the health of families, and the growing concern by enterprises over meeting the needs and interests of today's complex and demanding work force. The changing roles of men and women—both at home and at work, the changing make-up of families with increasing numbers of single parents, and the aging of the population and the subsequent rise in elder care, all have led firms (and governments) to look for ways to make work more attractive while allowing more balance between the demands of work and home. At a time when there is a worldwide growing shortage of critical talent, firms are finding they must do everything possible to make their workplaces desirable. And, even though these concepts originated in developed countries, MNE leadership and IHR must decide how to apply them to operations in emerging markets and in developing economies.

The EU has pioneered the legal framework for family-friendly policies (such as paid time off for maternity and paternity responsibilities, for elder care and family illness needs, time limits on work hours, restrictions on night and shift work, provision of significant paid annual leave, and equal rights for part-time workers). There are many pressures (from governments and firms) for the development of family-friendly laws and policies, including the increased numbers of women in the work force, low birth rates and the resultant labor shortages, variances between countries in such policies creating cost differentials for firms, female participation in various industries, etc. The result is that MNEs need to become both familiar with the legal and cultural constraints in the countries in which they operate or are considering operating as well as incorporating in their global strategic planning knowledge about these concerns around the world.

The current conversations on talent management and employee engagement within HR have pushed the topic of work–life balance to the forefront. HR is increasingly being asked to play a role in balancing the needs for work performance in companies with the demands from employees for greater balance in their lives.[7] Work–life balance issues can be looked at from different perspectives, starting from a broad societal view, then moving to the view of an employing organization, and finally to the perspective of an individual employee. The issues under consideration at each level vary considerably. At the "macro" societal level, issues of work–life balance deal with different cultural, political, economic, demographic, and legal contexts that affect the work–life balance debate, often resulting in legislation that supports family obligations. The "meso" organizational level focuses on the new world of work which has created pressures for workers and the responses companies are proposing in terms of work–life balance-friendly policies and benefits. At the "micro" individual level, the work–life balance focus is on coping mechanisms of the individual (or groups of individuals) in their particular situations. Although work–life balance initiatives are often in the forefront in developed economies, the issue is also impacting people in emerging markets, as IHRM in Action 9.1 illustrates in Romania.

Acquired immune deficiency syndrome (AIDS)

AIDS creates a special situation in a number of countries, particularly in Central and Southern Africa and South and Southeast Asia, and is a concern to all countries. "AIDS, so often regarded as a public health or humanitarian issue, casts a looming shadow over global business and already has begun causing bottom-line losses."[8]

In 2006, 2.9 million people died from AIDS/HIV and an estimated 4.3 million people worldwide contracted HIV, the virus that causes AIDS (with the majority of new cases occurring in people under the age of twenty-five).[9] According to UNAIDS, the UN program on HIV/AIDS, the total number of people estimated to be living with HIV was 39.5 million, a number which continues to grow every year. This group obviously includes employees, family members on employee health care plans, the future hiring pool, customers, and policy and decision makers. Death or illness in any of these groups affects an organization's performance and bottom line. When they hit key personnel, it can even put business activity completely on hold.

WORK–LIFE BALANCE FOR YOUNG PROFESSIONALS IN EMERGING MARKETS

Western multinational enterprises are now increasingly operating in emerging markets. They bring their global perspective to the table and a discipline of hard work for the professionals to tackle. In the West, educated professionals usually have a well established career path and are recognized as high potentials early on in their careers. But young professionals in emerging markets are eager to prove themselves, explore the new opportunities, and take on the hard work that multinationals bring to their countries. While company policies and local national legislation may promote having work time restrictions for employees, they do not always take the further step of making sure these rules are followed. Therefore, the eagerness to succeed takes over and most employees in emerging markets end up working overtime and neglecting their private lives in stark contrast with the Western work–life balance (WLB) notions of their multinational companies.

While it was never her intention to work herself to death, that is literally what happened to Raluca Stroescu in Romania. She worked as an audit manager of the multinational Ernst and Young and died on 22 May 2007 due to a problem of a "complex nature." Her friends and family relate that she worked every day and her local management did not accept her missing even one day. Within the last three weeks prior to her death, she had been working on an important audit project and had lost a lot of weight reaching less than 40 kg (88 lb) at thirty-one years of age. Her case was widely discussed in Eastern Europe and according to local public opinion it is considered the first case of a death due to overwork! Raluca's case was troubling, and is bringing a lot of awareness to the WLB issue in emerging markets. As a result of the publicity of this case, there have been numerous HR events that focused on the need for WLB in emerging markets like Romania. Included among these events was the Corporate Social Responsibility Forum, an annual conference held in Bulgaria in the fall of 2007 which had WLB as a general theme. One result has been that a number of Romanian organizations are increasingly discussing the topic of WLB as it applies to their workplaces.

The central theme around all these discussions is the debate whether young professionals in emerging markets really do want WLB (as it is advocated in the developed world—especially throughout Western Europe) or would they much rather trade it for advancement, fame, and fortune. Apparently, at this point in time, the motivation for fame and fortune wins out. Most young professionals in emerging markets work very hard because exciting developmental opportunities are opening up in their countries and there are always new and interesting projects in which to become engaged. They want to deliver these projects on time and at their best quality. They do it because they receive recognition for their accomplishments, better annual reviews, and a chance for advancement. They also do it because they do not want to fail. They cannot slow down because they are afraid others will take their places if they stop to take a break. They choose to work very hard and, even, to work without getting paid. In many instances, the expectations of the multinational companies are of such a nature that the expected work cannot be completed within "normal" working hours.

Many people in developing countries feel that WLB is a concept that is valued in the West, but countries like Romania cannot fully embrace it. Employees in emerging markets do not yet have the level of financial comfort that allows them to aspire to a well paid job that actually requires a standard forty-hour work week. This poses a serious challenge for multinational companies that want to implement WLB policies within their global organizations. While they may have the long term well-being of their employees in mind, they must overcome the "We have to catch up with the rest of the world" mentality that the young professionals in their emerging market subsidiaries have. What happens when a multinational company wants to promote WLB but the young professional adults in emerging markets cannot really take advantage of it? For a Western concept, such as WLB, to take traction in emerging markets may require more than a well planned global HRD intervention.

Source Claus, L. and Bucur, S. (2007) Global HR in Action Vignettes, Willamette University, www.willamette.edu/agsm/global_hr.

In the worst-affected areas, HIV/AIDS affects one in four urban-based adults and a larger percentage in many rural areas. In such areas, health care systems are overwhelmed and organizations experience staffing shortages and productivity interruptions. UNAIDS reports: "AIDS . . . is decimating a limited pool of skilled workers and managers and eating away at the economy . . . Businesses are . . . [suffering]."[10]

Every area of international business is affected. Every business program from sales to employee education to employee benefit plans to business operations to visas for business travelers and IAs (e.g., many countries will not allow entry by employees who are HIV positive) is affected and must be taken into consideration as multinational enterprises plan their global businesses.

Health and safety for international assignees

Many of the above issues overlap with concerns for the health and safety of business travelers (BTs) and IAs and their families. Some are standard concerns for employees while traveling and some involve employees after arrival at their new assignments. These concerns involve many types of situations (for both business travelers and IAs and their families), including concerns about kidnapping; having disabling accidents (for example, car accidents) while on foreign assignment; encounters with local law enforcement; coping with major natural disasters such as earthquakes, volcanoes, floods, and hurricanes/monsoons which affect all employees and operations; getting ill and having inadequate local health care; being mugged and losing passports and money which have to be replaced; dying while on foreign assignment; and being hit by terrorist acts or civil unrest or just being traumatized by them or their possibility.

In addition, being involved with any of these situations can be made worse because of inability to speak the local language, lack of familiarity with and/or distrust of local legal and medical or emergency services, inability to use the local phone systems (including inadequate phone systems); and being in distant time zones when needing help from headquarters. The issue of language is a particularly important one when confronting emergencies. The simple act of calling for help in the location of the problem can pose a major obstacle, e.g., not speaking the local language (or not speaking it well enough to describe the emergency), not knowing whom to call for help, problems with the local phone system, and problems with the competency of local police and emergency workers and hospitals/clinics.

In response to the importance of these issues, international business travelers and IAs and their families need to be briefed on and prepared for dealing with problems of safety and health while traveling and in their new countries. They should be given an orientation to the different medical systems in the new countries, how to take care of prescriptions and any special medical conditions, the identification of doctors and hospitals to provide for health care in their new locations, and usually the acquisition of emergency medical and evacuation insurance to cover possible contingencies. IHR should also be prepared to provide assistance in case of crises in the firm's foreign operations as well as to aid in times of need for business travelers.

Specific health and safety concerns for business travelers and international asignees

Even though potential problems related to terrorism, crime, kidnapping, civil unrest and riots, natural disasters, and other traumatic events, can seem overwhelming, it is often more likely that MNEs and IHR will have to deal with a number of specific health problems unrelated to these sorts of traumas. Business travelers and IAs and their families frequently (if not usually) suffer from less serious health complaints ranging from intestinal disorders due to exposure to new bacteria to major exotic illnesses. There is even some evidence that health problems abroad are on the increase.[11] Key reasons include:

- Increasing poverty in developing countries.
- Increasing failure of the health infrastructure in many parts of the world, following political or economic instability.

- A changing pattern of disease, with increasing drug resistance.
- Increased accessibility of destinations that were previously remote.
- Increasing global competition for business opportunities in developing countries, so more travel to and from them and more people assigned to them.
- Increasing problems with the transfer of diseases around the globe due to increased travel, particularly by air, such as was experienced in 2003 with SARS, a virus that spread from China across the world by travelers before it was recognized and could be isolated and countered.
- Relaxation of health formalities on entry to countries, resulting in reduced "need" to seek medical advice (for example, about required immunizations) prior to travel.

Under all circumstances, business travelers and expatriates need to be briefed as to what to expect, how to prepare for conditions in the country or countries to which they are going, and how to react when confronted with health or safety problems. IHRM in Action 9.2 describes a situation in which the lack of attention to health issues when an individual was sent on foreign assignment caused major problems for both the individual involved and the organization.

Death while on assignment

Once in a while (thank goodness, it doesn't happen very often), someone dies while on business travel or while on an international posting.[12] As bad as these events are, someone has to deal with them, and that someone in most organizations is IHR. Coping with such situations includes dealing with the situation in the foreign locale as well as helping the family cope. Death can occur from natural causes (heart attack, stroke) or from some other event, such as an auto accident, a terrorist act, or a natural disaster. Whatever the cause, it usually catches everyone by surprise. Thus having thought about the possibility before it happens can make timely and adequate response much more likely. For example, IHR (and employees and their families) need to be aware that typical emergency medical insurance and programs do not take care of people after death.[13] The contracts end when death occurs. And the treatment of deceased people varies from country to country and among differing religions, so IHR needs to get involved quickly to make sure that the wishes and traditions of the family are accommodated.

Crisis management

One important way for IHR to add to the value of their services is to design and implement crisis management programs for dealing with the many forms of trauma and health and safety problems that individual employees and their employing organizations confront in today's global environment.

TRUTH AND CONSEQUENCES

Expatriate health abroad

This is the true story of Kate Cawthorn, a twenty-five-year-old London-based trainee solicitor, sent on a very short-notice (three days) traineeship assignment to Ghana. On her very first day she contracted a severe case of shigella dysentery. She continued to try to do her job for five weeks, with no medical tests or treatment, but finally decided to fly home. Her symptoms got worse, which left her unable to complete her internship and thus unable to qualify as a solicitor. She has never recovered well enough to go back to work. Kate Cawthorn claimed that her employers negligently failed to provide an adequate standard of immunization and pre-travel health advice for her trip. She was given just three days to prepare for departure and was referred to a local clinic that provided her with gravely inadequate travel advice—even failing to mention the high risk of malaria, for example. So, eventually, she sued her employer, asking for £633,000 for loss of her career as a lawyer, personal injury, and distress. The case was settled for a "high" six-figure sum.

The case attracted widespread publicity in the press, as well as within the legal profession. This case has many implications for the treatment of people sent on international assignments. For example, the firm involved did not provide enough lead time for the assignee to take care of critical concerns (such as the necessary vaccinations), she was not provided with adequate preparation and advice, she was not provided with adequate support when she arrived, and there was too little concern about the implications of the assignment and its consequences for her career.

Source Adapted from Dawood, R. (1998), Bills of health, *HR World*, winter, 57.

Assess the risk

The first area of focus for IHR crisis planning is to assess the risks. When experts are asked what to tell employees going on international assignments, they often reply, "Drive very carefully on the way to the airport." The point is that there is likely to be greater risk involved in the drive to the airport than in anything else the traveler will experience (with the possible exception of traffic accidents overseas)! When business travelers and IAs and their families leave home and their comfortable, familiar surroundings, their major fears are often of unpredictable and uncontrollable events like acts of terrorism or becoming a hostage or being kidnapped. These are the events that people are most familiar with, since they are the ones that make the headlines in the media. But, in reality, there is greater risk from being in an automobile accident driving across town than from serious problems associated with travel or living abroad, even in the post-September 11 world. Consider the:

● *Size of the risk.* Using US statistics (these are the most readily available, but are not so different for other countries), the chances are greater of dying from a dog bite (twenty per year), from being hit by lightning (100), or from drowning in a bathtub (150) than from any act of terrorism (fewer than twenty in a typical year). Other common risks include being electrocuted in one's home (900 per year), choking on food (3,000), and dying in auto accidents (about 50,000 per year). Indeed, these types of problems are much more common than unexpected acts of violence of all kinds. Ten thousand Americans even die overseas every year from natural causes like heart attacks and old age. Helping IAs and business travelers to understand the nature of the risks is a first step in planning ways to prepare for the risks that do exist.

● *Types of potential problems for each locale.* IHR needs to assess (or get assistance from consultants that provide this information) the specific risks that do exist in a particular location. Not every overseas location poses the same level or type of risk. The types of risk that should be assessed would include things like level of crime, food and waterborne illness, transport safety, potential for natural disasters, potential for political problems, labor unrest, integrity of local contacts, security of business facilities and employees and their homes, quality of medical services, product sabotage, and potential for environmental disasters.

● *Relative risk for each situation.* Not all travelers and IAs face the same risks. Well-known or prominent executives working in high-profile jobs or industries face greater risks than the typical business traveler or IA and thus require greater protection and attention. And not all foreign destinations present the same levels of risk, including any of the kinds of issues listed above as well as, for example, the nature of the local legal systems (whether it can or will provide the same sort of legal protections that a firm's business travelers and IAs are used to) and the local medical system (and whether it can deliver the type and quality of medical care that a firm's business travelers and IAs are used to and expect).

Prepare a crisis management plan

The second thing IHR needs to do to address global health, safety, and security issues is to prepare a plan for dealing with the issues identified.[14] This area, like so many others, receives little attention until crises occur. Getting a plan prepared (even quickly) may be more important than thoroughness. Sensitivity (particularly when dealing with family members and with media) may be more important than any other consideration. And when a crisis is handled poorly, the firm is likely to lose personnel. So the benefits in employee morale and productivity are likely to outweigh the costs of the resources needed to prepare a crisis management plan. Part of this action would involve tracking employees who are traveling or on foreign assignments and the status of their official documents, such as visas, exit permits, etc., so that the firm has a fairly clear idea of who is located in any particular location, so that when a crisis arises, IHR know who is at risk.

Orientation and training

The third component of any plan to deal with global health, safety, and security issues is to develop a program for preparing business travelers and IAs and their families for international travel and living. This orientation and training could include insurance for issues such as emergency medical and kidnapping ransom, information about potential risks in the areas of the world involved, pre-departure orientation, and post-departure follow-up. This preparation should also involve preparing security for IA homes and foreign facilities, plans for dealing with civil emergencies (such as plans for evacuation of foreign personnel), plans for dealing with media and family "back home," and developing lists of sources of information and help in case of real crises.

Summary of crisis management planning and execution

- Planning can lessen the risks and the fears. Plan design is important. Plan execution is key.
- IHR must take a leading role. If it doesn't, it is likely that no one else will—and it is IHR that deals most directly with travel and relocation/living issues for business travelers and IAs.
- Don't underestimate or ignore possible threats.
- Don't underestimate how important these issues are to business travellers and international assignees and their families.
- Communication with employees is key.

International assignments are expensive and important to global enterprises. Ensuring the health, safety, and security of this small but significant group of employees is essential. The three simple steps of obtaining the relevant information, using that information to create awareness, and being prepared to cope with a business traveller or international assignee-related crisis, will go a long way toward minimizing the risks and maximizing the security of business travelers/international assignees and, by extension, the international business, itself.

GLOBAL HUMAN RESOURCE SUPPORT SERVICES AND INFORMATION SYSTEMS

In the typical domestic HR department, a number of activities are performed that are referred to as support services for the core HR responsibilities. These include the HR information system (including maintaining records on employees and employee programs, such as health insurance, and providing HR reports), HR planning (including employee forecasts, career plans for managers, and succession planning for executives), job analysis and the writing of job descriptions (for recruiting and training purposes and the setting of performance expectations), job evaluations and wage surveys and the development of job classifications and wage rates, labor market analyses to determine the availability and abilities of potential employees, the development of performance appraisal systems, domestic relocation services, and personnel/HR research.

However, there is relatively little research on these topics in the international context. A glance at any traditional HR textbook (almost all of which are country-specific) will show that most of these topics receive considerable attention in the local or domestic setting. But little research or writing has been focused on these support services as applied to foreign operations, even though they can be a significant responsibility. Therefore, the following provides a short overview of four of these services that play a particularly important role in IHRM: IHR research, IHR information systems, international relocation and orientation, and global administrative services. Some of the other topics, such as work force planning and performance management, have been discussed earlier in the book.

International human resource research

A major support service in many large firms is HR research, an activity staffed, usually, by Ph.Ds in industrial psychology with the mission to study and verify the importance and contribution of HR programs and systems. Nevertheless, there appear to be few resources in large firms devoted to research on IHRM programs. Thus, many of the challenges mentioned in this text—for example, determining which hiring practice, job classification system, or compensation system works best in which national context for which type of international employee, or even which type of international assignment to use when—have not been researched.

Such research still needs to be done. The impact of culture on IHR practices and the management of expatriates have been fairly extensively researched (refer to the discussion on this in Chapter 3 on culture). But not much else in the total domain of IHR activity has received much more than cursory research examination, if that. Partly because of this lack of research and the newness of global business to many firms, MNEs often extend their domestic (headquarters') policies and practices to their international operations. As a consequence, IHR research could be fruitfully applied to most (if not all) areas of IHR responsibility in order to establish best practice and the best way to perform these responsibilities. And as IHR is increasingly expected to provide evidence of the effectiveness and contributions of its programs and proposals, developing expertise in IHR research would appear to be highly recommended.

International human resource information systems

As firms internationalize their business operations they eventually reach the point where they need to internationalize their information systems. This includes their human resource information systems (HRIS). But, because the formats and purposes of the HRIS were established to service only HR in firms' home country operations, internationalizing the HRIS can be a very complex and challenging activity, including integrating any existing foreign HRIS from developed or acquired subsidiaries or joint ventures.

Special problems

Global HRISs create special problems for HR. Global HRISs need to cope with all (and more) of the following special issues, all of which can create major problems. It is not the authors' intent in this section on global HRIS to make experts of the reader, but to introduce the special complexities that global HRISs offer to MNEs.

- Keeping track of work forces in each country of operation (a particularly difficult problem for firms that operate in dozens of—for some firms up to 200—countries, with hundreds of business units spread around the world).
- Keeping track of long-term IAs, including home country contact information as well as foreign addresses, etc.
- Keeping track of short-term IAs who may be commuting, on extended business trips, or on assignment that last only a few months.
- Keeping track of IA compensation and benefits (incentives and allowances) packages in some form of comparable information, since most IAs have unique compensation packages.
- Providing ID numbers for all employees around the globe (and a way to standardize these, since many countries have their own identification numbers).
- Having multilingual capabilities and fields that accommodate diverse requirements (length of names, addresses, even multiple wives, etc.)
- Foreign currency conversions for payroll, which can vary daily.
- Standard formatting for compensation and benefits variations from country to country.
- Budgeting and tracking payroll, given various currencies and currency fluctuations.
- Government versus private health and pension benefits in various countries.
- Major variances in leave of absence and paid time off from country to country (even standard definition of what constitutes time off and when someone is included in the active head count).
- Employment contracts (with their major variances from country to country).
- Number of hours worked and vacation days.
- Termination liabilities.
- Tracking visas (for various types of IAs and families and business travelers, schedules for renewal, etc.).
- Tracking family information for IAs, including educational support.
- International job postings—locations, timing, job responsibilities, applicable employment contracts.
- Terms and conditions of employment variances from country to country.
- Keeping track of all the firm's union contracts and their variances.

- Data privacy laws that protect personal information residing in HRIS and the back-up systems (often in another country).
- Laws regarding the transfer of personal data from one country to another.

Management considerations

There are a number of policy decisions that IHR must take to develop a global HRIS, including these types of concerns: developing separate (for each location or region, for example) or integrated information systems, which would involve questions about the treatment of wholly owned subsidiaries versus joint ventures and partnerships and the compatibility of computer hardware and software, language(s) to be used, form of HR data to be maintained, etc.; centralization or localization of the system; authority over and control of access to the information and movement of the data between locations (which may be regulated by country law); centralized or localized privacy protection rules; control and maintenance of data, accessibility, updating, and flow; and decisions about what data to maintain in the global HRIS, given the thousands of potential elements from various countries that might be included. Of course, there are additional issues that have to be resolved, such as dealing with country cultural differences in the creation and use of employee data, training in the use of the system, choice of vendors and technology, integration of new and old systems, etc. And then there are basic issues related to the actual design of the system and its capture of things like employee names (with the incredible variance in forms, lengths, languages), desirability of standardization of names of local firms (e.g., Inc., PLC, GmbH, FrOres, SLA, Oy, etc.), differences in postal addresses (or lack of such), even variances in calendars, which must also be resolved.

Special capabilities: international human resource websites

In addition to the development of a global HRIS, HR has its own uses for technology, which can greatly enhance its ability to perform its responsibilities. For example, HR can develop an intranet within its own operations that can both help HR to deliver services, such as benefits information, as well as knowledge transfer among various HR business centers around the world. Such intranet portals and HR web sites can promote and facilitate the sharing of ideas and resources across borders, allowing firms to benefit from pooled and archived IHR experience and expertise, relying less on outside consultants for routine information (and data bases for finding the best consultants for the specialist help that is not available in-house). Technology such as this also allows ever-increasing capabilities, such as language translation software and multilingual programming for conducting global employee surveys and benefits management.

Relocation and orientation

This area of service has traditionally been one of the most time-consuming for IHR. Increasingly, however, at least in larger MNEs, these services are being outsourced to external firms or relegated to internal, central shared-service centers that specialize in transactional services such as relocations. To ensure that employees being assigned to foreign posts receive the best possible attention to the very personal concerns that accompany relocation to another country, most of these related services are sourced from firms that specialize in the delivery of these such services directly to IAs and their families. These services typically involve helping relocating employees with problems such as the selling or renting of houses, the shipment of household goods internationally, the location of temporary living quarters in their new location, the purchase or rental of a new house or apartment (or provision of a company-owned or leased residence), managing the international move itself, the control of family in-transit time, and the control of overall relocation costs. These concerns can often be quite intense for IAs and families relocating internationally (as well as for IHR staff that manage the processes). So ensuring the quality of these services (within reasonable costs), whether provided directly through the firm or through outsourced specialists, is a critical IHR responsibility.

Other than the issues involved with the physical relocation, as stated above, there are a number of other critical concerns that IHR needs to make sure are met. These include providing tax and financial advice; arranging visas and work permits; arranging medical exams and counseling related to medical services in the foreign locale; providing training and orientation (about financial issues, the travel arrangements and experience, the country and its history, culture, and language) for IAs and their families; and arranging education and schooling for IAs and their families while on assignment in another country.

Administrative services

Many of the following support services could be provided elsewhere in the firm, but they are generally delegated to IHR staff. All of them are, at least initially, established to ease the process of transferring employees from one country to another. Then because IHR finds ways to resolve these challenges, they often find other responsibilities being sent their way. These services can include:

- Making *travel arrangements* (for international assignees and their families and also for all employees who travel internationally). These services can involve travel arrangements, travel visas, and travel insurance.
- Arranging *housing* in foreign locales. This can involve finding quality housing (hotel rooms, apartments), making reservations, negotiating contracts, and signing rental agreements.
- Determining the availability and operation of local *transport*, including rental cars, chauffeurs, metro maps, bus schedules, and rail systems.
- *Office services*, such as translation and translators, typing and printing documents such as contracts, housing and rental agreements, business letters, and business negotiations and locations.

- *Currency conversion.* International assignees and international business travelers may, initially, need assistance with issues related to conversion of their home country currency into that of host countries. IHR is often tasked with ensuring that these people understand whatever complications might arise as pay arrangements are worked out to accommodate different currencies and their varying exchange rates and varying local inflation rates.
- *Local bank accounts.* Since banking systems vary from country to country, and access to familiar banking operations may be limited in availability, IAs may need assistance in establishing local bank accounts (sometimes even this is restricted) as well as in understanding how the banking system operates in his or her new country of residence. In many developing countries the banking system is relatively undeveloped (particularly in relation to what the IA is used to) such that there may not be an established checking system for paying bills or ready access to reliable ATM machines for acquiring cash. These issues may affect business operations, as well, for example, for paying bills and meeting payroll obligations. IAs will need to be oriented to these realities.
- *Government relations.* This will initially involve familiarity with the proper offices to get visas and work permits (or the consultancies that provide these services). But it may eventually extend also to local government offices for establishing business services (as well as residential services for IAs) such as telephones, internet connections, and business licenses. IHR may find providing these services cumbersome and complex, but successful local operations must have access to them. It makes sense that they be provided by the IHR staff. And they do serve to keep IHR closely involved with the firm's international activity.

STRUCTURE OF GLOBAL HUMAN RESOURCES[15]

The last section of this last chapter describes the challenges that IHR is facing in today's chaotic and hyper-competitive global marketplace and how it is dealing with them. In some ways, what is described here is a look at the future. And in some ways and for many MNEs this is here, now. In both cases, MNEs must confront these issues, now and into the future. As was discussed in the second chapter, the emerging model for the twenty-first century is not the multinational company as it has come to be known (and which is at the core of the IHR practices described throughout this text), but rather a globally integrated enterprise that is very different in structure and operation.

Global human resource challenges

Almost every chapter in this book has included some discussion of the challenges that IHR faces in each relevant area of responsibility. In addition, a number of issues which present strategic challenges to the IHR function as a whole are beginning to arise. These include the following:

- There is a growing realization, particularly in large MNEs, that there is a lack of HR talent around the world. There are too few opportunities for university education in HR and IHR; firms do too little to develop IHR talent internally, including the use of expatriates in HR assignments; and the new structures for delivering IHR services are not being incorporated into HR development yet, either internally or externally.
- There are an increased number of employee relations issues—for example, comparisons between workers in various countries—making IHR programming and service delivery increasingly complex and difficult.
- Globalization and freer trade are leading many countries to change their legal frameworks (e.g., China joining WTO, India deregulating its economy), which impacts IHR practices and local country management.
- There is too little consistency in HR infrastructures for delivery of IHR programs around the world.
- And what employees want in various locations around the world is constantly changing and often creates new and difficult challenges:
  - Global work forces want top-level leadership from within their own countries, not just from headquarters.
  - Local work forces and local HR staffs want their local office dynamics to be respected by corporate headquarters.
  - Local subsidiary and joint venture managements want expatriates to take ownership of becoming part of the country they are assigned to.
  - Local employees want defined career paths for themselves and want to be included in corporate career planning, as well. They expect the parent firm to initiate development opportunities for local employees.
  - Local offices often feel left out of corporate planning. They want and expect to be included particularly in communication on upcoming organizational changes.
  - Local business units expect to be included in executive visits from headquarters, not to be taken for granted.
  - Increasingly, employees in foreign subsidiaries around the globe want variable compensation schemes to include them. And they also expect to be included in parent company total rewards planning.

The new multinational enterprise human resource organization

These employee interests, combined with the types of social changes described in the first two chapters of this book, are leading to the need for major organizational changes, as well. Many executives were trained and developed during an era with very different demands than what is required today. Thus, a major disconnect is occurring between what executives know and understand and what the global business environment needs.

The demands of this "new world" impact HR (and IHR) even more so than many other areas of organizational leadership. Shifts from personnel administration (primarily transactional) to strategic HR, from mostly domestic to largely global HR, from traditional (paper-and-pencil) HR to delivery of services via electronic interfaces (e-HR), and from soft sell (do it because it makes people feel good) to hard sell (measuring the results of HR programs and showing they make a positive impact on a firm's profitability and its resultant market capitalization), all have changed the nature of HR services and competencies.[16] Of course, the traditional HR transactions haven't disappeared. Rather, they are automated and/or outsourced, with domestic HR practices now being multiplied in the many different countries in which the firm operates. And tasks related to HR administration and legal compliance are now scrutinized and measured in terms of value-added contribution to the global business. As a result, HR practitioners are now challenged to develop new mind-sets and distinct new professional HR competencies, such as global mind-sets and skills in computers and HR process outcomes measurement.

In terms of traditional HR transactions, such as signing up new employees for payroll and benefits services and updating such services when changes are made, technology has made it possible to deliver these transactions through in-sourcing (i.e., shared services) and outsourcing (initially involving only specific individual HR business processes and now involving the entire HR function). So now HR professionals must focus on the integration of HR processes and managing HR projects across organizational and national boundaries.

As has been indicated a number of times in this book, one of the most significant challenges for IHR is that the HR function is, for many reasons, not a highly globalized function.[17] Within international business, HR is the most likely function to be localized. And, yet, many forces are driving firms to globalize even their HR (IHR) functions. As Brewster *et al.* put it:

> Initiatives aimed at improving [global] temporal, functional, or financial flexibility are being introduced side by side with integrated programmes intended to link work practices to the need to deliver radical cost improvements [around the world]. In increasing flexibility, firms also want to change the nature of employee identification and their sense of involvement, and this changed identity knows few national borders.[18]

To meet these pressures, MNEs are pursuing several different models of IHR organization, with their IHR functions facing a number of challenges:[19]

- Consequences of global business process redesign, the pursuit of a global centre of excellence strategy and the global redistribution and relocation of work that this often entails.
- Absorption of acquired businesses, merging of existing operations on a global scale, the staffing of strategic integration teams, and attempts to develop and harmonize core HR processes within these merged businesses.
- Rapid startup of international operations and organization development as they mature through different stages of the business cycle.

- Changing capabilities of international operations with increased needs for up-skilling of local operations and greater complexity.
- Need to capitalize on the potential that technology affords the delivery of HR through shared services, on a global basis, while ensuring that social and cultural insights are duly considered when it is imperative to do so.
- Changes being wrought in the HR service supply chain as the need for several intermediary service providers is being reduced, and as web-based HR provision increases.
- Articulation of appropriate pledges about the levels of performance that can be delivered to the business by the IHR function, and the requirement to meet these pledges under conditions of tight cost control.
- Learning about operating through formal or informal global HR networks, acting as knowledge brokers across international operations, and avoiding a "one best way" HR philosophy.
- Offering a compelling value proposition to the employees of the firm, and understanding and then marketing the brand that the firm represents across global labor markets that in practice have different values and different perceptions.
- And identity problems faced by HR professionals as they experience changes in the level of decentralization/centralization across constituent international businesses. As knowledge and ideas about best practice flow from both the centre to the operations and vice versa, it is not uncommon for HR professionals at all levels of the firm to feel that their ideas are being overridden by those of other nationalities or business systems.

In pursuing these developments, IHR has to cope with four underlying challenges: managing the shift from domestic HRM to international/global HRM, enabling IHR capability development on a global basis, ensuring effective knowledge management across national and business unit boundaries, and providing HR services cost-effectively. In order to deliver on these realities and challenges, then, today, many global companies are evolving their IHR into a three-tiered organizational structure.[20] At the top of these MNEs is an HR headquarters organization made up of a small team of senior HR executives who deal with strategic organizational and HR issues. They work very closely on the organizational side with senior management, providing HR insight on global strategy and on the HR side with two groups: a team of very specialized experts in the traditional functional areas of HR and a global team of country/regional HR managers who act as local business partners, dispersed throughout the MNE's global operations. At the bottom of this IHR organization are the traditional HR staff who administer the HR programs and functions at the level of the business unit. These services may be delivered internally through shared (by multiple business units) service centers or externally through outsourced vendors who deal on a day-to-day basis with the purely transactional issues—and which are largely delivered through the internet, not face-to-face.

What makes this structure work are the HR business partners in the middle, implementing at the local level the strategy designed at the top and designing and overseeing the transactional services at the bottom. These HR business partners play a critical role, whether it is figuring out how to engage employees and manage and retain talent across the many business units, customizing employment deals, building sustainable HR practices, or creating and measuring HR value. Each of these three levels requires different competencies. Thus herein lies the challenges for IHR today and into the future.[21]

Opportunities for strengthening international human resources

These shifts from the traditional MNE model with mostly self-contained HR offices at the country level, with oversight from headquarters, to this three-tiered model have led to debate over the quality of the contribution of IHR to the new global organizational strategy. Although most executives do not deny the important role that IHR can (and should) play in the global firm, critics claim that IHR is not doing an adequate job of playing that role, that HR is not being a true business partner, that they don't have the IHR competencies necessary to meet all the needs of the new three-tiered model and to meet the global organizational needs of human capital, innovation, and flexibility.

These next few paragraphs outline ways that IHR can and must change in order to strengthen its value to the organization. These opportunities lie in increasing its professionalization, filling the competency gap with better internal IHR development, better understanding the new IHR practice, and finding and filling HR's sustainability "sweet spot."

Professionalization of international human resources

HR is achieving significant professionalization worldwide. According to Claus and Collison's research on the HR profession in twenty-three countries, there is a growing convergence in terms of HR practitioners' educational backgrounds, skill sets, and their accepted body of knowledge.[22] In terms of accepted indicators of professionalism, such as an agreed body of knowledge, recognition as a profession, discretion and autonomy in the performance of responsibilities, credentialing and certification, and the growth of local, national, and international HR organizations, HR has certainly reached acceptance as a major profession. Even so, this research also suggests that there is still a need for greater acceptance, both from within the profession and from without. More HR (and IHR) practitioners need to acquire professional degrees in business and HR and their employers need to require such levels of education and fields of study for their HR and IHR staffs. More practitioners need to take advantage of seminars and conferences on HR and IHR and demand that their local and national professional societies (and local colleges and universities) deliver high quality education on HR and IHR.

IHRM still needs to be recognized by top executives, strategic planners, and line managers, in general, as critical to the success of the global enterprise. Research supports that a focus on progressive IHR programs is related to gaining global competitive advantage.[23] Thus IHRM programs and departments need to receive high-priority attention and resources. And IHR managers need to deliver on the promise. Global managers need to have experience in IHR assignments and IHR managers need to have experience in global line management, as well.[24]

Global human resources certification

The Human Resource Certification Institute (HRCI) in the US has implemented a testing procedure for certifying professional skill and knowledge in global HR.[25] The original work on identifying the "body of knowledge" in IHR was completed in 2003 and the first certification in IHR (GPHR—Global Professional in HR) was offered in 2004. Possessing this certificate (which is now being acquired by HR professionals around the world) signals to employers that the holder has demonstrated a high level of competency in IHR. The body of knowledge (BOK) required in global HR was identified through a practice analysis (i.e., global HR is what global HR practitioners are doing!) and initially included knowledge in six domains:

- Strategic international HR management.
- Organizational effectiveness and employee development.
- Global staffing.
- International assignment management.
- Global compensation and benefits.
- International employee relations and regulations.

The Society for Human Resource Management (SHRM), the US's (and world's) largest professional society for HR professionals developed the SHRM Global Learning System with help from IHR practitioners around the world to codify that body of knowledge. A more recent practice analysis conducted by HRCI in 2007 updated the body of knowledge and shows that the field of IHRM is evolving rapidly.

Narrowing the international human resource competency gap

Major shifts in the nature of work and organizations require major competency adjustments. Many organizations have focused on the new competency requirements of their work forces, but few have focused on the needed competencies of their HR practitioners.[26] Two researchers who have focused on HR competencies are Brockbank and Ulrich.[27] Their updated HR competency model identifies six broad roles for HR, each with corresponding competencies. These broad roles include being a cultural steward, a talent manager and organizational designer, a strategy architect, a business ally who knows how to contribute to the financial success of the business through people management, the operational executor who deals with the transactional and legacy services, and a senior role that masters the other roles and is, therefore, the central activist and advocate for human capital.

The new international human resource practice

The new challenge for IHR is to be able to provide added value in the middle realm (that of the IHR business partner) by developing organizational initiatives that effectively attract, retain, and engage employees on a global scale who can achieve the organization's strategic global objectives. This challenge will vary in scope, depending on the type of organization (for example, a large MNE, a relatively small employer, or a government-owned enterprise), but overall people management success depends on IHR execution. The new IHR value focuses on branding of the organization as a desirable place to work, customizing employment arrangements, engaging employees, managing employee performance around the globe, managing lateral projects of global (and often virtual) teams, developing sustainable IHR practices, and creating and measuring value.

Developing international human resource sustainability

A fourth IHR opportunity for value creation relates to the ability to create sustainable practices for the long term. Savitz and Weber describe the sustainability sweet spot as "the common ground shared by your business interests (those of your financial stakeholders) and the interests of the public (your non-financial stakeholders)."[28] That is, it refers to those activities and programs that satisfy both the demand for bottom-line results as well as for the satisfaction of other non-financial stakeholders, such as employees and customers. For IHR, the sustainability sweet spot is the place where the pursuit of organizational interests seamlessly blends with the pursuit of employee interests.

Increasingly, in the global marketplace, it falls to IHR professionals to strategically manage human talent and to examine and understand how to respond to the cultural and human challenges facing successful organizations. To accomplish this, they must build global HR competencies. The challenge for IHR professionals is to work in a fast-changing environment, adapt rapidly to new technologies and organizational forms, balance people and organizational needs, and gain the necessary competencies to add value to people, human capital, and the overall success of the organization.

The international human resources job of the future

This last subsection provides a summary and conclusion for this last section of the chapter. A few years ago, IBM sponsored studies by Towers Perrin to identify the skills which would be necessary for IHR in the future.[29] These capabilities were also identified as the ones for which the widest gaps exist between current IHR abilities and those which were perceived as needed in world-class organizations of the future. They included:

- The ability to educate and influence line managers on IHR policies, practices, and importance.

- Being computer and technology-literate, so as to be able to create and use global databases for IHR advice and decision making and for delivery worldwide of IHR transactional services.
- Being able to anticipate internal and external changes, particularly of importance to the availability and qualification of human resource talent around the world.
- Exhibiting leadership for the IHR function and within the corporation, at headquarters level and at the business unit level.
- Focusing on the quality of IHR services within the enterprise.
- Defining an IHR vision of the future and communicating that to the IHR department and to the organization.
- Developing broad knowledge of many IHR functions.
- Being willing to take appropriate risks in the development and implementation of innovative IHR policies and practices.
- Being able to demonstrate the financial impact of IHR policies and practices.

So, given the need for these capabilities, what must IHR of the future do? The following points summarize the suggestions and ideas made in this chapter (and throughout the book):

- *Hire for international experience.* IHR must convince managers of the MNE of the importance to global competitiveness of having a work force that knows and understands international business. Thus, the firm needs to appreciate the importance of including international knowledge and experience as criteria in the recruiting and hiring process.
- *Disperse people with international experience throughout the firm* (including in HR). One way to improve the firm's overall international business competency is to disperse the people who have global knowledge and experience throughout the enterprise.
- *Learn how to recruit and assign on a global basis.* IHR must develop the ability to recruit talent from around the world and to assign such global hires throughout the firm's global operations.
- *Increase the firm's international information diet.* IHR should take a proactive role in providing all locations of the enterprise with information (e.g., general international magazines and newspapers) about not just the firm's global operations, but about global affairs in general, including actions of governments and competitors in countries where the firm operates.
- *Train everyone in cross-cultural communication, etiquette, protocol, negotiation styles, and ethics.* This is one additional, but specific, aspect of providing information to the work force about global business. These are areas of concern that greatly increase a global firm's competency in the conduct of international business.
- *Ensure international developmental assignments.* IHR must make sure the global enterprise understands and supports the necessary system for ensuring that international assignments are kept as a major component in all executive development programs.

- *Pursue GPHR certification.* HR practitioners who want to work in the global arena should acquire the basic global HR body of knowledge.
- And, most important, IHR managers need to understand and appreciate the importance of developing themselves to better carry out their global mandates. This would include thoroughly understanding how the enterprise makes money globally and being able to articulate an IHR point of view using the language of business on all global strategy discussions, knowing how to measure global return on investment in IHR programs, developing and using a global HR balanced scorecard to measure the overall contribution of IHR to the firm's global success, developing relationships and networks throughout the global enterprise, and creating a global HR learning organization, to constantly improve and better meet its changing global challenges.

To conclude, then, this final statement: though the exact nature of the IHR role of the future is still evolving (and will continue to evolve), the following roles will likely be among the critical roles being performed by the global HR manager of the future:

- The CFO for global HR, that is, thoroughly knowledgeable about the financial impact of IHR programs.
- The global IHR vendor manager, that is, effectively managing the vendors to whom IHR has outsourced its administrative and transactional functions.
- The internal consultant to the global business on issues related to the enterprise's human capital knowledge management.
- The global leader for HR.

CONCLUSION

This chapter has discussed three topics of great importance to the IHR professional: employee well-being, IHR support services, and the new structure of global HR. All three of these areas of responsibility play major roles in defining IHR's ability to achieve a strategic contribution to MNEs' global success. First, the chapter described why MNEs must understand and cope with local and international health, safety, and security regulations and needs and develop programs and policies that protect their global work forces in their many locations. The chapter explained the nature of the problems associated with these issues, in general, and for business travelers and international assignees and their families, in particular, and described the best practices that have developed for dealing with them, including crisis management and programs.

Second, the chapter described four particular support services that IHR provides for the international enterprise. These included IHR research, global HR information systems, relocation services, and special administrative services, such as providing translation and office services and developing information about local banking and transport services for business travelers and international assignees.

And, lastly, the chapter (and book) ended with a description of the challenges to the nature of IHR in the new global economy and how IHR is redesigning itself in responses to these challenges. New IHR competencies are described and a new IHR organizational structure is explained.

This book has provided a comprehensive view of the role and nature of International Human Resource Management in the enterprises that compete in today's global economy. It provided, first, an overview of the nature of that global economy and its impact on organizations, leading into an explanation of how that has influenced the development of IHRM and how it has contributed to strategic international business. Next the book described the influences of national culture, national legislation and regulation, and international labor standards and ethics in the development of HR policy and practice in MNEs.

The rest of the book provided descriptions and analyses of the major responsibilities of IHR: work force planning and staffing, training and management development, compensation and benefits, employee performance management, and the support services and new structures of IHRM. As the theme of the text has pointed to continually, the nature of business is rapidly changing and this is forcing rapid changes in the design and conduct of IHRM. The challenges are great but the opportunities are large. Hopefully, this text has provided the knowledge and the inspiration to meet those challenges and to take advantage of those opportunities.

As the challenges are met and IHR managers further develop their global HR competencies, multinational firms will find themselves developing world-class IHR capabilities with these characteristics:

- Responsive to a highly competitive marketplace and global business structure.
- Closely linked with global business strategic plans.
- Jointly conceived and implemented by line and international HR managers in an equal partnership.
- Focused on global quality, customer service, productivity, employee involvement, teamwork, and work force flexibility in all the enterprise's operations around the globe.

Only when such an integrated, responsive, and accepted IHRM is developed will IHRM reach its potential and take its rightful place in the management of today's successful global enterprises.

GUIDED DISCUSSION QUESTIONS

1 What makes managing employee health and safety programs around the world so difficult?

2 Why have family-friendly and work–life balance programs become so important?

3 Describe the kinds of health, safety, and security problems that international employees encounter and design a crisis management program to deal with them.

4 Why is designing and implementing a global human resource information system so difficult? What kinds of problems need to be overcome?

5 What actions would you suggest to HR managers in order to increase their professionalism and competency in handling global HR issues?

VIGNETTE 9.1 HR STRATEGY IMPLEMENTATION IN ACTION

Balanced scorecard at Pliva (a member of the Barr Group)

Established in 1929, Pliva is a generic pharmaceutical company based in Zagreb, Croatia. Pliva operates in over thirty markets worldwide with strong roots in Central and Eastern Europe. For nearly forty years since its first Federal Drug Administration approval, the company has had a strong history in both the highly demanding and rigorous quality and regulatory environments of the US and Western Europe. Pliva develops, manufactures and markets both final dosage form generic pharmaceutical products and active pharmaceutical ingredients (API), with products ranging from over-the-counter, commodity to value-added generics, biosimilars and cytostatics. In 2006, Barr Pharmaceuticals (a US holding company operating through its principal subsidiaries) acquired Pliva and deemed its headquarters for its European operations, making the group the third largest generic pharmaceutical company in the world.

Prior to the acquisition, the management board at Pliva engaged in a three-year goal-setting process. Goals were set at the corporate level for the Pliva Group, Marketing and Sales (M&S), Research and Development (R&D), Global Product Supply (GPS), Quality and all corporate support functions. These goals and targets were then cascaded through the company, reaching about 100 organizational units at the senior management level. Group Controlling and Finance set the targets for financial measures based on the approved financial plan. Other targets were set at the corporate level. Goals and targets were not explicitly cascaded further down in the organization below the organizational units. Experience taught that setting goals and targets at such levels is perceived as being too bureaucratic. Tasks can quickly become outdated during the year due to the speed of developments within Pliva. Employees at lower-level organizational units were bound to the goals and targets of the first upper-level organizational unit, with additional goals and targets supporting the Pliva values of teamwork and knowledge sharing.

The Balanced Scorecard (BSC) format, a tool that integrates strategy with operations, was used to set short-term performance goals that reflect long-term strategy. The balanced scorecard focused on selected key performance indicators (KPIs) to ensure achievement of the long-term goals. It was also used as a link for team performance between organizational units and the reward system.

The balanced scorecard reporting tool included objectives, risks to fulfill objectives, how progress is measured, required level of performance, and projects needed to achieve objectives across five balanced scorecard perspectives: financial (what financial objectives must be achieved?), customers (what value do we have to deliver to customers?), processes (in which business processes must we excel?), innovation (what do we have to do differently?) and people (what skills and systems do our people need?).

Led by Johan Swarts, executive director of Global HR, Human Resources also engaged in a three-step strategic thinking process:

- What is the corporate strategy—strategic statements?
- What are the HR strategic objectives to achieve these corporate goals (strategy maps) from the five perspectives (financial, customers, internal processes, innovation, and people)?
- What is the HR operational plan to achieve the HR objectives—KPIs, targets, risks involved and supporting projects?

The HR strategy map (Figure 9.1) illustrates how the various HR roles support the five perspectives of the balanced scorecard with regard to a specific Pliva strategic statement that aims to increase profitability through vertical integration.

Balanced scorecard results are reported in management meetings after each quarter results. Each scorecard "owner" reports the actual versus plan per each measure as well as the deviations or causes to be explained. Pliva developed its own software for standardized balanced scorecard reporting on line. Balanced scorecard is also incorporated in the performance management and reward system to strengthen the focus on Pliva group and business results, to reward for achieving strategic goals and planned business results as set out in the scorecard, and to reward for living Pliva values and operating principles.

The bonus formula is: Cb * Ib * Target bonus. The Cb factor is a mix between Pliva group EBIT, lines of business, and organizational unit results (balanced scorecard) and the Ib factor is a mix between how the employee is contributing to his/her applicable organizational unit goals/targets and his/her behavior in term of being a role model towards living the Pliva values and operating principles.

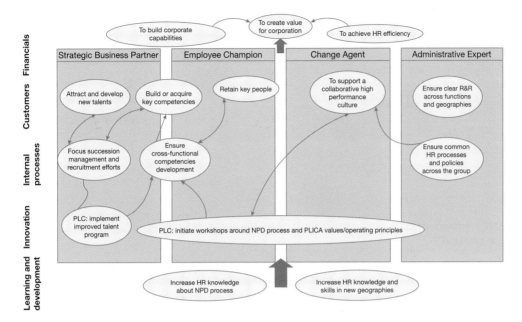

Figure 9.1 Pliva's human resources strategy map

At Pliva, HR is an integral part of strategy development and implementation. The HR strategy maps guide the activities of the HR team in alignment with corporate objectives and provide a true opportunity for business partnering.

Questions

1 How is HR at Pliva aligned with the corporate strategy?

2 How does the bonus formula at Pliva support the balanced scorecard efforts?

3 What is the impact of the Barr acquisition of Pliva on the strategic planning and balanced scorecard process?

Source Claus, L. (2007), "Global HR in Action Vignettes," Willamette University, www.willamette.edu/agsm/global_hr.

Notes

Part I Introduction to international human resource management: the context

1 The globalization of human resouce management

1 There have been many books and articles written about globalization and its impact. Here are only a few of these references: Bhagwati, J. (2004), *In Defense of Globalization*, Oxford/New York: Oxford University Press; Fernandez, F. (2005), *Globalization and Human Resource Management: Adapting Successful UN Practices for the Private and Public Sectors*, New York: HNB Publishing; Friedman, T. L. (1999), *The Lexus and the Olive Tree: Understanding Globalization*, New York: Farar Straus and Giroux; Friedman, T. L. (2005), *The World is Flat: A Brief History of the Twenty-first Century*, New York: Farar Straus and Giroux; Greider, W. (1997), *One World, Ready or Not: The Manic Logic of Global Capitalism*, New York: Simon and Schuster; Micklethwait, J. and Wooldridge, A. (2000), *A Future Perfect. The Challenge and Hidden Promise of Globalization*, New York: Crown Business; Rosenberg, J. (2000), *The Follies of Globalization Theory*, London/New York: Verso; Steger, M. B. (2003), *Globalization: A Very Short Introduction*, New York: Oxford University Press; Stiglitz, J. E. (2002, 2003), *Globalization and its Discontents*, New York: Norton; and Yergin, D. and Stanislaw, J. (1998, 2002), *Commanding Heights: The Battle for the World Economy*, New York: Simon and Schuster/Touchstone.

2 Friedman (2005) Prestowitz, C. (2005), *Three Billion New Capitalists*, New York: Basic Books.

3 For example, Kuruvilla, S., Frenkel, S., and Peetz, D. (2003), MNCs as diffusers of best practices in HRM/LR in developing countries, in W. M. Cooke (ed.), *Multinational Companies and Global Human Resource Strategies*, Westport, CT: Quorum Books, pp. 167–199.

4 Friedman (1999).

5 United Nations Conference on Trade and Development (UNCTAD), *World Investment Report 2005*, New York: United Nations; and www.unctad.org/wir.

6 See, for example, Wilson, D. and Purushothaman, R. (2003), *Dreaming with BRICs: The Path to 2050*, Global Economics Paper 99, New York: Goldman Sachs.

7 Data published by Dealogic, as reported in Cauchi, M. (2006), Wheelin', dealin' hits new high, *Boulder Daily Camera*, November 18: 8B; *CIA World Factbook* (2006), retrieved from http://www.photius.com.ranking/economy.

8 *CIA World Factbook* (2006), http://www.cia.gov/cia/publications/factbook; World Bank: http://www.worldbank.org/WEBSITE/EXTERNAL/DATASTATISTICS; Bureau of Economic Analysis, US Department of Commerce: http://www.bea.gov/national/xls/gdplev.xls.

9 *Fortune* (2006), The *Fortune* Global 500, July 24: 91–96.

10 *Business Week* (2004), Global 1000, July 24: www.businessweek.com.

11 *Forbes* (2006), Global 2000, April 17: www.forbes.com.

12 *Financial Times* (2006), Global 500, June 10: www.ft.com.

13 *Fortune* (2006), Global power 50, October 16: 191–192.

14 Simon, H. (1996), *Hidden Champions: Lessons from 500 of the World's Best Unknown Companies*, Boston, MA: Harvard Business School Press.

15 See the references on globalization in note 1. Also: Davis, S. and Meyer, C. (1998), *Blur: The Speed of Change in the Connected Economy*, Reading, MA: Perseus Books; Enriquez, J. (2000, 2001), *As the Future Catches You*, New York: Crown Business; Evans, P., Pucik, V., and Barsoux, J.-L. (2002), *The Global Challenge: Frameworks for International Human Resource Management*, New York: McGraw-Hill Irwin; Lawrence, P. (2002), *The Change Game: How Today's Global Trends are Shaping Tomorrow's Companies*, London/Sterling, VA: Kogan Page; Marquardt, M. J. (1999), *The Gobal Advantage: How World-class Organizations Improve Performance through Globalization*, Houston, TX: Gulf Publishing; and Thurow, L. (2003), *Fortune Favors the Bold*, New York: HarperCollins.

16 Thompson, A. A., Jr. and Strickland, A. J., III (1998), *Strategic Management: Concepts and Cases*, New York: McGraw-Hill.

17 Bartlett, C. (1983), How multinational organizations evolve, *Journal of Business Strategy*, summer: 10–32; Beechler, S., Bhatt, B. and Nath, R. (1986), The relationship between the global strategic planning process and the human resource management function, *Human Resource Planning* 9 (1): 9–23; Fadel, J. J. and Petti, M. (2001), International policy basics, in Albrecht, M. H. (ed.), *International HRM*, Oxford: Blackwell, 76–79; Harzing, A. H. (2004),Strategy and structure in multinational companies, in Harzing, A. H. and Ruysseveldt, J. V. (eds), *International Human Resource Management* (2nd ed), London: Sage, 33–64; Pucik, V. and Evans, P. (2004), *People Strategies for MNEs*, London: Routledge; Tung, R. L. (1984), Strategic management of human resources in multinational enterprises, *Human Resource Management*, 23: 129–143; and Walker, J. W. (2001), Are we global yet? in Albrecht, M. H. (ed.), *International HRM*, Oxford: Blackwell.

18 Calof, J. and Beamish, P. (1994), The right attitude for international success, *Business Quarterly*, 59 (1): 105–110; Kobrin, S. J. (1994), Is there a relationship between a geocentric mind-set and multinational strategy? *Journal of International Business Studies*, 25 (3): 493–511; Perlmutter, H. V. (1969), The tortuous evolution of the multinational corporation, *Columbia Journal of World Business* (January–February): 9–18; Perlmutter, H. V. and Heenan, D. A. (1974), How multinational should your top managers be? *Harvard Business Review*, 6: 121–132.

19 Gupta, A. K. and Govindarajan, V. (2002), Cultivating a global mind-set, *Academy of Management Executive*, 16 (1): 116–126; Kedia, B. L. and Mukherji, A. (1999), Global managers: Developing a mind-set for global competitiveness, *Journal of World Business* 34 (3): 230–251.

20 Stroh, L. K. and Caligiuri, P. M. (1998), Strategic human resources: A new source for competitive advantage in the global arena, *International Journal of Human Resource Management*, 9 (1): 1–17.

21 At least one text has been written focusing on the global HR practices of one of these organizations: Fernandez, F. (2005), *Globalization and Human Resource Management: Adapting Successful UN Practices for the Private and Public Sectors*, New York: HNB Publishing.

22 *Ibid*. 47.

23 *Business Week* (2006), Emerging giants, July 31: 41–49.

24 Fernandez (2005).

25 Adapted from Dowling, P. J. (1988), International and domestic personnel/human resource management: Similarities and differences, in Schuler, R. S., Youngblood, S. A. and Huber, V. L. (eds) *Readings in Personnel and Human Resource Management*, St. Paul, MN: West, pp. 456–462.

26 Claus, L. (1998), The role of international human resource management in leading a company from a domestic to a global corporate culture, *Human Resource Development International*, 1 (3): 309–326; Hendry, C. (1994), *Human Resource Strategies for International Growth*, London: Routledge, particularly chapter 1; Perkins, S. J. and Shortland, S. M. (2006), *Strategic International Human Resource Management*, London/Philadelphia: Kogan Page; and Vance, C. M. and Paik, Y. (2006), *Managing a Global Work force: Challenges and Opportunities in International Human Resource, Management*, New York: Sharpe.

27 Claus (1998).

28 Adler, N. and Ghadar, F. (1990), Strategic human resource management: A global perspective, in Pieper, R. (ed.), *Human Resource Management: An International Comparison*, Berlin: de Gruyter.

29 The phrase "suddenly global" was coined by global HR practitioner Lance Richards.

30 See, for example, Doz, Y. and Prahalad, C. K. (1986), Controlled variety: A challenge for human resource management in the MNC, *Human Resource Management*, 25 (1): 55–71; Evans, P. A. L., Lank, E. and Farquhar, A. (1989), Managing human resources in the international firm: Lessons from practice, in Evans, P. A. L., Doz, Y. and Laurant, A. (eds), *Human Resource Management in International Firms*, London: Macmillan; Evans, P. A. L. and Doz, Y. (1989), The dualistic organization, in Evans, *et al.* (eds) *Human Resource Management in International Firms*, London: Macmillan; Evans, P. A. L., Pucik, V., and Barsoux, J.-L. (2002), *The Global Challenge: Frameworks for International Human Resource Management*, New York: McGraw-Hill Irwin; Halley, J. (1999), Localization as an ethical response to internationalization, in Brewster, C. and Harris, H. (eds), *International HRM*, London: Routledge; Hendry (1994); Perkins and Shortland (2006); and Sparrow, P., Brewster, C., and Harris, H. (2004), *Globalizing Human Resource Management*, London: Routledge.

31 Laurent, A. (1986), The cross-cultural puzzle of international human resource management, *Human Resource Management*, 25 (1): 97.

32 Taylor, W. (1991), The logic of global business: An interview with ABB's Percy Barnevik, *Harvard Business Review*, March–April: 92.

33 Lorange, P. and Vancil, R. (1977), *Strategic Planning Systems*, Englewood Cliffs, NJ: Prentice Hall.

34 Arthur Andersen (2000), The globalization of human resources: A benchmarking study, Human Capital Consulting Practice: authors.

35 See, for example, Cheng, J. L. and Cooper, D. (2003), A strategic context approach to international human resource management research: Towards greater integration of theory and practice, in Rugman, A. M. (ed.), *Leadership in International Business Education and Research*, London: Elsevier Science/JAI Press; Fenwick, M. (2005), Extending strategic international human resource management research and pedagogy to the non-profit multinational, *International Journal of Human Resource Management*, 16 (4): 497–512; Gupta, A. K. and Govindarajan, V. (2001), Converting global presence into global competitive advantage, *Academy of Management Executive*, 15 (2): 45–58; Milliman, J., Von Glinow, M. A., and Nathan, M. (1991), Organizational life cycles and strategic international human resource management in multinational companies: Implications for congruence theory, *Academy of Management Review*, 16 (2): 318–339; Perkins and Shortland (2006); Schuler, R. S., Budhwar, P. S., and Florkowski, G. W. (2002), International human resource management: Review and critique, *International Journal of Management Reviews*, 4 (1): 41–70; Schuler, R. S., Dowling, P. J., and De Cieri, H. (1993), An integrative framework of strategic international human resource management,

Journal of Management, 19 (2): 419–459; Schuler, R. S. and Tarique, I. (2007), International HRM: A North American perspective, a thematic update and suggestions for future research, *International Journal of Human Resource Management*, 18 (5): 717–744; Stroh, L. K. and Caliguiri, P. M. (1998), Strategic human resources: A new source for competitive advantage in the global arena, *International Journal of Human Resource Management*, 9 (1): 1–17; Takeda, M. and Helms, M. M. (2007), The influence of human resource management identity on strategic intent in the multinational enterprise, *International Journal of Human Resource Development and Management*, 7 (2): 139–160; and Taylor, S., Beechler, S., Najjar, M. and Ghosh, B. C. (1998), A partial test of a model of strategic international human resource management, *Advances in International Comparative Management*, 12: 207–236.

36 Beechler, S., Bird, A. and Raghuram, S. (1993), Linking business strategy and human resource management practices in multinational corporations: A theoretical framework, *Advances in International Comparative Management*, 8: 199–215; Hannon, J. M., Huang, I.-C. and Jaw, B.-S. (1995), International human resource strategy and its determinants: The case of subsidiaries in Taiwan, *Journal of International Business Studies*, third quarter: 531–554; Harris, H. and Holden, L. (2001), Between autonomy and control: Expatriate managers and strategic international human resource management in SMEs, Thunderbird *International Business Review*, 43 (1): 77–100; Kobrin, S. J. (1994), Is there a relationship between geocentric mind-set and multinational strategy? *Journal of International Business Studies*, 25 (3): 493–511; Lei, D., Slocum, J. W., Jr. and Slater, R. W. (1990), Global strategy and reward systems: The key roles of management development and corporate culture, *Organizational Dynamics*, 18: 63–77; Rosenzweig, P. M. and Nohria, N. (1994), Influences on human resource management practices in multinational corporations, *Journal of International Business Studies*, second quarter: 229–251; Sheridan, W. R. and Hansen, P. T. (1996), Linking international business and expatriate compensation strategies, *ACA Journal*, 5 (2): 66–79.

37 Caliguiri, P. M. and Stroh, L. K. (1995), Multinational corporation management strategies and international human resource practices: Bringing international HR to the bottom line, *International Journal of Human Resource Management*, 6 (3): 494–507; Milligan *et al.* (1991); Pucik, V. and Evans, P. (2004), *People Strategies for MNEs*, London: Routledge; Stroh and Caliguiri (1998).

38 Yip, G. S., Johansson, J. K. and Ross, J. (1997), Effects of nationality on global strategy, *Management International Review*, 37 (4): 365–385.

39 See, e.g., Perkins and Shortland (2006)

40 Evans *et al.* (2002); and Sparrow *et al.* (2004).

41 Perkins and Shortland (2006); Sparrow *et al.* (2004); Reynolds, C. (2000) The future of global compensation and benefits, in C. Reynolds (ed.), *2000 Guide to Global Compensation and Benefits*, San Diego, CA: Harcourt; Tichy, N. M. (1988) Setting the global human resource management agenda for the 1990s, *Human Resource Management*, 27: 1–18; and Vance and Paik (2006).

42 Fernandez (2005); and Vance and Paik (2006).

2 Creating the international organization: strategy and structure

1 Bartlett, C. A. and Ghoshal, S. (1998), *Managing across Borders: The Transnational Solution*, 2d ed., Boston, MA: Harvard Business School Press; Evans, P., Pucik, V. and Barsoux, J.-L. (2002), *The Global Challenge: Frameworks for International Human Resource Management*, New York: McGraw-Hill; Galbraith, J. R. (1998), Structuring global organizations, in Mohaman, S. A., Galbraith, J. R. and Lawler, E. E. III (eds), *Tomorrow's Organization: Crafting Winning Capabilities in a Dynamic World*, San Francisco: Jossey Bass; Galbraith, J. R. (2000), *Designing the Global Corporation*,

San Francisco: Jossey Bass; Galbraith, J. R. (2001), Building organizations around the global customer, *Ivey Business Journal*, 66 (1); Lane, H. W., DiStefano, J. J. and Maznevski, M. L (2006), *International Management Behavior*, 5th ed., Oxford: Blackwell Publishing.

2 Friedman, T. L. (2005), *The World is Flat*, New York: Farrar Straus and Giroux; Gupta, A. K. and Govindarajan, V. (2002), Cultivating a global mind-set, *Academy of Management Executive*, 16 (1): 116–126; Moore, K. (2003), Great global managers, *Across the Board*, May–June: 40–44.

3 The term "suddenly global" was introduced by Lance Richards and is used here with his permission.

4 Gupta, A. K. and Govindarajan, V. (2001), Converting global presence into global competitive advantage, *Academy of Management Executive*, 15 (2): 45–58.

5 Bartlett and Ghoshal, S. (1998); Harzing, A.-W. (2000), An empirical analysis and extension of the Bartlett and Ghoshal typology of multinational companies, *Journal of International Business Studies*, 31 (1): 101–120.

6 Bartlett and Ghoshal (1998).

7 There is a good summary of these issues in Segal-Horn, S. and Faulkner, D. (1999), *The Dynamics of International Strategy*, London: International Thomson; and in Galbraith (2000).

8 For example, L. Claus is finding that at least one-third of the participants in SHRM's training programs for their GPHR exam are domestic HR managers seeking to increase their IHR competencies.

9 Bartlett and Ghoshal (1998); and Calori, R., Atamer, T., Nunes, P. *et al.* (2000), *The Dynamics of International Competition*, London/New York: Simon and Schuster.

10 Main, J. (1989), How to go global—and why, *Fortune*, August 28: 70.

11 Bartlett and Ghoshal (1989).

12 Segal-Horn and Faulkner (1999).

13 Bartlett, C. A. and Ghoshal, S. (1998), op. cit.

14 Palmisano, S. J. (2006), Multinationals have to be superseded, *Financial Times*, June 12: 19.

15 See, for example, Lapid, K. (2006), Outsourcing and offshoring under the Gernal Agreement on Trade in Services, *Journal of World Trade*, 40 (2): 431–364; Robinson, M. and Kalakota, R. (2005), *Offshore Outsourcing: Business Models, ROI and Best Practices*, 2d ed., Alpharetta, GA: Mivar Press; and Robinson, M., Kalakota, R. and Sharma, S. (2006), *Global Outsourcing: Executing an Onshore, Nearshore or Offshore Strategy*, Alpharetta, GA: Mivar Press.

16 "Outsourcing—what is outsourcing?" retrieved from www.sourcingmag.com, November 12 2006.

17 Definition retrieved from http://en.wikipedia.org and www.investordictionary.com. See also, Blinder, A. E. (2006), Offshoring: The next industrial revolution? *Foreign Affairs*, 85 (2): 113–128; Erber, G. and Sayed-Ahmed, A. (2005), Offshore outsourcing—A global shift in the present IT industry, *Intereconomics*, 40 (2): 100–112; and Friedman, T. L. (2005), *The World is Flat: A Brief History of the Twenty-first Century*, New York: Farrar Straus and Giroux.

18 Schramm, J. (2004), Offshoring, *Workplace Visions: Exploring the Future of Work*, Society for Human Resource Management Research 2.

19 *Ibid.*

20 Robinson, M. and Kalakota, R. (2005), *op cit.*

21 Cauchi, M. (2006), Wheelin', dealin' hits high, *Boulder Daily Camera*, November 18: 8B.

22 Schuler, R. S., Jackson, S. E. and Luo, Y. (2004), *Managing Human Resources in Cross-border Alliances*, London/New York: Routledge.

23 Shenkar, O. and Zeira, Y. (1987), Human resources management in international joint ventures: Directions for research, *Academy of Management Review*, 12 (3): 547.

24 Cyr, D. J. (1995), *The Human Resource Challenge of International Joint Ventures*, Westport, CT: Quorum Books; Schuler, R. S., Jackson, S. E. and Luo, Y. (2004), *Managing Human Resources in Cross-border Alliances*, London/New York: Routledge.

25 Cyr (1995), 116.

26 Lawson, S. (2006), Verizon and MCI close merger, *InfoWorld*, January 2006; "Thriving on Chaos," seminar (course notebook), Career Track Seminars, presented in San Diego, CA (1990); and Wikipedia: MCI Inc., http://en.wikipedia.org/wiki/WorldCom (retrieved August 10 2007).

27 "Thriving on Chaos," 21.

28 There are many sources of information about *maquiladoras*, but here are three from the internet that provide the basic information used to develop this section (all retrieved July 25 2007): http://www.mexconnect.com/business/mex2000maquiladora2.html; http://www.gao.gov/new.items/d03891.pdf (GAO July 2003 report to Congress: "International Trade: Mexico's Maquiladora Decline Affects US–Mexico Border Communities and Trade)"; http://www.madeinmexicoinc.com/FAQs.htm.

29 McKinsey & Co., Coopers & Lybrand, and American Management Association, reported in Marks, M. L. (1997), *From Turmoil to Triumph: New Life after Mergers, Acquisitions, and Alliances*, New York: Lexington Books.

30 Reported in Bates, S. (2002), Few business alliances succeed, report reveals, in Executive Briefing, *HR Magazine*, May: 12.

31 Schuler *et al.* (2004).

32 Beard, M., quoted in Bourne, S. R. (1996), Merger misery, *Colorado Business*, October: 82.

33 There have been many publications on mergers and acquisitions, joint ventures, and partnerships. Here are just a few of them: Charman, A. (1999), *Global Mergers and Acquisitions: The Human Resource Challenge*, Focus Paper, Alexandria, VA: Institute for International Human Resource Management, Society for Human Resource Management; Clemente, M. N. and Greenspan, D. S. (1998), *Winning at Mergers and Acquisitions: The Guide to Market-focused Planning and Integration*, New York: Wiley; Clemente, M. N. and Greenspan, D. S. (1999), *Empowering Human Resources in the Merger and Acquisition Process: Guide for HR Professionals in the Key Areas of M&A Planning and Integration*, Glen Rock, NJ: Clement Greenspan; Coffey, J., Garrow, V. and Holbeche, L. (2002), *Reaping the Benefits of Mergers and Acquisitions: In Search of the Golden Fleece*, Oxford: Butterworth Heinemann; Galpin, T. J. and Herndon, M. (2000), *The Complete Guide to Mergers and Acquisitions: Process Tools to Support M&A Integration at Every Level*, San Francisco: Jossey Bass; Gertsen, M. C., Siderberg, A.-M. and Torp, J. E. (eds) (1998), *Cultural Dimensions of International Mergers and Acquisitions*, Berlin: de Gruyter; Lajoux, A. R. and Elson, C. M. (2000), *The Art of Merger and Acquisition Due Diligence*, New York: McGraw-Hill; Marks, M. L. and Mirvis, P. H. (2000), Managing mergers, acquisitions, and alliances: Creating an effective transition structure, *Organizational Dynamics*, winter: 35–47; Morosim, P. (1998), *Cultural Differences: Effective Strategy and Execution across Cultures in Global Corporate Alliances*, Oxford: Pergamon Press; Rails, J. G., Jr. and Webb, K. A. (1999), *Managing the Chaos of Mergers and Acquisitions: How to Plan, Negotiate, and Implement Alliances and Partnerships in a Complex World*, Houston, TX: Cashman Dudley; Schmidt, J. A. (ed.) (2002), *Making Mergers Work: The Strategic Importance of People*, Alexandria, VA: Towers Perrin and Society for Human Resource Management; Schuler, R. S. and Jackson, S. E. (2001), HR issues and activities in mergers and acquisitions, *European Management Journal*, 19 (3): 239–253; and Sherman, A. J. and Hart, M. A. (2006), *Mergers and Acquisitions from A to Z*, New York: AMACOM.

34 Ohmae, K. (1989), The global logic of strategic alliances, *Harvard Business Review*, March–April: 143.

35 Berry, J. W. (1980), Acculturation as varieties of adaptation, in Padilla, A. M. (ed.), *Acculturation Theory, Models and Some New Findings*, Boulder, CO: Westview Press; Gertsen, M. C., Siderberg, A. M. and Torp, J. E. (1998), Different approaches to the understanding of culture in mergers and acquisitions, in Gertsen *et al.*

36 Galbraith (1998).

37 Evans *et al.* (2002); Bartlett and Ghoshal (1998); Galbraith (2000).

38 Evans *et al.* (2002); Galbraith (2000).

39 Galbraith (2000) 1.

40 Galbraith (2000); Greenwood, R., Rose, T., Brown, J. L., Cooper, D. J. and Hinings, B. (1999), The global management of professional services: the example of accounting, in Clegg, S. R., Ibarra-Colado, E. and Bueno-Rodriquez (eds), *Global Management: Universal Theories and Local Realities*, London: Sage Publications.

41 Bartlett, C., Doz, Y. and Hedlund, G. (1990), Introduction, in Bartlett, C., Doz, Y. and Hedlund, G. (eds), *Managing the Global Firm*, London: Routledge, 1

42 For example, Bartlett and Ghoshal (1998); Johansson, J. K. and Yip, G. S. (1995), Exploiting globalization potential: US and Japanese strategies, *Strategic Management Journal*, October: 579–601; and Porter, M. E. (1986), Competition in global industries: A conceptual framework, in Porter, M. E. (ed.), *Competition in Global Industries*, Boston, MA: Harvard University Press.

43 For example, Aharoni, Y. (ed.) (1993), *Coalitions and Competition: The Globalization of Professional Business Services*, New York: Routledge; Giarini, D. (ed.) (1987), *The Emerging Service Economy*, Oxford: Pergamon Press; and Schmenner, R. W. (1986), How can service business survive and prosper? *Sloan Management Review*, spring: 21–31.

44 Aharoni (1993); Fladmore-Lindquist, K. (1993), The impact of bargaining and negotiating on the globalization of professional service firms, in Aharoni (1993).

45 For example, Morrison, A. J. (1990), *Strategies in Global Industries: How US Businesses Compete*, Westpoint, CT: Quorum Books; Porter, M. E. (1990), *Competitive Advantage of Nations*, New York: Free Press; and Yip, G. S. (1995), *Total Global Strategy*, Englewood Cliffs, NJ: Prentice Hall.

46 Ghoshal, S. and Westney, E. (1993), *Organizational Theory and the Multinational Corporation*, New York: St. Martin's Press.

47 *Ibid.*, 53.

48 Hout, T., Porter, M. E. and Rudden, E. (1982), How global companies win out, *Harvard Business Review*, September–October: 98–108.

49 See, for example, Galbraith (2000); Farnko, L. (1976), The move toward a multi-divisional structure in European organizations, *Administrative Science Quarterly*, 19 (4): 493–506; and Stopford, J. and Wells, L. (1972), *Managing the Multinational Enterprise*, New York: Basic Books.

50 Johansson and Yip (1994); Martinez, J. and Jarillo, J. (1989), The evolution of research on co-ordination mechanisms in multinational corporations, *Journal of International Business Studies*, 20 (3): 489–514.

51 Bartlett, C. and Ghoshal, S. (1987), Managing across borders: New organizational responses, *Sloan Management Review*, fall: 43–53; Bartlett, C. and Ghoshal, S. (1988), Organizing for worldwide effectiveness: The transnational solution, *California Management Review*, fall 3 (1): 54–74; Bartlett and Ghoshal (1998); Egelhoff, W. G. (1984), Strategy and Structure in multinational corporations: A version of the Stopford and Wells model, *Strategic Management Journal*, 9: 1–14; Evans *et al.* (2002); Galbraith (2000); Galbraith, J. R. and Karanjian, R. R. (1986), Organizing to implement strategies of diversity and globalization: The role of matrix designs, *Human Resource Management*, spring: 37–54; Ohmae, K. (1990), *The Borderless World*, New York: Harper Business; Prahalad, C. and Doz, Y. (1987), *The Multinational Mission*, New York: Free Press.

52 For example, Bartlett and Ghoshal (1998); and Evans, *et al.* (2002),

53 See, for example, Ahmed, P. K., Kok, L. K. and Loh, A. Y. (2002), *Learning through Knowledge Management*, Oxford: Butterworth Heinemann; Cerny, K. (1996), Making local knowledge global, *Harvard Business Review*, May–June: 22–38; Davenport, T. H. (2005), *Thinking for a Living*, Boston: Harvard Business School Press; Evans, *et al.* (2002); Fuller, S. (2002), *Knowledge Management Foundations*, Boston, MA: Harvard Business School Press; Marquardt, M. J. (2002), *Building the Learning Organization*, 2nd ed., Palo Alto, CA: Davies Black; Marquardt, M. J. and Reynolds, A. (1994), *The Global Learning Organization*, Burr Ridge, IL: Irwin; Schwandt, D. R. and Marquardt, M. J. (2000), *Organizational Learning: From World-class Theories to Global Best Practices*, Boca Raton, FL: St. Lucie Press.

54 Daft, R. (2002), *The Leadership Experience*, 2nd ed., Orlando, FL: Harcourt, 582.

55 Prokesch, S. E. (1997), Unleashing the power of learning: An interview with British Petroleum's John Browne, *Harvard Business Review*, September–October: 148.

56 Senge, P. (1990*), The Fifth Discipline,* New York: Doubleday Currency, 69.

57 Jackson, S. E. and Schuler, R. S. (2001), Turning knowledge to business advantage, *Financial Times*, January 15, special section, part fourteen.

3 International human resource management and culture

1 Schell, M. S. and Solomon, C. M. (1997), *Capitalizing on the Global Work force*, Chicago: Irwin: 9.

2 The World Economic Forum and the International Institute for Management Development, *The World Competitiveness Report 1995*, reported in *World Business*, January–February, 1996: 15.

3 *Ibid.*, 8.

4 See, for example, Hofstede, G. (1991), *Cultures and Organizations: Software of the Mind*, Maidenhead: McGraw-Hill, chapter 1; Moore, K. (2003), Great global managers, *Across the Board*, May–June: 40–44; Stroh, L. K., Black, J. S., Mendenhall, M. E. and Gregersen, H. B. (2005), *International Assignments*, Mahwah, NJ/London: Erlbaum; Trompenaars, F. (1992/1993), *Riding the Waves of Culture: Understanding Diversity in Global Business*, Burr Ridge, IL: Irwin, chapter 1.

5 Schell and Solomon (1997); Hofstede (1991); Trompenaars (1992/1993).

6 McCall, M. W., Jr. and Hollenbeck, G. P. (2002), *Developing Global Executives: The Lessons of International Experience*, Boston, MA: Harvard Business School Press.

7 Hofstede, G. (1980), *Culture's Consequences: International Differences in Work-related Values*, Beverly Hills, CA/London: Sage; Hofstede (1991); Hofstede, G. (2001), *Culture and Organizations: Comparing Values, Behaviors, Institutions and Organizations across Nations*, 2nd ed., Thousand Oaks, CA: Sage; Hofstede, G. (2002), Cultural constraints in management theories, *CRN News*, 7 (4): 1–3, 12–13, 16, 19, 22–23.

8 See, for example, Hofstede, G. (1984), Clustering countries on attitudinal dimensions: A review and synthesis, *Academy of Management Review*, 9 (3): 389–398; Hofstede, G. (1983), The cultural relativity of organizational theories, *Journal of International Business Studies*, 14 (2): 75–90.

9 Saari, L. and Schneider, B. (2001), Global Employee Surveys: Practical Considerations and Insights, paper presented at "Going global: Surveys and beyond," workshop at the annual conference, Society of Industrial/Organizational Psychology, San Diego, CA: April.

10 Hampden-Turner, C. and Trompenaars, F. (1993), *The Seven Cultures of Capitalism*, New York: Currency/Doubleday; Trompenaars, F. (1992/1993); and Trompenaars and Hampden-Turner, C. (2004), *Managing People across Cultures*, Chichester, England: Capstone Publishing.

11 Trompenaars (1992/1993), 31–32.

12 To learn more about GLOBE see Javidan, M. and House, R. J. (2000), Cultural acumen for the global manager, *Organizational Dynamics*, 29 (4): 289–305; Globe Research Team (2002), *Culture, Leadership, and Organizational Practices: The GLOBE Findings*, Thousand Oaks, CA: Sage.

13 Ronen, S. and Shenkar, O. (1985), Clustering countries on attitudinal dimensions: A review and synthesis, *Academy of Management Review*, 10 (3): 435–454; Ronen, S. and Shenkar, O. (1988), Using employee attitudes to establish MNC regional divisions, *Personnel*, August: 32–39.

14 See, for example, Earley, P. C. and Erez, M. (eds) (1997), *New Perspectives on International Industrial/Organizational Psychology*, San Francisco: New Lexington Press; Gesteland, R. R. (1999), *Cross-cultural Business Behavior: Marketing, Negotiating and Managing across Cultures*, Copenhagen, Denmark: Copenhagen Business School Press; Hodge, S. (2000), *Global Smarts: The Art of Communicating and Deal-making Anywhere in the World*, New York: Wiley; Moran, R. T., Harris, P. H. and Moran, S. V. (2007), *Managing Cultural Differences*, 7th ed., Burlington, MA: Butterworth-Heinemann; and Scherer, C. W. (2000), *The Internationalists*, Wilsonville, OR: Book Partners.

15 Gesteland (1999).

16 Brannen, M. Y. (1999), The many faces of cultural data, *AIB Newsletter*, first quarter: 6–7.

17 *Ibid.*

18 For a good discussion of this topic, refer to Vance, C. M. and Paik, Y. (2006), *Managing a Global Work force: Challenges and Opportunities in International Human Resource Management*, Armonk, NY/London: Sharpe, 50–54. Also refer to Dunphy, D. (1987), Convergence/divergence: A temporal view of the Japanese enterprise and its management, *Academy of Management Review*, 12: 445–459; Sparrow, P., Schuler, R. S. and Jackson, S. (1994), Convergence or divergence: Human resource practice and policies for competitive advantage worldwide, *International Journal of Human Resource Management*, 5 (2): 267–299.

19 Huo, Y. P., Huang, H. J. and Napier, N. K. (2002), Divergence or convergence: A cross-national comparison of personnel selection practices, *Human Resource Management*, 41 (1): 31–44; Von Glinow, M. A., Drost, E. and Teagarden, M. (2002), Converging on IHRM best practices: Lessons learned from a globally distributed consortium on the theory and practice, *Human Resource Management*, 41 (1): 123–140.

20 Drost, E., Frayne, C., Lowe, K. and Geringer, M. (2002), Benchmarking training and development practices: A multi-country comparative analysis, *Human Resource Management*, 41 (1): 67–85; Pucik, V. (1997), Human resources in the future: An obstacle or a champion of globalization? *Human Resource Management*, 36 (1): 163–167.

21 Vance, C. and Paik, Y. (2006) 52–53. The concept of "crossvergence" originated in Ralston, D., Holt, D., Terpstra, R. H. and Yu, K.-C. (1997), The impact of national culture and economic ideology on managerial work values: A study of the United States, Russia, Japan, and China, *Journal of International Business Studies*, 28 (1): 177–207.

22 Pierce, B. and Garvin, G. (1995), Publishing international business research: A survey of leading journals, *Journal of International Business Studies*, 26 (1): 69–89.

23 Adler, N. J. (1983), Cross-cultural management research: The ostrich and the trend, *Academy of Management Review*, 8 (2): 226–232; Pierce and Garvin (1995).

24 Boyacigillar, N. and Adler, N. J. (1991), The parochial dinosaur: Organizational science in a global context, *Academy of Management Review*, 16 (2): 262–290.

25 Thomas, A. S., Shenkar, O. and Clarke, L. (1994), The globalization of our mental maps: Evaluating the geographic scope of JIBS coverage, *Journal of International Business Studies*, 25 (4): 675–686.

26 *Ibid.*; Hickson, D. J. (1996), The ASQ years then and now through the eyes of a Euro-Brit, *Administrative Science Quarterly*, 41 (2): 217–228.

27 Inkpen, A. and Beamish, P. (1994), An analysis of twenty-five years of research in the *Journal of International Business Studies*, *Journal of International Business Studies*,

25 (4): 703–713; Melin, L. (1992), Internationalization as a strategy process, *Strategic Management Journal*, 13: 99–118; Parker, B. (1998), *Globalization and Business Practice: Managing across Borders*, Thousand Oaks, CA: Sage; Thomas *et al.* (1994).

28 Dowling, P. J. (1988), International HRM, in Dyer, L. (ed.), *Human Resource Management: Evolving Roles and Responsibilities*, Washington, DC: Bureau of National Affairs; Earley, P. C. and Singh, S. H. (2000), Introduction: New approaches to international and cross-cultural management research, in Earley, P. C. and Singh, S. H. (eds), *Innovations in International Cross-cultural Management*, Thousand Oaks, CA: Sage; McEvoy, G. M. and Buller, P. F. (1993), New directions in international human resource management research, paper presented at the Academy of International Business annual meeting, Maui, HI, October 21–24; Tayeb, M. (2001), Conducting research across cultures: Overcoming drawbacks and obstacles, *International Journal of Cross-cultural Management*, 1 (1): 91–108; Triandis, H. C. (1998), Vertical and horizontal individualism and collectivism: Theory and research implications for international comparative management, *Advances in International Comparative Management*, XII, Greenwich, CT: JAI Press.

29 See, for example, Aguinis, H. and Henley, C. (2003), The search for universals in cross-cultural organizational behavior, *Organizational Behavior: The State of the Science*, 2nd ed., Mahwah, NJ/London: Erlbaum; Baruch, Y. (2001), Global or North American? A geographical-based comparative analysis of publications in top management journals, *International Journal of Cross-cultural Management*, 1 (1): 109–125; Bond, M. H. (1997), Adding value to the cross-cultural study of organizational behavior: Reculer pour mieux sauter, in Earley, P. C. and Erez, M. (eds), *New Perspectives on International Industrial/Organizational Psychology*, San Francisco: New Lexington Press; Earley, P. C. and Mosakowski, E. (1995), Experimental international management research, in Punnett, B. J. and Shenkar, O. (eds) *Handbook for International Management Research*, Cambridge, MA: Blackwell Publishers; Gelfand, M. J., Holcombe, K. M. and Raver, J. L. (2002), Methodological issues in cross-cultural organizational research, in Rogelberg, S. G. (ed.), *Handbook of Research Methods in Industrial and Organizational Psychology*, Malden, MA: Blackwell Publishers; GLOBE Research Team (2002), *Culture, Leadership, and Organizational Practices: The GLOBE Findings*, Thousand Oaks, CA: Sage; Graen, G. B., Hui, C., Wakabayashi, M. and Wang, Z.-M. (1997), Cross-cultural research alliances in organizational research, in Earley, P. C. and Erez, M. (eds), *New Perspectives on International Industrial/Organizational Psychology*, San Francisco: New Lexington Press; House, R. *et al.* (eds), *Designing and Conducting Large Multi-country Research Projects: The GLOBE Study of 62 Cultures*, Thousand Oaks, CA: Sage; Mattl, C. (1999), Qualitative research strategies in international HRM, in Brewster, C. and Harris, H. (eds), *International HRM: Contemporary Issues in Europe*, London: Routledge; and Wright, L. L. (1995), Qualitative international management research, in Punnett, B. J. and Shenkar, O. (eds), *Handbook for International Management Research*, Cambridge, MA: Blackwell Publishers.

30 See, for example, Claus, L. and Briscoe, D. R. (2008), Employee performance management across borders: A review of relevant academic literature, *International Journal of Management Reviews* (in press).

31 For example, Aycan, Z., Kanungo, R. N., Mendonca, M., Yu, K., Deller, J., Stahl, G. and Kurshid, A. (2000), Impact of culture on human resource management practices: A ten-country comparison, *Applied Psychology: An International Review*, 49: 192–221.

32 Caligiuri, P. M. (1999), The ranking of scholarly journals in the field of international human resource management, *International Journal of Human Resource Management*, 10 (3): 515–518; House, R. H., Hanges, P. J., Antonio Ruiz-Quintanilla, S., Dorfman, P. W., Javidan, M., Dickson, M., Gupta, V. and GLOBE country co-investigators (1999), Cultural influences on leadership and organizations: Project GLOBE, in Mobley, W. H., Gessner, M. J. and Arnold, V. (eds), *Advances in Global Leadership*, Vol. I, Stamford, CT:

JAI Press; House, R. J., Wright, N. S. and Aditya, R. N. (1997), Cross-cultural research on organizational leadership: A critical analysis and a proposed theory, in Earley, P. C. and Erez, M. (eds), *New Perspectives on International/Industrial/Organizational Psychology*, San Francisco: New Lexington Press.

33 Saari, L. and Schneider, B. (2001), Global employee surveys: Practical considerations and insights, paper presented at "Going Global: Surveys and Beyond," workshop at the annual conference of the Society for Industrial/Organizational Psychology, San Diego, CA, April.

34 Lubatkin, M. H., Ndiaye, M. and Vengroff, R. (1997), The nature of managerial work in developing countries: A limited test of the universalist hypothesis, *Journal of International Business Studies*, fourth quarter: 711–733; Punnett, B. J. and Shenkar, O. (eds) (1996), *Handbook for International Management Research*, Cambridge, MA: Blackwell Publishers; Sparrow, P., Brewster, C. and Harris, H. (2004), *Globalizing Human Resource Management*, London: Routledge; and Vance, C. M. and Paik, Y. (2006), *Managing a Global Workforce: Challenges and Opportunities in International Human Resource Management*, Armonk, NY/London: Sharpe.

35 Mullen, M. R. (1995), Diagnosing measurement equivalence in cross-national research, *Journal of International Business Studies*, 15 (3): 573–596.

36 Cavusgil, S, T. and Das, A. (1997), Methodological issues in empirical cross-cultural research: A survey of the management literature and a framework, *Management International Review*, 37 (1): 81.

37 *Ibid.*; Douglas, S. P. and Craig, S. (1983), *International Marketing Research*, Englewood Cliffs, NJ: Prentice Hall; Samiee, S. and Jeong, I. (1994), Cross-cultural research in advertising: An assessment of methodologies, *Journal of the Academy of Marketing Science*, 22 (3): 205–217.

38 Mullen (1995).

39 Yu, J. H., Keown, C. F. and Jacobs, L. W. (1993), Attitude scale methodology: Cross-cultural implications, *Journal of International Consumer Marketing*, 6 (2): 45–64.

40 Mattl (1999).

4 Global employment law, industrial relations and international ethics

1 Much of the information in this section comes from documents of the International Labour Organisation, Geneva, Switzerland, such as the report on International Organizations by their Working Party of the Social Dimensions of the Liberalization of International Trade.

2 Berkowitz, P. M. (2003), Avoidance of Risks and Liabilities through Effective Corporate Compliance, paper presented at the 4th Annual Program on International Labor and Employment Law, Center for American and International Law, Dallas, TX, September 10.

3 See, for example, the *World Investment Report* (most recent edition, 2003), published by UNCTAD. Refer to the UNCTAD web site at http://www.unctad.org for information on UNCTAD's work and access to extensive data about various countries and transnational corporations.

4 Berkowitz (2003).

5 Murphy, E. E., Jr. (2001), The World Trade Organization, in Keller, W. L. (editor-in-chief), *International Labor and Employment Laws*, 2001 Cumulative Supplement to Vol. 1, Washington, DC: Bureau of National Affairs, for the International Labor Law Committee of the Section of Labor and Employment Law of the American Bar Association, 44–1 to 44–13.

6 Manley, T. and Lauredo, L. (2003) International labor standards in free trade agreements of the Americas, paper delivered at the 4th Annual Program on International Labor and Employment Law, Dallas, TX, September 30–October 1.

7 Official web site of the FTAA, www.ftaa-alca.org.

8 See, for example, Nielsen, R. and Szyszczak, E. (1997), *The Social Dimension of the European Union*, 3rd ed., Copenhagen: Handelshøjskolens Forlag/Copenhagen Business School Press.

9 There are only limited reference works available for information about employment law on a global basis. Other than individual articles in mostly the practitioner and consultant press, these general references include two volumes in this series: Florkowski, G. W. (2006), *Managing Global Legal* Systems, London/New York: Routledge; and Morley, M. J., Gunnigle, P. and Collings, D. G. (eds) (2006), *Global Industrial Relations*, London/New York: Routledge; plus the following: Bamber, J., Lansbury D. and Wailes, N., (2003) *International and Comparative Employment Relations: Globalisation and the Developed Market Economies*, Sydney: Allen and Unwin (London/Thousand Oaks, CA: Sage); Blanpain, R., Bisom-Rapp, S., Corbwett, W. R., Josephs, H. K. and Simmer, M. J. (2007), *The Global Workplace: International and Comparative Employment Law*, New York: Cambridge University Press; Keller, W. L. (editor-in-chief) (1997 with extensive annual updates), *International Labor and Employment Laws*, Washington, DC: Bureau of National Affairs, for the International Labor Law Committee of the Section of Labor and Employment Law of the American Bar Association; Maatman, G. L., Jr. (ed.) (2000), *Worldwide Guide to Termination, Employment Discrimination, and Workplace Harassment Laws*, Chicago: Baker and McKenzie; and Feu, V. D., Edmunds, V., Gillow, E. and Hopkins, M. (general editors) (2000 plus annual updates), *EU and International Employment Law*, Bristol: Jordans Publishing, for Eversheds.

10 Darby, T. J. (2001), Extraterritorial application of US laws, in W. L. Keller (ed.) *International Labor and Employment Laws*, 2001 Cumulative Supplement to Vol. 1, Washington, DC: Bureau of National Affairs, for the International Labor Law Committee of the Section of Labor and Employment Law of the American Bar Association, 50 (52): 50–74.

11 Hall, L. (2001b), Data dangers, *Global HR*, October: 24–28; Kremer-Jones, B. (2002), Think before you send, *Global HR*, July/August: 52–59; Protecting the privacy of employees based in Europe (2000), *SHRM Global Perspectives* 1 (1): 1, 6–7 (originally published in *HRWIRE*, by the West Group).

12 Are you EU privacy-compliant? (2000), *International Update* (newsletter of the SHRM Institute for International HRM, now the SHRM Global Forum), No. 3: 10; Martinez, M. N. (1999), European law aims to protect employee data, *International Update* (newsletter of the SHRM Institute for International HRM, now the SHRM Global Forum), No. 1: 1, 3; Minehan, M. (2001), Complying with the European privacy data directive, *SHRM Global Perspective*, No. 5: 1, 6–8; Minehan, M. and Overman, S. (2000), Companies to begin EU safe harbor registration, *HR News*, December, 19 (12), 1–2; Wellbery, B. S. and Warrington, J. P. (2001), EU Data Protection Requirements and Employee Data: December 2001, International Focus White Paper of the SHRM Global Forum, Alexandria, VA: Society for Human Resource Management; and Wellbery, B. S., Warrington, J. P. and Howell, R. (2002), EU data protection requirements: An overview for employers, *Employment Law* (Morrison and Foerster Newsletter), 14 (1): 1–12.

13 See, for example, Maatman (2000); Conway, M. E. (1998), Sexual harassment abroad, *Global Workforce*, September: 8–9; Javaid, M. (2002), Race for knowledge, *Global HR*, November: 59–60; Keller, W. L. (ed.) (1997 and annual updates), *International Labor and Employment Laws*; and Mackay, R. and Cormican, D. (2002), The trouble with religion, *Global HR*, December/January: 26–30.

14 Webb, S. (1994) Shockwaves: *The Global Impact of Sexual Harassment*, London: MasterMedia.

15 www.de2.psu.edu/harassment/generalinfo/international.html (retrieved February 11 2007).

16 Keller, W. L. and Darby, T. J. (editors-in-chief), (2003), *International Labor and Employment Law*, Vols. 1 and 2, 2d ed., Washington, DC: Bureau of National Affairs.

17 Adapted from International Labour Organization (2000) *Termination of Employment Digest: A Legislative Review*, Geneva: author; and Shillingford, J. (1999), Goodbye, adios,

sayonara, *HR World*, July/August: 27–31 (data on separation practices from Drake Beam Morin).

18 Maatman (2000); Keller and Darby (2003); International Labor Organization (2000), *Termination of Employment Digest: A Legislative Review*, Geneva: author; and Shillingford (1999).

19 Hall, L. (2001a), Protecting your vital assets, *Global HR*, July/August: 46–52.

20 Visser, J. (2006), Union membership statistics in twenty-four countries, *Monthly Labor Review*, January: 38–49.

21 This short summary is based on the following: Baker and McKenzie, *Worldwide Guide to Trade Unions and Works Councils* (2001), Chicago: Commerce Clearing House; Bamber (2003); Ferner, A. and Hyman, R. (1998) (eds), *Changing Industrial Relations in Europe*, 2d ed., Oxford, UK/Malden, MA: Blackwell Publishers; Hansen, E. D. (2001), *European Economic History*, Copenhagen, DK: Copenhagen Business School Press; Hyman, R. (2001), *Understanding European Trade Unionism*, London/Thousand Oaks, CA: Sage Publications; Keller and Darby (2003), Vol. 1; Morley, M. J., Gunnigle, P. and Collings, D. G. (eds) (2006), *Global Industrial Relations*, London/New York: Routledge.

22 ICTUR *et al.*, (2005) *Trade Unions of the World*, 6th ed., London: John Harper.

23 William, F. and Williamson, H. (2006) International unions form body to defend workers' rights in era of globalization, *Financial Times*, November 2.

24 Rothman *et al.* (1992); Levinson, D. L., Jr. and Maddox, R. C. (1982), Multinational corporations and labor relations: Changes in the wind? *Personnel*, May–June: 70–77.

25 Bamber, G. J. and Lansbury, R. D. (eds) (1998) *International and Comparative Employment Relations*, 3rd ed., London: Sage Publications; Rothman, M., Briscoe, D. R. and Nacamulli, R. C. D. (eds) (1992) *Industrial Relations around the World: Labor Relations for Multinational Companies*, Berlin: de Gruyter.

26 Excerpted from a presentation by David Killinger, Director, International Labor Affairs, on Ford Motor Company's global labor relations, delivered at the Faculty Development Seminar on International HRM at the University of Colorado, Denver, June 8 2000.

27 Baker and McKenzie (2001); Goetschy, J. (1998), France: The limits of reform, in Ferner, A. and Hyman, R. (eds), *Changing Industrial Relations in Europe*, Oxford/Malden, MA: Blackwell Publishers; Keller and Darby (2003); Schneider, B. (2004), "Global Industrial Relations", presentation to the Faculty Development Program in International Human Resource Management, Denver, CO: June 7–11.

28 Frege, C. (2006), International trends in unionization, in Morley, M. J., Gunnigle, P. and Collings, D. G. (eds), *Global Industrial Relations*, London/New York: Routledge.

29 Refer to Part II, Contemporary developments in global industrial relations, in Morley *et al.* (2006).

30 Bamber *et al.* (2003); and Rothman, M., Briscoe, D. R. and Nacamulli, R.C.D. (eds) (1993) *Industrial Relations Around the World: Labor Relations for Multinational Companies*, Berlin: de Gruyter.

31 See, for example, Baker and McKenzie (2001); Gill, C. (2006), Industrial relations in Western Europe, in Morley *et al.*; and Keller and Darby (2003), Vols 1 and 2 and annual updates.

32 Fox, A. (2003), To consult and inform, *HR Magazine*, October: 87–92.

33 Paskoff, S. M. (2003), Around the world without the daze: Communicating international codes of conduct, paper presented to the 4th Annual Program on International Labor and Employment Law, Center for American and International Law, Dallas, TX, October 1.

34 Briscoe, D. R. (2000), *International Focus: Global Ethics, Labor Standards, and International HRM*, Alexandria, VA: Society for Human Resource Management White Paper, winter; Digh, P. (1997), Shades of gray in the global marketplace, *HR Magazine*, April: 91–98; Florkowski, G., Schuler, R. S. and Briscoe, D. R. (2004), Global ethics and international HRM, in Berndt, R. (ed.), *Challenges in Management*, Vol. 11: *Competitiveness and Ethics*, Berlin: Springer; Kumar, B. N. and Steinman, H. (eds)

(1998), *Ethics in International Management,* Berlin: de Gruyter; Gesteland, R. R. (1999), *Cross-cultural Business Behavior,* Copenhagen, Denmark: Copenhagen Business School Press; and Morgan, E. (1998), *Navigating Cross-cultural Ethics: What Global Managers do Right to keep from Going Wrong,* Burlington, MA: Butterworth-Heineman.

35 Buller, P. F. and McEvoy, G. M. (1999), Creating and sustaining ethical capability in the multinational corporation, *Journal of World Business,* 34 (4): 326–343.

36 Donaldson, T. (1996), Values in tension: Ethics away from home, *Harvard Business Review,* September–October: 48–62; Singer, A. W. (1991), Ethics: Are standards lower overseas? *Across the Board,* September: 31–34.

37 Schlegelmilch, B. B. and Robertson, D.C. (1995), The influence of country and industry on ethical perceptions of senior executives in the US and Europe, *Journal of International Business Studies,* fourth quarter: 859–881.

38 Fleming, J. E. (1997), Problems in teaching international ethics, *Academy of Management News,* March: 17; Armstrong, R. W. (1996), The relationship between culture and perception of ethical problems in international marketing, *Journal of Business Ethics* 15 (11): 1199–1208.

39 The story was related in Digh (1997).

40 Buller and McEvoy (1999).

41 De George, R. T. (1993), *Competing with Integrity in International Business,* New York: Oxford University Press; Hausman, C. (1996), Ethics issues circle the globe, *Insights on Global Ethics,* 6 (3): 1, 5.

42 Bribes can cost the US an edge, *Business Week,* April 15 1996, p. 30; Foreign practices: bribery and pressure tactics are costing American business overseas, *Across the Board,* October 1996: 11–12; Kaltenheuser, S., *Across the Board,* November–December 1988: 36–42.

43 Transparency International is a global civil society organization leading the fight against corruption, see http://www.transparency.org.

44 Wiehen, M. H. (1998), Corruption in international business relations: Problems and solutions, in Kumar, B. N. and Steinmann, H. (eds), *Ethics in International Management,* Berlin: de Gruyter.

45 A good overview of this subject can be found in *ibid.* Other references include: *Business Week* (1996), Bribes can cost the US an edge, April 15: 30; *Across the Board* (1996), Foreign practices: Bribery and pressure tactics are costing American business overseas, October: 11–12; *Workplace Visions* (1998), International attention turns to corruption (Society for Human Resource Management), July/August: 4–5; James, B. (1997), OECD takes a first step in the battle over bribery, *International Herald Tribune,* May 29: 11; Kaltenheuser, S. (1998), Schmiergeld, *Across the Board,* November–December: 36–42; Minehan, M. (1998), International attention turns to corruption, *HR Magazine,* March: 152; Patel, T. (1996), US seeks to end greasing of palms, *Journal of Commerce,* May 3: 1A, 3A; and Webley, S. (1998), The interfaith declaration: Context, issues and problems of application of a code of ethics for international business among those of three major religions, in Kumar, B. N. and Steinman, H. (eds), *Ethics in International Management,* Berlin: de Gruyter.

46 James, B. (1997), OECD takes a first step in the battle over bribery, *International Herald Tribune,* May 29: 11; Patel, T. (1996), US seeks to end greasing of palms, *Journal of Commerce,* May 3: 1A, 3A; (1988), International attention turns to corruption, *Workplace Visions,* July–August: 4–5; Solberg, J., Strong, K. C. and McGuirre, C. Jr. (1995) Living (not learning) ethics, *Journal of Business Ethics,* 14 (1): 71–81. Minehan, M. (1998), International attention turns to corruption, *HR Magazine,* March: 152; Kaltenheuser, (1983).

47 A good discussion of this issue can be found in Gesteland (1999) and in Wiehen (1998).

48 This section is adapted from Fisher, C. D., Shoenfeldt, L. F. and Shaw, J. B. (1993) *Human Resource Management,* 2d ed., Boston, MA.: Houghton Mifflin, Original sources: Stace, W. T. (1988), Ethical relativity and ethical absolutism, in Donaldson, T. and

Werhane, P. H. (eds), *Ethical Issues in Business*, Englewood Cliffs, NJ: Prentice Hall; Shaw, W. and Barry, V. (1989) *Moral Issues in Business*, Belmont, CA: Wadsworth, pp. 11–13; and Donaldson, T. (1989) *The Ethics of International Business*, New York: Oxford University Press.

49 See, for example, Donaldson (1996).
50 Donaldson (1989), 103.
51 *Ibid.*, 104.
52 Donaldson (1996).
53 Digh, P. (1997), Shades of gray in the global marketplace, *HR Magazine*, April: 91–98.
54 Adapted from Tansey, L. A. (1996), Taking ethics abroad, *Across the Board*, June: 56, 58; Donaldson (1996), HBR.
55 Sweeney, J. J. (1998), *Making the Global Economy work for America*, presentation by the president of the AFL-CIO to the Economic Strategy Institute Conference, May 5, http://www.aflcio.org/publ/speech98/sp0505.htm.
56 In Digh (1997).
57 Donaldson (1996).
58 *Ibid.*
59 Phillips, R. and Claus, L. (2002), Corporate social responsibility and global HR: Balancing the needs of the corporation and its stakeholders, *International Focus* (SHRM).
60 Savitz, A. and Weber, K. (2006), *The Triple Bottom Line*. San Francisco, CA: Jossey Bass.

Part II International human resource management in the multinational enterprise: politics and practices

5 Global talent management and staffing

1 Baron, A. and Armstrong, M. (2007), *Human Capital Management: Achieving Added Value Through People*, London/Philadelphia: Kogan Page; Berger, L. A. (2004), Creating a talent management system for organization excellence: Connecting the dots, in Berger, L. A. and Berger, D. R. (eds) (2003), *The Talent Management Handbook*, New York: McGraw-Hill; Briscoe, D. R. (2008), Talent management and the global learning organization, in Vaiman, V. and Vance, C. M. (eds), *Smart Talent Management: Building Knowledge Capital for Competitive Advantage*, Cheltenham, UK/Northhampton, MA: 195–216; Edward Elgar; Javidan, M., Stahl, G. K., Brodbeck, F. and Wilderom, C. P. M. (2005), Cross-border-transfer of knowledge: Cultural lessons from Project GLOBE, *Academy of Management Executive*, 19 (2): 59–76; Knez, M. and Ruse, D. H. (2004), Optimizing your investment in your employees, in Berger and Berger (2003); Lunnan, R., Lervik, J. E. B., Traavik, L. E. M., Nilsen, S., Amdam, R. P. and Hennestad, B. W. (2005), Global transfer of management practices across nations and MNC subcultures, *Academy of Management Executive*, 19 (2): 77–80; Marquardt, M. and Reynolds, A. (1994), *The Global Learning Organization*, Burr Ridge, IL: Irwin; Moore, K. and Birkinshaw, J. (1998), Managing knowledge in global service firms: Centers of excellence, *Academy of Management Executive*, 12 (4): 81–92; Thorne, K. and Pellant, A. (2007), *The Essential Guide to Managing Talent*, London/Philadelphia: Kogan Page.
2 This term refers to the ability of firms to use the input of non-employees for in-house projects, much like the development of "open source" software. Sometimes this is referred to as the "Wiki Workplace," which refers to the use of mass collaboration, which is taking root in the workplace, connecting internal teams to external networks or individuals facilitated by the Web 2.0 platform for collaboration. As a result, the boundaries of the organization are extended in terms of the work force that can be accessed by the firm. See "The Wiki Workplace," in Tapscott, D. and Williams, A. D. (2006), *Wikinomics: How Mass Collaboration Changes Everything*, New York: Portfolio Penguin Group.

3   Kelly, L. K., (2007), *Mapping Global Talent: Essays and Insights*, Chicago: Heidrick and Struggles/Economist Intelligence Unit.

4   There are many references on this subject. Here are only a few: Boardman, M. (1999), Worker "dearth" in the twenty-first century, *HR Magazine*, June: 304; Golzen, G. (1998), Skill shortages around the globe, *HR World*, November–December: 41–53; Herman, R., Olivo, T. and Gioia, J. (2003), *Impending Crisis: Too Many Jobs, Too Few People*, Winchester, VA: Oakhill Press; Johnston, W. B. (1991), Global work force 2000: The new world labor market, *Harvard Business Review*, March–April: 115–127; Leonard, S. (2000), The labor shortage, *Workplace Visions*, 4: 1–7; Patel, D. (2001), HR trends and analysis: The effect of changing demographics and globalization on HR, *Global HR*, July–August: 9–10; Richman, L. S. (1992), The coming world labor shortage, *Fortune*, April 6, 70–75; Sappal, P. (2000), Just can't get the staff (includes articles on skill shortages in various regions of the world), *HR World*, July–August: 53–62.

5   Female Labor Force Participation (Percent of Active Population), OECD, 2006.

6   Country participation rates are available on the OECD web site: www.oecd.org.

7   Estimates from data provided by the World Bank, *World Development Indicators*, http://web.worldbank.org/WBSITE/EXTERNAL/DATASTATISTICS.

8   Hall, L. (2001), Talent mapped out, *Global HR*, April: 30, quoting Alan Tsang, managing director for Asia of the search and selection firm Norman Broadbent.

9   Friedman, T. L. (2005), *The World is Flat*, New York: Farrar Straus and Giroux.

10 Sullivan, J. (2002), Plan of action, *Global HR*, October: 22.

11 Perlmutter, H. V. and Heenan, D. A. (1986), Cooperate to compete globally, *Harvard Business Review*, March/April: 135–152.

12 See, for example, Borg, M. and Harzing, A.-W. (2004), Composing an international staff, in Harzing, A.-W. and Van Ruysseveldt, J. (eds), *International Human Resource Management*, 2d ed., Thousand Oaks, CA/London: Sage Publications; Fernandez, F. (2005), *Globalization and Human Resource Management*, New York: HNB Publishing; Gross, A. and McDonald, R. (1998), Vast shortages in talent keep employers searching, *International HR Update*, July: 6; Melton, W. R. (2005), *The New American Expat*, Yarmouth, ME: Intercultural Press; Schell, M. S. and Solomon, C. M. (1997), *Capitalizing on the Global Workforce*, Chicago: Irwin; Stroh, L. K., Black, J. S., Mendenhall, M. E. and Gregersen, H. B. (2005), *International Assignments: An Integration of Strategy, Research, and Practice*, Mahwah, NJ/London: Erlbaum; Vance, C. M. and Paik, Y. (2006), *Managing a Global Workforce*, Armonk, NY/London: Sharpe. The terms PCN, TCN and HCN, were introduced into the IHRM literature by Patrick Morgan, at that time director of international HR at Bechtel, in 1986. Morgan, P. (1986), International human resource management: Fact or fiction? *Personnel Administrator*, 31 (9): 43–47.

13 See, for example, Edström, A. and Galbraith, J. R. (1977), Transfer of managers as a coordination and control strategy in multinational organizations, *Administrative Science Quarterly*, 22 (June): 248–263; Harzing, A.-W. (2001a), Of bears, bumble-bees, and spiders: The role of expatriates in controlling foreign subsidiaries, *Journal of World Business*, 36 (4): 366–379; Hays, R. (1974), Expatriate selection: Insuring success and avoiding failure, *Journal of International Business Studies*, 5 (1): 25–37; Roberts, K., Kossek, E. E. and Ozeki, C. (1998), Managing the global work force: Challenges and strategies, *Academy of Management Executive*, 12 (4): 6–16; Tahvanainen, M. (1998), *Expatriate Performance Management*, Helsinki: Helsinki School of Economics Press; and Tung, R. L. (1991), Selection and training of personnel for overseas assignments, *Columbia Journal of World Business*, 16 (1): 68–78.

14 Carpenter, M. A., Sanders, W. G. and Gregersen, H. B. (2001), Bundling human capital with organizational context: The impact of international assignment experience on multinational firm performance and CEO pay, *Academy of Management Journal*, 44 (3): 493–511; Harzing, A.-W. (2001a); Harzing, A.-W. (2001b), Who's in charge? An empirical study of executive staffing practices in foreign subsidiaries, *Human Resource Management*, 40 (2): 139–158; Stahl, G. T., Miller, E. L. and Tung, R. L. (2002), Toward

the boundaryless career: A closer look at the expatriate career concept and the perceived implications of an international assignment, *Journal of World Business*, 37 (3): 216–227; and Tung, R. L. (1998), American expatriates abroad: From neophytes to cosmopolitans, *Journal of World Business*, 33 (2): 125–144.

15 Adler, N. J. with Gundersen, A. (2008), *International Dimensions of Organizational Behavior*, 5th ed., Mason, OH: Thomson/South Western; Bachler, C. (1996), Global inpats: Don't let them surprise you, *Personnel Journal*, June: 54–56; Forster, N. (2000), The myth of the international manager, *International Journal of Human Resource Management*, 11: 126; Groh, K. and Allen, M. (1998), Global staffing: Are expatriates the only answer? Special report on expatriate management, *HR Focus*, March: 75–78; Minehan, M. (1996), Skills shortage in Asia, *HR Magazine*, 41: 152; Tung, R. (1987), Expatriate assignments: Enhancing success and minimizing failure, *Academy of Management Executive*, 1 (2): 117–126.

16 Roberts *et al.* (1998), 96.

17 Mendenhall, M.E., Osland, J.S., Bird, A., Oddou, G.R. and Mazenevski, M.L. (2008) *Global Leadership: Research, Practice and Development*, London: Routledge; Black, J. S., Morrison, A. J. and Gregersen, H. B. (1999), *Global Explorers: The Next Generation of Leaders*, New York/London: Routledge; Fatima (2005); Ferraro, G. (2002), *Global Brains: Knowledge and Competencies for the Twenty-first Century*, Charlotte, NC: Intercultural Associates; Hodge, S. (2000), *Global Smarts: The Art of Communicating and Deal-making Anywhere in the World*, New York: Wiley; Keys, J. B. and Fulmer, R. M. (eds) (1998), *Executive Development and Organizational Learning for Global Business*, New York/London: International Business Press; McCall, M. W., Jr. and Hollenbeck, G. P. (2002), *Developing Global Executives: The Lessons of International Experience*, Boston, MA: Harvard Business School Press; Moran, R. T., Harris, P. R. and Moran, S. V. (2007), *Managing Cultural Differences*, 7th ed., Burlington, MA/Oxford: Butterworth-Heinemann; Rosen, R., Digh, P., Singer, M. and Phillips, C. (2000), *Global Literacies: Lessons on Business Leadership and National Cultures*, New York: Simon and Schuster; Scherer, C. W. (2000), *The Internationalists: Business Strategies for Globalization*, Wilsonville, OR: Book Partners; Stroh *et al.* (2005); Vance and Paik (2006).

18 This is just a summary. If the reader would like more information, more complete descriptions, and references to support these different types of international employees, please contact the lead author, Dr. Dennis Briscoe, at drbriscoe1@aol.com.

19 For more complete discussion of the management of expatriates, refer to the following sources: Brewster, C. (1991), *The Management of Expatriates*, London: Kogan Page; Fernandez, F. (2005), *Globalization and Human Resource Management*, New York: HNB Publishing; Lomax, S. (2001), *Best Practices for Managers and Expatriates*, New York: Wiley; Melton, W. R. (2005), *The New American Expat*, Yarmouth, ME: Intercultural Press; Schell, M. and Solomon, C. (1997), *Capitalizing on the Global Workforce: A Strategic Guide to Expatriate Management*, Chicago: Irwin; Scullion, H. and Collings, D. G. (eds) (2006), *Global Staffing*, London/New York: Routledge; Stroh, L. K., Black, J. S., Mendenhall, M. E. and Gregersen, H. B. (2005), *International Assignments: An Integration of Strategy, Research, and Practice*, Mahwah, NJ/London: Erlbaum; Thomas, D. C. (1998), The expatriate experience: A critical review and synthesis, *Advances in International Comparative Management*, 12: 237–273.

20 GMAC Global Relocation Services/Windham International, National Foreign Trade Council, and SHRM Global Forum (2008 and previous years), *Global Relocation Trends Annual Survey Report*, New York: GMAC GRS/Windham International.

21 Keichell, M., III (1983), Our person in Pomparippu: The successful expatriate executive learns to cool heels, live with servants—and come home again, *Fortune*, October 17: 213.

22 Stroh *et al.* (2005).

23 For example, yearly surveys such as the *Global Relocation Trends Survey Report*, by the National Foreign Trade Council, Society for Human Resource Management (SHRM) Global Forum, and GMAC Global Relocation Services; *Global Assignment Policies and*

Practices Survey, by KPMG; and the *Survey of Short-term International Assignment Policies*, by ORC Worldwide, the MI Group, and Worldwide ERC.

24 Harvey, M. G., Novicevich, M. M. and Speier, C. (2000), An innovative global management staffing system: A competency-based perspective, *Human Resource Management*, 39 (4): 381–394; Hauser, J. A. (2000), Filling the candidate pool, *World at Work Journal*, second quarter: 26–33.

25 Source: Briscoe, D. R. and Gazda, G. M. (1989), The successful expatriate, *Proceedings*, "Managing in a Global Economy," third biannual international conference, Eastern Academy of Management, Hong Kong, November.

26 See, for example, Black, J. S. and Mendenhall, M. (1990), Cross-cultural effectiveness: A review and a theoretical framework for future research, *Academy of Management Review*, 115: 113–136; Brocklyn, P. (1989), Developing the international executive, *Personnel*, March: 44–48; Caliguiri, P. M. (1989), Preparing the new global manager, *Training and Development Journal*, March: 29–31; Hixon, A. L. (1986), Why corporations make haphazard overseas staffing decisions, *Personnel Administrator*, March: 91–94; Hogan, G. W. and Goodson, J. R. (1979), The key to expatriate success, *Training and Development Journal*, January: 50–52; Lanier, A. R. (1979), Selecting and preparing personnel for overseas transfers, *Personnel Journal*, March: 71–78; Stroh *et al.* (2005); Tung, R. L. (1987), Expatriate assignments: Enhancing success and minimizing failure, *Academy of Management Executive*, 1 (2): 117–126.

27 Miller, E. L. and Cheng, J. (1978), A closer look at the decision to accept an overseas position, *Management International Review*, 18: 25–33.

28 Quoted in Howard, C. G. (1992), Profile of the twenty-first-century expatriate manager, *HR Magazine*, June: 96.

29 See, for example, Donegan, J. (2002), Effective expatriate selection: The first step in avoiding assignment failure, *Expatiate Advisor*, spring: 14–16; Ondrack, D. (1996), Key managers "make or break" a new international operation, *International HR Update*, November: 1, 4; Solomon, C. M. (1994), Staff selection impacts global success, *Personnel Journal*, January: 12–19.

30 Hawley-Wildmoser, L. (1997), Selecting the right employee for assignments abroad, *Cultural Diversity at Work*, 9 (3): 1, 12–13.

31 See, for example, the discussion of this point in Black *et al.* (1999).

32 Briscoe, D. R. (1997), Assessment centers: Cross-cultural and cross-national issues, in Riggio, R. E. and Mayes, B. T. (eds), *Assessment Centers: Research and Application*, special issue of the *Journal of Social Behavior and Personality*, 12 (5): 261–270.

33 For overviews of these issues, look at Dowling *et al.* (2005); Stroh *et al.* (2005); Vance and Paik (2006).

34 Nasif, E. G., Thibodeaux, M. S. and Ebrahimi, B. (1987), Variables associated with success as an expatriate manager, *Proceedings*, Academy of International Business, Southeast Region, annual meeting, New Orleans, November 4–7: 169–179.

35 Refer to sources in previous notes plus Black, J. S. and Gregersen, H. B. (1991), The other half of the picture: Antecedents of spouse cross-cultural adjustment, *Journal of International Business Studies*, second quarter: 225–247; Fuchsberg, G. (1990), As costs of overseas assignments climb, firms select expatriates more carefully, *Wall Street Journal*, April 5: B-1, B-5; Gomez-Mejia, L. and Balkin, D. B. (1987), The determinants of managerial satisfaction with the expatriation and repatriation process, *Journal of Management Development*, 6 (1): 7–18; Savich, R. S. and Rodgers, W. (1988), Assignment overseas: Easing the transition before and after, *Personnel*, August: 44–48; Tung, R. L. (1988), Career issues in international assignments, *Academy of Management Executive*, 2 (3): 241–244.

36 Conway (1984); Harvey, M. G. (1983), The multinational corporation's expatriate problem: An application of Murphy's Law, *Business Horizons*, January–February: 72; Henry, E. R. (1965), What business can learn from Peace Corps selection and training, *Personnel*, 42

(4): 17–25; Misa, K. F. and Fabricatore, J. M. (1979), Return on investment of overseas personnel, *Financial Executive*, 47 (4): 42–46; Murray and Murray (1986); Rahim, A. (1983), A model for developing key expatriate executives, *Personnel Journal*, April: 312; Tung (1981, 1987).

37 Tung, R. L. (1982), Selection and training procedures of US, European, and Japanese multinationals, *California Management Review*, fall: 57–71; Tung, R. L. (1984), *Key to Japan's Economic Strength: Human Power*, Lexington, MA: Heath.

38 Based on Perraud, P. and Davis, A. (1997), Assignment success or failure: It's all in the family, presented to the annual conference of the Institute for International Human Resource Management (now the Global Forum, division of the US Society for Human Resource Management), Los Angeles, CA, April 15–17.

39 Reported in Bennett, R. (1993), Solving the dual international career dilemma, *HR News*, January: C5.

40 *Ibid.*; see also Fitzgerald-Turner, B. (1997), Myths of expatriate life, *HR Magazine*, June: 65–74; Organization Resources Counselors (2005), Fifth Annual Dual Careers and International Assignments Survey, reported in *Expatriate Advisor*, autumn: 28–29; Punnett, B. J. (1997), Towards effective management of expatriate spouses, *Journal of World Business*, 32 (3): 243–257; Thaler-Carter, R. E. (1999), Vowing to go abroad, *HR Magazine*, November: 90–96.

41 Bennett (1993).

42 Dolainski, S. (1997), Are expats getting lost in translation? *Workforce*, February: 32–39.

43 Lester, T. (1994), Pulling down the language barrier, *International Management*, July–August: 44.

44 See, for example, Is there a problem, officer? Second time around expat describes benefits of language skills, *Global Voice*, Berlitz Newsletter of International Communication and Understanding (no date), 6 (1): 1; and *Reading across Boundaries* Newsletter of International Orientation Resources, July 1994: 1–6.

45 Reading across Boundaries (1994), 1.

46 *Ibid.*

47 *Ibid.*

48 Solon, L. (2000), The language of global business, *SHRM Global*, December: 12–14.

49 Naisbitt, J. and Aburdene, P. (1990), *Megatrends 2000*, New York: Morrow.

50 Refer to surveys by Mercer Human Resources Consulting (www.mercerhr.com) and GMAC Global Relocation Services/Windham International, Prudential Relocation, and Cendant International Assignment Services.

51 Adler, N. J. (1984a), Expecting international success: Female managers overseas, *Columbia Journal of World Business*, 19 (3): 79–85; Adler, N. J. (1987), Pacific Basin managers: A *gaijin*, not a woman, *Human Resource Management*, 26 (2): 169–191; Adler, N. J. (1984b), Women do not want international careers—and other myths about international management, *Organizational Dynamics*, 13 (2): 66–79; Adler, N. J. (1984c), Women in international management: Where are they? *California Management Review*, 26 (4): 78–89; Adler, N. J. and Izraeli, D. (eds) (1988), *Women in Management Worldwide*, Armonk, NY: Sharpe; Adler, N. J. and Izraeli, D. N. (eds) (1994), *Competitive Frontiers: Women Managers in a Global Economy*, Cambridge, MA/Oxford: Blackwell; Corporate women: A rush of recruits for overseas duty, *Business Week*, April 20 1981: 120 ff.; Jelinek, M. and Adler, N. J. (1988), Women: World-class managers for global competition, *Academy of Management Executive*, 2 (1): 11–19; Kirk, W. Q. and Maddox, R. C. (1988), International management: The new frontier for women, *Personnel*, March: 46–49; Lockwood, N. (2004), *The Glass Ceiling: Domestic and International Perspectives*, Alexandria, VA: SHRM Research Quarterly.

52 Adler, N. J. (1984d), Managers perceive greater barriers for women in international versus domestic management, *Columbia Journal of World Business*, 19 (1): 45–53.

53 *Ibid.*; Pomeroy, A. (2006), Outdated policies hinder female expats, *HR Magazine*, December: 16 (reporting on survey results from Mercer Human Resource Accounting); Mercer HR Consulting (2006), More females sent on international assignment than ever before, survey finds, retrieved from www.mercerhr.com, December 30 2006.

54 See above, plus surveys by GMAC Global Relocation Services/Windham International/SHRM Global annual reports.

55 Abraham, Y. (1985), Personnel policies and practices in Saudi Arabia, *Personnel Administrator*, April: 102; Thal, N. and Caleora, P. (1979), Opportunities for women in international business, *Business Horizons*: December, 21–27.

56 Adler (1984b); Golesorkhi, B. (1991), Why not a woman in overseas assignments? *HR News: International HR*, March: C4; Kirk and Maddox (1988).

57 See above, plus Brown, L. K. (1989), *Women in Management Worldwide*, Armonk, NY: Sharpe; Catalyst (2000), *Passport to Opportunity: US Women in global business*, New York: author; Maital, S. (1989), A long way to the top, *Across the Board*, December: 6–7.

58 Quoted in Grove, C. and Hallowell, W. (1997), Guidelines for women expatriates, *Solutions*, November: 42.

59 *Ibid*, 41–44; Sappal, P. (1999), Sometimes it's hard to be a woman, *HR World*, January–February: 21–24.

60 Caligiuri, P. M. and Cascio, W. F. (1998), Can we send her there? Maximizing the success of Western women on global assignments, *Journal of World Business*, 33 (4): 394–416; Caligiuri, P. M. and Cascio, W. F. (2000), Sending women on global assignments, *World at Work Journal*, second quarter: 34–41; Caligiuri, P. M. and Tung, R. L. (1999), Comparing the success of male and female expatriates from a US-based multinational company, *International Journal of Human Resource Management*, 10: 763–782; Taylor, S. and Napier, N. (1996), Working in Japan: Lessons from Western expatriates, *Sloan Management Review*, 37: 76–84.

61 Varma, A., Stroh, L. K. and Schmitt, L. B. (2001), Women and international assignments: The impact of supervisor–subordinate relationships, *Journal of World Business*, 36 (4): 380–388.

62 Harris, H. (1999), Women in international management, in Brewster, C. and Harris, H. (eds), *International Human Resource Management*, London: Routledge.

63 Joinson, C. (2002), No returns: "Localizing" expats saves companies big money and can be a smooth transition with a little due diligence by HR, *HR Magazine*, November: 70–77.

64 See, for example, Black, J. S., Gregersen, H. B., Mendenhall, M. E. and Stroh, L. K. (1999), *Globalizing People through International Assignments*, Reading, MA: Addison Wesley; Hauser, J. (1997), Leading practices in international assignment programs, *International HR Journal*, summer: 34–37; McCall, M. W., Jr. and Hollenbeck, G. P. (2002), *Developing Global Executives: The Lessons of International Experience*, Boston, MA: Harvard Business School Press; Stahl, G. K., Miller, E. L. and Tung, R. T. (2002), Toward the boundaryless career: A closer look at the expatriate career concept and the perceived implications of an international assignment, *Journal of World Business*, 37: 216–227; Stroh *et al.* (2005).

65 Gregson, K. (1997), Outsourcing international assignments, *International HR Journal*, fall: 38–40; Joinson, C. (2002), Save thousands per expatriate, *HR Magazine*, July: 73–77; Smith, J. J. (2006), Executives say HR needs to improve to attract top global talent, reporting on findings reported in the Economist Intelligence Unit's *CEO Briefing: Corporate Priorities for 2006 and Beyond*, retrieved from http://www.shrm.org/global/news_published/CMS_0117960.asp.

66 Smith, J. J. (2006), Firms say expats getting too costly; but few willing to act, reporting on findings of the KPMG *2006 Global Assignment Policies and Practices* survey, retrieved September 11 2006 from http://www.shrm.org/global/news_published/CMS_018300.asp.

67 Adler with Gundersen (2008); Black, J. S. (1991), Returning expatriates feel foreign in their native land, *HR Focus*, August: 17; Brewster, C. (1991), *The Management of*

Expatriates, London: Kogan Page; Harvey, M. G. (1989), Repatriation of corporate executives: An empirical study, *Journal of International Business Studies*, spring: 131–144; Howard, C. G. (1987), Out of sight—not out of mind, *Personnel Administrator*, June: 82–90; Stroh *et al.* (2005); Tyler, K. (2006), Retaining expatriates, *HR Magazine*, March: 92–102; Vance and Paik (2006); Welds, K. (1991), The return trip, *HR Magazine*, June: 113–114.

68 Shumsky, N. J. (1999), Repatriation can be the most difficult part of a global assignment, *CRN News*, May: 21.

69 Munkel, N. and Nghiem, L. (1999), Do multinationals face up to the challenges of repatriation? *KPMG Expatriate Administrator*, 4: 6–8.

70 The term "inpatriates" is a little more than ten years old. It is a term developed by MNEs to describe a particular type of international employee, as described in the text. Subsequently, most of the literature describing inpatriates has been written by practitioners, consultants, or journalists writing in magazines with a primarily practitioner readership. For example, refer to Bachler, C. J. (1996), Global inpats: Don't let them surprise you, *Personnel Journal*, June: 54–64; Cook, J. (1998), A whole new world, *Human Resource Executive*, March 19: 1–2; Copeland, A. P. (1995), Helping foreign nationals adapt to the US, *Personnel Journal*, February: 83–87; Finney, M. (2000), Culture shock in America? For foreign expatriates, absolutely, *Across the Board*, May: 28–33; Harvey, M. G. and Buckley, M. R. (1997), Managing inpatriates: Building a global core competency, *Journal of World Business*, 32 (1): 35–52; Harvey, M. G., Novicevic, M. M. and Speier, C. (2000), An innovative global management staffing system: A competency-based perspective, *Human Resource Management*, 39 (4): 381–394; Joinson, C. (1999), The impact of "inpats," *HR Magazine Focus*, April: 5–10; Kent, S. (2001), Welcome to our world, *Global HR*, February–March: 32–36; Lachnit, C. (2001), Low-cost tips for successful inpatriation, *Work force*, August: 42–47; Ladika, S. (2005), Unwelcome changes, *HR Magazine*, February: 83–90; Solomon, C. M. (1995), HR's helping hand pulls global inpatriates on board, *Personnel Journal*, November: 40–49; Solomon, C. M. (2000), Foreign relations, *Workforce*, November: 50–56.

71 Caligiuri, P. M. (1997), Assessing expatriate success: Beyond just "being there," *New Approaches to Employee Management*, 4 (1): 17–40.

72 *Ibid.*

73 Many of the references in this chapter deal with various aspects of best practice in the selection of IAs. In addition, refer to Berlitz International, PHH Relocation, and SHRM Institute for International HRM (1996–1997), executive summary, *International Assignee Research Project*, authors; Lomax, S. (2001), *Best Practices for Managers and Expatriates*, New York: Wiley; Black, J. S. and Gregersen, H. B. (1999), The right way to manage expats, *Harvard Business Review*, March–April: 52–63; Dolins, I. (2002), Ready, steady, go, *Global HR*, June: 1619; Foster, R. D. (1997), Strategic solutions for effective international assignments, *International HR Journal*, summer: 38–40; Hauser, J. (1997), Leading practices in international assignment programs, *International HR Journal*, summer: 34–37; Herring, L. and Greenwood, P. (2000), "Best practices" leverage international assignment success in the United States, *International HR Journal*, spring: 21–28; Institute of Personnel and Development (1999), *The IPD Guide on International Recruitment, Selection, and Assessment*, London: IPD; Melton (2005); Prudential Relocation Global Services (no date), *Leading Practices in International Assignment Programs*, Valhalla, NY: Prudential Relocation; Stroh *et al.* (2005); Toh, S. M. and DeNisi, A. S. (2005), A local perspective to expatriate success, *Academy of Management Executive*, 19 (1): 132–146; Usner, J. W. (1996), A primer on programs and policies for successful foreign assignments, *International HR Journal*, winter: 45–48.

74 Barboza, D. (2006), Sharp labor shortage in China may lead to world trade shift, *New York Times*, April 3: A1, A10; Clouse, T. (2006), Firms in China faced with tight supply of skilled labor, *Workforce Management*, September 11: 37–38; Fox, A. (2007), China: Land

of opportunity and challenge, *HR Magazine*, September: 38–44; Lee, D. (2006), Job hopping is rampant as China's economy chases skilled workers, *Los Angeles Times*, February 21: C1.

75 Kent, S. (1999), Cultivating home-grown talent, *HR World*, November–December: 24–28.

76 Halley, J. (1999), Localization as an ethical response to internationalization, in Brewster, C. and Harris, H. (eds), *International Human Resource Management*, London: Routledge; Kent, S. (1999), Cultivating home-grown talent, *HR World*, November–December: 24–28; Solomon, C. M. (1995), Learning to manage host-country nations, *Personnel Journal*, March: 21–26.

77 Robock, S. H. and Simmonds, K. (1989), *International Business and Multinational Enterprises*, 4th ed., Homewood, IL: Irwin, p. 559.

78 Smith, J. J. (2006), More third-country nationals being used, retrieved from the SHRM Global HR Focus Area: http://www.shrm.org/global/news_published/CMS_017348.asp.

79 Friedman (2005); Johnston, W. B. (1991), Global work force 2000: The new world labor market, *Harvard Business Review*, March–April: 115–127.

80 For example, refer to Briscoe, D. R. (in press, 2008), Talent management in the global learning organization, in Vaiman, V. and Vance, C. M. (eds), *Smart Talent Management: Building Knowledge Capital for Competitive Advantage*, Cheltenham, UK/Northhampton, MA: Edward Elgar; Herman, R., Olivo, T. and Gioia, J. (2003), *Impending Crisis: Too Many Jobs, Too Few People*, Winchester, VA: Oakhill Press; Johnston (1991); Leonard, B. (2006), Immigration rises sharply in most developed nations, retrieved from the SHRM Global HR Focus Area: http://www.shrm.org/global/news_published/CMS_017977.asp; Richman, L. S. (1990), The coming world labor shortage, *Fortune*, April 9, 70–77; Schramm, J. (2006), *Global Labor Mobility*, Workplace Visions, No. 2, Alexandria, VA: Society for Human Resource Management; Templeman, J., Wise, D. C., Lask, E. and Evans, R. (1989), Grappling with the graying of Europe, *Business Week*, March 13: 54–56.

6 Training and management development in the multinational enterprise

1 Evans, P., Pucik, V. and Barsoux, J. L. (2002), *The Global Challenge*, New York: McGraw-Hill Irwin.

2 Keys, J. B. and Fulmer, R. M. (1998), Introduction: Seven imperatives for executive education and organizational learning in the global world, in Keys, J. B. and Fulmer, R. M. (eds), *Executive Development and Organizational Learning for Global Business*, New York: International Business Press. Also see the entire special issue of *Human Resource Management*, summer/fall 2000, Nos 2 and 3; and Sparrow, P., Brewster, C. and Harris, H. (2004), *Globalizing Human Resource Management*, London: Routledge.

3 Slocum, J., Jr., McGill, M. and Lei, D. T. (1994), The new learning strategy: Anytime, anything, anywhere, *Organizational Dynamics*, 23 (2): 33–47.

4 Ohmae, K. (1990), *The Borderless World*, New York: HarperCollins, 18.

5 See, for example, Ahmed, P. K., Kok, L. K. and Loh, A. Y. E. (2002), *Learning through Knowledge Management*, Oxford and Woburn, MA: Butterworth-Heinemann; Argyris, C. (1999), *On Organizational Learning*, 2d ed., Oxford UK and Malden, MA: Blackwell Publishers; Chawla, S. and Renesch, J., eds (1995), *Learning Organizations: Developing Cultures for Tomorrow's Workplace*, Portland, OR: Productivity Press; Davenport, T. O. (1999), *Human Capital: What It Is and Why People Invest It*, San Francisco: Jossey Bass; DiBella, A. J. and Nevis, E. C. (1998), *How Organizations Learn*, San Francisco: Jossey Bass; Dotlich, D. L. and Noel, J. L. (1998), *Action Learning: How the World's Top Companies are Re-creating their Leaders and Themselves*, San Francisco: Jossey Bass; Leonard, D. (1995), *Wellsprings of Knowledge: Building and Sustaining the Sources of Innovation*, Boston, MA: Harvard Business School Press; Liebowitz, J. and Beckman, T. (1998), *Knowledge Organizations: What Every Manager Should Know*, Boca Raton, FL:

St. Lucie Press; Marquardt, M. J. (2002), *Building the Learning Organization*, 2d ed., Palo Alto, CA: Davies-Black Publishing; Marquardt, M. and Reynolds, A. (1994), *The Learning Organization: Gaining Competitive Advantage through Continuous Learning*, Burr Ridge, IL: Irwin; Sparrow, J. (1998), *Knowledge in Organizations: Access to Thinking at Work*, London: Sage Publications; Stewart, T.A. (1997), *Intellectual Capital: The New Wealth of Organizations*, New York: Doubleday/Currency; Vaill, P. B. (1996), *Learning as a Way of Being: Strategies for Survival in a World of Permanent White Water*, San Francisco: Jossey Bass; and Watkins, K. E. and Marsick, V. J. (1993), *Sculpting the Learning Organization*, San Francisco: Jossey Bass.

6 De Geus, A. (1980), Planning is learning, *Harvard Business Review*, March–April: 71; and de Geus, A. (1997), *The Living Company*, Boston, MA: Harvard Business School Press; Sparrow *et al.* (2004).

7 For an explanation of the Addie model see Rothwell, W. J. and Kazanas, H. C. (2004), *Mastering the Instructional Design Process*, 3rd ed., San Francisco: Wiley.

8 Adapted from Geber, B. (1989), A global approach to training, *Training*, September, 42–47. See also Schuler, R. S., Tarique, I. and Jackson, S.E. (2004), Managing human resources in cross-border alliances, in Cooper, C. and Finkelstein (eds) *Advances in Mergers and Acquisitions*, New York: SAI Press; Odenwald, S. B. (1993), *Global Training: How to Design a Program for the Multinational Corporation*, Homewood, IL: Business One Irwin and Alexandria, VA: American Society for Training and Development; Reynolds, A. and Nadler, L. (1993), *Globalization: The International HRD Consultant and Practitioner*, Amherst, MA: Human Resource Development Press; and Miller, V. A. (1994), *Guidebook for Global Trainers*, Amherst, MA: Human Resource Development Press.

9 Sappal, P. (2000), ¿Entiendes? Capiche? Comprenez-vous? *HR World*, September/October: 28–32.

10 *Ibid.*

11 Francis, J. L. (1995), Training across cultures, *Human Resource Development Quarterly*, 6 (1), reprinted in Albrecht, M. H., ed. (2001), *International HRM*, Oxford, UK/Malden, MA: Blackwell Publishers, adapted from Hofstede, G. (1991), *Cultures and Organizations: Software of the Mind*, New York: McGraw-Hill; and Pfeiffer, J. W. and Jones, J. E. (1983), *Reference Guide to Handbooks and Annuals*, San Diego, CA: University Associates. Similar efforts are reported in Keys, J. B. and Bleicken, L. M. (1998), Selecting training methodology for international managers, in Keys and Fulmer (2002).

12 Adapted from Jones, M. L. (1989), Management development: An African focus, *International Studies of Management and Organization*, 19 (1): 74–90.

13 Tyler, K. (1999), Offering English lessons at work, *HR Magazine*, December: 112–120.

14 Gratton, L. and Erickson, T. J. (2007), Eight ways to build collaborative teams. *Harvard Business Review*, November: 100–109.

15 Katzenback, J. R. and Smith, D. K. (2003), *The Wisdom of Teams*, New York: Harper Business Essentials.

16 See Oh, H., Labianca, G. and Chung, M-H. (2006) A multilevel model of group social capital, *Academy of Management Review*, 3: 569–582; Labianca, J. (2004) The ties that bind, *Harvard Business Review*, October: 19.

17 Belbin, R. M. (1996), *Management Teams: Why they Succeed or Fail*, London: Butterworth-Heinemann. See also www.belbin.com.

18 DiStefano, J. J. and Maznevski, M. L. (2000) Creating value with diverse teams in global management. *Organizational Dynamics*, 29 (1): 45–63.

19 Maitland, A. (2004), Virtual teams' endeavors to build trust, *Financial Times*, September 8.

20 Malhotra, A., Majchrzak, A. and Rosen, B. (2007), Leading virtual teams, *Academy of Management Perspective*, 21 (1): 60–70.

21 Gratton, L. (2006), *Hot Spots: Why some Teams, Workplaces, and Organizations Buzz with Energy—and Others Don't*. San Francisco: Berrett-Koehler Publications.

22 Gratton and Erickson (2007).

23 Leadership books that take a more global perspective and question the Western-centric view of leadership are: Mendenhall, M. E., Osland, J. S., Bird, A., Oddou, G. R. and Maznevski, M. L. (2008), *Global Leadership: Research, Practice, and Development*, London: Routledge; Trompenaars, F. and Hampden-Turner, C. M. (2000), *Twenty-one Leaders for the Twenty-first Century*, Oxford: Capstone; Evans *et al.* (2002); Lipman-Blumen, J. C. (2000), *Connective Leadership: Managing in a Changing World*, New York: Oxford University Press; Black, J. S., Morrison, A. J. and Gregersen, H. B. (1999), *Global Explorers: The Next Generation of Leaders*, New York/London: Routledge; Kets de Vries, M. F. R. (2006), *The Leadership Mystique: Leading Behavior in the Human Enterprise*, Englewood Cliffs, NJ: FT Prentice Hall.

24 House, R. J., Hanges, P. J., Javidan, M., Dorfman, P. and Gupta, V. (eds) (2004), *Leadership, Culture, and Organizations: The GLOBE Study of Sixty-two Societies*, Thousand Oaks, CA: Sage Publications; House, R. J., Hanges, P. J., Ruiz-Quinanilla, S. A., Dorfman, P. W., Javidan, M., Dickson, M. W., Gupta, V. *et al.* (1999), Cultural influences on leadership and organizations: Project GLOBE, in Mobley, W. H., Gessner, M. J. and Arnold, V. (eds), *Advances in Global Leadership*, Stamford, CT: JAI Press; and Javidan, M., Stahl, G. K., Brodbeck, F. and Wilderom, C. P. M. (2005), Cross-border transfer of knowledge: Cultural lessons from Project GLOBE, *Academy of Management Executive*, 19 (2): 59–80.

25 Avolio, B. (1999), *Full Leadership Development: Building the Vital Forces in Organizations*. Thousand Oaks, CA and London: Sage Publications.

26 Trompenaars *et al.* (2000).

27 Kets de Vries, M. F. R. and Mead, C. (1992), The development of the global leader within the multinational organization, in Pucik, V., Tichy, N. M. and Barnett, C. K. (eds), *Globalizing Management: Creating and Leading the Competitive Organization*, New York: Wiley.

28 Evans *et al.* (2002).

29 Black, Morrison *et al.* (1999).

30 Marquardt has published extensively on the subject of organizational learning and the learning organization, including in the global context. This particular information is adapted from Marquardt, M. J. (1999), *Action Learning in Action*, Palo Alto, CA: Davies-Black Publishing.

31 Adler, N. J. and Bartholomew, S. (1992), Managing globally competent people, *Academy of Management Executive,* 6 (3): 52–65.

32 See, for example, Briscoe, D. R. (2007), Developing a global mind-set: Its role in global careers, *Proceedings*, Ninth Bi-annual Conference, International Human Resource Management, June 12–15: Tallinn, Estonia; Gupta, A. K. and Govindarajan, V. (2002), Cultivating a global mind-set, *Academy of Management Executive*, 16 (1): 116–126; and Morrison, A. J. (2000), Developing a global leadership model, *Human Resource Management*, summer/fall, 39 (2–3): 117–131.

33 Evans *et al.* (2002); and Mendenhall and Stahl (2000).

34 See, for example, Bartlett, C. A. and Ghoshal, S. (1998), *Managing across Borders*, 2d ed., Boston, MA: Harvard Business School Press; Dalton, M., Ernst, C., Deal, J. and Leslie, J. (2002), *Success for the New Global Manager: How to Work across Distances, Countries, and Cultures*, San Francisco: Jossey Bass; Evans *et al.* (2002); Ferraro, G. (2002), *Global Brains: Knowledge and Competencies for the Twenty-first Century*, Charlotte, NC: Intercultural Associates; Hodge, S. (2000), *Global Smarts*, New York: Wiley and McCall and Hollenbeck (2002); Rosen, R. (2000), *Global Literacies: Lessons on Business Leadership and National Cultures*, New York: Simon and Schuster.

35 Kedia, B. L. and Mukherji, A. (1999), Global managers: Developing a mind-set for global competitiveness, *Journal of World Business*, 34 (3): 230–251.

36 Scherer, C. W. (2000), *The Internationalists: Business Strategies for Globalization*, Wilsonville, OR: Book Partners.

37 McCall and Hollenbeck (2002).

38 Rhinesmith, S. H. (1993), *A Manager's Guide to Globalization: Six Keys to Success in a Changing World*, Homewood, IL: Business One Irwin and Alexandria, VA: American Society for Training and Development, 24.

39 Evans *et al.* (2002), 385–387.

40 Rhinesmith, S. H. (1992), Global mind-sets for global managers, *Training and Development Journal*, 46 (10): 63–68; and Rhinesmith (1993).

41 Evans *et al.* (2002), 396–397.

42 See, for example, Black, J. S., Gregersen, H. B., Mendenhall, M. E. and Stroh, L. K. (1999), *Globalizing People through International Assignments*, Reading, MA: Addison Wesley; Black, Morrison and Gregersen (1999); Claus, L. (1999), Globalization and HR professional competencies, paper presented at the 22nd Annual Forum, Institute for International Human Resources (now called the Global Forum), Society for Human Resource Management, Orlando, FL, April 13; Dalton *et al.* (2002); Evans *et al.* (2002); Ferraro (2002); Harris, P. R. and Moran, R. T. (1996), European leadership in globalization, *European Business Review*, 96 (2), reprinted in Albrecht, M. H. (ed) (2001), *International HRM: Managing Diversity in the Workplace*, Oxford, UK/Malden, MA: Blackwell Publishers; Harris, P. R. and Moran, R. T. (1999), *Managing Cultural Differences: Leadership Strategies for a New World of Business*, 5th ed., Woburn, MA: Butterworth-Heinemann, 41–54; Hodge (2000); McCall and Hollenbeck (2002); Rosen, R., with Digh, P., Singer, M. and Phillips, C. (2000), *Global Literacies: Lessons on Business Leadership and National Cultures*, New York: Simon and Schuster; and Scherer (2000).

43 Adler, N. J. and Bartholomew, S. (1992), Managing globally competent people, *Academy of Management Executive*, 6 (3): 52–65; Evans *et al.* (2002).

44 Kets de Vries, M. F. R. and Mead, C. (1992), The development of the global leader within the multinational corporation, in Pucik, V., Tichy, N. M. and Barnett, C. K. (eds), *Globalizing Management: Creating and Leading the Competitive Organization*, New York: Wiley.

45 Lancaster, H. (1998), Managing your career, *Wall Street Journal*, June 2: C1.

46 Lobel, S. A. (1990), Global leadership competencies, *Human Resource Management*, 29 (1): 39–47.

47 Barham, K. and Wills, S. (1992), *Management across Frontiers*, Ashridge, England: Ashridge Management Research Group.

48 Lancaster (1998).

49 Palmisano, S. (2007) The globally integrated enterprise, address to the Forum on Global Leadership, Washington, DC, July 25 (also in *Foreign Affairs*, 2006).

50 Black *et al.* (1999).

51 Claus, L. *et al.* (2004), *Worldwide Benchmark Study. Trends in Global Mobility: the Assignee Perspective Research Report*, Swindon: Cendant Mobility.

52 McCall and Hollenbeck (2002).

53 Hall, D. T., Zhu, G. and Yan, A. (2001), Developing global leaders: To hold on to them, let them go! in Mobley, W. and McCall, M. W., Jr. (eds), *Advances in Global Leadership*, Vol. 2, Stamford, CT: JAI Press.

54 McCall and Hollenbeck (2002).

55 Bennett, J. M. and Bennett, M. J. (2003), Developing intercultural sensitivity: An integrative approach to global and domestic diversity, in Landis, D., Bennett, J. M. and Bennett, M. J. (eds), *The Handbook of Intercultural Training*, Thousand Oaks, CA: Sage; and Hodge (2000).

56 See, for example, Seibert, K. W., Hall, D. T. and Kram, K. E. (1995), Strengthening the weak link in strategic executive development: Integrating individual development and global business strategy, *Human Resource Management*, 34: 549–567; and Yan, A.,

Zhu, G. and Hall, D. T. (2002), International assignments for career building: A model of agency relationships and psychological contracts, *Academy of Management Review*, 27 (3): 373–391.

57 Yan *et al.* (2002).

58 Baker, J. C. and Ivancevich, J. M. (1971), The assignment of American executives abroad: Systematic, haphazard, or chaotic? *California Management Review*, 13 (3): 39–41; Black, J. S. (1988), Work role transitions: A study of expatriate managers in Japan, *Journal of International Business Studies*, 19: 277–294; Oddou, G. and Mendenhall, M. (1991), Succession planning for the twenty-first century: How well are we grooming our future business leaders? *Business Horizons*, 34 (1): 26–34; and Tung, R. L. (1981), Selecting and training of personnel for overseas assignments, *Columbia Journal of World Business*, 16 (1): 68–78.

59 See, for example, Black, Gregersen *et al.* (1999); Brewster, C. (1991), *The Management of Expatriates*, London: Kogan Page; and Schell, M. and Solomon, C. (1997), *Capitalizing on the Global Work force: A Strategic Guide to Expatriate Management*, Chicago: Irwin.

60 Quoted in Blocklyn, P. L. (1989), Developing the international executive, *Personnel*, March: 44–45.

61 Black, Gregersen *et al.* (1999); Sparrow *et al.* (2004); Stroh, L. K., Black, J. S., Mendenhall, M. E. and Gregersen, H. B. (2005), *International Assignments: An Integration of Strategy, Research, and Practice*, Mahwah, NJ/London: Erlbaum.

62 Stroh *et al.* (2005); and Ward, C. and Kennedy, A. (1993), Where's the "culture" in cross-cultural transition? *Journal of Cross-cultural Psychology*, 24: 221–249.

63 Refer to the references in note 59 as well as Bennett, R., Aston, A. and Colquhoun (2000), Cross-cultural training: A critical step in ensuring the success of international assignments, *Human Resource Management*, summer/fall, 39 (2–3): 239–250.

64 Based on Rahim, A. (1983), A model for developing key expatriate executives, *Personnel Journal*, April: 23–28.

65 Stroh *et al.* (2005); Francis (1995); Keys and Bleicken (1998); and Ronen, S. (1989), Training the international assignee, in I. L. Goldstein and Associates (eds), *Training and Development in Organizations*, San Francisco: Jossey Bass.

66 A good summary of this research and application to training programs for IAs is found in Keys and Bleicken (1998); also see Stroh *et al.* (2005); and Mendenhall, M. E. and Stahl, G. K. (2000), Expatriate training and development: Where do we go from here? *Human Resource Management*, summer/fall, 39 (2–3): 251–265.

67 Keys and Bleicken (1998).

68 See Blocklyn (1989); Stroh *et al.* (2005); and Moran, R. T., Harris, P. R. and Moran, S. V. (2007), *Managing Cultural Differences: Global Leadership Strategies for the Twenty-first Century* (7th ed.), Burlington, MA/Oxford: Butterworth-Heinemann.

69 Described in Blocklyn (1989).

70 Lanier, A. R. (1979), Selecting and preparing personnel for overseas transfers, *Personnel Journal*, March: 160–163.

71 Black, J. S., Gregersen, H. B. and Mendenhall, M. E. (1992), *Global Assignments*, San Francisco: Jossey Bass; Black, Gregersen *et al.* (1999); Black, J. S. and Mendenhall, M. E. (1989), Selecting cross-cultural training methods: A practical yet theory-based approach, *Human Resource Management*, 28 (4): 511–540; Black, J. S. and Mendenhall, M. E. (1990), Cross-cultural training effectiveness: A review and a theoretical framework for future research, *Academy of Management Review*, 15 (1): 113–136; Caudron, S. (1991), Training ensures success overseas, *Personnel Journal*, December: 27–30; Earley, P. C. (1987), Intercultural training for managers: A comparison of documentary and interpersonal methods, *Academy of Management Journal*, 30 (4): 685–698; and Stroh *et al.* (2005).

72 Kohls, L. R. (1993), Preparing yourself for work overseas, in Reynolds, A. and Nadler, L. (eds), *Globalization: The International HRD Consultant and Practitioner*, Amherst, MA:

Human Resource Development Press; and Budhwar, P. S. and Baruch, Y. (2003) Career management practices in India: An empirical study, *International Journal of Manpower*, 24 (6): 69–719.

73 Kohls (1993).

74 Stroh *et al.* (2005); and Mendenhall and Stahl (2000).

75 Stroh *et al.* (2005); Black and Mendenhall (1990); and Keys and Bleicken (1998).

76 Black, J. S., Morrison, A. J. and Gregersen, H. B. (1999), *Global Explorers: The Next Generation of Leaders*, New York and London: Routledge; McCall, M. W., Jr. and Hollenbeck, G. P. (2002), *Developing Global Executives: The Lessons of International Experience*, Boston, MA: Harvard Business School Press; Pucik, V. (1992), Globalization and human resource management, in Pucik, V., Tichy, N. M. and Barnett, C. K. (eds), *Globalizing Management: Creating and Leading the Competitive Organization*, New York: Wiley; and Scherer, C. W. (2000), *The Internationalists: Business Strategies for Globalization*, Wilsonville, OR: Book Partners.

77 See, for example, *Competing in a Global Economy* (1998), Executive Summary of the Watson Wyatt Study of Senior Executives Across the Globe, Bethesda, MD/Reigate, England: Watson Wyatt Worldwide.

78 These paragraphs draw heavily on Evans, P. A. L. (1992), Human resource management and globalization, keynote address presented to the third Biannual Conference on International Personnel and Human Resource Management, Ashridge Management College, Berkhamsted, July 2–4; Evans, P., Lank, E. and Farquhar, A. (1989), Managing human resources in the international firm: Lessons from practice, in Evans, P., Doz, Y. and Laurent, A. (eds), *Human Resource Management in International Firms*, London: Macmillan; Evans *et al.* (2002); and McCall and Hollenbeck (2002). For a broader look at executive development programs, particularly looking at executive training programs, refer to Keys and Fulmer (1998).

79 Quoted in Evans *et al.* (1989).

80 In addition to the other major references on global management development, most of which make reference to the importance of early identification of candidates for global development, see Spreitzer, G.M., McCall, M. W., Jr. and Mahoney, J. D. (1997), Early identification of international executive potential, *Journal of Applied Psychology*, 82 (1): 6–29.

81 See, for example, Adler, N. J. and Bartholomew, S. (1992), Managing globally competent people, *Academy of Management Executive*, 6 (2): 52–65; Black, Morrison *et al.* (1999); Cascio, W. and Bailey, E. (1995), International human resource management, in Shenkar, O. (ed.), *Global Perspectives of Human Resource Management*, Englewood Cliffs, NJ: Prentice Hall; McCall and Hollenbeck (2002); Minehan, M. E. (1996), The shortage of global managers [reports on two major studies, one from thirty countries and one from Europe], *Issues in HR*, Alexandria, VA: Society for Human Resource Management, March/April: 2–3; Rosen, R. (2000), *Global Literacies: Lessons on Business Leadership and National Cultures*, New York: Simon and Schuster; and Thaler-Carter, R. E. (2000), Whither global leaders? *HR Magazine*, May: 82–88.

82 Bartlett and Ghoshal (1998).

7 Global compensation, benefits, and taxes

1 Reynolds, C. (2000), *Guide to Global Compensation Benefits*, New York: Harcourt; Reynolds, C. (1992), Are you ready to make IHR a global function? *HR News: International HR*, February: C1–C3; Reynolds, C. (1997), Expatriate compensation in historical perspective, *Journal of World Business*, 32 (2): 118–132.

2 See, for example, Gomez-Mejia, L. and Werner, S. (2008), *Global Compensation: Foundations and Perspectives*, London: Routledge; Crandall, L. P. and Phelps, M. I.

(1991), Pay for a global work force, *Personnel Journal*, February: 28–33; Czinkota, R. M., Rivoli, P., and Ronkainen, I. A. (1989), International human resource management, *International Business*, Chicago: Dryden Press; Green, W. E. and Walls, G. D. (1984), Human resources: Hiring internationally, *Personnel Administrator*, July: 61–64, 66; Gross, R. E. and Kujawa, D. (1995), Personnel management, *International Business: Theory and Managerial Applications*, 3d ed., Homewood, IL: Irwin; *Fortune* (1984), Are you underpaid? 19 March: 20–25; Stuart, P. (1991), Global payroll: A taxing problem, *Personnel Journal*, October: 80–90.

3 See, for example, Overman, S. (1992), The right package, *HR Magazine*, July: 71–74; Senko, J. P. (1991), Controlling expatriate execs' costs, *Management Review*, March: 38–39.

4 Mercer Traavik, L. E. and Lunnan, R. (2005), Is standardization of performance appraisal perceived as fair across cultures? Paper presented at the Academy of Management in Honolulu, HI, August.

5 Adapted from Hait, A. G. (1992), Employee benefits in the global economy, *Benefits Quarterly*, fourth quarter, reprint.

6 Latta, G. W. (1995), Innovative ideas in international compensation, *Benefits and Compensation International*, July–August: 3–7; Luebbers, L. A. (1999), Laying the foundation for global compensation, *Workforce Supplement*, September: 1–4; Minehan, M. (2000), The new face of global compensation, *SHRM Global*, December: 4–7; Murphy, E. (1998), Payday around the world, *IBIS Review*, July: 17–20; Ritchie, A. J. and Seltz, S. P. (2000), Globalization of the compensation and benefits function, in C. Reynolds, (ed.), *Guide to Global Compensation and Benefits*, San Diego, CA: Harcourt; Sutro, P. J. (1999) Thinking about a global share plan? Think smart, *Compensation and Benefits Review*, reprint (no pages); and Townley, G. (1999), Leveling the global paying field, *HR World*, March–April: 75–80.

7 Abowd, J. M. and Kaplan, S. D. (1998), Executive compensation: Six questions that need answering, US Department of Labor, Bureau of Labor Statistics, Working Paper 319.

8 See ftp://ftp.bls.gov/pub/special.requests/ForeignLabor/industrynaics.txt.

9 See the references in notes 46 and 51 as well as Hempel, P. S. (1998), Designing multinational benefits programs: The role of national culture, *Journal of World Business*, 33 (3): 277–294; and Outram, R. (2000), Cherry pickings, *HR World*, March–April: 30–34.

10 Adapted from Kaplan, C. Y. and Bernstein, Z. S. (2000), Other benefits, in Reynolds (2000); Working practices around the world, *HR World*, November–December: 18–19.

11 Bernstein, Z. S. and Kaplan, C. Y. (2000) Benefits: Introduction and retirement programs, in C. Reynolds (ed.), *Guide to Global Compensation and Benefits*, San Diego, CA: Harcourt; Spencer, B. F. (1998), Governments continue to hinder development of centralized approach to funding pensions, *IBIS Review*, July: 10–12; and Townley, G. (1999), In the twilight zone, *HR World*, January–February: 76–79.

12 Di Leonardi, F. A. (1991), Money Makes the World Go Round, interview with Eugene Barron, assistant treasurer of Johnson & Johnson, *Wyatt Communicator*, spring: 15–19.

13 Reported in Kaplan, C. Y. and Bernstein, Z. S. (2000), Other benefits, in Reynolds (2000); Most nations require employers to provide maternity leave, meeting told (1990), *BNA's Employee Relations Weekly*, April 2: 433. For current information on maternity and related leave, refer to Keller, W. L. (ed.-in-chief) (Vol. 1, 1997; Vol. 2, 2001, and annual updates), *International Labor and Employment Laws*, International Labor Law Committee section of Labor and Employment Law, American Bar Association, Washington DC: Bureau of National Affairs.

14 Johnson, R. E. (1991), Flexible benefit programs: International style, *Employee Benefits Journal*, 16(3): 22–25.

15 Freedman, R. (1997), Incentive programs go global, *Worldwide Pay and Benefits Headlines* (Towers Perrin Newsletter), February: 1; Gross, A. and Lepage, S. (2001), Stock options in Asia, *SHRM Global Perspective*, 3 (1): 8–9; Andersen, A (2001), New global share plan

survey data released, *International Mobility Management Newsletter*, fourth quarter: 7; Pacific Bridge (2001), Stock options in Asia: Legal and regulatory roadblocks, *Asian HR eNewsletter*, May 10: 1–2; Perkins, S. J. (1998), The search for global incentives, *HR World*, November–December: 62–65; William M. Mercer International and Arthur Andersen & Co. (1990), *Globalizing Compensation: Extending Stock Option and Equity Participation Plans Abroad*; Solomon, C. M. (1999), Incentives that go the distance, *HR World*, May–June: 40–44; Thompson, R. W. (1999), U.S. subsidiaries of foreign parents favor pay incentives, *HR Magazine*, April: 10; US-based long-term incentive plans go global (2000), *International Update* (reporting on a Towers Perrin report: *The Globalization of Long-term Incentive Plans by US-based Companies*) 3: 8; U.S. version stock plans filter into Europe (1999), *International Update*, February, 9; and Veloitis, S. (2000), Offshore equity compensation plans: Focus of audit activity in many countries, *KPMG eNewsletter, The Expatriate Administrator*, August 28: 1–4.

16 Hewitt Associates (1993) *Granting Stock Options and Restricted Stock to Overseas Employees*, New York.

17 Hall, B. J.(2000), What you need to know about stock options, *Harvard Business Review* 78 (2): 121–129; Rosen, C., Case, J. and Staubus, M. (2005), Every employee an owner, *Harvard Business Review* 83 (6): 122–130; Corporate Secretary Guide, *Global stock plan management*, www.fidelity.com/stockplans (2006).

18 Adapted from *Fortune* (2002), Canon loves to compete, July 22: S5.

19 Adapted from Lublin, J. S. (1991), Employee stock plans run into foreign snags, *The Wall Street Journal*, September 16: B1.

20 Krupp, N. B. (1986), Managing benefits in multinational organizations, *Personnel*, September: 76–78; Murdock, B. A. and Ramamurthy, B. (1986), Containing benefits costs for multinational corporations, *Personnel Journal*, May: 80–85.

21 Towards a global compensation model: Two key concepts (2001), *International Mobility Management Newsletter* (Arthur Andersen), second quarter, 2–3.

22 Black, J. S. (1991), Returning expatriates feel foreign in their native land, *Personnel*, August: 17.

23 Clague, L. (1999), Expatriate compensation: Whence we came, where we are, whither we go, *Corporate Relocation News*, April: 24, 25, 31; Reynolds, C. (1994), *Compensation Basics for North American Expatriates,* Scottsdale, AZ: American Compensation Association; Reynolds, C. (1997), Expatriate compensation in historical perspective, *Journal of World Business*, 32 (2): 118–132; Reynolds, C. (2000), Global compensation and benefits in transition, *Compensation and Benefits Review*, January–February: 28–38; Reynolds, C. (1996), What goes around comes around, *International HR* (Organization Resources Counselors, Inc.), spring: 1–10; and Ritchie, A. J. and Seltz, S. P. (2000), Globalizaation of the compensation and benefits function, in C. Reynolds (ed.), *Guide to Global Compensation and Benefits*, San Diego, CA: Harcourt Professional Publishing, 19–30.

24 Stone, R. J. (1986), Compensation: Pay and perks for overseas executives, *Personnel Journal*, January: 64–69.

25 Czinkota, M. R., Rovoli, P. and Ronkainen, I. A. (1989), International human resource management, *International Business*, Chicago: Dryden Press, 580; Stone (1986).

26 Black, J. S., Gregersen, H. B., Mendenhall, M. E. and Stroh, L. K. (1999) *Globalizing People through International Assignments*, Reading, MA: Addison Wesley; Chesters, A. (1995), The balance sheet approach: Problem or solution? *International HR Journal*, fall: 9–15; Frazee, V. (1998), Is the balance sheet right for your expats? *Global Workforce*, September: 19–26; Infante, V. D. (2001), Three ways to design international pay: headquarters, home country, host country, *Workforce*, January: 22–24; Organization Resources Counselors (1998), *Understanding the Balance Sheet Approach to Expatriate Compensation,* (pamphlet), New York: Organization Resources Counselors.

27 O'Reilly, M. (1995), Reinventing the expatriate package, *International HR Journal*, fall: 58–59; Reynolds, C. (2000), Global compensation and benefits in transition, *Compensation*

& Benefits Review, January–February: 28–38; and Sheridan, W. R. and Hansen, P. T. (1996), Linking international business and expatriate compensation strategies, *ACA Journal*, spring: 66–79.

28 Crandall, L. P. and Phelps, M. A. (1991), Pay for a global work force, *Personnel Journal*, February: 28–33.

29 For discussions of these issues, see Gould, C. (1995), Expatriate compensation, *International Insight*, winter: 6–10; Gould, C. (1998), Expatriate policy development, in Gould, C, and Schmidt-Kemp, B. (eds), *International Human Resources Guide*, Boston, MA: Warren Gorham and Lamont, 7–1 to 7–45; Infante (2001); Kearley (1996); Overman, S. (1992), The right package, *HR Magazine*, July: 71–74; Pollard, J. (2000), Expatriate practices, in Reynolds (2000), 117–152; Reynolds (1996); Reynolds (2000); and Solomon (1999).

30 *Global Relocation Trends Annual Survey Report*, New York: GMAC Global Relocation Services/Windham International, New York: National Foreign Trade Council, and Alexandria, VA: Society for Human Resource Management (SHRM) Global Forum; and Society for Human Resource Management/Commerce Clearing House, *1992 SHRM/CCH Survey on International HR Practices*, Chicago: Commerce Clearing House.

31 Pollard (2000).

32 Overman, S. (1992), The right package, *HR Magazine*, July: 71–74.

33 Senko, J. P. (1990), The foreign service premium & hardship differential, *Mobility*, May: 10–12.

34 *Ibid.*; and New York (2005), *Global Relocation Trends Annual Survey Report*, New York: GMAC GRS/Windham International, New York: National Foreign Trade Council, and Society for Human Resource Management (SHRM) Global Forum.

35 Senko (1990).

36 Runzheimer International (1991) reproduced in *HR Focus*, September 8.

37 Senko, J. P. (1991), Controlling expatriate execs' costs, *Management Review*, March: 38–39.

38 See, for example, Bishko, M. J. (1990), Compensating your overseas executives, Part 1: Strategies for the 1990s, *Compensation and Benefits Review*, May–June: 33–43; Brooks, B. J. (1988), Long-term incentives: international executives,: *Personnel*, August: 40–42; Brooks, B. J. (1987), Trends in international executive compensation, *Personnel*, May: 67–70.

39 Global relocation survey (2005).

40 Gould (1998), chapter 7; Littlewood, M. (1995), Total compensation: A new way of doing things, *International HR Journal*, fall: 17–21; Reynolds (2000), chapter 5; and Runzheimer International (2000), Lump-sum allowances: The efficient approach to handling relocation expenses, pamphlet published by Runzheimer International, Rochester, WI.

41 Gregsen, K. J. (1996), Flexpatriate remuneration: An alternative method for compensating foreign assignees, *International HR Journal*, winter: 24–28; Reynolds, C. (2000), chapter 5: Expatriate compensation strategies.

42 Milliman, J., Nason, S., Von Glinow, M. A., Huo, P., Lowe, K. and Kim, N. (1995), In search of "best" strategic pay practices: An exploratory study of Japan, Korea, Taiwan, and the United States, *Advances in International Comparative Management* 10: 227–252; Schuler, R. S. (1998), Understanding compensation practice variations across firms: The impact of national culture, *Journal of International Business Studies*, 29 (1): 159–177; and Toh, S. M. and Denisi, A. S. (2003), Host country national reactions to expatriate pay policies: A model and implications, *Academy of Management Review*, 28 (4): 606–621.

43 http://www.ssa.gov/international/agreements_overview.html.

44 See, for example, Russo, S. M. and Orchant, D. (2000), Expatriate taxation, in Reynolds (2000), 153–176; Stuart, P. (1991), Global payroll: A taxing problem, *Personnel Journal*, October: 80–90.

45 Presented in Stuart (1991), 81. See also surveys such as the Global Relocation Trends Annual Report from GMAC Global Relocation Services/Windham, National Foreign Trade Council, and SHRM Global Forum.
46 Adapted from Stuart (1991), 84.
47 Adapted from Outram, R. (2001), The taxman cometh, *Global HR*, February–March: 22–25.
48 Bernstein, Z. S. and Kaplan, C. Y. (2000), Benefits: Introduction and retirement programs, in Reynolds (2000); Gould (1998); Holleman, W. J. (1991), Taxation of expatriate executives, *International Executive*, May–June: 30–33; Russo and Orchant (2000); and Stuart (1991).
49 Holleman (1991).
50 Nemerov, D. S. (1994), How foreign-owned companies pay their US executives, *Journal of International Compensation and Benefits*, January–February: 9–14.
51 See, for instance, the *Annual CEO Scorecard: International Comparison* from Towers Perrin.
52 *Ibid.*
53 Sparrow, P. R. (1998), International rewards systems: To converge or not to converge? in Brewster, C. and Harris, H. (eds), *International HRM: Contemporary Issues in Europe*, London: Routledge; and Sparrow, P. R. (1999), International reward management, in White, G. and Drucker, J. (eds), *Reward Management: A Critical Text*, London: Pittman.
54 Carey, B. P. (1993), Why inpatriates need special remuneration packages, *Journal of European Business*, May–June: 46–49; and De Leon, J. (2000), International assignments to US headquarters, in Reynolds (2000).
55 Crandall, L. P. (1992), Getting through the global payroll maze, *Personnel Journal*, August: 76–77; Dowling, P. J. (1989), Hot Issues Overseas, *Personnel Administrator*, January: 66–72.
56 Crandall (1992).
57 See, for example, Gibbons, D. (2002), Employee benefits for expatriates, *Expatriate Advisor*, spring: 40–41; Joinson, C. (1999), Companies tailor benefits, compensation for overseas workers, *HR News*, April: 1, 20; Milkovich, G. T. and Bloom, M. (2000), Rethinking international compensation, in Mendenhall, M. and Oddou, G. (eds), *Readings and Cases in International Human Resource Management*, Cincinnati, OH: South Western College Publishing; Pollard (2000); Reynolds (2000), Global compensation and benefits in transition; Reynolds (2000), chapter 4 and chapter 5; Ritchie, A. J. and Seltz, S. P. (2000), Globalization of the compensation and benefits function, in Reynolds (2000); Russo and Orchant (2000); and Sheridan and Hansen (1996).
58 Thanks to Cal Reynolds of ORC, New York, for this phrase.

8 International employee performance management

1 See, Greene, R. J. (2005), *Effective Performance Appraisal: A Global Perspective*, Alexandria, VA: SHRM; Pulakos, E. D. (2004), *Performance Management. A Roadmap for Developing, Implementing, and Evaluating Performance Management Systems*, Effective Practice Guidelines, Alexandria, VA: SHRM Foundation.
2 See, for example, Varma, A., Budhwar, P. and DeNisi, A. (2008), *Performance Management around the Globe*, London: Routledge; Black, J. S., Gregersen, H. B., Mendenhall, M. E. and Stroh, L. K. (1999), Appraising: Determining if people are doing the right things, in *Globalizing People through International Assignments*, Reading, MA: Addison Wesley; Brewster, C. (1991), Monitoring performance—and coming home, in *The Management of Expatriates*, London: Kogan Page; Caligiuri, P. M. (1997), Assessing expatriate success: Beyond just "being there", in Aycan, Z. (ed.), *New Approaches to*

Employee Management, Vol. IV, New York: JAI Press; Davis, D. D. (1998), International performance measurement and management, in Smither, J. (ed.), *Performance Appraisal*, San Francisco: Jossey Bass; Dowling, P. J., Welch, D. E. and Schuler, R. S. (1999), Performance management, *International Human Resource Management*, 3d ed., Cincinnati, OH: Southwestern College Publishing; Gregersen, H. B., Black, J. S., and Hite, J. M. (1995), Expatriate performance appraisal: Principles, practice, and challenges, in Selmer, J. (ed.), *Expatriate Management: New Ideas for International Business*, Westport, CT: Quorum; Gregersen, H. B., Hite, J. M. and Black, J. S. (1996), Expatriate performance appraisal in US multinational firms, *Journal of International Business Studies*, fourth quarter: 711–738; Harvey, M. (1997), Focusing on the international personnel performance appraisal process, *Human Resource Development Journal*, 8 (1): 41–62; Janssens, M. (1994), Evaluating international managers' performance: Parent company standards as control mechanisms, *International Journal of Human Resource Management*, 5 (4): 853–873; Kleiman, L. S. (2004), *Human Resource Management*, 3d ed., Cincinnati, OH: Atomic Dog; Milliman, J., Nason, S., Gallagher, E., Huo, P., Von Glinow, M. A. and Lowe, K. B. (1998), The impact of national culture on human resource management practices: The case of performance appraisal, *Advances in International Comparative Management*, 12: 157–183; Oddou, G., and Mendenhall, M. (2000), Expatriate performance appraisal: Problems and solutions, in Mendenhall, M. and Oddou, G. (eds), *Readings and Cases in International Human Resource Management*, Cincinnati, OH: Southwestern College Publishing; Schuler, R. S., Fulkerson, J. R. and Dowling, P. J. (1991), Strategic performance measurement and management in multinational corporations, *Human Resource Management*, 30 (3): 365–392; Vance, C. M., McClaine, S. R., Boje, D. M. and Stage, H. D. (1992), An examination of the transferability of traditional performance appraisal principles across cultural boundaries, *Management International Review*, 32 (4): 313–326.

3 Beer, M. (1981), Performance appraisal: Dilemmas and possibilities, *Organizational Dynamics*, 10: 24–36; Cascio, W. F. (2002), *Managing Human Resources: Productivity, Quality of Work Life, Profits*, 6th ed., New York: McGraw-Hill Irwin.

4 Dowling *et al.* (1999).

5 Claus, L. M. and Briscoe, D. R. (2006), What we know and don't know about performance management from an international/global perspective: A review and analysis of empirical research, paper presented at the annual conference of the Academy of Management, August 11–16, Atlanta, GA.

6 See: Kluckhohn, F. and Strodtbeck, F. (1961), *Variations in Value Orientations*, Westport, CT: Greenwood Press; Hofstede, G. (1980), *Culture's Consequences: International Differences in Work-related Values*, Newbury Park, CA: Sage; Hall, E. T. and Hall, M. R. (1964), *Understanding Cultural Differences*, Intercultural Press; Trompenaars, F. and Hampden-Turner, C. (1992), *Riding the Waves of Culture: Understanding Diversity in Global Business*, London: Economist Books.

7 See, for example, Chow, I. H. S. (1994), An opinion survey of performance appraisal practices in Hong Kong and the People's Republic of China, *Asia Pacific Journal of Human Resource Management*, 32: 67–79; Easterby-Smith, M., Malina, D. and Yuan, L. (1995), How culture sensitive is HRM? A comparative analysis of practice in Chinese and UK companies, *International Journal of Human Resource Management*, 6: 31–59; Vallance, S. (1999), Performance appraisal in Singapore, Thailand and the Philippines: A cultural perspective, *Australian Journal of Public Administration*, 58: 78–95; Entrekin, L. and Chung, Y. (2001), Attitudes towards different sources of executive appraisal: A comparison of Hong Kong Chinese and American managers in Hong Kong, *International Journal of Human Resource Management*, 12: 965–987.; Bai, X. and Bennington, L. (2005), Performance appraisal in the Chinese state-owned coal industry, *International Journal of Business Performance Management*, 7: 275–287.

8 Sullivan, J., Suzuki, T. and Kondo, Y. (1985), *Managerial Theories and the Performance Control Process in Japanese and American Work Groups*, National Academy of Management Proceedings, 98–102.

9 Arthur, W. Jr., Woehr, A., Adebowale D. J. and Strong, M. (1995) Human resource management in West Africa: Practices and perspectives, *International Journal of Human Resource Management*, 6: 347–366.

10 Faulkner, D., Pitkethly, R. and Child, J. (2002), International mergers and acquisitions in the UK 1985–1994: A comparison of national HRM practices, *International Journal of Human Resource Management*, 13: 106–122.

11 Shadur, M.A., Rodwell, J. and Bamber, G. J. (1995), The adoption of international best practices in a Western culture: East meets West, *International Journal of Human Resource Management*, 6: 735–757.

12 Bai, X. and Bennington, L. (2005), Performance appraisal in the Chinese state-owned coal industry, *International Journal of Business Performance Management*, 7: 275–287.

13 Easterby-Smith, M., Malina, D. and Yuan, L. (1995), How culture sensitive is HRM? A comparative analysis of practice in Chinese and UK companies, *International Journal of Human Resource Management*, 6: 31–59.

14 Paik, Y., Vance, C. and Stage, H. D. (2000), A test of assumed cluster homogeneity for performance appraisal in four Southeast Asian countries, *International Journal of Human Resource Management*, 11: 736–750; Vance, C. M., McClaine, S., Boje, D. M. and Stage, H. D. (1992), An examination of the transferability of traditional performance appraisal principles across cultural boundaries, *Management International Review*, 32: 313–326.

15 Paik, Y. and Choi, D. Y. (2005), The shortcomings of a standardized global knowledge management system: The case study of Accenture, *Academy of Management Executive*, 19: 81–84.

16 Björkman, I. and Lu, Y. (1999), The management of human resources in Chinese–Western ventures, *Journal of World Business*, 34: 306–324.

17 Von Glinow, M.A., Drost, E. and Teagarden, M. (2002), Convergence of IHRM practices: Lessons learned from a globally distributed consortium of theory and practice, *Human Resource Management*, 41: 123–141.

18 Entrekin, L. and Chung, Y. (2001), Attitudes towards different sources of executive appraisal: A comparison of Hong Kong Chinese and American managers in Hong Kong, *International Journal of Human Resource Management*, 12: 965–987.

19 Galang, M. C. (2004), The transferability question: Comparing HRM practices in the Philippines with the US and Canada, *International Journal of Human Resource Management*, 15: 1207–1233.

20 Mendonca, M. and Kanungo, R.N. (1996), Impact of culture on performance, *International Journal of Manpower*, 17: 65–69; Aycan, Z. (2005), The interplay between cultural and institutional contingencies in human resource management practices, *International Journal of Human Resource Management*, 16: 1083–119.

21 Aycan (2005).

22 Davis, D. D. (1998), International performance measurement and management, in Smither, J. W. (ed.), *Performance Appraisal: State of the Art in Practice*, San Francisco, CA: Jossey Bass.

23 Suutari, V. and Tahvanainen, M. (2002), The antecedents of performance management among Finnish expatriates, *International Journal of Human Resource Management*, 13: 55–75.

24 Davis (1998); Stroh, L. K., Black, J. S., Mendenhall, M. E. and Gregersen, H. B. (2005), *International Assignments: An Integration of Strategy, Research, and Practice*, Mahwah, NJ/London: Erlbaum; other studies show a similar range of findings, e.g. Woods, P. (2003), Performance management of Australian and Singaporean expatriates, *International Journal of Manpower*, 24: 517–534.

25 Vance, C. M. (2006), Strategic upstream and downstream considerations for effective global performance management, *International Journal of Cross-cultural Management*, 6: 37–56.

26 Briscoe, D. R. and Claus, L. (2008), PMS policies and practices in MNEs, in Varma, A., Budhwar, P. S. and DeNisi, A. (eds), *Performance Management Systems Around the Globe*, London/New York: Routledge.

27 Claus, L. (2008), Employee performance management in MNCs: Reconciling the need for global integration and local responsiveness, *European Journal of Management* (forthcoming).

28 Cascio, W. F. (2002), *Managing Human Resources: Productivity, Quality of Work Life, Profits*, 6th ed., New York: McGraw-Hill Irwin.

29 Figures from a survey by the former Arthur Andersen's Human Capital Services practice, reported in Juday, H. (1999), Employee development during international assignments, *Corporate Relocation News*, August: 18, 35.

30 See, for example, Oddou, G. and Mendenhall, M. (2000), Expatriate performance appraisal: Problems and solutions, in Mendenhall, M. and Oddou, G. (eds), *Readings and Cases in International Human Resource Management*, Cincinnati, OH: Southwestern College Publishing;

31 See, for example, Trompenaars, F. (1994), *Riding the Waves of Culture: Understanding Diversity in Global Business*, New York: Irwin. Dr Trompenaars found that managers from various countries ranked qualities for evaluation in significantly different orders.

32 Oddou and Mendenhall (2000); Harvey, M. G. (1997), Focusing on the international personnel performance appraisal process, Human Resource Development Journal, 8 (1): 41–62.

33 Harvey, M. G. and Buckley, M. R. (1997), Managing inpatriates: Building a global core competency, *Journal of World Business*, 32 (1): 35–52.

34 See for example, Adler (2002); Black *et al.* (1999); Bonache *et al.* (2001); Brewster and Harris (1999); Brewster and Larsen (1990); Brewster and Scullion (1997); Briscoe (1995); Briscoe and Schuler (2004); Cullen (1999); Deresky (1997); Dowling *et al.* (1999); Francesco and Gold (1998); Gooderham and Nordhaug (2003); Gregersen *et al.* (1995); Harris and Moran (1991); Hill (2003); Joint and Morton (1999); Kleiman (2004); Mendenhall *et al.* (1995); McFarlin and Sweeney (1998); Oddou and Mendenhall (1995, 2000); Petersen *et al.* (1996); Rhinesmith (1993); Scullion and Brewster (2001); Shenkar and Luo (2004).

35 Dowling *et al.* (1999); Janssens (1994).

36 Birdseye, M. G. and Hill, J. S., (1995), Individual, organization/work and environmental influences on expatriate turnover tendencies: an empirical study, *Journal of International Business Studies*, 26 (4): 795–809; Feldman, D. C., and Thompson, H. B. (1993), Expatriation, repatriation, and domestic geographic relocation: An empirical investigation of adjustment to new job assignments, *Journal of International Business Studies*, 24 (3): 507–529.

37 Torbiörn, I. (1985), The structure of managerial roles in cross-cultural settings, *International Studies of Management and Organization*, 15 (1): 52–74.

38 Adapted from Logger, E. and Vinke, R. (1995), Compensation and appraisals of international staff, in Harzing, A.-W. and Van Ruysseveldt, J. (eds), *International Human Resource Management*, London: Sage in association with the Open University of the Netherlands.

39 Borkowski, S. C. (1999), International managerial performance evaluation: A five-country comparison, *Journal of International Business Studies*, 30 (3): 533–555.

40 Black *et al.* (1999), 166.

41 Most of the references in note 2 made this point. In addition, see Lomax, S. (2001), *Best Practices for Managers and Expatriates: A Guide on Selecting, Hiring, and Compensation*, New York: Wiley.

42 Based on Black *et al.* (1999).
43 *Global Relocation Trends*, 1998 and 1998 Survey Reports, New York: Windham International and National Foreign Trade Council, and Alexandria, VA: Society for Human Resource Management.
44 Black *et al.* (1999.
45 Logger and Vinke (1995).
46 Gregersen *et al.* (1996).
47 *Ibid.*
48 Cascio (2002), 302–303.
49 Black *et al.* (1999).
50 Tahvanainen, M. (2000), Expatriate performance management: The case of Nokia Telecommunications, *Human Resource Management*, summer–fall, 39 (2–3): 267–275.
51 Oddou and Mendenhall (2000), 274.
52 *Ibid.*

9 The well-being of the global work force, global human resource information systems, and the structure of today's international human resource management

1 The most important reference on country health and safety practices is the International Labour Organization's four-volume *Encyclopaedia of Occupational Health and Safety*, by Jeanne Mager and Ed. Stellman. The most recent edition is the 4th edition, published in 1998, in Geneva, Switzerland, by the ILO. Current databases, publications on specific aspects of health and safety issues, linkages to other organizations and national health and safety agencies, and other services related to global health and safety, are available at the International Occupational Safety and Health Information Center (CIS) at the ILO. The CIS is a network of health and safety centers from over 100 countries. The CIS's web site can be found at: http://www.ilo.org.
2 Locke, R. M., Fei Qin and Brause, A. (2007), Does monitoring improve labor standards? Lessons from Nike, *Industrial and Labor Relations Review*, 61 (1): 3–31; Roggero, P., Mangiaterra, V., Bustreo, F. and Rosati, F. (2007), The health impact of child labor in developing countries: Evidence from cross-country data, *American Journal of Public Health*, 97 (2): 271–275; Takala, J. (1999), *Introductory Report of the International Labour Office, Occupational Safety and Health Branch*, Geneva, CH: International Labor Organization; Wilson, D. (2007), The ratification status of ILO conventions related to occupational safety and health and its relationship with reported occupational fatality rates, *Journal of Occupational Health*, 49 (1): 72–79.
3 Reported in "Half of the world's workers employed in risky jobs" (1996), *Manpower Argus*, February: 5.
4 Elling, R. H. (1986), *The Struggle for Workers' Health: A Study of Six Industrialized Countries*, Farmingdale, NY: Baywood.
5 Morse, T. (2002), International occupational health and safety, online lecture, retrieved November 7 2007 from http://iier.isciii.es/supercourse/lecture/lec8271/001.
6 This section is adapted from Ackers, P. and El-Sawad, A. (2006), Family-friendly policies and work–life balance, in Redman, T. and Wilkinson, A. (eds), *Contemporary Human Resource Management*, 2d ed., Harlow: Prentice-Hall/Financial Times.
7 Claus, L. *An HR Framework for Work/Life Balance: An Exploratory Survey of the CEE Country HR Managers of MNCs.* Paper accepted at the International Human Resource Conference, Tallinn, Estonia, June 2007.
8 Breuer, N. (2000), AIDS threatens global business, *Workforce*, February: 52.
9 The most recent UNAIDS/WHO data, retrieved on November 9 2007 from Avert, an international AIDS charity, at http://www.avert.org/worldstats.htm.

10 Quoted in Breuer (2000), 53.

11 See, for example, Dawood, R. (1998), Bills of health, *HR World*, winter: 57–62.

12 American is killed in Mexico City cab holdup (1997), *San Diego Union Tribune*, September 17: A-21; Evans, G. (2001), Last rites, *Global HR*, June: 36–40; Evans, G. (1999), Victim support, *HR World*, May–June: 46–52; Preston, A. (2002), The international assignment taboo: Expatriate death, *KPMG Expatriate Administrator*, summer: 1–3; Tragedy on a Turkish roadway (1998), *USAA Magazine*, March–April: 20–22; York, G. (1996), American's murder sows fear: Moscow a sinister business partner, *Rocky Mountain News*, November 14: 2A, 58A.

13 Evans (2001).

14 See, for example, Davidson, C. and Busch, E. (1996), How to cope with international emergency situations, *KPMG Expatriate Administrator*, April: 6–10; Kroll Associates (2000), *Secure Travel Guide and Guide to Personal Security*, New York: Kroll Associates.

15 Much of this section is drawn from Claus, L. (2007), Operating in an uncertain world: New opportunities for global HR, Paper presented at the NHRMA conference, Seattle, WA; and Claus, L. (2007), Get a virtual grip, *People Management*, August 23. In addition, refer to Brewster, C. and Sparrow, P. (2007), The new roles and challenges of the IHRM function, in Barmeyer, C. and Waxin, M.-R. (eds), *Gestion des Resources Humaines Internationales*, Paris: Connections; and Buyens, D. (2007), Keynote address. Strategic HRM: The three pillar model: A blueprint for future HR, ninth bi-annual Conference, International Human Resource Management, Tallinn, Estonia, June.

16 Claus (2007), Operating in an uncertain world; and Brewster and Sparrow (2007).

17 Brewster and Sparrow (2007).

18 Brewster, C., Sparrow, P. R. and Harris, H. (2005), Towards a new model of globalizing human resource management, *International Journal of Human Resource Management*, 16 (6): 957.

19 Brewster and Sparrow (2007).

20 Based on Claus, L. (2007), "Building global HR competencies," master class presentation at the CIPD annual conference and exhibition, Harrogate, UK; with some reference to Buyens (2007).

21 Claus, L. (2001), The future of HR, *Workplace Visions*, 6: 2–3.

22 Claus, L. and Collison, J. (2005), *The Maturing Profession of Human Reources: Worldwide and Regional View. Survey Report*, Alexandria, VA: Society for Human Resource Management; Claus, L. (2004), *The HR Profession Worldwide*, presentation at the World Congress of the WFPMA, Rio de Janeiro, Brazil.

23 Buyens, D. and de Vos, A. (1999), The added value of the HR department, in Brewster, C. and Harris, H. (eds), *International Human Resource Management*, London: Routledge; Stroh, L. K. and Caligiuri, P. M. (1998), Increasing global competitiveness through effective people management, *Journal of World Business*, 33 (1): 1–16; Stroh, L. K. and Caligiuri, P. M. (1998), Strategic human resources: A new source for competitive advantage in the global arena, *International Journal of Human Resource Management*, 9 (1): 1–17.

24 Frase-Blunt, M. (2003), Raising the bar, *HR Magazine*, March: 74–78; Grossman, R. J. (2003), Putting HR in rotation, *HR Magazine*, March: 50–57; Poe, A. C. (2000), Destination everywhere, *HR Magazine*, October: 67–75.

25 Refer to the Human Resource Certification Institute's web site, www.hrci.org/about/intl.html.

26 Grossman, R. J. (2007), New competencies for HR, *HR Magazine*, June, 58–62.

27 Reported on in *ibid.*

28 Savitz, A. W. and Weber, K. (2006), *The Triple Bottom Line*, San Francisco: Jossey Bass.

29 Towers Perrin (studies conducted for IBM) (1990), *A Twenty-first Century Vision: A Worldwide Human Resources Study* and (1992), *Priorities for Competitive Advantage*, New York: authors.

Author index

Subject index

ASIAN BUSINESS BOOKS

FROM ROUTLEDGE

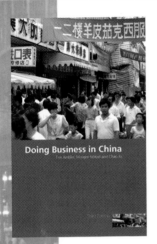

3rd Edition
Doing Business in China

Tim Ambler, University of Exeter, UK
Morgan Witzel, London Business School, UK and
Chao Xi, School of Oriental and African Studies, University of London, UK

Doing Business in China is the number one resource for students of international business and managements studies and practitioners with an eye on China.

This book offers a theoretical framework for understanding Chinese business culture and a practical guide to business practices, market conditions, negotiations, organizations, networks and the business environment in China and the factors that can lead to business success.

The authors guide the reader through the processes of market entry, marketing and managing operations in this unique social and cultural context by including:

- case studies and examples of business ventures as diverse as ornamental lamps, car washes, sausages and outdoor clothing
- discussions of the issues surrounding products, pricing, distribution and advertising
- advice on choosing business partners, negotiating and entering Chinese Overseas markets
- guides to further resources in local cultures to help businesses tailor their strategies to local conditions.

Hb: 978-0-415-43632-8: **£85.00**
Pb: 978-0-415-43631-1: **£19.99**
e-Book: 978-0-203-94649-7

Doing Business in India

Pawan S. Budhwar, Aston Business School, UK and
Arup Warmar, Loyola University, Chicago, USA

This brand new and indispensable textbook covers a wide range of issues and topics for students and researchers in the fields of International Management, International HRM, Cross-Cultural Management, Business Communication and Asian Business.

Written by academic experts, the book presents key information on topics including:

- geography
- politics
- legal system
- historical background
- economy and economic factors
- national infrastructure
- regulatory environment (convertibility of local currency, sectors open to foreign investors, extent of foreign ownership allowed)
- how to negotiate in India
- privatisation
- hot sectors for investors

- incentives for foreign investors
- competitive environment
- advertising and marketing
- promotion
- distribution
- conducting / implementing business (i.e. strategies for investing in India, mode of entry)
- possible business structures
- culture, business customs, practices and etiquette
- greetings, gestures, conversation and related issues.

Hb: 978-0-415-77754-4: **£85.00**
Pb: 978-0-415-77755-1: **£22.99**

Visit **www.routledge.com/asianstudies** to order copies or for further information

an **informa** business